Human Geography

A Short Introduction

John Rennie Short

*University of Maryland,
Baltimore County*

New York   Oxford
OXFORD UNIVERSITY PRESS

Oxford University Press is a department of the University of Oxford. It furthers the University's objective of excellence in research, scholarship, and education by publishing worldwide.

Oxford New York
Auckland Cape Town Dar es Salaam Hong Kong Karachi
Kuala Lumpur Madrid Melbourne Mexico City Nairobi
New Delhi Shanghai Taipei Toronto

With offices in
Argentina Austria Brazil Chile Czech Republic France Greece
Guatemala Hungary Italy Japan Poland Portugal Singapore
South Korea Switzerland Thailand Turkey Ukraine Vietnam

For titles covered by Section 112 of the US Higher Education Opportunity Act, please visit www.oup.com/us/he for the latest information about pricing and alternate formats.

Published in the United States of America by
Oxford University Press
198 Madison Avenue, New York, NY 10016
http://www.oup.com

Oxford is a registered trade mark of Oxford University Press.

Cataloging-in-Publication Data is on file with the Library of Congress.

ISBN 978-0-19-992512-4

Printing number: 9 8 7 6 5 4 3 2 1

Printed in the United States of America
on acid-free paper

Dedication

I **dedicate this** book to the memory of two of my grandparents.

My paternal grandmother, Janet Adamson Craig Short (1895–1966) had a profound respect for learning and social justice, an endless devotion to my education, and an almost infinite patience with my spelling lessons. I think of her often, especially when my thoughts turn to the connections between love and teaching, devotion and education, wonder and learning.

My maternal grandfather, John Rennie (1903–1963) was a coalminer who spent all his working years in the darkness and the danger. Perhaps because he worked in such cramped and tight spaces, in one memorable holiday, just the two of us, he gave me a sense of limitless freedom.

Contents

Contents

Preface

The aim of this book is to introduce students to a wide range of important and exciting work in human geography. The primary audience is students in colleges and universities. I decided to write this book because many of the standard texts are too big, and increasingly too expensive, to provide the accessible and affordable base most of us need for our human geography courses. I sense a pushback by teachers and students against the overly large and expensive books available now. They have grown into, to use Henry James's description of many nineteenth century novels, "loose and baggy monsters." There is room for a more interesting and subtle book than the standard texts. This briefer and more accessible alternative is written in a more familiar style and intended to be augmented by other resources.

As a former mountain climber I will use as metaphor the attempts on the big Himalayan peaks. In the 1970s, the attempts were increasingly organized as large teams with many climbers and elaborate systems of camps and base camps. Then, in the late 1970s, a number of climbers dispensed with the large teams and sought to climb alone or with one other climber. Less burdened by organizational weight, they were much more successful in reaching the summits in quick direct assaults. This book adapts a similar ethic of "light and fast" that relies more on instructor expertise and input—and affords more flexibility to instructors—than a traditional textbook. Not an exact metaphor, to be sure, but close enough to give you a sense of the book's character and mission.

The title, *Human Geography: A Short Introduction*, employs the word "short" in two ways. First, it indicates a relatively brief introduction rather than a wide survey—although only in the word-rich world of college textbooks can a 100,000-word text be described as short; "concise" may be a more appropriate term. Second, the play on my own name is to signal that it is a book with a distinctive authorial voice. Textbooks are written at specific times in specific places by specific people, and these three basic facts color and shape the material covered and the nature of the coverage. I have drawn heavily on much of my own work conducted over the past thirty-five years. The main title announces the subject matter, while the subtitle lets the reader know that it is the world of human geography as seen by just one person. This is less an act of egotism than a reminder to the reader that the text is not revealed truth but the singular vision of just one scholar.

The aim is to be both engaging and comprehensive. The text is intended to be both student- and instructor-friendly. The structure, while providing a coherent whole, also allows sectional choices to meet the different needs, time constraints, and interests of individual instructors. Each chapter has a list of further readings and websites that instructors can employ in teaching and develop as resources in ways suitable for the size and constitution of their particular classes.

This is an ambitious book that gives readers a sense of the complex human geography of the contemporary world. It brings together a global perspective with an understanding of national concerns and the growth of select urban regions. Broad arguments are enlivened with detailed case studies. The writing style is accessible to the general reader, and the scholarship is comprehensive, so that different interpretations are presented. Five large themes dominate:

- the relationships between people, environment and resources,
- the economic organization of space,
- the global organization of space,
- the political organization of space,
- the urban organization of space.

Running through a discussion of these broad themes are case studies that include examples of specific places as well as examples of the geographical imaginations—models, ideas, and theories—that inform and shape the relationship between people and their environments.

Part 1 sets the context. The first chapter provides a brief introduction to the physical geography of the world, while the second provides an intellectual context by discussing major themes in the development of the discipline of human geography. Not all human geography courses include these topics, but I feel they have a place. To understand contemporary human geography, it is necessary to have a basic grounding in the physical geography of the planet and the intellectual history of the discipline. This section is an elective for those with the time to set the course in its broader physical and intellectual history. Some may elect to move straight to part 2, which makes the connections between population, environment, and resources. Part 3 discusses the economic organization of space. Part 4 centers on the analysis of global trends and processes. Many introductory texts have only one chapter devoted to globalization, almost as an afterthought. An important part of contemporary scholarship identifies the global scale as important for understanding a wide variety of the world's most pressing issues. The book will enable readers to make sense of complex and seemingly unrelated global and regional phenomenon. Part 5 examines the political organization of space. Here I take as the starting point the idea that space embodies and contains power relations. Part 6 focuses on cities, now home to the majority of the world's population. Specific chapters look at the trends of urbanization, urban networks, and the internal structure of the city.

The text is constructed so that instructors can tailor the readings to suit class needs. The entire book may be used, but some may want to exclude the introductory chapter, while others may want to focus on just four of the five major topic areas.

Those with a more economic interest, for example, will certainly want to include part 3, while those with more cultural emphasis will definitely use parts 4 and 5. Those with an interest in cities will use part 6. Each of the six sections is self-contained, so an instructor may elect to choose any four or five and leave more time for other class activities.

TEACHING AND LEARNING PACKAGE

This book is supported by a carefully crafted ancillary package designed to support both professors' and students' efforts in the course:

- *Digital files of all the graphics in the book.* Instructors will find all of the images from the book available to them, both as raw jpegs and pre-inserted into PowerPoint.

- *Test questions and testing software.* Written by experienced instructors and answerable directly from the text, these questions provide professors and instructors with a useful tool for creating and administering tests.

- *Review questions for students.* Carefully crafted by experienced instructors, these computer-graded review questions accompany each unit of the textbook. Professors can assign them for homework, or students can use them independently to check their understanding of the topics presented in the book.

- *Interactive exercises.* These exercises—more extensive than chapter review exercises—guide students through visualizations and animations about key geographic phenomena.

- *Dashboard.* A text-specific, integrated learning system designed with clear and consistent navigation. It delivers quality content and tools to track student progress in an intuitive, web-based learning environment. Dashboard features a streamlined interface that connects instructors and students with the functions they perform most, simplifying the learning experience to save time and put student progress first.

- *Course cartridges.* Instructors may order selected digital supplements in a ready-to-upload form for the most popular course management systems, including Blackboard, D2L, Moodle, Canvas, and Angel, by contacting their Oxford University Press sales representative.

Instructors should contact their Oxford University Press representative for more information about the supplements package.

ACKNOWLEDGMENTS

I'd like to thank the many thoughtful scholars who, during the writing process, dedicated valuable time to reviewing and offering comments on the manuscript. Their comments improved the book significantly.

Jeff Baldwin, Sonoma State University

Brian Blouet, The College of William and Mary

Karl Byrand, University of Wisconsin Colleges

Thomas Chapman, Old Dominion University

Timothy W. Collins, University of Texas-El Paso

Elizabeth Dunn, University of Colorado Boulder

Owen Dwyer, Indiana University–Purdue University Indianapolis

Kyle T. Evered, Michigan State University

Steven M. Graves, California State University, Northridge

Ann Fletchall, Western Carolina University

Joshua Hagen, Marshall University

Stephen Healy, Worcester State University

Peter R. Hoffman, Loyola Marymount University

Jonathan Leib, Old Dominion University

Donald Lyons, University of North Texas

Heather J. McAfee, Clark College

Richard Medina, George Mason University

Darren Purcell, University of Oklahoma

William Rowe, Louisiana State University

James C. Saku, Frostburg State University

Arun Saldanha, University of Minnesota

Richard H. Schein, University of Kentucky

Roger M. Selya, University of Cincinnati

Thomas Sullivan, University of Montana

Selima Sultana, University of North Carolina at Greensboro

Kate Swanson, San Diego State University

Rajiv Thakur, University of Tennessee

Scott Therkalsen, Grossmont Community College

Paul M. Torrens, University of Maryland, College Park

Amy Trauger, University of Georgia

Erika Trigoso, University of Denver

Nicholas Vaughn, Indiana University

Jamie Winders, Syracuse University

David J. Wishart, University of Nebraska-Lincoln

Ryan Weichelt, University of Wisconsin-Eau Claire

The book has also benefited tremendously from the team of professionals at Oxford University Press, and I am grateful to be associated with them. Here I thank my editorial team: Dan Kaveney, Executive Editor, for shepherding the project from the idea stage through to publication; Christine Mahon, Assistant Editor, for helping to attend to the many details involved in preparing a manuscript for production; and Editorial Assistant Nathaniel Rosenthalis, who ably assembled the diverse and helpful review panels mentioned above. The book you are holding wouldn't have been possible without Production Editor Theresa Stockton's steady hand on the tiller coordinating the myriad of tasks required to turn a manuscript into composited, edited pages supported by a terrific art program. Finally, I wish to thank Marketing Manager David Jurman for his tireless work and travel in support of the book.

Lisa Benton-Short is a constant source of love and endless encouragement with just the right amount of sass to keep me firmly grounded.

Welcome to human geography: an endlessly fascinating and always rewarding subject!

Human Geography

PART 1

The Context

This section sets the stage. Chapter 1 gives a brief account of the planet we call home. Attention is paid to the evolution of the Earth, its emerging physical geography, and its humanization. The term "geography" derives from the Greek for "earth description." Chapter 2 looks at the evolution of earth description from its earliest roots to current concerns.

1 The Home Planet

THE BIG PICTURE

According to the aptly named Big Bang Theory, it all started with a very big explosion that produced enough energy to expand a single point outward to infinity. From a singular point in space-time of intense heat and pressure, the universe began to expand, cooling as it spread outward. The universe is still moving outward from this specific moment and particular location. Measuring the speed of the expansion allows us to calculate the approximate moment of the "birth" of our universe, around 13.7 billion years ago. A billion years after the Big Bang (a term coined by Fred Hoyle in 1949), galaxies first came into being from the gravitational pull of small differences in the young universe.

The Big Bang expansion exacerbated minutely small differences in density into sites of star clusters and galaxies. For the first 7 to 9 billion years, the pull of this matter slowed down the rate of expansion of the universe in a cosmic pull of competing forces, the explosive energy of the Big Bang dampened by the gravitational pull of the matter that it created in its wake. Then, the universe began to accelerate as a mysterious energy source, with the foreboding name of dark energy, overcame gravity. Almost three-quarters of the universe is made up of this mysterious force, a little under a quarter is made up of dark matter that does not reflect or emit light, and only around 4 percent is the matter in the universe that we can see and, as yet, understand. We live in a dark universe. And to add to the pervasive strangeness of it all, there is also the intriguing proposition that there was more than one big bang. We are living in the aftermath of a big bang, but perhaps there was more than one, with the possibility of an infinite number, perhaps, as the universe expands and contracts, each big bang leading to a giant implosion followed in turn by another big bang in an endless cycle.

The universe consists of around 200 billion galaxies and 30 billion trillion stars. Our home planet is situated in the Milky Way, a galaxy composed of 100 to 400 billion stars bound together by gravitational pull that stretches across 100,000 light years. One light year is the equivalent of 5.8 trillion miles; it is calculated from the speed of light in a vacuum, which travels at 186,000 miles per second, or 700 million miles an hour. One of the stars, located 24,000 light years from the center of this galaxy, is the Sun, the center of our planetary system and rightfully deserving its capitalization. Eight planets revolve around this star. From near to far they are Mercury, Venus,

Earth, Mars, Jupiter, Saturn, Uranus, and Neptune. The four nearest to the sun are relatively small and composed of rock and metal; the four furthest, the gas planets, are larger, with planetary rings of particles and cosmic dust. Jupiter and Saturn are composed of hydrogen and helium, and the two furthest planets, Uranus and Neptune, circling the darker, colder edges of the solar system, are ice giants made up of water, ammonia, and methane.

We are situated close enough to the Sun to get more heat and light than the furthest planets but not so close as to be burned up by the intense heat experienced by the two planets closer to the Sun. The third planet out from the Sun has enough oxygen and water to support life.

We live on a planet in motion. It revolves around the sun once every 365.25 days. A year marks how long it takes the Earth to complete one full movement around the Sun. The Earth is tilted approximately 23 degrees from the perpendicular in its orbit. This creates the seasons, especially marked further away from the equator, where the distance from the Sun varies more substantially when the tilt is angled away or toward the sun. The tilt of the Earth divides this yearly cycle into seasons; closer to the poles, the seasonal effects are exaggerated as intense cold turns into a marked warming when the long dark days of winter become the light-filled days of summer. At the equator the seasons are less pronounced and the daily division into light and dark more even throughout the year. At the poles the annual cycle moves from a sun that never sets to a sun that is barely visible over the dark horizon. At the equator the sun is a more constant and reliable presence.

Our planet rotates its own axis on a roughly twenty-four-hour cycle. The daily cycle is created as the Earth turns toward and then away from the sun. Although we continue to use the terms "rising" and "setting" sun, it is the Earth that moves. Our planet revolves around the sun and rotates on its own axis.

The Earth does not revolve in a perfect circle. It wobbles, the angle of tilt moves, and its orbit around the sun varies in its eccentricity (departure from circularity).

 Box 1.1   POOR PLUTO

From 1930 to 2006, there were nine planets, a period during which Pluto was discovered, identified as a planet, and then dropped from the list of major planets. The American astronomer Clyde W. Tombaugh discovered the planet in 1930 from the Lowell Observatory in Arizona. Before this date it was too small—only 18 percent of the Earth's diameter—and too far to be visible. It was designated as the ninth and furthest planet from the Sun, but in 2006 it was reclassified as one of the dwarf planets, now classified as plutoids, and dropped from the list of major planets. While denied membership in the club of major planets, poor Pluto still makes its eccentric orbit at the edge of the solar system. In a touching moment of solidarity with the marginalized and the shunned, the supporters of the Turkish soccer club Beşiktaş carried banners that proclaimed, "We Are All Pluto."

These small differences in distance from the sun may account for very long-term climate changes on the Earth, especially the rise and fall of ice ages.

Soon after the formation of the solar system—after only 30 to 50 million years—a giant asteroid, almost half the size of the Earth, hit the Earth. The impact created the Moon, which now revolves around the Earth every 27.3 days, its pitted surface a silent witness to the destructive forces still at work in the universe. The gravitational effect of the Moon on the Earth is responsible for the tides that move the oceans and seas in ceaseless and regular vertical motion. The lunar cycle is the source of our division of time into months.

The yearly, monthly, and daily cycles that are such important rhythms of our lives are caused by the movement of our planet and the Moon in the vast inky darkness of deep space. Even in a more electronic age we are affected by the beats of the cosmos. Two researchers, Scott Golder and Michael Macy, examined millions of tweets over a two-year period. Using selected words in messages to connote moods, they found that there was distinct periodicity, with more positive words in the early morning. Each new dawn offers the promise of a new beginning. Our moods also vary over the seasons. Seasonal Affective Disorder (SAD) is the tendency for more negative moods among normally healthy people during distinct seasons. Winter blues are more common in northern latitudes because of the rapid decrease in sunlight. SAD varies with latitude, with only 1.4 percent experiencing it in Florida but 9.7 percent in colder, darker New Hampshire.

SHAKY GROUND: PLATE TECTONICS

Look at any map of the world. The continents sitting in the blue seas and vast oceans look solid, firm, permanent. From a very long perspective the image is deceptive. The present distribution of landmasses is just the most recent frame in a dynamic, complex picture of continents forming, reforming, splitting up, and moving across the Earth's surface.

Earth came into being around 4.55 billion years ago. Soon afterwards, around 4.51 billion years ago, the Earth was hit by a giant asteroid, turning it into a fiery ball of intense heat. Over the years the surface cooled more than the interior. The Earth's surface, the "solid ground" of so many metaphors, is in fact a thin brittle crust, no more than four to sixty-five miles thick, that floats precariously on a viscous mass of molten metal. The crust that we occupy is the cold top level that is formed just as the skin forms when boiling milk cools. Below is the hot mantle and, even deeper, the extremely hot core. The crust is a solidified surface that fractures on the large round object of the Earth, breaking up into distinct plates. There are nine large plates and numerous small ones (Figure 1.1). They sit atop powerful currents. Below them the mantle of molten metal heaves as the hotter liquid moves up in convection currents from the boiling mass at the Earth's core while the cooler liquid closer to the surface sinks to the bottom. This continual subterranean motion moves the plates. The plates on the surface are like bumper cars in a fairground ride that move in a restricted space. Driven by the upward convection currents deep in

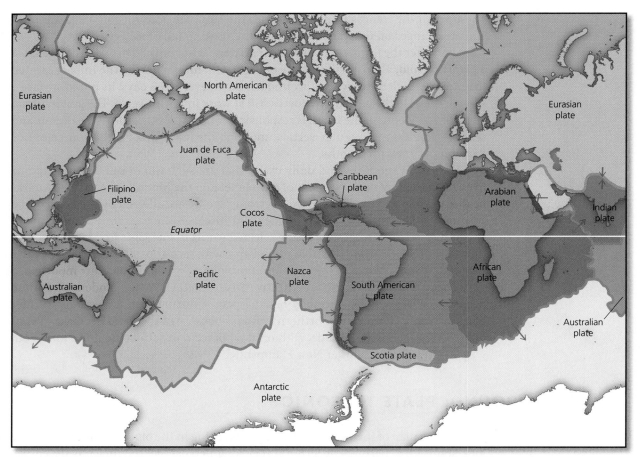

1.1   Plate boundaries

the Earth's mantle, they bump up against each other, slide past each other, and move away from each other. Mountains are formed, trenches are created, earthquakes occur, and boiling magma spews out in volcanic eruptions to reveal the fiery material that shapes the Earth's geological formations. The surface that we live on is a fragile membrane across deep and powerful subterranean forces. Volcanic and earthquake activity is particularly severe at the edges where plates meet (Figures 1.2 and Figure 1.3).

The plates are always on the move. In the geological equivalent of political empires, giant landmasses rise and fall. Over 1.4 billion years ago, small masses of land collided to form the supercontinent of Rodinia. This landmass was rent asunder into different blocs including Avalonia; Baltica; Laurentia, eventually to become North America; and Gondwana, the source continent for South America, Africa, India, Antarctica, Australia, and New Zealand. When Baltica and Laurentia joined up with Gondwana around 300 million years ago, a new supercontinent, Pangaea, was created. It took up almost one entire side of the globe—the other side

1.2 Along the line of mountains in Central America is a zone of active volcanic and earthquake events. This is a volcano just outside the city of Antigua in Guatemala. It belches smoke every day. The locals say the time to worry is when the daily outburst does not occur.

was mostly water—and it was centered on the South Pole. This began to break up, but the large landmass of Gondwana remained. Beginning around 200 to 160 million years ago, it too began to break up, as South America broke off and drifted west and a landmass of what was to become India began a 150-million-year journey northwards to Asia, and when it crashed into the Eurasian plate the Himalayas were formed. Around 60 million years ago, another landmass, what we now call Australia, broke off from what is now Antarctica and began a 45-million-year, 500-mile journey north through various climate zones toward the warmth of a more northerly location. Australia was on the move. Slowly. It is still moving northward away from Antarctica at a rate of around 2.7 inches per year. There are many traces of the long journey. Australia shares with South America similar species of marsupials, turtles, and lungfish that are over 400 million years old, a biotic reminder of when the two continents were joined in Gondwana. And the distribution of an extinct fern, *Glossopteris*, in Antarctica, Africa, Australia, India, and South America is a biological reminder of the supercontinent.

The Indo-Australian plate eventually crunched up against the Eurasian plate around 15 million years ago (Figure 1.4). The border area between the two plates is still one of the most active volcanic zones in the world. Let us consider three events. Around 74,000 years ago, a giant volcano exploded at Mount Toba in Sumatra (now part of Indonesia). Almost a billion tons of ash and dust were thrown up into the atmosphere, darkening the skies and reducing global temperatures by around 5°C for up to five years. One anthropologist, Stanley Ambrose, writes of a long volcanic winter, an instant Ice Age that severely reduced early human populations. The total human population in the world was probably reduced to around 10,000, so that local variations became more pronounced in human evolution, creating the contemporary racial differentiation. The huge, violent explosion caused global climate change that further impacted human populations. The extent to which the consequent environmental stressors may have promoted social cooperation and thus facilitated the human dispersal from Africa is a debatable but intriguing proposition.

The region saw another massive volcanic explosion when the island of Krakatoa exploded on August 27, 1883. Not as violent as the Mount Toba explosion, it was still a devastating volcanic eruption; the resultant tsunami killed approximately 36,500 people in the region as tidal waves drowned towns and villages along the

1.3 The cloud-covered top of Mount Vesuvius looms over the Gulf of Naples. It erupted in 70 CE and drowned the city of Pompeii in a sea of ash. It is one of the most active volcanoes in mainland Europe, last erupting in 1944.

coast. The waves swept around the world. A wave height increase of three inches was noted in Biarritz, France, more than 10,000 miles from the explosion. The air pollution caused by all the dust and ash blotted out the sun's heat and light and reduced the world's temperature by about 1°F. The volcanic ash and dust made sunsets all over the world more dramatically red. The bright colors are recorded in the paintings of the time, including Frederic Edwin Church's watercolor based upon a trip to the New York–Canadian border in 1883 and titled *Sunset over the Ice on Chaumont Bay, Lake Ontario*. The painting is aglow with a sunset infused with dust from Krakatoa. Simon Winchester also argues that Krakatoa influenced political developments. He suggests that the 1888 Banten Peasants' Revolt, which pitted local people against Dutch colonial rule, was in part influenced by the cataclysm that befell local people and fed into an Islamic fundamentalist and an anticolonial narrative that "explained" the explosion and the mass deaths as the work of a wrathful Allah signaling displeasure at colonial control and lax religious practices.

On December 26, 2004, movement along the plate caused another major disaster. The Sumatra-Andaman earthquake occurred nineteen miles below sea level off the coast of Sumatra. Along a 1,000-mile zone, plates shifted almost fifty feet and raised the surface of the seabed, displacing millions of gallons of water that caused the tsunami, the post-earthquake tidal waves that suddenly overwhelmed coastal communities in fourteen countries fringing the Indian Ocean. As wave crests reaching 100 feet crashed into unsuspecting communities, more than 230,000 people died, 125,000 were injured, and almost 1.7 million were displaced from their homes.

1.4 This section of a physiographic diagram of the Indian Ocean by Bruce Heezen and Maria Tharp highlights the plate boundary off the coast of Java and Sumatra.

LIFE ON EARTH

For half of its entire existence the Earth did not sustain life. It took a long time for the planet to cool down and its landmasses to become more stable. The beginnings of life around 2.2 billion years ago were in the modest form of blue-green algae. Evolution was slow until the development of sexual reproduction. An explosion of life took place around 545 million years ago in the Cambrian period of the Early Paleozoic era as living forms with skeletons first appeared. The growth of the amount and diversity of life was not a simple upward trajectory. The same era also marked the first global mass extinction as many species of shallow water fauna were killed off by rising sea levels.

Around 418 million years ago, the first land animals appeared. Insects and amphibians emerged. In the Mesozoic era, from 248 to 65 million years ago, the first dinosaur appeared, as did the first mammal, a tiny shrew-like animal dwarfed by the giant reptiles around it. In the late Mesozoic there was another mass extinction of animal life. Dinosaurs became extinct, and birds lost almost 80 percent of their species, as did the marsupials. Some scientists suggest that colossal volcanic eruptions in a mountain chain in eastern India spewed huge amount of carbon dioxide and sulfur dioxide into the atmosphere, poisoning the air. Other scientists point to an asteroid hitting the Earth around the same time, 65 million years ago. A crater measuring 100 miles wide and 6 miles deep was discovered in the Yucatan peninsula near the town of Chicxulub. The impact of the asteroid created global fires that sucked oxygen out of the atmosphere and caused huge shock waves that triggered volcanoes and earthquakes. The volcanic eruptions in India and the asteroid strike in the Yucatan created devastating global environmental conditions. Dust covered the Earth, leading to temperature decrease. Acid rain fell. Dark and coldness settled on the Earth, plants stopped growing, and animals died. More than 90 percent of all marine life died as the seas became acid baths. The dinosaurs became extinct, as they could not survive in the wasteland of permanent winter. They starved to death.

The Tertiary period, from 65 million to 1.8 million years ago, is the age of mammals. Whales appear, as do elephants, cats, and dogs. Around 50 million years ago, the first primate appears, a little lemur-like creature barely more than two pounds in weight. The primates diversified and spread. Four million years ago, the first hominid to stand upright, *Australopithecus,* walked on the Earth. Between 2 and 3 million years ago, at least eight different hominid species emerged from this one species, correlating with a time of increased climate change. The rapidly changing conditions rewarded species that could adapt quickly, especially those that had the brain capacity to adjust to constant environmental change. Adaptability to diverse environmental conditions is one of the defining hallmarks of our human species.

A HUMANIZED WORLD

Tracing human origins was long the preserve of archeologists and physical anthropologists. Digging in old sites and dating the old bones was the preferred method. Dates were always provisional, and the ambiguity of the information always provided lots of room for debate. Things began to change when scientists could use live humans to chart the past. Our bodies, it appears, are the equivalent of an archeological site, containing memories and traces of the far distant past. Plotting the distribution of the information in our bodies allows us to map possible sites of human origin and paths of human dispersal.

In the 1950s, differences in blood group protein were identified that allowed a picture of human ancestry. A more sophisticated analysis was made possible in 1987, when scientists first used the DNA in mitochondria, the rod-shaped "power batteries" of cells, to construct a genetic tree. This allowed the examination of generic materials passed from mother to child. Using this method allowed scientists to come to the startling conclusion that we are all descended from one woman who lived in Africa around 200,000 years ago.

After decades of competing ideas and dueling theories, there is an emerging consensus that all humans are descended from a group of people who left Africa. Human origins lie in Africa. The first humans stepped out of Africa to populate and humanize the world (Figure 1.5). Evidence of genetic variation sustains this out-of-Africa hypothesis. Peoples in central and southern Africa have more genetic variation than elsewhere in the world. The highest levels of genetic diversity in the world are among the Namibian and Khomani Bushmen of southern Africa, the Biaka Pygmies of Central Africa, and the Sandawe of East Africa. There is a decrease of genetic diversity with increasing distance from Africa, suggesting a founder's group in Africa as the basis for all subsequent human population. As smaller subgroups broke off to settle in different places, the amount of genetic diversity decreased. The amount of genetic variation declines with distance from Africa—a classic case of the distance-decay effect—suggesting that humans came out of Africa to populate the Earth. It was the first wave of globalization.

The human diffusion from Africa, around 120,000 to 70,000 years ago, initially involved a tiny population of probably only around 3,000 people. Notice the implied leeway in the term "around." We have gotten a general idea, not a sure fix. The movement out of Africa took different routes at different times. The oldest was a group that moved out through the Horn of Africa into the Middle East. One group then moved along a coastal route skirting the Indian Ocean. They took around 20,000 years to migrate around the Indian Ocean, taking the beachcomber route into Southeast Asia and Oceania. The migration took the form of budding, as small subgroups

1.5 The peopling of the world

broke away to settle new places. Traveling along the coast and up rivers, they avoided the difficulties of passing through deserts and across mountains. Consider, as just one example, the settling of Australia. Around 50,000 years ago, when sea levels were lower, Australia was linked to Papua New Guinea, and there was only a relatively short distance, probably no more than sixty-five miles, between the edge of Asia and the coast of Australia. Bamboo rafts probably were constructed to make the sea crossing. The current archeological evidence dates the human presence in Australia to between 55,000 to 42,000 years ago. Most of the early Australian sites have deep charcoal deposits that suggest both early settlement and a long record of occupation. The migrants traveled quickly up the rivers and along the coast. Colonization was rapid, as there are sites scattered throughout the vast continent in the north, northwest, southwest, and southeast and sites as far south as Tasmania, all dated to around 32,000 to 40,000 years ago. Central Australia was settled last, as there were no easy coastal or riverine routes to follow. People had to venture into a dry, forbidding interior. But venture they did. We have a site, the Puritjarra Cave Rock Shelter, with rock art suggesting occupancy as far back as 32,000 years ago.

Another later wave of human migration around 50,000 years ago moved into Eurasia. Giant walls of ice restricted movement north; it was still the Ice Age, also known as the Pleistocene era. However, sea levels were much lower in the Pleistocene, exposing land bridges that are now covered with seawater.

Box 1.2   WALLACE'S LINE: A BIOGEOGRAPHICAL BOUNDARY

In the mid-ineteenth century, Alfred Russell Wallace (1828–1913) spent eight years travelling the Malay Archipelago. He travelled over 14,000 miles and collected over 100,000 samples. He was less well known than Darwin, and his letters back to members of England's scientific community indicating a theory of natural selection for the origin of species prompted some to counsel Darwin to publish his own work in 1859. In 1863 Wallace published a paper in the *Journal of the Royal Geographical Society* that identified a boundary line between two realms. This line, now known as Wallace's Line, divides the Australian and Asian biotas.

Wallace's work was part of a surge of mapping in the nineteenth-century natural sciences. Maps were used as a conceptual framework and as a tool for presenting vast amounts of data in simple yet suggestive ways. Wallace's Line evolved from papers he wrote in 1855 and 1860 as well as the 1863

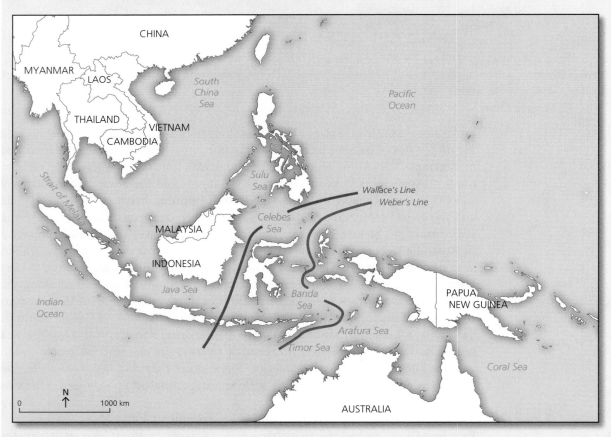

Wallace's Line

Box 1.2 CONTINUED

paper. Later, the zoologist and biogeographer Max Carl Wilhelm Weber drew his own line based on surveys of mammalian fauna. His line is further to the east than Wallace's Line. The difference between the two lines is because flora found it easier to move across the "line," while the seas constituted a larger barrier to animal movement. The area between the Wallace and Weber lines can be considered a zone of transition.

The biogeographical boundaries identified by Wallace and Weber are a result of plate tectonics. The northward drift of the Australian plate made it crash against the Eurasian plate around 15 million years ago. Previously separate biological realms were brought into contact. The Australian plate was like a raft filled with distinctive flora and marsupial animals now abutting the Asian flora and fauna. Without a theory of plate tectonics, the theory was only first mooted by Alfred Wegener in 1912 and published in 1915, Wallace could not discern the geological basis for the division. However, his careful mapping highlighted the benefits of fieldwork and the representation of these data in maps. Wallace's Line is the biological equivalent of plate boundaries, even although Wallace was not aware of the plates and the theory of continental drift.

References

Camerini, J. R. (1993) Evolution, Biogeography and Maps: An Early History of Wallace's Line. *Isis* 84: 700–727.

Vetter, J. (2006) Wallace's Other Line: Human Biogeography and Field Practice in the Eastern Colonial Tropics. *Journal of the History of Biology* 39: 89–123.

Wallace, A. J. (1863) On the Physical Geography of the Malay Archipelago. *Journal of the Royal Geographical Society* 33: 217–234.

The English Channel was dry land, allowing people and animals to move from Europe into what is now Britain and Ireland. On the other side of the world, the land bridge between the northeasternmost edge of Eurasia and the northwest edge of America allowed people and animals to make the journey across the continents around 22,000–25,000 years ago.

Humans groups were restless, continually moving and settling new areas. People even sailed across the vast expanses of the Pacific Ocean to settle on such distant specks of islands as Hawaii. The early humans explored the world, settled in different habitats, and impacted their environment.

The human colonizers had an immediate impact on their environment. Despite early interpretations of them as docile elements in the landscape, they were very much active agents in modifying and changing the environment. The early humans first shared the Eurasian landmass with other hominids such as the Neanderthals and the Denisovans. These were cousins to humans on the evolutionary tree, emerging as separate subspecies around 500,000 years ago. The Neanderthals were not as dumb as common characterizations assume. They walked upright and effectively communicated with each other. They emerged in and lived throughout Eurasia. With the entry of *Homo sapiens,* these two

Box 1.3 MAPS AS EVIDENCE

Mapping is an enormously productive way of not only showing things but also suggesting things. We should be careful, however. Similar patterns may emerge from different processes, so there is no easy way to read processes from spatial patterns. So mapping can merely suggest different processes, but mapping, in association with strong theory, can be a very powerful way to confirm theories.

We have already noted in this chapter how mapping genetic and language diversity has confirmed the out-of-Africa hypothesis. The distance-decay of genetic and linguistic complexity further from Africa is very suggestive of an African origin of human settlement of the

Earth. The theory of plate tectonics is also confirmed by the spatial correlation of plate boundaries with seismic activity.

Even spatial anomalies can be productive sources of ideas. Hippopotamus fossils are found in southern England. Dating back 120,000 years, they remind us of an interglacial period of rising temperatures that increased the warming effect of the Gulf Stream. During the next cold snap, between 38,000 and 10,000 years ago, the ice sheet was so extensive that polar bears could travel as far as Ireland, where they interbred with local brown bears. That explains why today we can trace the genetic origin of polar bears back to Ireland's now extinct brown bears.

hominid species died out around 30,000 years ago, just as the human population spread across the Eurasian landmass. We effectively annihilated our closest competition for food and environmental resources. One competitive advantage was the division of labor. Among human populations, women and young children were responsible for skill-intensive crafts such as making clothing and shelter as well as gathering food. Men were primarily responsible for hunting. The division of labor allowed access to a wider range of food sources compared to the other hominids, who, because they did not have the gender and age division of labor that allowed economic specialization, were almost entirely dependent on hunting game. When the game disappeared, they starved and died out. The gender and age division of labor in early human populations created more specialized economic roles that allowed a more efficient use of labor and gave access to a wider food resource base.

The other hominid groups died out, but they live on in our genetic makeup. They must have been close enough to humans so that interbreeding occurred. Hybrid humans, the outcome of sexual liaisons between humans and the two other groups, survived, breeding in turn. We have a genetic record of the process. All non-Africans have between 1 and 4 percent of Neanderthal DNA. The people of New Guinea have around 5 percent of Denisovan DNA. Most of the world's non-African population carry this genetic reminder of the width of human sexual appetite and willingness to "interact" with their evolutionary cousins. The distinction between human and nonhuman hominids was more of a liminal area than a sharp and fixed boundary.

The early human colonization of the Earth was also marked by ecological changes. The most pronounced is the Pleistocene Overkill, which refers to the extinction of megafauna such as the mammoth and the mastodon. This extinction occurred in every continent and was experienced by every community of large terrestrial vertebrates at a time of humans' increased technological sophistication in hunting. While there has been some debate about the relative role that climate change played in the mass extinction, human hunting was a definitive contributing cause. In some continents both hunting and climate change were important, while in others the primary causal explanation lies with human hunting. The extinction was particularly marked in North America around 20,000 years ago.

America is a test case of the overkill, since human entry into the region was relatively late, and there are no records of other hominids. John Alroy created a grid of 754 spatial cells of one degree of latitude and one degree of longitude. His computer simulation model for North America clearly shows that human population growth and hunting led to mass extinction 1,200 years after humans first appeared.

The larger and slower megafauna were very vulnerable to skilled hunters. The megafauna, weighing more than 220 pounds and thus slower, became especially vulnerable. In Australia, for example, many megafauna became extinct around 46,000 years ago, soon after the entry of humans into Australia. We will never again see the three-meter-high giant kangaroo, the rhino-sized wombat, or the marsupial lion. We do have a visual record from rock paintings in Arnhem Land in northern Australia, which may depict a *Palorchestes*, a large browsing animal; a *Genyornis*, similar to an emu but three times as tall; and a marsupial lion. Further west in Kimberley, rock paintings depict giant kangaroos and huge echidnas. The paintings are a reminder of the time when megafauna and humans shared the same space and an early example of the immense role that humans played and continue to play in shaping the global ecosystem.

Cited References

Alroy, J. (2001) A Multispecies Overkill Simulation of the End-Pleistocene Megafaunal Extinction. *Science* 292: 1893–1896.

Ambrose, S. (1998) Late Pleistocene Human Population Bottlenecks, Volcanic Winter, and Differentiation of Modern Humans. *Journal of Human Evolution* 34: 623–651.

Golder, S. A. and Macy, M. W. (2011) Diurnal and Seasonal Moods Vary with Work, Sleep, and Daylength across Diverse Cultures. *Science* 333: 1878–1881.

Grove, M. (2011) Change and Variability in Plio-Pleistocene Climates: Modelling the Hominin Response. *Journal of Archaeological Science* 38: 3038–3047.

Kuhn, S. L. and M. C. Stiner (2006) What's a Mother to Do? The Division of Labor among Neandertals and Modern Humans in Eurasia." *Current Anthropology* 47:953–980.

Winchester, S. (2003) *Krakatoa: The Day the World Exploded: August 27, 1883*. New York: Viking.

Select Guide to Further Reading

On human peopling of the world:

Oppenheimer, S. (2003) *Out of Eden: The Peopling of the World*. London: Constable.

Stix, G. (2008) Traces of a Distant Past. *Scientific American* 299, 1: 56–63.

Stringer, C. (2011) *The Origin of Our Species*. London: Allen Lane.

Tattersall, I. (2009) Human Origins: Out of Africa. *Proceedings of National Academy of Sciences* 106: 16018–16021.

Selected Websites

Shifting plates
http://www.nasa.gov/audience/forstudents/5-8/features/F_Earth_Has_Faults_prt.htm

An interactive map of earthquakes, plates, and volcanoes
http://nhb-arcims.si.edu/ThisDynamicPlanet/index.html

An interactive atlas of human origins and dispersal
https://genographic.nationalgeographic.com/genographic/atlas.html

The Biodiversity Heritage Library
http://www.biodiversitylibrary.org

Convention on Biological Diversity
http://www.cbd.int

The World Meteorological Organization is a specialized agency of the United Nations that provides information on the state and behavior of the Earth's atmosphere, its interaction with the oceans, the climate it produces, and the resulting distribution of water resources.
http://www.wmo.int/pages/index_en.html

The Intergovernmental Panel on Climate Change (IPCC) is the leading international body for the assessment of climate change.
http://ipcc.ch

2 | The Intellectual Context

In this chapter I will place the contemporary study of human geography in a deeper historical context. Human geography of today is shaped by the debates of the past. I will identify five particular themes that resonate down through the years: coordinating absolute space, the emergence of geography from cosmography, the discussion of relative space, environment and society, and the links between geography and society. A discussion of these themes is a revealing entry point into the history of human geography.

MAPPING ABSOLUTE SPACE

A significant and recurring theme in geography is the attempt to accurately represent the world we live in through maps. It is an important element of the geographical imagination. One of the earliest geographers who sought to measure and coordinate the world was Claudius Ptolemy. He was a Greek-Egyptian who worked in the great library of Alexandria. He lived sometime between 90 CE and 168 CE and spent his adult life in Alexandria, a Greek city founded in 331 BCE and named after Alexander the Great. The city was one of the wonders of the classical world, and its population grew to almost half a million. There were palaces and large public buildings, and at the heart of the intellectual life of the city was the library. It was a major center of scholarship with over 700,000 volumes. Euclid and Archimedes worked at the library, and Eratosthenes was, for a time, the chief librarian.

The *Almagest* is Ptolemy's earliest major work. The title comes from an Arabic form of the Greek word for "greatest"; the *Almagest* maps the heavens and plots the location of the sun, moon, stars, and planets and their trajectory across the sky. He assumed that the universe revolved around the Earth. If the *Almagest* plotted the celestial universe, his *Geography* sought to map the terrestrial world. He defined latitude and longitude, discussed methods of mapmaking, and posed the problem of how to represent the round world on a flat surface. He proposed two map projections, a conic projection and a partial conic projection, on which to represent the habitable world. Conic projections map the earth on a cone and then show it as flattened with lines of latitude as concentric circles, so you can see that Ptolemy has some nifty mathematical abilities (Figure 2.1). He compiled lists of the latitude and longitude of places in the world known to him, basically a world centered on the Mediterranean. Ptolemy was also an astrologist. His *Tetrabiblos* was an extended astrological treatise. At that time, there was no distinction between astrology and astronomy. Mathematics, geometry, and astrology formed more of a coherent whole than they do today. The universe was studied for intimations of cosmic influence, and human understanding of the world was bound up with a sense of connection between the internal world of human psychology and temperament and the external world of planetary alignment.

In the European Dark Ages, Ptolemy's influence quickly disappeared. His work, however, was kept alive in the Arab world. Ptolemy's work was translated by the Arab cosmologists of the Abbasid court in Baghdad. Al-Battani (ca. 880) restated the *Almagest* with improved measurements, and *Geography* was revised by al-Khwarizmi around 820 in his *Face of the Earth*, which included a map of the world.

Al-Idrisi (ca. 1100–1166) was born in Ceuta, Morocco. He studied at Cordoba in Spain and was employed by Roger the Second of Sicily. Al-Idrisi was a practicing geographer who traveled through the Arab world. He constructed a celestial sphere and a map of the world. He was part of a larger geographical school of scholarship in the Arab world, involving book knowledge as well as geographical fieldwork and travel, that included the *Book of Countries* by Al-Yaqubi (ca. 891), Al-Balkhis's *Figures of The Climates* (921), Al-Muqaddasi's *The Best Description for*

2.1 Ptolemy's map of the world in a conic projection, ca.1300

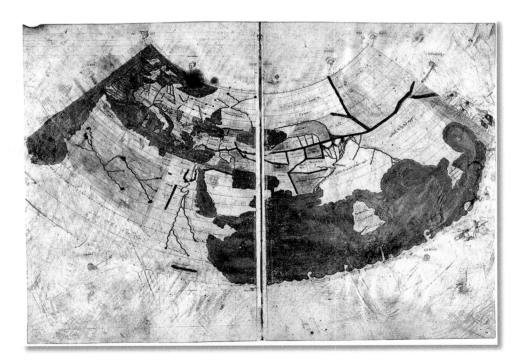

Box 2.1 MEASURING THE WORLD

The measuring of the world is a significant part in the early history of geography. By the fifth century BCE, the Greeks knew that the world was a sphere. Eratosthenes (ca. 276 BCE–ca. 194 BCE), who, like Ptolemy, worked at the great Library of Alexandria, calculated the circumference of the Earth. Assuming a spherical Earth, he calculated the circumference with only a 1–2 percent difference from the correct figure of 24,901 miles.

Ptolemy's measurement of the circumference was much less accurate, around 18,000 miles. The wide diffusion of Ptolemy's writings meant that this figure was taken as fact during the early modern period. Columbus probably had this much smaller value in mind when he was planning to sail to the East Indies; Ptolemy's shorter value made the voyage that much less intimidating.

In 1669–1670, the Frenchman Jean Picard tried to accurately measure the earth by extrapolating from the distance of one degree of latitude measured in the French countryside. However, similar surveys of a degree of latitude undertaken in Peru and Scandinavia at the same time had different values. The reason was not an instrumentation error but because the earth is an oblate, flattened at the poles. A degree of latitude is shorter closer to the equator than the poles. We live on a less than perfect sphere in all its misshapen complexity.

an *Understanding of All Provinces* (ca. 985), and Al-Bakri's *Book of Roads and Kingdoms* (ca. 1050).

In the early 1400s, Byzantine scholars brought their Greek manuscripts, including manuscripts of Ptolemy's writings, to Italy. The first printed copy of *Geography* appeared in Vicenza in 1475. Other editions appeared in Rome (1477), Florence (1480), and Ulm (1482). The Ulm edition, with its richly colored woodblock maps with deep blue seas and bright yellow borders, is arguably one of the most beautiful. After 1508, editions of Ptolemy's *Geography* included maps that incorporated the discoveries of the New World. The first printed map of the New World appears in an edition of *Geography.*

Ptolemy's *Geography* stimulated new knowledge and innovative cartographic techniques. His continuing legacy includes orientating maps with north at the top, the grid of latitude and longitude, using gazetteers in maps and atlases, and employing a variety of map projections. Ptolemy introduced us to the idea and practice of a coordinated world.

It is important to remember, however, that Ptolemy's view of the world was centered on the West. It was not the only view. Figure 2.2 is one of the oldest world maps from East Asia, created around 1389, roughly the same time as the world's map shown in Figure 2.1. Notice how China sits in the center of the map, the pivot of the world's landmass, with a hazily outlined Europe located on the far western periphery.

2.2 Korean map of the world, ca.1389

THE SHIFT FROM COSMOGRAPHY TO GEOGRAPHY

Geography was part of a much wider cosmographical understanding of an interconnected cosmos that included astronomy, astrology, and magic as well. The history of geography in the past five hundred years is the dismemberment of this cosmological enterprise.

It begins in the Renaissance, where there is evidence of both continuances and ruptures. There was an esoteric side to the Renaissance that included alchemy, astrology, and magic. These were not marginal concerns but rather central to the life and work of influential Renaissance scholars. John Dee (1527–1608) was a mathematician, mapmaker, and astrologist. His writings combine an interest in exploration and travel, magic and alchemy, mathematics and geography. Dee, like Ptolemy, had a concern with a cosmography that linked the Earth and the heavens, people and their wider environment.

We sometimes assume that the Scientific Revolution marked a major change: before was superstition; after was rational, enlightened thought. Recent scholarship has questioned the traditional assumption of such a radical break in intellectual practice as to constitute the epistemological rupture. The revisionist argument has

Box 2.2 THINKING ABOUT MAPS

Maps and mapmaking are an integral part of the history of geography. The history of cartography was long dominated by a narrative that stressed mapping as a steady rise in greater knowledge and increased understanding of the world. It was a tale of the increasing scientific rationality of mapmaking from a dim and distant premodern past to an increasingly enlightened present. Maps were milestones along this journey. This discourse was undermined by the postmodern turn, which emphasized maps as social constructions, stories with a purpose full of erasures and silences as well as inscriptions and disclosures. Maps were deconstructed according to their ideological basis, their political undertones, and their social contexts. Maps are now no longer seen as uncomplicated pictures of the world. They reflect power relations and embody the knowledge and ignorance, articulations and silences, of the wider social world. The accuracy or provenance of maps is no longer the only consideration in the new history of cartography. It is important to uncover their narrative context—their truths as well as their lies. Mapping is not innocent science, it is a political act.

References

Harley, B. (2001) *The New Nature of Maps*. Johns Hopkins University Press: Baltimore and London.

been put most cogently by Steven Shapin, who argues for a diverse array of cultural practices aimed at understanding, explaining, and controlling the world; these practices involved a continuity with the medieval world rather than a sharp break.

The shift from magus to scientist and from cosmography to geography was neither sudden nor abrupt. The new scientific order bears the mark of the old cosmologies. These connections are clear when we look at some of the early cosmographer/geographers. The great mapmaker Gerard Mercator (1512–1594) had a religious dimension to his work. Born Gerard Kremer in the small town of Rupelmonde near Antwerp into a modest household, he went to Louvain in 1530 and Latinized his surname to Mercator. He was always interested in theology, he wrote religious tracts, and his first map was a map of the Holy Land. In 1544 he was accused of heresy, one of forty-three accused in Louvain. Two of the accused were burned at the stake, one was beheaded, and a woman was buried alive. Supported by friends and colleagues at the university, he was released. Mercator was a friend of John Dee; they corresponded, and Dee visited him in 1547. Mercator is best known today for his maps. In 1585 he published volumes covering France, Belgium, and Germany. In 1589 he published twenty-two maps, including those of Italy, Slovakia, and Greece. He died in 1594, but his son Rumold collected all the maps in one volume, entitled it *Atlas,* and published it in 1595. We continue to use the term *atlas* to describe a collection of printed maps.

Perhaps the last cosmographer and first modern geographer was Baron Friedrich Wilhelm Heinrich Alexander von Humboldt (1769–1859; see Figure 2.3). Born

2.3 Portrait of von Humboldt, 1843

in Berlin, he was privately tutored as a young boy and then studied at universities in Frankfurt, Göttingen, Hamburg, and Freiburg. He traveled widely. A voracious reader, he had interests in economics, geology, botany, and mining. He was also, for his time, a radical. He arrived in Paris shortly before the storming of the Bastille; he wrote later that it "stirred his soul." He had a lifelong social concern with social reform and improvement. A recurring theme of his intellectual curiosity was to identify the "life force." His belief in universal harmony echoed concerns of John Dee. And, like Mercator, he had a fascination with geomagnetism. He was also deeply empirical; measurement and numbers were important to him.

After 1796, when he inherited money after his mother's death, he was able to pursue his dream of traveling, exploring, and writing about the world. He traveled to France and Spain, a "measuring expedition" he called it, so he could practice surveying techniques. He traveled to South America in 1799 with his friend the French botanist Aimé Bonpland, and stayed until 1804. He passed through Cuba, Colombia, Ecuador, Mexico, and Venezuela, recording, measuring, and explaining. He gathered 60,000 plant specimens, made maps, and amassed a range of data from climate to linguistics. His careful mapping of plants in different places demonstrated the effect of altitude and latitude on plant communities.

Humboldt was an influential figure. His fame and reputation stimulated the adoption of measurement and observation in various expeditions and surveys throughout the world. He stimulated geographical measurement and observation. Figure 2.4 is an 1823 isothermal map of the world, as the text notes, "drawn from the account of Humboldt and others." Humboldt traveled throughout his life, in later years venturing east to Siberia and covering almost 9,000 miles at a time when transport was rudimentary. His travel journal consisted of thirty-four volumes.

His best-known work, *Cosmos*, was published from 1845 to 1862. He sought to make it accessible to a wider public. Four volumes were published during his lifetime. Volume 1 is a general view of nature—from a discussion of stars to the geographic distribution of plants. Volume 2 deals with responses to the physical environment and explores the world of perception and feelings. There is extensive treatment of poetic descriptions of nature, from the Greeks to modern travelers. Volumes 3 and 4 are more standard scientific works that discuss astronomy, geology, and physical geography. Humboldt thought of calling his work *Cosmography* but stayed with *Cosmos* because it implied order. On the pivot of intellectual change,

2.4 Isothermal chart, 1823

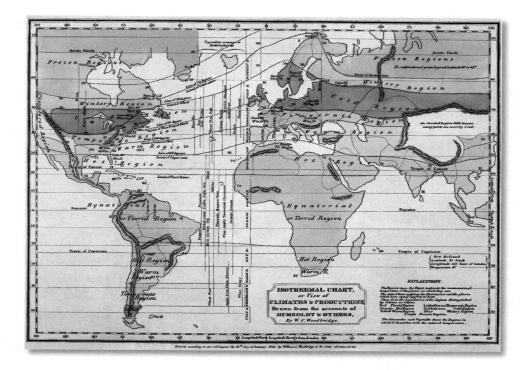

he shared some of the concerns of the older cosmographical tradition while inaugurating modern geography.

MAPPING RELATIVE SPACE

Absolute space is the grid of latitude and longitude. It is now easy to note that as I type these lines I am located at 39.09 degrees north, 76.88 degrees west. We have come very far in giving an accurate spatial fix. In absolute terms, the earth is accurately mapped, gridded, and coordinated. However, this locational fix says little about the neighborhood where I live. What kind of people live here? What are the housing conditions and neighborhood characteristics? Absolute location tells us nothing about the character of places. Much of contemporary human geography is concerned with the relative space of social connections, political arrangements, and economic conditions. We can consider the development of relative space by sampling some varied endeavors: the history of the mappings of crime, health, and social deprivation.

Crime

The term "moral statistics" first appears in an essay by André-Michel Guerry in 1833. It was used to refer to crime, pauperism, and a wide range of social phenomena. Such statistics were an important part of nineteenth-century thematic

Box 2.3 CARTOGRAPHIC ENCOUNTERS

Europeans "explored" and mapped large parts of Africa, America, and Asia. Despite the traditional view that Europeans created such maps on their own, local and indigenous peoples helped considerably in the mapping. It is more accurate to consider the notion of cartographic encounters involving Europeans and local peoples, rather than a simple cartographic appropriation by Europeans. The mapping of the continents was underpinned by native knowledge. There is a hidden stratum of indigenous geographical knowledge that is only now being uncovered.

Take the case of North America. The Europeans landed in a populated place. In order to find their way and move around the unfamiliar landscape, they relied upon the indigenous people to provide information, advice, and guidance. In return, the indigenous people obtained trade goods, spatial information, and the possibility of new alliances against longstanding enemies. This exchange was invaluable to the Europeans over both the short and long term. For the Native Americans, the exchange over the short and medium term could prove useful, but over the long term it sealed their fate. The cartographic encounters resulted in Native Americans losing control over their territory. No longer needed, they were moved and marginalized. In the case of North America, the mapping of the land embodied a *symbiotically destructive* relationship. It was a relationship that allowed Native Americans to parlay their deeper and wider knowledge of the land into a strong bargaining position, but in this very exchange, where they had some leverage, lay the roots of their loss of the land. They used what resources they had in gain a short-term advantage, but over the long term the cartographic encounter gave the newcomers more power. There were cartographic encounters between Europeans, European Americans, and Native Americans. The maps made by the explorers drew heavily upon an indigenous cartographic contribution.

References

Short, J. R. (2009) *Cartographic Encounters: Indigenous Peoples and the Exploration of the New World*. London: Reaktion.

mapping. Maps of crime in France first appeared in 1829, when Guerry used data from 1825 to 1827 to plot, for each of the *départements* in the country, the incidence of crime against persons, crimes against property, and educational instruction. Mapping in the early nineteenth century predated the development of statistical techniques. Maps and mapping were thus an important way to identify and suggest causal connections. The Belgian statistician Adolphe Quetelet also used maps to suggest connections. His carefully gradated shading maps of France, the Low Countries, and parts of the Rhineland published in 1831, show statistics on crimes against the property and crimes against people. Quetelet was an influential figure in Europe, and his work and maps were translated into other languages. In the United States, Chicago was an early laboratory of social analysis and spatial mapping. A 1942 study by Shaw and McKay, for example, maps the covariation of various social conditions with reported incidences of juvenile delinquency.

Today the mapping of crime is an important element in policing. Keith Harries summarizes the now vast material on the mapping of crime. Maps of crime allow a spatial visualization vital to patrol officers, investigators, police managers, policy makers, and community organizations. Improvements in GIS (geographic information systems) now allow data to be mapped, presented, and correlated. Maps are used to identify areas of high crime activity (so-called hot spots), and mapping the timing and spacing of crimes allows a more efficient use of police resources. Crime maps of local areas are regularly posted by police departments.

Mapping is also used helps to solve crimes. Geographic profiling, like psychological profiling, has become an important part of law enforcement. Geographic profiling assumes that criminal activity is place-specific and that criminals like to use known areas that are not too close to their home location. Criminals do not travel very far from their anchor points to commit crime. Plotting a series of crimes can thus be used to create a probability surface of the location of criminals. Dates and places of crime are mapped in order to provide clues to the location of the criminal.

The background to the mapping of these "moral" statistics is the concern to know where social deviance occurs but also to look for the covariance of other factors so that the deviance can be understood, controlled, and negated. The mapping of moral statistics is not innocent of wider political considerations. "Deviance," for example, is a politically freighted term whose definition tells us about those with power and their concerns and perceived threats. Contemporary human geographers no longer just concern themselves with mapping crime. A large body of work is now concerned with exploring the socio-spatial nature of crime and the policing of space. Phil Hubbard, for example, looks at the geographies of prostitution, while Katherine Beckett and Steve Herbert look at the spatial strategies of policing in Seattle to banish certain types of people, especially the poor and indigent, and enforce zones of exclusion in the city.

Public Health and Disease

The first maps of the incidence of disease, at least in the United States, were by Valentine Seaman (1770–1817), who identified individual cases of yellow fever along the New York City waterfront. In the nineteenth century, mapping the spread of disease became more common. Public anxiety over the public health of industrial cities in Britain led to the creation of the Poor Law Commission, which prompted the Ordnance Survey, the government mapping agency, to produce detailed maps of towns and cities.

One of the most famous sets of medical maps was drawn by John Snow, a doctor working in mid-nineteenth-century London. He was convinced that cholera was communicated by contaminated water. The 1855 second edition of his work *On the Mode of Communication of Cholera* contained two maps. The first showed the areas of London served by two different water companies. These companies

Box 2.4 ALTERNATIVE GEOGRAPHIES: LOOKING TO THE GROUND

The Canadian explorer and geographer David Thompson (1770–1857) was traveling in western North America when he recorded the following encounter:

> Both Canadians [French-Native Americans] and Indians often inquired of me why I observed the sun, and sometimes the moon, in the day-time, and passed whole nights with my instruments looking at the moon and stars. I told them it was to determine the distance and direction from the place I observed to other places; neither the Canadians nor the Indians believed me; for both argued that if what I said was the truth, I ought to look to the ground.

This encounter encapsulates the difference between the search for the coordinates of the grid and a reliance on a more intuitive sense of place. We now look with more sympathy upon the "Canadians and Indians" than the Enlightenment figure of David Thompson struggling to measure and map the world.

We now have accurate measurements of the Earth. Latitude and longitude can now be easily and precisely calibrated. Handheld GPS (global positioning systems) allow observers to get a very accurate and almost immediate reckoning of their coordinates in the grid. But perhaps because this avenue has been so fully explored and developed, there is a renewed interest in the areas outside the arc of traditional geography. We also need to develop the more empathetic understanding that made the Canadians and Indians tell Thompson to "look to the ground."

References

Short, J. R. (2000) *Alternative Geographies*. New York: Prentice Hall.

used different sources for their water, and one drew upon polluted water from the river Thames. While the area served by the company with fresh water had death rates due to cholera of 5 per 1,000, the one with a polluted water source had rates of 71 per 1,000. Snow's second map plotted the distribution of cholera cases at a more finely grained level and showed that they clustered around particular pumps. People using the water pump in Broad Street, poisoned by a leaking cesspool, were more likely to come down with cholera than those using water from unaffected pumps. The maps highlighted the fact that cholera was due to contaminated water and not, as the prevailing view at the time believed, though contact with polluted air.

Social geographers have long mapped diseases and epidemics. A worldwide cholera epidemic began in India in 1817, and the American mapmaker Henry Schenck Tanner (1786–1858) produced *A Geographical and Statistical Account of the Epidemic Cholera from its Commencement in India to its Entrance into the United States* in 1832. One map shows how the disease spread up the Hudson River and along the Champlain and Erie Canals.

The interest in mapping disease continues. Two human geographers, Andy Cliff and Peter Haggett, along with various colleagues have produced a large body of work plotting the diffusion of diseases. They have produced studies of the diffusion of disease through islands as well as case studies of individual diseases such as AIDS, influenza, and measles.

There is more to the contemporary social geography of health and disease than mapping. More recent work examines the geographies of health inequalities, healthcare provision, health, and well-being.

Deprivation and Inequality

London in the 1880s was a place of turmoil: an economic depression in the middle of the decade increased unemployment and heightened social unrest. Charles Booth, a wealthy shipowner, established a social survey, one of the first. His multivolume *Life and Labour of the People in London* (1892–1903) quantified social problems in the metropolis. Booth's use of social statistics to measure and map urban inequality inaugurated an important strand of urban research in which empirical methods were tied to welfare reform objectives. This strand of urban investigation became a common feature of urban studies in the the early twentieth century.

2.5 Jane Addams, 1914

Jane Addams was a social activist (Figure 2.5). In 1889 she founded Hull House on Chicago's Near West Side. She worked from there until her death in 1935. She and the other residents of the settlement provided services for the neighborhood, such as kindergarten and daycare facilities for children of working mothers, an employment bureau, an art gallery, libraries, and music and art classes. Hull House surveys of the local areas, similar to Booth's survey, led to the construction of maps of household income levels and ethnicity (Figure 2.6). One interesting feature of Hull House was the important role of women. Eight out of ten of the contributors to the 1895 volume *Hull-House Maps and Papers* were women. The Hull House residents and their supporters forged a powerful reform movement that launched the Immigrants' Protective League, the Juvenile Protective Association, the first juvenile court in the nation, and a Juvenile Psychopathic Clinic. They lobbied the Illinois legislature to enact protective legislation for women and children and to pass, in 1903, a strong child labor law and an accompanying compulsory education law. The Keating-Owen Child Labor Act of 1916 was the legislative result of their efforts. Jane

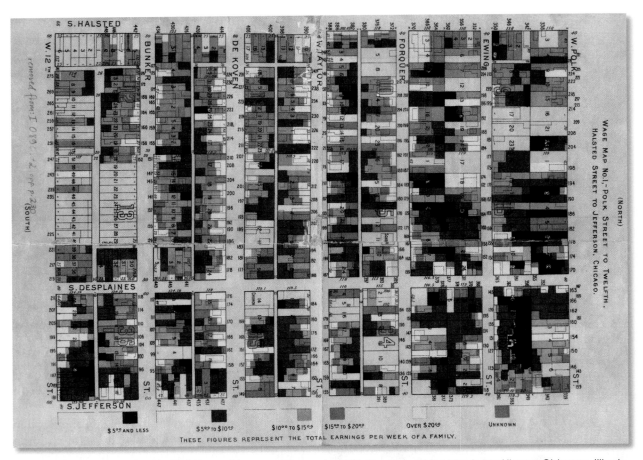

2.6 Wage map published in *Hull-House Maps and Papers* in 1895. Courtesy of the Newberry Library, Chicago, Illinois.

Addams was tireless in her dedication. She wrote many popular books and numerous articles, maintained speaking engagements around the world, and played an important role in many local and national organizations, such as the Consumers League, the National Conference of Charities and Corrections (later the National Conference of Social Work), Campfire Girls, the National Playground Association, the National Child Labor Committee, the National Association for the Advancement of Colored People, and the American Civil Liberties Union. She was awarded the Nobel Peace Prize in 1931.

The concern with urban social difference continues to be an important part of urban social geography. To take just one example from thousands: Alasdair Rae highlights areas of deprivation in the English city of Sheffield as he maps health, education, skills, and crime and plots the trajectory of change from 2004 to 2010. While the maps and techniques have become more sophisticated, there remains at the core of human geography a consistent interest in documenting, mapping, and explaining the socio-spatial patterns of inequality.

ENVIRONMENT AND SOCIETY

One goal of early-twentieth-century geography was to study the causal effects of environment on society. Ellsworth Huntington (1876–1947), a professor of geography at Yale University, argued that certain climatic conditions are "especially favorable to human progress." His environmental determinism was a form of racism. In his 1924 book *Civilization and Climate* he argued, "We know that the denizens of the torrid zone are slow and backward, and we almost universally agree that this is connected with the damp, steady heat" (Huntington, 1924, p. 2). Climate, for Huntington, created culture.

Geography, like all intellectual disciplines, reflects and embodies current beliefs and ideologies. In the late nineteenth and early twentieth century, geography was often used to justify imperial adventures as well as to back up belief systems that ranked humans and societies. At the top were the white Protestant people and societies of Northwest Europe and North America. At the bottom were the black and brown peoples of the world. Racism and imperialism were an integral part of geography.

Ellen Churchill Semple (1863–1932), who taught geography at the University of Chicago and Clark University, writing at approximately the same time as Huntington, developed a more probabilistic view of the role of environment. She was concerned with examining the relationships less deterministically and with less emphasis on racial differences and cultural hierarchies. Her writing needs to be placed in context. At a time when technological triumphalism was dominant, she was suggesting a counter-narrative that humans are connected to the land. In her classic work *Influences of Geographic Environment* (first published in 1911), she writes on page 2: "Man has been so noisy about the way he has 'conquered Nature,' and Nature has been so silent in her persistent influence over man, that the geographic factor in the equation of human development has been overlooked." Semple's book, a product of its time in its use of such terms as "savage," is still worth reading for both its eloquent style and its sensitivity to the relationship between people and environment.

Modern geography has long moved past issues of environmental determinism. However, a socially sensitive environmentalism still has some value. At the macro level, for example, climate change plays an important role in the rise and fall of civilizations. Mesopotamian civilization collapsed around 3,400 years ago due in part to a severe 200-year drought. The Mayan civilization of Central America collapsed almost 1,100 years ago, again due to a combination of social and environmental factors. The environmental context is an important one for looking at the big picture of societies' rise and fall. Echoing the basic theme of Huntington, but with a very different emphasis, Christian Parenti in his book *Tropic of Chaos* considers the area between the Tropics of Cancer and Capricorn. The tropical zone is one where issues of climate change and especially water availability are partial causes behind social conflict and political ruptures. Parenti draws a connection between climate change and violence through preexisting conditions, such as the legacy of Cold War militarism and the destructive consequences of neoliberal economics. He describes a catastrophic convergence of societies littered with cheap weapons and fractured by the lack of social connectivities now worsened by the wrenching effects of climate change. In an even broader perspective, Jared Diamond identifies the links behind social collapse and environmental degradation. This is not the simple determinism of earlier geographers but a more nuanced account that shows how social change is embedded and embodied in environmental relations.

GEOGRAPHY AND SOCIETY

The history of an academic discipline is tightly bound up in broader social developments. Three themes spring to mind when discussing the evolving relationship between geography and society: the connection with wider intellectual debates, the varied relationships to political power, and contemporary concerns.

Intellectual Debates

One historian of geography, David Livingston, describes the discipline as a contested tradition. He argues for a history of geography that does not assume an unchanging metaphysical core but rather a series of situated geographies: geographies that are shaped and shaped in turn by the time and place of their making; to write a global geography in London in 1910 or Washington, DC, in 1945 is a very different enterprise from a global geography written in twenty-first-century Beijing. A comparison of the different world views embodied in Figures 2.1 and 2.2 is instructive. Practices and procedures vary, and this variation is not incidental to the evolution of geographic writing but fundamental. What interests are advanced, what assumptions are made, and what underlying model of how the world hangs together all depend on the time and place. Historians of the discipline, for example, are often appalled at the casual racism prevalent in the work of geographers writing in decades past. In other words, there is a historical geography to the evolution of human geography.

The situated and compromised nature of knowledge production is best summarized in the title and subheading of Steven Shapin's 2010 book on the history of science, *Never Pure: Historical Studies of Science as If It Was Produced by People with Bodies, Situated in Time, Space, Culture, and Society, and Struggling for Credibility and Authority*. The history of geographic thought is intimately bound up in the historical geography of ideas.

Geography and Politics

The development of human geography is intimately connected to the interests of powerful groups, whether they are private and corporate or public and governmental. John Dee was an important intellectual figure in Renaissance England. He cast horoscopes for Queen Elizabeth, promoted the expansion of English mercantile interest, and "proved" English claims in the New World. The production of geographical knowledge is intimately connected to national economic interest. Fast-forward over three hundred years: geography, according to Sir Halford Mackinder (1861–1947), was an aid to statecraft. What he meant by that was that geography could help frame geopolitical strategies for the nation state; in his particular case, Britain and the British Empire. He developed a heartland theory that argues that whoever ruled the central part of the Eurasian landmass ruled the world. The idea was first formulated in 1904 and appeared in book form in 1919. At the time he was a fervent anti-Bolshevik, and so his argument can be seen in one light as a rationale for providing a cordon around Bolshevik Russia. His ideas influenced Nazi strategic thinking and US Cold War strategy.

Isaiah Bowman (1878–1950), a contemporary of Mackinder, was Director of the American Geographical Society for over twenty years. He was also the chief territorial advisor to President Wilson and to the US State Department during the Second World War. He had a strong belief in US expansionism based on penetration of foreign markets by US capitalism. He provided a geographical imagination to ideas of US global superiority and dominance. His book *The New World*, written in 1921, is still a very well written and accessible account of geopolitical issues and problems facing the world in the aftermath of the First World War and in the wake of the fragmentation of prewar empires.

Dee, Mackinder, and Bowman are at one end of the applied geography scale, their work and ideas directly shaping and influencing national interests. At the other end are more antiestablishment figures. Peter Kropotkin (1842–1921) provides an interesting contrast. He was born into the privileged life of pre-Revolutionary Russian aristocratic society; his father owned vast tracts of land and over 1,200 serfs.

Box 2.5 SUBALTERN GEOGRAPHIES

For much of the history of geography in the past two hundred years, the subject was written about by a relatively small sample of people. Generally, it was men in positions of power and authority in the richer countries of the world. Geography was linked to the existing global and national power structure. In recent years, however, there is a growing body of work that we can call subaltern geographies, having two characteristics. First, more geography is being written by groups outside the usual suspects. For example, more female scholars and scholars from developing countries are beginning to shift the angle of vision. Second, there are now more geographical studies of marginalized groups: women, children, migrant workers, peasants, slum dwellers, sexual minorities, etc. Geography is enriched by these developments.

References

Featherstone, D. (2009) *Resistance, Space and Political Identities*. Chichester: Wiley.

McFarlane, C. (2011) In the Space of Resistance: Network, Subaltern and Relationality. *Area* 43: 232–233.

In 1864 he led a geographical expedition to Siberia, and on his return to St. Petersburg he became secretary to the Imperial Russian Geographical Society. His interests widened to include a more radical vision of society: an anarcho-communist society based on mutual aid and voluntary associations. In 1875 he was imprisoned, but because of his social status was allowed to finish a geographical report on the last Ice Age, based on the fieldwork he had conducted earlier in Finland and Sweden. Students who are late with their work might like to think of Kropotkin, who finished his geography report even while in jail. He managed to leave Russia and lived in Switzerland and England, but returned in 1917 after the February Revolution overthrew the czar. He spoke out against the authoritarian socialism inaugurated with the October Revolution and the Bolshevik accession to power. Since 1957 a Moscow subway station bears his name.

A more intellectual radicalism shapes the work of contemporary human geographers. David Harvey (b. 1935) is a human geographer whose PhD work was on hop production in the English county of Kent. His first book, *Explanation in Geography* (1969), was an argument for the adoption of the deductive approach in geography. *Explanation* concerned the academic world. The context for Harvey's next book, *Social Justice and The City* (1973), was the wider world of the Vietnam War, the persistence of poverty in the richest countries, intractable racial divisions, and the decline of the long postwar economic boom, exposing inequalities and social discontent. There was a growing dissatisfaction in the academy with traditional methods of scholarship. In *Social Justice*, Harvey reflects upon and informs the debates surrounding these societal and academic issues. *Social Justice*, then, is really two books. The first part, "Liberal Formulations," focuses geographical inquiry on socially relevant topics. The second, "Social Formulations," marks a distinct epistemological break. Now ideas derive from a particular context. The concept of the city is radically altered between parts one and two. Rather than being an independent object of inquiry, it is an important element mediating and expressing social processes. Through considerations of Marxist rent theory and the history of urbanism, the main objective in the second part is to explore the relationship between the city and society from the perspective of historical materialism. In subsequent books, Harvey continues to provide radical critiques of capitalism in his development of a radical geography. His 2010 *The Enigma of Capital* outlines the tendency of crisis in capitalism, while *Rebel Cities* (2012) argues for the importance of the city and the neighborhood as sites of political struggle.

CONTEMPORARY DEBATES

Human geography has undergone profound change in the past fifty years. A number of "turns" can be identified. The quantitative turn, associated with such people as Peter Haggett and Brian Berry in the 1960s, was concerned with measurement, calibration, the creation of spatial models, and the testing of hypotheses. The quantifiers also excavated previously neglected scholars such as the 1930s German geographer Walter Christaller, whose work we will consider in another chapter. This excavation of previously ignored work is a consistent theme of all the different approaches and leads to a constant recreation of the history of human geography.

But the quantitative turn was not a revolution that came to dominate the entire discipline. It is more appropriate to think of it as a seismic shudder with multiple epicenters: Cambridge and Bristol in Britain and the University of Washington in the United States. In many places the seismic shift was scarcely recorded, and if it was, it was dismissed as of minor, ephemeral significance. And here we come to another trait of contemporary human geography: no turn has involved all of the discipline, because it is just too big and too varied.

The quantifiers had an uphill task against the entrenched forces of reaction. Old men (and most of them were men) with established reputations rarely take much heed of young scholars in a hurry who make very negative statements about the work of their elders. It was in one sense a generational struggle for power and status. But scarcely had the quantifiers established a beachhead in the discipline through creating mandatory courses on statistical techniques and establishing their own publishing outlets before counter-critiques and new turns emerged from the early 1970s. We can identify four from the many.

First, the notion of dispassionate, objective observers was criticized for its lack of social relevance and its connections with the corporate world. In effect, the "scientific" endeavor was neither socially neutral nor politically innocent. The emphasis shifted from identifying the spatial structure of society—a world of surfaces, edges, nodes, hierarchies, and flows—to the analysis of the social organization of space. This involved a more radicalized human geography.

Second, there was a criticism of the quantifiers from a humanist perspective. The humanist critique pointed to the lack of concern with personal geographies, the fact that statistical averaging ignored the whole realm of feeling, perception, and inter-subjectivity. The work of Peter Jackson and Susan Smith showed what a radically informed cultural geography could look like. In the United States, cultural geography was revived through a concern with landscape as a socially contested, materially produced cultural artifact. Geographers like Jim Duncan and Denis Cosgrove reinvigorated old concerns of landscape with the new interest in social theory.

Third, in the 1980s feminists appeared as a significant voice in the struggle for the hearts and minds of human geography. The feminist critique drew attention to the bias in the academic practice of geography and geographical writings. It was a discipline dominated by men and a discourse that rarely connected with the reality of gendered spaces and gendered lives. There is now a considerable body of work on the gendered separation of productive and reproductive spheres, issues of domestic labor, work-home separation, and the overall living and working experience of women. The feminist perspective also shows how gender interacts with race, class, and sexuality to produce socio-spatial patterns of inequality and marginalization. Geographers such as Doreen Massey, Linda Macdowell, and Gill Valentine, to name just a few feminist scholars, have widened my own angle of vision.

Fourth, in the 1990s postmodernists such as Michael Dear, Gillian Rose and Ed Soja also shifted the debates by introducing notions of hybridity, alternative rather than dominant narratives, and a multiplicity of ways of knowing.

2.7 Two young people studying a globe in a park in Vienna, Austria

Today human geography is a rich area of intellectual inquiry. The discipline continues to be contested in a lively fashion as geographers look at space and society from a variety of scales from the global to the local; encompass a variety of approaches from GIS, remote sensing, and statistical analysis techniques to qualitative ethnographic studies; and intersect with other researchers in a consideration of such important topics as the flexible identities of gender, ethnicity and nationality, the measurement and explanation and understanding of globalization, the connections between space and place, the recurring question of how we represent the world around us, and the pressing concerns of sustainability, environmental transformation, and climate change. At its very best, the discipline exhibits an environmental sensitivity with a social awareness. And like the two young people in Vienna shown in Figure 2.7, it looks at the world as a constant source of fascination and interest.

As you read these lines you are now an active participant and cocreator in this fascinating discourse. Welcome to one of the most exciting and engaging academic subjects.

Cited References

Balch, E. (1895) *Hull House Maps and Papers.* http://www.jstor.org/stable/2276290

Beckett, K., and Herbert, S. (2009) *Banished: The New Social Control in Urban America.* New York: Oxford University Press.

Booth, C. (1903) *Life and Labour of the People in London.* London: Macmillan.

Bowman, I. (1921) *The New World: Problems in Political Geography.* Yonkers: World Book Company.

Diamond, J. (2005) *Collapse: How Societies Choose to Fail or Succeed.* New York: Penguin.

Harries, K. (1999) *Mapping Crime: Principle and Practice.* Washington, DC: Department of Justice. NCJ 178919.

Harvey, D. (1973) *Social Justice and the City.* London: Arnold.

Harvey, D. (2010) *The Enigma of Capital.* London: Profile.

Harvey, D. (2012) *Rebel Cities: From the Right to the City to the Urban Revolution.* London: Verso.

Hubbard, P. (1999) *Sex and the City: Geographies of Prostitution in the Urban West.* Aldershot: Ashgate.

Humboldt, A. (1897) *Cosmos: A Sketch of a Physical Description of the Universe.* New York: Harper.

Huntington, E. (1924) *Civilization and Climate.* New Haven: Yale University Press.

Livingstone, D. N. (1993) *The Geographical Tradition: Episodes in the History of a Contested Enterprise.* Oxford: Blackwell.

Parenti, C. (2011) *Tropic of Chaos: Climate Change and the New Geography of Violence.* New York: Nation.

Rae, A. (2011) Deprivation in Sheffield. http://www.sheffield.ac.uk/polopoly_fs/1.137936!/file/ajr_sheffield_deprivation_nov_2011.pdf

Shapin, S. (1996) *The Scientific Revolution.* Chicago: University of Chicago Press.

Shapin, S. (2010) *Never Pure: Historical Studies of Science as If It Was Produced by People with Bodies, Situated in Time, Space, Culture, and Society, and Struggling for Credibility and Authority.* Baltimore: Johns Hopkins University Press.

Semple, E. C. (1911) *Influences of Geographic Environment on the Basis of Ratzel's System of Anthropo-geography.* New York: Holt. https://archive.org/details/influencesofgeog00semp

Snow, J. (1855) *On the Mode of Communication of Cholera.* London: John Churchill. http://www.ph.ucla.edu/epi/snow/snowbook.html

Ptolemee, C., Berggren, J. L., and Jones, A. (2001). *Ptolemy's Geography: An Annotated Translation of the Theoretical Chapters.* Princeton: Princeton University Press.

Tanner, H. S. (1832). *A Geographical and Statistical Account of the Epidemic Cholera: From Its Commencement in India to Its Entrance Into the United States: Comprehended in a Series of Maps and Tables, Exhibiting the Names of Places Visited by the Pestilence, the Time of Its Commencement, the Number of Cases, and Deaths, and Duration, at Each Place: Compiled from a Great Variety of Printed and Manuscript Documents.* Philadelphia: author. http://collections.nlm.nih.gov/catalog/nlm:nlmuid-64760030R-bk

Select Guide to Further Reading

For contemporary discussion of the geographies of health:

Anthamatten, P. and Hazen, H. (2011) *An Introduction to the Geography of Health.* Routledge: New York.

Brown, T., McLafferty, S., and Moon, G. (2010) *A Companion to Health and Medical Geography*. Malden: Wiley-Blackwell.

Cliff, A. D., Haggett, P., and Raynor, M. S. (2004). *World Atlas of Epidemic Diseases*. London: Hodder Arnold.

Koch, T. (2011) *Disease Maps: Epidemics on the Ground*. Chicago: University of Chicago Press.

Two sample papers on crime:

Andresen, M. A., and Brantingham, P. L. (2012). Visualizing the Directional Bias in Property Crime Incidents for Five Canadian Municipalities. *The Canadian Geographer/ Le Geographe Canadien* 57: 31–42.

Rossmo, D. K., and Harries, K. (2011) The Geospatial Structure of Terrorist Cells. *Justice Quarterly* 28: 221–248.

A useful entry point into the history of an intellectual discipline is to read the biographies and autobiographies of its practitioners. Here is a very small sample of a range of human geographers:

French, P. J. (1987) *John Dee: The World of an Elizabethan Magus*. London: Routledge.

Gould, P. (1999) *Becoming a Geographer*. Syracuse: Syracuse University Press.

Gould, P. and Pitts, F. (eds.) (2002) *Geographical Voices*. Syracuse: Syracuse University Press.

Haggett, P. (1990) *The Geographer's Art*. Oxford: Blackwell.

Hubbard, P. and Kitchin, R. (eds) (2011) *Key Thinkers on Space and Place*. London: Sage.

Kearns. G. (2009) *Geopolitics and Empire: The Legacy of Halford Mackinder*. Oxford: Oxford University Press.

Kropotkin, P. (1927) *Memoirs of a Revolutionist*. London: Smith Elder. First published 1899. http://theanarchistlibrary.org/library/petr-kropotkin-memoirs-of-a-revolutionist

Moss, P. (ed.) (2000) *Placing Autobiography in Geography*. Syracuse: Syracuse University Press.

Rupke, N. A. (2008) *Alexander von Humboldt*. Chicago: University of Chicago Press.

Smith, N. (2004) *American Empire: Roosevelt's Geographer and the Prelude to Globalization*. Berkeley and Los Angeles: University of California Press.

On human geography, ancient and modern:

Agnew, J. A. and Livingstone, D. N. (eds.) (2011) *The Sage Handbook of Geographical Knowledge*. Thousand Oaks: Sage.

Cresswell, T. (2013) *Geographic Thought: A Critical Introduction*. Chichester: Wiley-Blackwell.

Gregory, D., Johnston, R., Pratt, G., Watts, M., and Whatmore, S. (eds.). (2011). *The Dictionary of Human Geography*. Chichester: Wiley-Blackwell.

Martin, G. J. (2005) *All Possible Worlds: A History of Geographical Ideas*. 4th ed. Oxford: Oxford University Press.

Thomson, J. O. (2013) *History of Ancient Geography*. Cambridge: Cambridge University Press.

Selected Websites

Alasdair Rae maintains interactive websites that plot deprivation in cities
http://imd040710.blogspot.co.uk
https://sites.google.com/site/scotdep2012/).
Just one of the many urban police websites that map crime
http://oakland.crimespotting.org/map
A website run by geographers that maps and analyzes user generated geocoded data; it
uses social media to produce some very cool maps
http://www.floatingsheep.org/

PART 2

People, Resources, and Environment

Part 2 takes up the general themes of population geography. Chapter 3 outlines the basic trends of growth and decline and examines the dynamics of the demographic transition. The relations between population and food supply are detailed in chapter 4 and those between population and resources in chapter 5. Chapter 6 examines people-environment relations through exploring environmental impacts on society and human impacts on environment change.

3 Population Trends

The world's population is now more than 7 billion people. It grew from a very small base. The number of humans poised to leave Africa to populate the world probably did not exceed 5,000 souls. This tiny group was the basis for the spread and growth of human population around the globe. Global population remained small and steady until 4,000 years ago, when there was a slow, steady rise until an explosive upward growth beginning around 1800 (Figure 3.1). Population growth accelerated in the past century. It took thirty years, from 1930 to 1959, for an extra billion people to be added. It took only eleven years, from 1998 to 2011, for yet another billion to be added.

Throughout most of human history, the world's population was relatively small. Specific bottlenecks occurred when the human population came precariously close to extinction. Around 70,000 years ago, the eruption of Toba in Sumatra caused a volcanic winter. The total human population may have been reduced to only thousands. The result was a very small pool of genetic diversity. Today's huge population is genetically very close. We share a common ancestry, and despite the cultural production of racial and ethnic differences, we are biologically really just part of one large extended family.

Despite such setbacks, humans prospered. They were adaptable, smart, and mobile. They transformed their surroundings, trapping animals, creating gardens, and efficiently developing gender divisions of labor between male hunting and female gathering and foraging. Men and women accumulated a long-term, deep, and sophisticated knowledge of the environment. The total world population, before the advent of agriculture, did not exceed 10 million people, fluctuating between 5 million to 15 million, and it was spread thinly across the surface of the globe. Despite its small size, the preagricultural human population still had an enormous impact on the environment; the most obvious is the hunting of megafauna in the Pleistocene Overkill that we discussed in chapter 1. Environmental changes were wrought as grass was burned in regular cycles, trees were felled, and animals were hunted. The early hunting-gathering societies, small in absolute numbers, modified their physical environments through dramatic intervention rather than through the weight of their population.

3.1 World population
growth

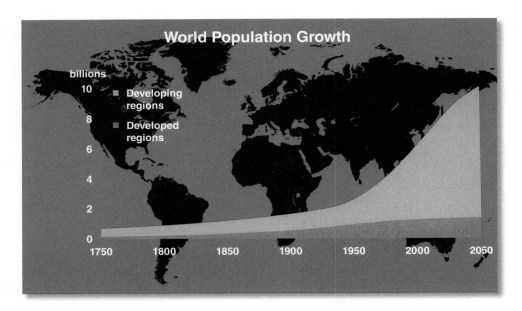

POPULATION AND AGRICULTURE

Agriculture first developed around 10,000 years ago. There was no one single source area, as it developed independently in various regions of the world, including the Nile Valley, Mesopotamia, the Indus Valley, West Africa, Mesoamerica and the Andes, and New Guinea. The exact set of reasons behind the transition from hunting-gathering to settled agriculture are complex, and a number of competing theories have been suggested. These include the idea that ostentatious feasting by tribal leaders and the competition to outmatch competitors led to an increasing drive to find greater and more reliable sources of food. Another theory, based on the existence of giant megaliths built by hunting-gathering groups that have been discovered in present-day Turkey, is that it was the need to build and maintain religious complexes that first compelled people to establish permanent sites, which in turn led to the development of agriculture. Ruling elites then emerged, and as societies became more complex, with more layers of personnel not directly concerned with hunting and gathering, more food needed to be produced. Whatever the precise combination of factors, it is clear that the initial development of agriculture required some form of compulsion, often a mixture of force and religious ideology, as people were now commanded to produce food for others rather than merely for their immediate kin. The development of agriculture is intimately connected with the development of centralized power, hierarchical control, and the creation of authoritarian societies. The origins of agriculture lie in a social revolution in political organization.

Settled agriculture allowed an increase in population because the food resource base was increased and made more reliable. With a specialized division of labor, effective utilization of crops and animals, and centralized political control, population could increase beyond the limits of hunting-gathering societies. By 2,000 years ago, the population had increased to 200 million. Improvements in agricultural technology, such as the use of the plow and hybrid crops, enabled more food to be produced, sometimes by extending the amount of arable land and sometimes by increasing the productivity of existing agricultural land. The areas of greatest population density had rich fertile soils and reliable sources of water as well as centralized political control.

The development of agriculture made human population more dependent on agricultural productivity. A decline in agricultural output could increase mortality and lead to fewer births. The decline in food supply occurred especially when climate change reduced the length of the growing season. Patrick Galloway noted a connection between population change and fluctuations in climate change for the mid-latitude regions of the world. Across these regions there was a warming trend, peaking around 1200, followed by cooling until 1450; then warming until 1600, followed by a rapid cooling until around 1650. These changing temperatures caused a decline in agricultural productivity—colder weather reduced harvests and increased the risk of hunger and starvation—that suppressed population growth. In England, for example, during the cooling period of 1600 to 1650, population levels declined because, with low supplies of food, women had fewer children.

Harry Lee and colleagues, testing Galloway's model, examined the data for China over the past thousand years. They found that five major population contractions occurred during cooler temperatures. Long-term cooling led to falling harvest yields, fewer births, and increasing mortality rates.

POPULATION AND DISEASE

The agricultural revolution and the attendant growth in the size and density of human settlements also created the preconditions for disease and its rapid spread, often with fatal outcomes. In Athens between 430 BCE and 427 BCE almost a third of the population of the city-state died from a disease as yet undetermined, though likely to be a form of typhus. Sometimes disease could reach pandemic proportions. A pandemic is an epidemic on a wide geographic scale. We can consider three examples.

The first was the bubonic plague that swept in a series of waves across the world from 541 to 747. It was especially pronounced in the Byzantine Empire. The first wave occurred from 541 to 544 and is named after the ruling emperor of the time, Justinian. It spread quickly along the trade routes. The total death rate is estimated at 25 million people. In Constantinople, at the height of the first wave, almost 5,000 people were dying every day, ultimately halving the city's population.

Box 3.1   THE REPRODUCTIVE REVOLUTION

The demographic transition is less a natural fact than a social revolution. It is a result of changes in public health and nutrition that extend the average life span. It is also the consequence of a reproductive revolution. The reproduction capacity of women is potentially very high. In theory, each fertile woman can have up to, and in some cases have had more than, fifteen children. Before the demographic transition, the reproductive efficiency was low, with few women living to puberty, high infant mortality rates, and low life expectancy. Fewer than one in ten girls reached the age of puberty. The result was a relatively low reproductive capacity. Each child born had limited chance of reaching adulthood. Emphasis was thus placed on each and every woman having as many children as possible. This largely defined the role of women and is the fundamental basis of patriarchy, the belief system and practice that men are the authority figures and women are restricted to home, hearth, and the bearing and rearing of children. Patriarchy—although mediated through different cultural and religious filters—is an attribute of low reproductive efficiency.

After the demographic transition, more women survive into their fertile years, and there is a reduction in infant mortality rates. This higher reproductive capacity means that women can have fewer children. As the risk of each child dying declines women do not need to have so many children in order to ensure that they some survive into adulthood. The increased life expectancy also extends more women's lives beyond childbearing ages. The reproductive revolution calls into question the basis of patriarchy. McInnes and Diaz argue that the origin of other social changes, including the deregulation and privatization of sexuality and the rise of the importance of individual identity, also ultimately resides in the increased efficiency of reproduction. Their case is suggestive and intriguing, yet like all ambitious arguments it is open to debate and discussion, criticism, improvement, and refinement.

References

McInnes, J. and Diaz, J. P (2009) The Reproductive Revolution. *Sociological Review* 57: 262–284.

The disease spread as far west as England and as far east as Persia. The mass death created social confusion, caused economic dislocations, and prompted political upheaval. Villages were abandoned. Arable land lay fallow, and labor was in short supply. The lack of labor stimulated technological improvements such as improved plow design and new crop rotations. The pandemic impeded the growth of the Byzantine Empire and led to what some describe as the birth of Europe, as there was a localization of economies and political systems rather than unification under an empire. It was the pivot of large-scale social change, including the shift from antiquity to the Middle Ages and the opening stage of the rise of Western Europe to continental and then global dominance.

A second pandemic, a recurrence of bubonic plague, swept throughout Asia, North Africa, and Europe: the "Black Death," first mentioned in written records in 1346, by 1353 had killed between 30 and 40 percent of the population, with some estimates of up to 60 percent mortality in Europe. The population of Europe probably declined from 80 million to 30 million. The effects of such a rapid population loss were immense. There was forest regrowth throughout Europe as a direct consequence of the population reduction. Societies dominated by low wages, high rents, and high prices were quickly transformed into ones of high wages, low rents, and low prices. The lack of population forced more efficient, less labor-intensive, technologies. Landowners switched from the labor-intensive arable agriculture of grain production to the less labor-intensive pastoral farming of producing meat, wool, and dairy products. The switch "from corn to horn" also gave more employment opportunities for women, who were traditionally employed in the pastoral sector. There were also social upheavals. In England the 1381 Peasant's Revolt was the organized resistance to attempts by authorities to reduce wage levels to pre–Black Death levels. The wider significance of the Black Death is debatable. There are those who argue for continuities before and after, while others see a more profound shift from the medieval world to the modern world—a world where religious devotion was undermined for some, strengthened for others; a world where minorities, especially Jews, could become scapegoats for disasters; a world where the authorities were made responsible for public health; a world where the relationship between rich and poor was dramatically revealed as based less on unchanging custom and tradition than on the brute facts of labor supply and demand.

Perhaps the most dramatic relationship between disease and population declines involves the Columbian Encounter that took place when Europeans discovered and colonized the Americas. The impact on the indigenous population was devastating. The pre-Columbian population of the Americas is difficult to gauge precisely, but estimates put the figure between 50 million and 100 million. The indigenous population was descended from peoples who had come from Eurasia before the development of agriculture, in which the resultant close association between animals and people made the transfer of diseases from animals to humans, such as influenza and measles, less fatal, as those fatally susceptible died out, leaving behind a more resilient human population. This process did not occur in the New World, making its indigenous inhabitants fatally susceptible to everyday diseases from the Old. Diseases such as influenza, measles, and smallpox proved fatal to the people of the Americas. Soon after contact, the population of indigenous peoples collapsed as fatal diseases spread quickly with devastating effect. "Great was the stench of the dead," noted a report from 1571 of an epidemic in Guatemala. In the northwest region of Guatemala, the population fell from 260,000 in 1520 to 47,000 in 1575. Across the entire continent over the period from 1492 to 1640, the indigenous population was reduced by close to 90 percent. Later European colonists arrived in a land largely emptied of its original inhabitants. The wilderness that nineteenth-century observers noted—the vast forests, empty plains, and abundant animal life—was not a pristine landscape but an environment of much reduced human impact. The geographer William Denevan deconstructs the "pristine myth" that North America was a vast wilderness before the coming of the Europeans. The later colonists encountered not what they thought of and described as a "natural" wilderness but what was in fact a regenerated wilderness, the product of a dramatic decline in the indigenous population and its environmental impact. The American landscape of the eighteenth and nineteenth centuries was not an unchanging wilderness but the result of the population collapse of the sixteenth and seventeenth centuries. The Columbian Encounter did not reveal the American wilderness but created it.

Societies develop equilibrium when demographic trends stay the same or exhibit only slight increase or decrease. Change, even large change, if it develops slowly can be easily incorporated into social institutions. But when population levels fall drastically, the resultant ruptures and tears in social norms and social relationships produce dramatic changes and long-term unfolding consequences. All three pandemics had dramatic effects. The rise of Western Europe, the creation of modernity, and the decline of the indigenous people of America all have rapid population loss as part of their origin.

THE DEMOGRAPHIC TRANSITION

Until 1800, global demographics was characterized by short life expectancy, high fertility, a young population, and slow population growth. In 1800 the average lifespan was only twenty-seven years, most fertile women gave birth to six children, one in three people were less than fifteen years old, and the annual population growth rate was around 0.51 percent. People's lives were short, women spent much of their time having and raising children, and there were very few old people.

Around 1800, changes in mortality and fertility, known as the demographic transition, altered this global pattern. The transition has two dominant trends. First, there was the decline in mortality rates, initially in the richer parts of the world, such as Western Europe and North America, brought about by improved personal hygiene, public health measures, and increased affluence, which led to better diets. These all combined to reduce death rates and lengthen life expectancy. More people lived longer. A benign cycle was created in which increased affluence led to better diets, which led to longer and more productive lives, which in turn led to increased economic development. In 1950 the average life expectancy in Japan was 63.5. By 2010 it had reached 82.5 years. Lower-income countries have taken longer to increase life expectancies. Zimbabwe, for example, still has an average life expectancy of only 49.6 years. Malaria, largely eradicated elsewhere, annually sickens more than 200 million people and kills close to 800,000 children in Africa, where it is the leading cause of death for those aged under five. There are still global disparities in healthcare provision that have led to marked spatial differences in child mortality and overall life expectancy.

Second, the increase in life expectancy was soon followed by a decline in fertility, at first only in the richer countries and then later more widely diffused. In 1800 there were an average of 6 births for every woman, by 2010 the figure was 2.5. This is very close to the replacement rate, or the number of births needed to

Box 3.2 IRELAND: THE DEMOGRAPHIC BASE OF THE CELTIC TIGER

The demography of Ireland is an interesting one. The graph of its demographic history, like most of the rest of the world, shows a steady increase from 1700 with acceleration from 1800 until it peaks at over 6 million in 1840. After the Great Famine of 1845–1849, the population plummeted as one million died and 2 million more left the land. It leveled off at around 4 million. The country was slow to pass through the demographic transition, with 3.5 births per woman even into the early 1980s. High levels of emigration to Australia, Britain, and the United States kept the population level down. Then two things happened. First, after 1979 contraception was readily available, and the birth rate fell sharply. The demographic dividend of increasing working-age population was a factor in accelerated economic growth, which reached almost 6 percent annually in the 1990s. Ireland became the Celtic tiger of rapid economic and demographic growth. Second, as the economy grew

stronger, providing more employment opportunities, fewer young people left the country's shores, and indeed there was increased immigration, with Poland being a rich source. So while birth rates fell, the population increased. There was also a marked increase in female participation rates.

Since 2008, the economy has been badly hit by the global recession and risky investments by banks that were underwritten by the government, which in turn led to fiscal crisis, deep cuts in public spending, and a decline in economic growth. Immigration has fallen off, emigration has increased, and Ireland joins Portugal, Greece, and Italy as ground zero for the European debt crisis.

References

Bloom, D. E. and Canning, D. (2003) Contraception and the Celtic Tiger. *Economic and Social Review* 34: 229–247.

keep the population stable. The replacement rate is 2.1 in richer countries and 2.3 in poorer countries. The difference is the result of increased juvenile mortality rates in poorer countries.

Many countries moved toward lower birth rates between 1890 and 1920. Today, in rich countries like Japan, for example, the birth rate is 1.2. In the United States, it is 2.1. In China, with its one-child policy for urban residents, the birth rate is 1.75. Many factors were involved, including access to more reliable birth control methods, changes in household economies such that children were not so much workers as dependents, and increased investment in an individual child's caring and rearing. Family size declined. In the lower-income countries the fertility rates began to drop later, beginning in the 1960s. They are still higher than in the richer countries—7.38 births per woman in Mali, for example—but across the world, there is a transition toward lower birth rates.

This demographic transition has transformed the human population. Life is now longer as life expectancy increases and mortality rates decline. There is also a steady graying of the population. In 1950 only 4 percent of the total global population was aged more than sixty-five; by 2000 this had increased to almost 6 percent. By 2100 it is estimated to be 21 percent. The world's population is aging. The aging trend is especially marked in the richer countries of the world.

These demographic changes have cultural consequences. Consider, for example, gender roles and representations. Masculinity was often constructed around the image of the strong, virile body. But what of masculinity when men live long past their peak physical strength and virility? Similarly, as birth rates drop women are freed from constant childrearing. As their lives extend beyond their fertility, we need new models of what it means to be woman. Family size declines, so that large families are now replaced by smaller, nuclear families. The family is less a large group of people than a tight nexus of a few individuals. Family life takes on a new hue from how it was long imagined and lived. And what of the elderly? When they were a small group, they were revered and often subsidized. But when this group grows in size and lives long past its economic productivity, they can become a fiscal liability as well as an important resource of accumulated knowledge and wealth. With a rapidly aging population, intergenerational inequities and conflicts can become more pronounced, just as intergenerational transfers of wealth can become more important.

PHASES OF THE DEMOGRAPHIC TRANSITION

There is a chronology and a geography to the demographic transition. In the richer countries, the transition is more fully developed. Life expectancy has increased, and birth rates have dropped. In poorer countries, while life expectancy has increased, the birth rate has declined more slowly. The result is a complex pattern of different demographic regimes in countries at different phases of the transition.

Figure 3.2 highlights four distinct phases of the demographic transition. Figure 3.3 depicts the population pyramid of four individual countries at different

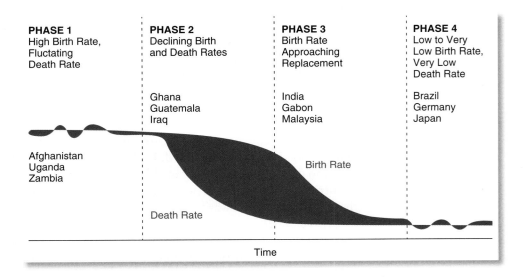

3.2 Phases of the demographic transition

3.3 Population pyramids

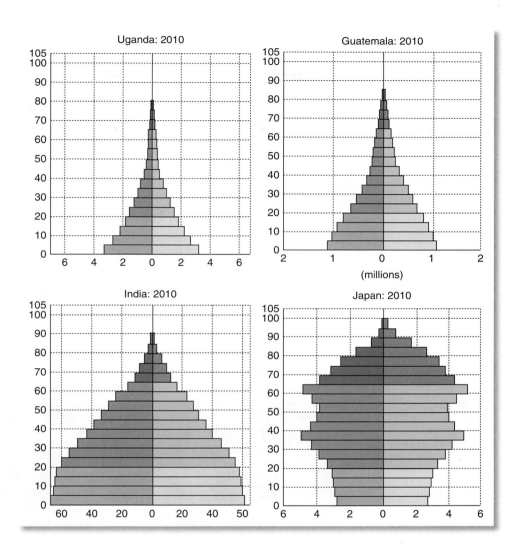

stages in this transition. The pyramids are the graphic representation of the national population along the vertical axis in five-year age cohorts, males to the left, females to the right of the vertical line through the middle of the pyramid.

The first phase is one of high birth rate and fluctuating death rate. Countries with this profile include Afghanistan, Uganda, and Zambia. In Uganda, with a population of 35 million, for example, population growth is around 3.3 percent, driven by the high average birthrate of 6.5 births for every woman. The population pyramid shows the typical pattern of a large youthful base, because of the high birth rates, tapering off quickly because of the relatively low life expectancies. Birth rates are high because there is little effective contraception and cultural mores inhibit its use. The net result is a very young population with high growth rates. Almost half of the population of Uganda is younger than fifteen. There are also considerable gender inequalities in income and job opportunities, since a woman's role is largely defined as giving birth to many children. The challenge for Uganda, as for all first-phase countries (which now constitute 9 percent of the world's population), is how to slow down the rate of growth to provide enough jobs and opportunities for a young population coming on to the job market and to extend the economic opportunities for women.

Countries in phase 2 have declining death and birth rates. They constitute 7 percent of the world's total population and include middle-income countries such as Ghana, Guatemala, and Iraq. In Guatemala, because of improved public health, life expectancy is now seventy-one years. The birth rate has declined to three births per woman. The decline is due to increased use of modern family planning methods. Almost half of all women in Guatemala use modern family planning methods. The population growth rate is still high at 2.5 percent, and more than half of the population is aged below nineteen, so Guatemala, like Uganda, shares the problems of finding opportunities for its many young people. A distinctive feature in Guatemala is the difference between the indigenous Mayan and non-Mayan populations. The indigenous Mayan population has a birth rate of over five per woman, whereas it is less than two for the richer, non-Mayan women. National population statistics can hide marked differences in income, race, and ethnicity (Figure 3.4). In the case of Guatemala, there is a difference between the indigenous Mayan population and the non-Mayan, which tends to be more affluent.

Phase 3 countries, which now constitute 38 percent of the world's population, are characterized by sharply falling birth rates below three per woman. Figure 3.3

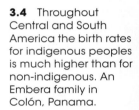

3.4 Throughout Central and South America the birth rates for indigenous peoples is much higher than for non-indigenous. An Embera family in Colón, Panama.

shows the population pyramid of India. Compared to Uganda and Guatemala, there is a thickening in the middle cohorts, from ages twenty to fifty, and less marked tapering as the population ages. India has seen a remarkable decline in birth rates from over 5 births per woman in the 1950s to around 2.6 by 2010. There are marked regional variations. Birth rates per woman in the southern state of Kerala have dropped below 2, while they are still high in the poorer states of the north. In Uttar Pradesh, with a population of 200 million, the rate is 4 births per woman. With 1.2 billion people, India is one of the most populous countries in the world. In ten years' time, it may overtake China as the most populous country on the planet.

For countries at this stage and even phase 2, there is the possibility of a demographic dividend. The dividend occurs when birth rates fall substantially, requiring less investment in the very young, and before the population starts to age dramatically, requiring more money spent on caring for the elderly. As the cohorts from previous growth spurts enter the job market, there are proportionately more people of working age compared to the very young (as birth rates decline) or the very old (as life expectancy for the older groups is still relatively low). The net effect is a relative and absolute increase of younger, more productive workers. One way to highlight the demographic dividend is to estimate the dependency ratio. One measure is calculated by dividing the working age population, those aged fifteen to sixty-five, by the non–working age population, those aged zero to fourteen and those older than sixty-five: the higher the ratio, the larger the demographic dividend. Figure 3.5 shows how the ratio and the dividend decline as societies pass through to the later stages of the demographic transition.

The dividend pays out in several ways. It increases the labor supply and reduces the relative size of the dependent population of the very young and the very old. More public and private investment can thus be devoted to increasing productive capacity as less public money is spent supporting the very young and very old. Working-age

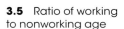

3.5 Ratio of working to nonworking age

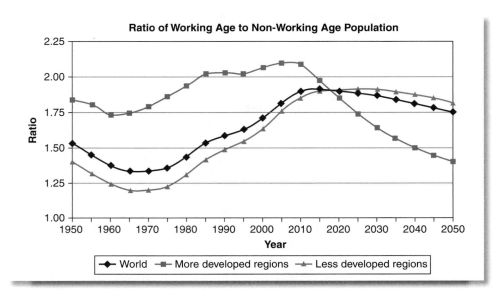

Box 3.3 BRAZIL AND THE DEMOGRAPHIC DIVIDEND

At the time of its first official census in 1872, the population of Brazil was only 10 million. In 2010 it was estimated at 190 million. After a century of rapid demographic growth, the country is undergoing a major demographic transition. Birth rates are dropping; the number of births per woman declined from 6.3 in 1960 to 1.9 in 2010. This remarkable fall is a product of many things, including rapid urbanization, the secularization of Brazilians, and the increasing use of contraception. The religious codes of the Catholic Church no longer exercise much influence. Popular soap operas with their emphasis on modernity play a hugely influential part in creating new gender roles and generating alternative models of family life and size. Better access to reproductive health and increasing female participation are part cause and part effect of the rapid fall in birth rates. It is not only the affluent who are able to limit family size. The cause and affects feed off each other. Economic growth makes it possible for poorer families to have fewer children, which means that more can be spent on each child's education, which in turn means children are better educated and more able to find employment.

Brazil has experienced a demographic dividend since 1970 as the rapid fall in fertility has reduced the absolute and relative proportion of dependents. From 1970 to 2010, more than half of all economic growth could be explained by the dividend, which will be in operation until 2025. On the basis of this economic growth and increased democratization, recent decades have witnessed the creation of relatively generous social welfare programs of social security and a public education system. However, as the increasing life expectancy grays the population, the number of beneficiaries to workers will increase. Mortality rates have also fallen dramatically to the extent that life expectancy has increased from 53.7 in 1960 to 72.5 in 2011. While the social welfare programs reduce inequality and promote economic growth, they also will be a significant source of political debate as the population ages. How to balance old-age security and income equality with sustaining economy growth will become a significant policy issue for Brazil and for the many other countries moving into the latter stages of the transition.

adults tend to save more, and this can create a larger pool of capital available for investment. The human capital of the country is increased, because with many fewer children, women are able to join the workforce, and because family income is spread across fewer children, more can be invested in each child's education.

Part of the economic growth of countries such as South Korea was based on this demographic dividend. More recently, the rapid economic growth of countries in the past twenty years, such as Brazil, China, and India, is based on the demographic engine of the absolute and relative increase in its working population. In these three countries, the proportion of the population aged between fifteen and sixty-five—generally considered the most economically active age range—is 67, 73, and 64 percent respectively. In poorer countries such as Afghanistan, Bangladesh, and Cameroon, the respective figures are 55, 61, and 56 percent.

The opportunity for this demographic dividend is relatively short, because increasing life expectancy soon ages the population, quickly reducing the ratio of workers to nonworkers. There is a short window of time when there is a rising share of people of working age and the demographic profile is weighted toward the most productive. During this time, holding everything else constant, average per capita income rises, both reflecting and prompting enhanced economic growth. Between one-third and one-half of economic growth in states such as India may be due to the demographic dividend.

A full dividend is only possible if female participation rates are high. If societies continue to restrict the employment opportunities of women, the full benefits of the dividend are unrealized. One reason behind China's spectacular growth is not simply the demographic dividend but its full implementation. Female participation rates are very high at 94 percent for women aged twenty-five to thirty-four. The dividend is fully realized if the workforce is educated and skilled and the benefits of the growth are spread across the population rather than garnered by only a few. The tigers of rapid economic growth, such as Japan and South Korea from 1960 to 1990 and China since 1990, capitalized on their demographic dividend by increasing employment opportunities fast enough to maintain labor productivity growth.

The demographic dividend may provide a supply of relatively cheap labor, but only for a limited period. The Lewis Turning Point, named after the economist William Arthur Lewis, occurs when the supply of cheap labor runs out. The increased demand for labor pushes up wages, and benefits are increased. Wages rise, profits may fall, and the economy loses its cheap labor cost advantages. A vital question for China, with its below-replacement birth rate, is whether it is reaching or passing through a Lewis Turning Point.

In the early and middle stages of the demographic transition, a youth bulge occurs (Figure 3.6). This is the rapid increase in the number of people aged between fifteen and twenty-four. It occurs when a rapid reduction in child mortality occurs before a rapid falloff in fertility. In ten years' time, the increase in the number of people aged under fourteen becomes the youth bulge of fifteen to twenty-four. When this bulge constitutes more than 20 percent of the population, it has been linked to an increase in political instability and the possibility of increased political violence. Two political geographers, Gary Fuller and Forrest Pitts, looked at the emergence of this youth cohort in South Korea in the 1970s and 1980s and its correlation with the rise of political unrest.

A number of social scientists have sought to test the connection between youth bulges and social conflict in more detail. Using data from 1998–2005 covering 127 countries, Alfred Marcus and colleagues found that youth bulges are correlated with violent conflict. They also found that violence did fall off when the youth bulge was followed by a decline in the youth cohort. Henrik Urdal also tested this idea against empirical data. He found that an increase in the youth bulge of 1 percent increases the likelihood of domestic armed conflict in a society by 7 percent. Countries with particularly large youth bulges are three times more likely to experience serious armed conflict. Economic stagnation plays an important role in turning a youth bulge into a tinderbox of armed conflict. In a more detailed study, he looked at

3.6 A youth bulge can occur at the middle stages of the demographic transition. Young people in Tunis, Tunisia.

fifty-five large urban centers in Asia and sub-Saharan Africa for the 1960–2006 period. The male youth population bulge did not increase levels of social disorder. A more important factor was youth exclusion from economic opportunity, even in the absence of extraordinarily large urban youth population bulges. It is not simply the number of youth but their range of opportunity for active and meaningful participation in economic and political life that influences political conflict.

Across the Middle East and North Africa, the proportion of fifteen- to twenty-four-year-olds is 21 percent of the total population and 34 percent of the working-age population. The unemployed rate among this group is a very high 26 percent. The Arab Spring had many causes, but a disenfranchised youth bulge was certainly a significant factor.

The relative and absolute size of specific cohorts does have wider social implications, even for the more affluent countries. The Easterlin hypothesis is named after the economist Richard Easterlin, who suggested that the fortunes of a cohort depends on the size of that cohort relative to the total population. There are luckier times to be born than others. If you were born in the United States in the 1930s, you experienced a demographic trough—only 18.7 babies were born for every 1,000 people, compared to 29.5 in 1915 or 24.1 in 1950. Holding everything else constant, you had smaller class sizes, easier access to college, and more employment opportunities. While we imagine our economic success or failure to be a result of personal characteristics, it is also a matter of demographic luck.

Demographic troughs also have wider social effects. Crime rates, for example, showed a marked decline across several countries, including Brazil, Canada, and the United States, as the percentage of the population aged fifteen to twenty-four declined. This occurred in Canada and the United States in the 1990s and in Brazil in the early 2000s. Very different types of societies at different times all show the falloff in crime rates as the percentage of the fifteen to twenty-four age group declined. Demography is behind the fall in crime rates, as the cohort more likely to commit crime diminishes in numbers and relative weight.

Phase 4 of the demographic transition is categorized by low birth rates and high life expectancy. Countries in this category constitute 46 percent of the world's population. The population pyramids of these countries, like those of Japan shown in Figure 3.3, have a narrower base because of low birth rates and less obvious tapering because of longer life expectancies. There are fewer young people compared to the increasing proportion of old people. Japan has one of the highest life expectancies and lowest birth rates in the world. The average life expectancy in the world is seventy, while in Japan it is eighty-three, and while across the world there are twenty births per 1000 population, in Japan the figure is eight. With only 1.2 births per woman, Japan is falling below replacement levels. A similar trend can be noted for other East Asian countries, including South Korea (1.2 births per women), Taiwan (1.1), Singapore (1.0), and Hong Kong (1.0) (Figure 3.7). In Japan the result is a declining population, a trend that is particularly marked in rural areas of the country. There is an effective depopulation of much of rural and small-town Japan as the young people move to the larger cities for jobs and services. Across the nation, the population is aging. Almost one in four of Japanese are over sixty-five.

One major reason behind the decrease in fertility in Japan, and throughout East Asia and elsewhere, is that women of reproductive age are not getting married and not having children. Because of job discrimination, only about one-third of Japanese women remain in the workforce after having a child, compared to two-thirds of women in the United States. Because of the cultural mores

3.7 In richer societies with low birth rates, children are often the recipients of significant public and private investment. Schoolchildren in South Korea.

Box 3.4   RUSSIA'S DECLINING POPULATION

In 2010 the Russian government offered the equivalent of $9,000 in cash to have a second child, evidence of a pronounced demographic shift. At the end of the Soviet era, the population of Russia was around 148 million, having risen steadily from a 1950 population of around 102 million. It fell to around 138 million in 2011 and is likely to fall further to 111 million by midcentury. What is behind this remarkable collapse, which may reduce the country's population close to what it was a hundred years earlier?

First, unlike most countries Russia experienced increased mortality rates. Russia is one of the few countries to experience a decline in life expectancy for males; it was sixty-five in 1989 but fell to a staggering fifty-nine by 2010. Life expectancy for females is seventy-two, the disparity a direct effect of heavier alcoholism rates among men compared to women. The second is the decline of the old Soviet system with its extensive welfare programs and its replacement, especially in the earlier years of reform, by a harsh market-driven approach that initially led to a decline in general public health provision, increased unemployment, and declining living standards. This economic shock therapy led very quickly to a decline in general social welfare and an increase in mortality. The number of deaths increased from 1.58 million in 1989 to 2.36 million in 2003 as the death rate rose from 10.7 to 16.4 per thousand.

Second, there was a decline in birth rates from 1.89 in 1989 to a historic low of 1.16 in 1999, well below replacement level. There were 2.1 million births in 1989 but only 1.4 million in 2003. More Russian women, with very easy access to abortion, simply limited the number of children they were willing to have. Economic uncertainty and social dislocation made having children a more difficult choice, and with fewer males there were fewer available male partners to start or raise a family.

The population decline occurred because more people died and fewer children were born. Immigration was tightly controlled and kept low, so the foreign-born did not contribute very much to population increase. The most pronounced population decline occurred between five and fifteen years after the fall of communism. There is some indication of demographic recovery. Yet even with slightly lower mortality, longer life expectancy, and higher birth rates, the overall population of Russia will continue to decline.

---

against out-of-wedlock children and the heavy pressure to look after their husbands, for most Japanese women the choice is a stark one: stay single and have a career and financial independence or get married and devote oneself to husband and child. The percent of Japanese women who have opted to remain single has doubled over the past twenty years. Over the coming decades, the proportion of working-age Japanese will continue to dwindle. This situation is the opposite of the demographic dividend: it is the demographic deficit of a declining workforce and an increasingly dependent population. The Japanese workforce will decline by 70 percent by 2050. In countries with a similar age profile, immigration from outside the country fills some of the job vacancies. In Japan, there are strict restrictions on foreign immigration. Less than 2 percent of the population is foreign-born, compared to the United States, where the figure is 12 percent, or Australia, where it is 22 percent. Japan will experience a major crisis when its anti-immigration posture crashes against the reality of its demographic deficit. Another solution to this impending crisis would be to make it easier for women with children to enter the workforce. Again, however, this policy goes against traditional cultural norms. In 2011 a government think tank in South Korea, the Korea Development Institute, made the case for reducing the social taboos in the country associated with out-of-wedlock pregnancies, as one way to counter the declining fertility. With a fertility rate of 1.2 births per women, South Korea ranks 217th out of 222 countries in fertility. As the number of single women increases, easing legal safeguards of children born outside of marriage is one way to counter falling population.

At current rates, the world's population aged over sixty-five is likely to double in fifty years. Tod Fishman uses the phrase "shock of grey" to refer to the reality of rapidly aging societies. The old will become an increasingly large part of the population in both absolute and relative terms. As people live longer, what it is to be old is redefined. The above-sixty-five cohort is growing so large and so quickly that new categories are developed: the young-old aged sixty-five to seventy-four, the old-old aged seventy-five to eighty-four, and the oldest aged eighty-five and above. We can also reconceptualize old age in a more positive light as an age of personal fulfillment rather than one of degeneration and dependency. People previously considered old now live longer and more engaged lives. And with more elderly, there are new market niches, such as retirement communities. Some residential developments in the United States, for example, have minimum age requirements as the affluent elderly sequester themselves into homogenous communities.

3.8 The elderly will double in population over the next fifty years. An elderly lady in Inchon, South Korea.

Another form of demographic dividend is the increase in the number of older persons who are able to share their life assets with the younger generation. This is an important phenomenon in countries with, on the one hand, strong extended family ties and, on the other, limited social welfare programs. Intergenerational transfers of wealth and income from an older generation to a younger generation are an important part of economic growth in East and Southeast Asia and Latin America. In South Africa, Monde Makiwane conducted fieldwork on intergenerational transfers of wealth and concluded, "Most of the elderly in South Africa use their meager old age pensions to support unemployed children and orphaned and vulnerable children."

This fourth phase of the demographic transition has developed in some richer countries where it is associated with very low fertility levels, more pronounced aging,

3.9 As the elderly become a larger proportion of the population, retirement communities like this will become more important features of the urban landscape.

more reliance on immigration to fill job vacancies, especially at the lower wage levels, and a disconnect between marriage and children. More children are born out of wedlock and more couples do not have children. A variety of household living arrangements occur as traditional marriage is no longer such a dominant model of household formation. These trends are especially marked in the countries of Northwest and Eastern Europe. In Norway and Sweden, 54 and 55 percent respectively of all births are to unmarried women. The figures reflect increasing cohabiting between couples rather than marriage and more single-parent households, in part the result of choices of women and their families. These choices may have some negative economic consequences in some countries. In the United States, almost 41 percent of all births are to unmarried women. One in three households that experience child poverty are single-parent, female-headed households, and only 6.4 percent are from married, two-parent families. In many northern European countries, in contrast, children born out of wedlock are generally born to stable, cohabiting couples or to those with access to more generous social welfare and public health programs.

PROBLEMS AND OPPORTUNITIES OF THE DEMOGRAPHIC TRANSITION

At a very fundamental level, the demographic transition is an enormously life-enhancing phenomenon. People now live longer, healthier lives. The crushing tragedy of infant mortality and the lost opportunity of short lives, if not eradicated, are much reduced. People get to enjoy the gift of life for longer and in a healthier state, and they lead more productive lives.

Each stage of the demographic transition creates both problems and opportunities. In the initial stages, as death rates decline, more people live longer, healthier lives. However, the still high birth rate means that a society at this stage has to cope with a very youthful population with a limited number of people in the most economically productive cohorts. There is the potential instability of a youth bulge.

In the middle phases of the demographic dividend, there is an increasing proportion of the economically active population. This demographic dividend can turn into a demographic time bomb, however, if economic growth does not keep up with the number of people coming in to the job market. An increase in the working-age population can produce a demographic dividend but also raise the possibility of social unrest if the army of young people fails to find gainful and rewarding employment. It is too simple to assign the Arab Spring, for example, only to the large number of young people in the societies without job prospects—there are other countries with similar conditions that did not experience social uprisings—but it was an important demographic context. When there are a large number of young people—the median age in Egypt and Tunisia is twenty-four and thirty, respectively, compared to 44 in Germany—there is the possibility, in association with anemic economic growth and sclerotic political systems, of social unrest. Other things being equal, younger people more easily take to the streets than older people. And if the demography is weighted toward to the young while the economy is geared toward the more elderly, there is the increasing possibility of social unrest.

In the later phases of the transition, birthrates drop and life expectancies stretch out the length of the average life. There are more people with the advantage of a long life experience. A society with more of these people should be wiser, more able to take the sage, long-term perspective. Again opportunity and crises are possibilities at the later stages of the transition. On the one hand, there is the possibility of a second demographic dividend as the elderly, able to amass a long lifetime of assets, pass on their wealth to their children and younger family members. On the other hand, there may be little dividend if the elderly hang on to their assets and continue to receive and demand public benefits.

The aging of the population can be measured by the ratio of retired to working population. One standard measure divides the number of people aged over sixty-five by those aged fifteen to sixty-five and multiplies by 100. This gives a figure for the number of the dependent population for every 100 of the more economically active. The world average is ten and likely to grow to twenty-four. A ratio for a range of countries is shown in Figure 3.10. At the later stages of the demographic transitions, there is an increase in the elderly nonworking population. We can follow one of the consequences by looking at Social Security in the United States, a social insurance fund that current workers pay into to support retired workers. When it was first introduced, there were many more workers paying into the system than recipients receiving benefits. In 1950, for example, the number of workers per beneficiary was 16.4. In 1960 the number of workers per beneficiary was 5.1,

3.10 Dependency ratio by country

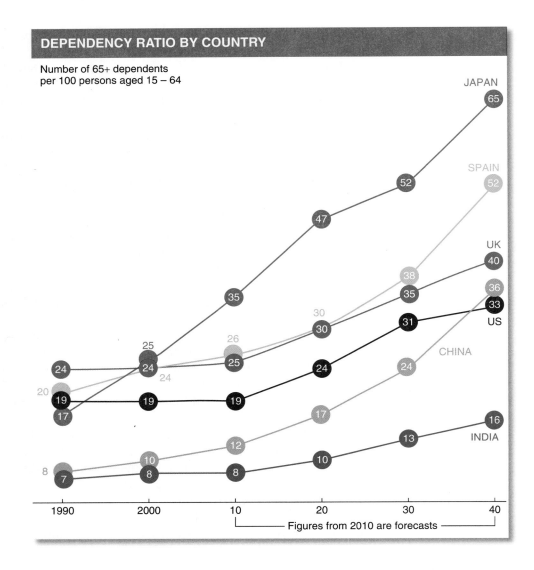

DEPENDENCY RATIO BY COUNTRY

Number of 65+ dependents
per 100 persons aged 15 – 64

JAPAN 65

SPAIN 52

UK 40

36

33 US

CHINA

INDIA

52

47

38

35

31

35

30

30

26

25

25

24

24

24

24

24

20

19

19

19

17

17

13

16

12

10

10

10

8

8

8

8

7

1990 2000 10 20 30 40

Figures from 2010 are forecasts

by 2010 it had fallen to 2.9, and it is likely to fall to 2 in twenty years' time. In 1950 48.2 million workers supported 2.9 million beneficiaries, but by 2010 the respective numbers were 156 million workers and 53 million beneficiaries. As more retirees live longer, they are supported by relatively fewer number of workers. Over the longer term, this may be fiscally unsustainable. In social democracies with generous social insurance programs, the aging of the population creates a fiscal crisis for the welfare state. It can lead to generational inequalities, as fewer workers have to support more retirees.

Generational inequity really kicks in if those paying for the elderly are unlikely to see the same benefits. In the United States, for example, older adults are advantaged because they have publicly provided pensions and healthcare that are unlikely be so generous to future generations. The net worth of a typical US household member aged over sixty-five is forty-seven times that of one younger than thirty-five. The disparity was ten to one just twenty-five years ago. Over a quarter of a century, there has been a relative shift of wealth from the young to the elderly and the creation of an intergenerational divide in life chances and benefits. Around the world, in countries with social welfare programs, the aging of the population creates fiscal tensions and the possibility of intergenerational conflicts. Class, race, and gender have long been identified as sources of difference, advantage, and disadvantage. We need to add to that list both age and the cohort's position in the demographic transition.

The shift toward a more elderly population can have major implications for continued economic growth, as without younger workers the number of dependents will exceed the number of productive workers and there will be increasing pressure on generous social welfare systems. In some rich countries, there is now a greater reliance on foreign immigrants to fill job vacancies. However, this can create tensions as the issue of citizenship, for example, becomes more problematic with more "foreign" workers. As welfare costs mount, there is increasing concern with noncitizen access to generous welfare arrangements. The economic need for increased immigration can sometime clash with a cultural debate about national identity and emerging political debates on citizenship.

There is a distinct global geography to the demographic transition, and it interconnects with levels of economic development and rates of growth. We can identify three types of countries:

1. Aging countries, such as Japan and Russia, with aging populations.

2. Demographic and economic growth countries, such as Brazil and Thailand, with rapidly growing populations but developing economies, with the possibility of a positive demographic dividend.

3. Rapid demographic growth with limited economic growth countries, such as Afghanistan.

Youth revolts, crime levels, culture wars about the family, discussions about welfare reform and national identity: there is a demographic context to some of these interesting social changes. Demographic changes are at the heart of some of most profound cultural transformations and intense political debates occurring around the world.

Cited References

Denevan, W. (ed) (1992) *The Native Population of the Americas in 1492*. Madison: University of Wisconsin Press.

Fishman, T. C. (2010) *Shock of Grey*. New York: Scribner.

Fuller, G. and Pitts, F. R. (1990) Youth Cohorts and Political Unrest in South Korea. *Political Geography Quarterly* 9: 9–22.

Galloway, P. R. (1986) Long-Term Fluctuations in Climate and Population in the Preindustrial Era. *Population and Development Review* 12: 1–24.

Lee, H. F. and Zhang, D. D. (2010) Changes in Climate and Secular Population Cycles in China, 1000 CE to 1911. *Climate Research* 42: 235–246.

Lee, H. F., Fok. L., and Zhang, D. D. (2008) Climate Change and Chinese Population Growth Dynamics over the Last Millennium. *Climate Change* 88: 131–156.

Makiwane. M. (2011) Intergenerational Relations in Africa with a Focus on South Africa. Paper presented at the United Nations Expert Group Meeting on Adolescents, Youth and Employment. Population Division, United Nations Secretariat. http://www.un.org/esa/population/meetings/egm-adolescents/p09_makiwane.pdf Accessed November 7, 2011.

Marcus, A. A., Islam, M. and Moloney, J. (2008) Youth Bulges, Busts, and Doing Business in Violence-Prone Nations. *Business and Politics* 10 DOI: 10.2202/1469-3569.1227 http://www.bepress.com/bap/vol10/iss3/art4 Accessed November 8, 2011.

Urdal, H. (2004) *The Devil in the Demographics: The Effect of Youth Bulges on Domestic Armed Conflict 1950–2000.* World Bank: Social Development Paper No. 14. Washington, DC.

Urdal, H. and Hoelscher, K. (2009) *Urban Youth Bulges and Urban Social Disorder.* World Bank. Washington, DC.

Select Guide to Further Reading

Benedictow. O. J. (2004) *The Black Death, 1346–1353: The Complete History.* Woodbridge: Boydell.

Bongaarts, J. (2009) Human Population Growth and the Demographic Transition. *Philosophical Transactions of the Royal Society B: Biological Sciences.* 364: 2985–2990.

Cai, F. (2010) Demographic Transition, Demographic Dividend, and Lewis Turning Point in China. *China Economic Review* 3: 107–119.

Demeny, P. (2011) Population Policy and the Demographic Transition: Performance, Prospects, and Options. *Population and Development Review* 37 (supplement): 249–274.

Dyson, T. (2010) *Population and Development: The Demographic Transition.* New York: Zed Books.

Laslett, P. (1989) *A Fresh Map of Life: The Emergence of the Third Age.* London: Weidenfeld and Nicholson.

Lee, R. (2003) The Demographic Transition: Three Centuries of Fundamental Change. *Journal of Economic Perspectives* 17: 167–190.

Lee, R. and Reher, D. (2011) Introduction: The Landscape of Demographic Transition and Its Aftermath. *Population and Development Review* 3: 1–7.

Lesthaeghe, R. (2010) The Unfolding Story of the Second Demographic Transition. *Population and Development Review* 36: 211–251.

Little, L. L. (ed.) (2006) *Plague and the End of Antiquity: The Pandemic of 541–750.* Cambridge: Cambridge University Press.

Lovell, W. G. (1992) "Heavy Shadows and Black Night": Disease and Depopulation in Colonial Spanish America. *Annals of Association of American Geographers* 82: 426–443.

Rosen, W. (2007) *Justinian's Flea: Plague, Empire and the Birth of Europe.* New York: Viking.

Tuchman, B. W. (1978) *The Distant Mirror: The Calamitous 14th Century.* New York: Knopf.

Websites

Spread of the Black Death in Europe 1346–1353
http://en.wikipedia.org/wiki/File:Blackdeath2.gif

Population Reference Bureau
http://www.prb.org/

Interactive world population map
http://www.prb.org/Publications/Datasheets/2011/world-population-data-sheet/world-map.aspx#/map/population

United Nations Population Data
http://www.un.org/esa/population/
http://www.un.org/popin/data.html

Global demography of aging
http://www.hsph.harvard.edu/pgda/

Human mortality database
http://www.gapminder.org/communityproxy/ChartDataServlet?key=p2p2lQFK9sM2aZxRc4f2ndA#$majorMode=chart$is;shi=t;ly=2003;lb=f;il=t;fs=11;al=30;stl=t;st=t;nsl=t;se=t$wst;tts=C$ts;sp=6;ti=1760$zpv;v=0$inc_x;mmid=XCOORDS;iid=p2p2lQFK9sM2avvuSFHXBVw;by=ind$inc_y;mmid=YCOORDS;iid=p2p2lQFK9sM2SxRWYSSUGNQ;by=ind$inc_s;uniValue=20;iid=phAwcNAVuyj0XOoBL_n5tAQ;by=ind$inc_c;uniValue=255;gid=CATID2;iid=p2p2lQFK9sM3QMNESzxcmQw;by=grp$map_x;scale=log;dataMin=0.0156;dataMax=0.805$map_y;scale=log;dataMin=0.0022;dataMax=0.6168$map_s;sma=84;smi=7.66$cd;bd=0$inds=

Data for demographic research
http://www.icpsr.umich.edu/icpsrweb/DSDR/

4 Population and Food

In the last chapter we looked at population numbers and their change over time and across space. Absolute numbers are significant, but they take on extra meaning when we look at them relative to resources. In this chapter, we will consider how population connects with one of the most important resources, food.

MALTHUSIAN MELANCHOLY

The relationship between food and population has long interested social observers. One has left a permanent intellectual legacy. Thomas Robert Malthus (1766–1834) was one of eight children born to a prosperous middle-class family in Surrey, England. He is best known for his work *An Essay on The Principle of Population*, of which he worked on six successive editions from 1798 and 1826.

The historical context is important. Writing in the convulsive times of the French Revolution, Malthus was one of the many English reactionaries who were wary of radical change, distrustful of social progress, and skeptical of massive improvement and the idea of upward progress. His basic argument is that while population increases at a geometric rate, food supply only grows at an arithmetic rate. The end result is that there are more people than food. When things are good, people have more children, but eventually this population growth exceeds the food supply. Families respond to this dire situation by having less children, and so population decreases until things are back in equilibrium, when the cycle starts all over again. Human history is one of population increase overshooting the available food supply. Misery, poverty, and famine, the so-called Malthusian checks, are "natural" elements that bring population growth back into alignment with the food supply.

This simple model has policy implications. As a social conservative, Malthus was against social policy that disrupted the existing social order and its workings. He was highly critical of policies aimed to help the poor. Social welfare provision, Malthus believed, allowed the poor to have children and, for him and his followers, that simply made things worse. The number of children born to the poor should be limited.

His ideas influenced contemporary British politicians, who introduced the census in 1801 as a means of counting the population and the New Poor Law of 1834, which launched workhouses for the poor, so familiar to the readers of Charles Dickens.

His ideas filtered out to social theorists such as Herbert Spencer (1820–1903), who espoused Social Darwinism, based on the idea of the survival of the fittest. Malthus's works were roundly criticized in the radical working-class journals of the day. In 1820 William Godwin calculated that, using China as his model, the world's population could comfortably reach 9 billion. He was writing at a time when the population was little more than one billion and few at the time could even imagine today's population of 7 billion.

Malthus's work was socially specific, written at a time of intense political debates and just as the demographic transition and the agricultural and industrial revolutions were taking off. Yet his ideas have proven very influential, echoing down through the subsequent years.

A continuing legacy is a pessimism regarding the ability to expand population beyond a fixed base because the food supply is considered as relatively fixed or capable of only slow increase. Malthus presents a specter of population increasing greater than the food supply. He was writing just as the agricultural revolution was transforming agricultural productivity. Since then, in the past two hundred years, agricultural productivity has increased remarkably, creating a much larger food supply base. In one important way, Malthus's gloomy predictions proved incorrect. The global population has increased to over 7 billion, and yet global hunger is not inevitable, even with a larger population. According to the Food and Agriculture Organization (FAO), the proportion of people in developing countries with food intakes below 2,200 calories per day fell from 57 percent in 1965 to just 10 percent in 1998. For those with access to food, the price has steadily declined by 60 percent in the last 40 years, according to FAO estimates.

4.1 Grocery store in Budapest, Hungary. Local, national, and international food chains converge on this one store in Budapest to ensure fresh fruit and vegetables in January.

The Danish economist Ester Boserup (1910–1999) reversed the Malthusian argument. Rather than agricultural technology determining population, it is population that determines agricultural technology. Necessity, in this case population pressure, is the mother of invention. In the history of agriculture, when population levels are low shifting agriculture can be employed, but when population increases more emphasis is placed on using fields on a permanent basis, and this incentive spurs agricultural innovation. Innovations include the use of irrigation, the development of hybrid plants, weed control, and the use of fertilizers. Agriculture intensifies as population pressure mounts.

In one sense, at least, Malthus's prophecy of doom has failed to materialize, while Boserup's more optimistic view is sustained. Population has increased, yet so has global food supply (Figures 4.1 and 4.2). All the evidence suggests that world agricultural production can grow even more in line with increased demand. Charles Godfray and colleagues looked at the ability of the global food production system to meet the demand of 9 billion people by 2050. They suggest that it is possible through a variety of methods:

- closing the yield gap, that is, the difference between possible and actual productivity. In Southeast Asia, for example, there is a 60 percent difference between average and maximum rice yields. Yield gaps are larger in failed or dysfunctional states or in poor countries with limited access to the world markets or to easy and cheap credit. Political stability and world trade can increase yields by making it profitable for farmers to invest more.

4.2 Food preparation and sale in Grenada. Women constitute the vast majority of food preparers and sellers at this weekly market in Grenada's capital city, St. George's, as they do in much of the world.

Box 4.1 OVERFISHING

The oceans of the world have long been an important food source. Along the coast and deep in the ocean, fish stocks are protein-rich sources of food and nutrition. However, as industrial-style fishing with large boats and fish-detecting sonar now sweep the oceans, the supply of fish is endangered. Wilf Swartz and colleagues looked at fish catches from 1950 to 2005 and mapped the levels of exploitation. Heavily exploited areas are highlighted in red. The global increase in the

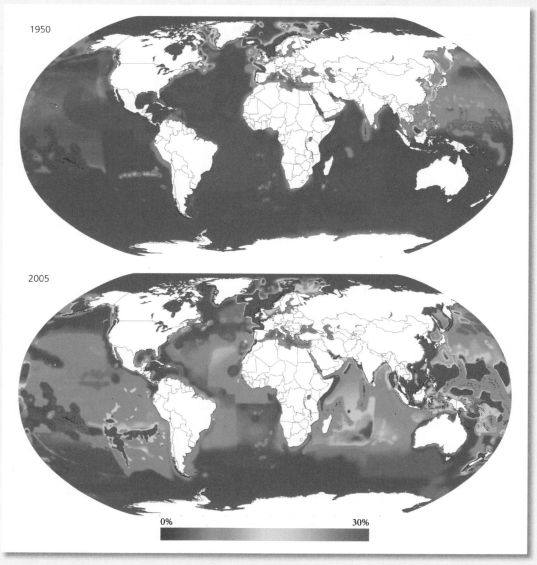

Fisheries exploitation, 1950 and 2005

Box 4.1   CONTINUED

distribution of severe exploitation is vividly demonstrated in the comparison of the two maps. The global depletion of fish supply is one reason behind the growth of fish farming. Some wild species, such as the bluefin tuna, are on the verge of extinction due to overfishing. As the fleets go into deeper and deeper water, deep-sea fish that mature and reproduce slowly (such as the orange roughy, with a lifespan of 149 years) are particularly vulnerable. With nonselective fishing and a weak regulatory system, deep-sea fishing will soon exhaust the fish stock. Wild fish supplies peaked in the 1980s, and the decline of global fish supplies will put extra pressure on farming to replace the protein provided by the world's fisheries.

References

Greenberg, P. (2010) *Four Fish: The Future of the Last Wild Food.* New York: Penguin.

Norse, E. A., Brooke, S., Cheung, W. W. L., Clark, M. R., Ekeland, I., Froese, R., Gjerde, K. M., Haedrich, R. L., Heppell, S. S., Morato, T., Morgan, L. E., Pauly, F., Sumaila, R., and Watson, R. (2012) Sustainability of Deep-Sea Fisheries. *Marine Policy* 36:307–320.

Pauly, D. (2010) *Five Easy Pieces: How Fishing Impacts Marine Ecosystems.* Washington, DC: Island Press.

Swartz, W., Sala, E., Tracey, S., Watson, R., and Pauly, D. (2010) The Spatial Expansion and Ecological Footprint of Fisheries: 1950 to Present. *PLoS ONE* 5(12): e15143. doi:10.1371/journal.pone.0015143

- increasing production limits. The Green Revolution successfully increased agricultural production throughout the world from the 1960s and 1970s by developing hybrid varieties of maize, rice, and wheat and increasing use of fertilizers and pesticides. Genetically modified crops can increase productivity. However, there is mounting public disquiet about the long-term implications of engineering our food supply and the unfolding consequences of genetically modified elements in the food chain.

- reducing waste. Around 35 percent of food in the world is wasted. The reason varies from lack of cold storage to "supersized" portions. Food is so cheap in some places that there is little incentive to avoid waste.

- changing diet. As societies get richer they tend to consume more meat. This involves growing grain to feed to livestock. Reducing the consumption of meat allows grassland for animals to be turned into arable farming. Reducing meat consumption also has a positive health benefit, since it reduces heart disease rates.

- expanding aquaculture. Fish farming increases the amount of relatively cheap protein. There are, however, issues of environmental pollution and genetic contamination with an increase in aquaculture.

Despite the tremendous increases in agricultural productivity that have rendered Malthus's original predictions obsolete, problems remain. Let us consider four of them: hunger, sustainability, nutrition, and ethics.

HUNGER, FAMINE, AND FOOD INSECURITY

The declining levels of hunger and malnutrition are testament to the ability of agricultural production to surpass the Malthusian limits. Yet hunger remains. Figure 4.3 shows the distribution of a global hunger. Notice the extreme concentration in tropical Africa.

The term "food security" is employed to refer to food's availability. Food security is when people have relatively easy access to safe and nutritious food. Food insecurity occurs when this does not occur, either on a permanent or transitory basis; it leads to hunger and undernourishment, making people more susceptible to disease and illness. Figure 4.4 plots the global distribution of undernourishment. Worldwide, it is estimated that there are approximately one billion without enough calories and a further one billion who are malnourished in a form of hidden hunger because they do not consume enough nutrients for a healthy life. Almost 160 million children lack vitamin A, and 500 million women have an iron deficiency that causes 60,000 deaths each year during pregnancy.

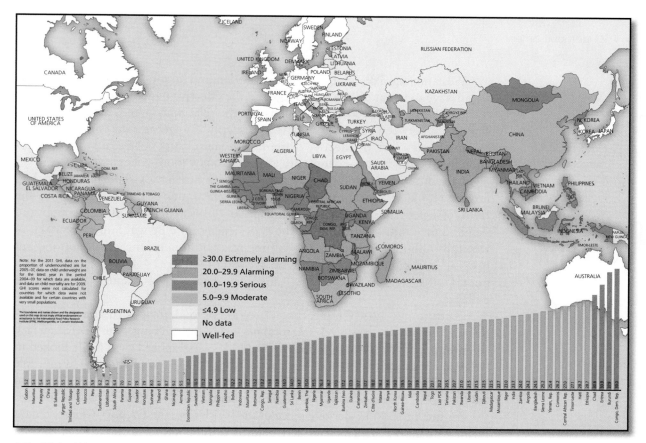

4.3 Global Hunger Index

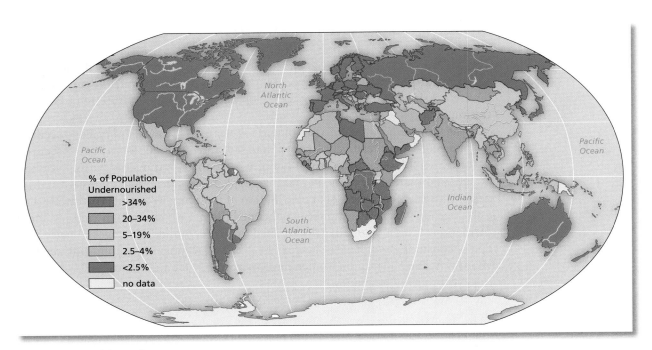

4.4 Undernourishment

We can make a distinction between the demand for food—a universal need, as we all have to to eat to remain alive—and the effective demand for food, which is the ability to pay for food. The issue is not the relationship between demand and supply but between effective demand and supply. Hunger is not a function of lack of supply but a lack of effective demand. Hunger occurs not because there is not enough food but because people are too poor to buy food.

Lack of access to food is also a major cause of hunger. Extreme hunger such as famine regularly affects millions. Amartya Sen argues that famines are less the result of lack of food and more the collapse of the system that links the supply and demand for food. He drew upon the experience of the Bengal famine of 1943, in which 3 million people died. The famine was not because there was no food but because wages did not keep up with growing food prices. Food price inflation, poor food distribution, hoarding, and poor government responses caused the collapse.

Three things cause famine: the redirection of food, the destruction of the productive capacity to grow food, and total neglect of the starving. Famines reflect lack of power more than lack of food. The historical geographer David Nally looked in detail at the famine in Ireland that began when the potato blight created multiple harvest failures beginning in 1845. More than a million people died, and 2 million left the land. He looked at the effect of the Irish Poor Law system developed prior to the famine, in 1838. Under one piece of the legislation, the Gregory Clause, tenant farmers on more than a quarter-acre holding could not receive public relief without leaving the land and entering the workhouse. Once tenants left, their dwellings

Box 4.2 FOOD DESERTS

The rich world of developed economies is a place of relative food plenty. Yet even there, access to food varies. At the most extreme end are "food deserts," parts of a city or region with very limited access to cheap, nutritious food. The US Department of Agriculture identifies food deserts at the level of census tracts, areas containing a population of approximately 5,000 (http://www.ers.usda.gov/data/fooddesert/fooddesert.html). Almost 24 million people in the United States live more than a mile from a supermarket. Almost 2 million households live more than a mile from a supermarket and are without access to a vehicle. In total, 5.7 percent of all US households had problems getting access to the food that they wanted. Food deserts are most prevalent in areas with low to median incomes and the highest proportion of African Americans. There are fewer food deserts in areas with predominantly white middle- and upper-income households. And the groceries that are in food deserts have higher prices. Many studies show a correlation between food deserts and lower consumption of fruit and vegetables and higher levels of obesity.

References

Beaulac, J., Kristjansson, E., and Cummins, S. (2009) A Systematic Review of Food Deserts, 1966–2007. *Preventive Chronic Disease* 6: A105.

Gordon, C., Purciel-Hill, M., Ghai, NR., Kaufman, L., Graham, R., and Van Wye, G. (2011) Measuring Food Deserts in New York City's Low-Income Neighborhoods. *Health Place.* 17:696–700.

Walker, R. E., Keane, C.R., and Burke, J. G. (2010) Disparities and Access to Healthy Food in the United States: A Review of Food Deserts Literature. *Health and Place* 16:876–884.

Wrigley, N. (2002) Food Deserts in British Cities. *Urban Studies* 39:2029–2040.

were knocked down and the landholdings were consolidated. The famine provided an opportunity for the British authorities to clear "excess" population from the land and rationalize the landholding system. A colonial state used the famine to advance its agenda of agricultural rationalization and social improvement. Nally notes, "For those holding political and economic power, famine became the function of new regulatory and corrective mechanisms that unleashed the terror of the possible."

Famine occurs when the usual markets collapse, food is taken away, or the hungry are wantonly ignored. The great famine in China that occurred from 1959 to 1962 was a result of a forced collectivization of agriculture. Family farms were turned into people's communes, and impossibly high quotas were established. Grain production plummeted, but in order to fill their quotas, local officials continued to ship the dwindling grain supply to the cities. It is estimated that around 35 million people died in a famine that was entirely human-made. Heavy police control meant that people were unable to leave their villages. People were reduced to eating tree bark.

Famines continue to be present on the world stage. They rarely appear in democracies, even poor democracies. Their connection with deeply authoritarian regimes is exemplified in the recent famine in North Korea, when between 1 and 3 million people, out of a total population of 22 million, died due to a collapse of the food distribution system and government incompetence. The country suffers from chronic food insecurity, with almost half of all children malnourished.

The Horn of Africa is a scene of recurrent famines. Almost 12 million people are currently at risk from famine. In 1984–1985, more than one million died in a famine in Ethiopia caused by conflict, drought, and economic mismanagement. Between 2010 and 2012, more than 260,000 people died in Somalia, half of them aged under five. Persistent hunger in sub-Saharan Africa is one of the major failures of the global food system. Many causes are at work. Consider the case of Niger, which is one of the poorest countries of the world, with at least 40 percent of the population chronically malnourished. Food shortages affect more than 7 million people. Household vulnerability is made more severe by land degradation that is reducing the supply of farmland and forcing more people onto marginal lands. Low income, erratic rainfall, and the low status afforded to women are just some of the many reasons behind the recurring famine and food shortages. The growing reliance on food aid paradoxically depresses even farther local agriculture production. The result is a population with precarious access to food too easily pushed over into hunger and famine by even small changes in food supply, food prices, and climate. In these circumstances, drought does not cause hunger as much as it pushes an already vulnerable population into famine.

4.5 Irrigation in Midwest United States. Central pivot irrigation systems ensure high agricultural productivity in the drier parts of the United States. However, freshwater sources are being used up, questioning the long-term sustainability of such practices.

SUSTAINABLE AGRICULTURE

The enormous gains in agricultural productivity have passed the limits imagined by Malthus. Agricultural production has increased food supply enough to dispel the original Malthusian prediction. And yet there are some who see a global food system precariously balanced. While Charles Godfray and colleagues look to increased gains to be made, Carleton Schade and David Pimental point to problems. A comparison of the data and arguments in the two papers makes for a compelling case study of a situation's alternative readings and a reminder that arguments vary even when using the same facts. Whereas Godfray et al. highlight the ability of the global food system to produce even more food, Schade and Pimental point to systemic problems. They suggest that the rapid increase in food supply was the result of available land, water, and energy, a benign climate, and improving crop yields, conditions unlikely to be repeated. They estimate that if the population increases to 9.2 billion there is likely to be only enough food for only 6–8 billion. Food insecurity and famine are likely to afflict anywhere between 1 and 3 billion people. The problems they identify include declining land and water availability. The amount of land available for agriculture is unlikely to meet the demand for extra food production because increasing population reduces the amount of available land and degrades some of the most productive soil. They suggest a land deficit of between 0.1 and 0.9 billion hectares. Irrigated land is the most productive land on the planet (Figure 4.5). However, we are losing this land to salinization and erosion. The production of food requires large quantities of fresh water. We already have reached the ceiling of surface supply, and the supply of water from aquifers is fast running out. Climate change will also affect the global agricultural system through generating more extreme and damaging weather events, such as flooding. While the higher-latitude countries such as Canada and Russia may experience an extension of their growing season with global warming, other regions may be negatively affected. In general, the growth of population combined with their enlarging ecological footprint is having an environmental impact. We are losing rainforest cover in the tropical zones, wild fish stocks in the oceans are depleting, and reserves of fresh water in river basins around the world are diminishing. More than 1.4 billion people live in river basins where water sources are being depleted.

The two contrasting papers embody the different perspectives. Whereas Godfray and colleagues point to the slack in the system, Schade and Pimental point to its limits. They suggest that we have reached if not already passed peak water supply, peak land availability, and peak crop yields. The future that they see is one of Malthusian limits reimposed. Adherents of either side can look to current trends to bolster their claims. On the one hand, levels of food insecurity are being reduced. On the other, there is evidence of increasing food prices. There was rapid increase in 2006. Prices fell as the world economic crisis hit in 2008, but the trend, ominously, suggests more expensive food, which will have the biggest negative impact on the poor and vulnerable (Figure 4.6). Only time will tell which of these trends, declining insecurity or increasing costs, is temporary and which is persistent.

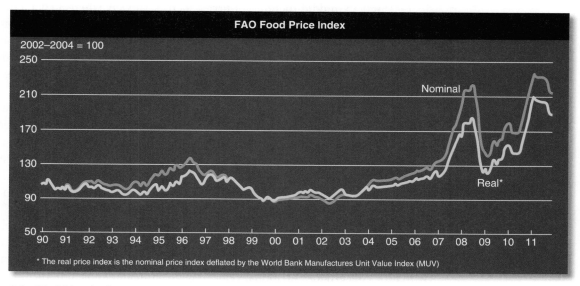

4.6 World food prices

QUESTIONING THE FOOD PRODUCTION SYSTEM

The Malthusian limits were bypassed because of the creation of a very efficient industrialized agricultural system that generated large amounts of relatively cheap food. Only seven countries produce more food than they need—the United States, Canada, France, Australia, Thailand, and Argentina—but a global trading system has widened the availability of food. In recent years this system has come under greater scrutiny.

The original Malthusian/Boserup debate was concerned only with the quantity of food, and in this regard food supply has largely kept up with population increases. Boserup triumphs over Malthus. Gains in productivity and the emergence of a global food system have ensured large amounts of cheap food to much of the world's population. Yet there are emerging questions regarding the quality of food and the wider implications of its nutritional and environmental impacts.

The rise of processed foods goes hand in hand with the increase of obesity. Much of the processed food is loaded with sugar and fats. The World Health Organization (WHO) now estimates that 1.5 billion adults are overweight and 500 million are obese, as defined by the Body Mass Index (BMI), which is a person's weight in kilograms divided by the square of their height in meters. Overweight people are defined as having a BMI greater than 25, and obesity is defined with a BMI greater than 30. It is a crude measure, as it does not distinguish between muscle and fat tissue, but until we have better metrics, it is a useful indicator. The obesity epidemic is associated with a population that is sedentary, sitting and driving rather than walking and exercising, and with diets that contain high-energy nutrients such as fat, starch, and sugar. Increasing obesity leads to cardiovascular disease and diabetes. The obesity epidemic is particularly prevalent among young children; the WHO estimates that 43 million children under the age of five are now overweight.

Figure 4.7 highlights the geographic distribution of obesity. There are high levels of obesity in affluent countries such as the United States. Obesity is also found increasingly in middle-income countries such as Mexico, where 30 percent of adults are defined as clinically obese. In such cases malnutrition, strangely enough, plays a role. The bodies of malnourished young children learn to retain fat, and in later life, with more income and food choices, the children of malnourishment can become obese adults. This process explains the rapidly rising obesity levels of countries transitioning from low to middle income in one generation.

Obesity has complex roots. Individuals can limit their energy intake and exercise more. Yet it is more than just a case of individual choice. Jamie Pearce and Karen Witten describe environments that create higher risk of obesity as obesogenic. The food industry could, and in some cases is starting to, reduce the fat, sugar, and salt content of the food it produces to ensure more nutritional choices. We could make our cities friendlier to walking and cycling rather than making them only convenient for sedentary motorists.

A food movement is emerging that shifts the debate from the basic supply of food to a wider concern with nutrition. It is a debate not just about the supply of food but the quality of the food. In many countries government subsidizes the production of crops with little concern for nutritional value or environmental impact. In the United States,

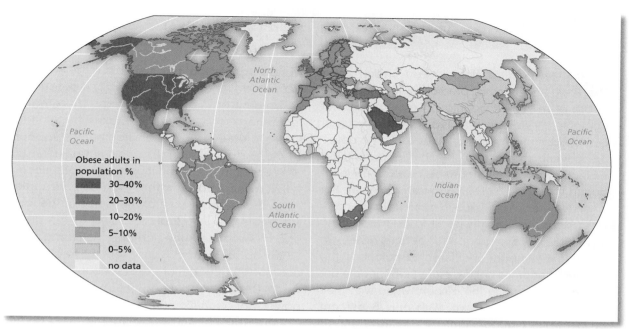

4.7 Obesity

around 90 million acres are devoted to growing corn. A huge corn surplus is created by the combination of efficient farming and generous government subsidies. The corn surplus is turned into corn syrup that is added to the food supply, which in turn adds extra calories to the average consumer. The rise of obesity in the United States is directly linked to the corn surplus and the heavy use of corn syrup in processed foods.

Food surpluses are also the result of heavy chemical usage. The main form of pollution in much of the United States, for example, comes not from factories but from farms and agribusiness, with the runoff of pesticides and animal wastes entering streams, rivers, and groundwater. Every year between 10,000 to 20,000 farm workers suffer acute pesticide poisoning.

The rise of a corporate industrialized food production system due to economies of scale and large investments has produced vast quantities of cheap food, but we are now beginning to question the wider costs of this system, its impact on public health and environmental quality. A new food movement is emerging that is concerned more with health, nutrition, sustainability, and access. It is a disparate movement with a wide variety of goals and concerns, including improving the plight of agricultural workers, raising issues of animal rights in factory farming, the slow food movement, the promotion of local food producers, and the encouragement of inner-city vegetable gardens. Fundamentally, it is concerned with the nature of the food that we produce, in particular questioning the emphasis of encouraging grain-fed meat production, assessing the wider costs of cheap fast food, highlighting the darker side of the food chain, and pointing out the issue of the sustainability of the entire global food system.

The global food system, while perhaps producing a supply of food, does little to effect a fair or even healthy supply of food. While obesity is emerging as a major

Box 4.3 OVERPOPULATION REEXAMINED

In 1968 the Stanford biologist Paul Ehrlich wrote *The Population Bomb,* predicting the imminent death of millions if population growth was not contained. It was, and still, is a common assumption. Since growth rates are highest in the developing world, the debate often hinges around the belief that population controls need to be introduced into these high-growth-rate countries. But when we look at the issue in more detail, a number of important points need to be made. First, it is not simply the number of people. When we factor in the impact of different populations, the problem becomes not too many poor people but too many people in the affluent world with their heavy ecological imprint. With only 5 percent of the world's population, the United States is responsible for 23.3 percent of the global total of carbon dioxide emissions. The average US citizen generates a much higher environmental impact and heavier ecological footprint than citizens of other countries, especially of lower-income countries. It is not that there are too many people, it is that there are too many with a heavy ecological imprint. Ehrlich saw the problem as too many other people, but in terms of environmental impact there are too many like him, affluent people living in the developed world, rather than too many poor people in the less-developed world.

It is perhaps useful to consider environmental impact as more than just a function of population. One useful general equation is

$$I = PAT$$

where I is the environmental impact, P is total population, A is a measure of that population's affluence, and T is the technological capacity available to that population. The environmental impact of a population is a function of its affluence and technology. It is not just population totals that have an environmental impact. Thus while the United States has only 5 percent of the world's population, because it is a rich country (A) with advanced technology (T) it consumes 20 percent of the world's energy. The greater technology and affluence makes the United States create a larger environmental impact (I) than its population (P) would suggest.

Second, there is a politics to population control. It reflects power rather than demographic analysis. The birth control measures of the last fifty years are invariably targeted at the poor and the weak, not the rich and the strong. The World Bank used to adopt fertility targets for countries, but none for the rich countries of the world. Debates about population control reflect power, not scientific neutrality.

Third, there is an adage from farming communities, "each mouth comes with two hands." It refers to the fact that people are a resource, not just a problem. The ultimate resource is the inventiveness of humans: the more humans, the larger the creative pool of talent.

It is not simply the amount of people that is the issue; it is their relationship to the land, their use of resources, and the economic system at the heart of the people/environment relationship. To talk about only reducing population is to pass the blame onto the poorest and weakest, when what is really required is a fundamental reassessment of our relationship with the environment and the nature of our economic system.

References

Caldecott, B., Howarth, N. and McSharry, P. (2014) *Stranded Assets in Agriculture: Protecting Value From Environment-Related Risks.* Smith School of Enterprise and the Environment. University of Oxford. http://www.smithschool.ox.ac.uk/research/stranded-assets/Stranded%20Assets%20Agriculture%20Report%20Final.pdf

Connelly, M. (2008) *Fatal Misconceptions: The Struggle to Control World Population.* Cambridge, MA: Belknap Press of Harvard University Press.

Box 4.3 CONTINUED

Ehrlich, P. (1968) *The Population Bomb.* New York: Ballantine.

Harvey, D. (1974) Population, Resources and the Ideology of Science. *Economic Geography* 50: 256–277.

Simon, J. L. (1981) *The Ultimate Resource.* Princeton: Princeton University Press.

Weisman, A (2013) *Countdown: Our Last, Best Hope For A Future on Earth.* New York: Little Brown and Company

Zehner, O. (2011) Population/Overpopulation. In *Green Culture*, edited by P. Robbins, K. Wehr, and J. G. Golson, 366–369. London: Sage.

health issue, food insecurity continues to be a problem for many. Parts of the world are overfed while others are undernourished, and yet other parts are, strangely, both overfed and undernourished.

We are what we eat, and for those who can afford it there are choices to be made about what we eat and how we eat it. A non-vegetarian diet requires 2.9 times more water, 2.5 times more primary energy, 13 times more fertilizer, and 1.4 times more pesticides than a vegetarian diet. When we move beyond worrying about the supply of food, we begin to question the nutritional quality of the food we buy and eat, its environmental impact, its ethical implications, and its wider imprint on the world we live in.

What to make of the gloomy prognostication of Malthus? The constraints of food supply have been transcended by incredible gains in agricultural productivity and a global supply chain of food that links importers and exports of food. Population has continued to increase long past the Malthusian limits. And yet if the basic limits of food supply no longer apply with the brutal force predicted by Malthus, problems remain. Out of 7 billion people, one billion are hungry, one billion are malnourished, and a further billion are obese. It is not only the supply of food that is the problem, although there are some who see food supply peaking and then declining as other resource inputs such as land and water become more problematic. Questions are also being raised about the distribution, quality, and price of food and the long-term sustainability of maintaining enough good-quality food for all of the world's population.

Cited References

Boserup, E. (1965) *The Conditions of Agricultural Growth: The Economics of Agrarian Change under Population Pressure.* London: Allen and Unwin.

Godfray, H. C. J., Beddington, J. R., Crute, I.R., Haddad, L., Lawrence, D., Muir, J. F., Pretty, J., Robinson, S., Thomas, S. M., and Toulmin, C. (2010) Food Security: The Challenge of Feeding 9 Billion People. *Science* 327: 812–818.

Keneally. T. (2010) *Three Famines: Starvation and Politics.* North Sydney: Knopf.

Nally, D. (2008) "That Coming Storm": The Irish Poor Law, Colonial Biopolitics, and the Great Famine. *Annals of the Association of American Geographers* 98: 714–741.

Pearce, J. and Witten, K. (eds) (2010) *Geographies of Obesity: Environmental Understandings of the Obesity Epidemic.* Burlington: Ashgate.

Schade, C. and Pimentel, D. (2010) Population Crash: Prospects for Famine in the Twenty-First Century. *Environment, Development and Sustainability* 12: 245–262.

Sen, A. (1981) *Poverty and Famines.* Oxford: Clarendon Press.

Selected Guide to Further Reading

Bassett, T. J. and Winter-Nelson, A. (2010) *The Atlas of World Hunger*. Chicago: University of Chicago Press.

Carolan, M. (2011) *The Real Cost of Cheap Food*. New York: Routledge.

Carolan, M. (2013) *Reclaiming Food Security*. New York: Routledge.

Cohen, D. A. (2013) *A Big Fat Crisis: The Hidden Forces Behind The Obesity Epidemic-and How We Can End It*. New York: Nation.

Guthman J, 2013, Too Much Food and too Little Sidewalk? Problematizing the Obesogenic Environment Thesis. *Environment and Planning A* 45: 142–158.

Hallett, L. and McDermott, D. (2011) Quantifying the Extent and Cost of Food Deserts in Lawrence, Kansas, USA. *Applied Geography* 31: 1210–1215.

Huzel, J. P. (2006) *The Popularization of Malthus in Early Nineteenth-Century England*. Burlingtion: Ashgate.

Jinseng, J. (2012) *Tombstone: The Great Chinese Famine 1958–1962*. New York: Farrar Straus and Giroux.

Kiple, K. F. and Ornelas, K.C. (eds) (2000) *The Cambridge World History of Food*. Cambridge: Cambridge University Press.

Lappe, F. M. (1971) *Diet for a Small Planet*. New York: Ballantine.

Marlow, H. J., Hayes, W.K., Soret, S., Carter, R.L., Schwab, E.R., and Sabaté, J. (2009) Diet and the Environment: Does What You Eat Matter? *American Journal of Clinical Nutrition* 89: 1699–1703.

Morrison, N.O. (2011) Mapping Spatial Variation in Food Consumption. *Applied Geography*. 31:1262–1267.

McMillan, T. (2012) *The American Way of Eating*. New York: Scribner.

Patel, R. (2008) *Stuffed and Starved: The Hidden Battle for the World Food System*. Brooklyn: Melville House.

Pilcher, J. M. (ed.) (2012) *The Oxford Handbook of Food History*. New York: Oxford University Press.

Pimentel, D. (2005) Economic and Environmental Costs of the Application of Pesticides Primarily in the USA. *Environment, Development and Sustainability* 7: 229–252.

Pollan, M. (2006) *The Omnivore's Dilemma: A Natural History of Four Meals*. New York: Penguin.

Pollan, M. (2008) *In Defence of Food*. New York: Penguin.

Roberts, P. (2008) *The End of Food*. Boston: Houghton Mifflin.

Schlosser, E. (2004) *Fast Food Nation: The Dark Side of the All-American Meal*. New York: Harper.

Woodham-Smith, C. (1962) *The Great Hunger, Ireland 1845–9*. London: Hamish Hamilton.

Websites

Data on food, food security, and many other issues are available at the Food and Agricultural Organization (FAO) of the United Nations
   http://www.fao.org/index_en.htm

Global hunger index
   http://chartsbin.com/view/3355

Issues of world population are discussed at
   http://www.worldpopulationbalance.org/
   http://www.worldwatch.org/

A number of nongovernment agencies are concerned with food security
   http://www.oxfam.org
   http://www.stophungernow.org/

Population and Resources

In this chapter, we will consider some of the general relationships between people and resources, using the nonrenewable resources of coal and oil as primary examples. Let us begin with some definitions. In the *Oxford English Dictionary*, among the many definitions of "resource," the primary one is "a means of supplying a deficiency or need." This sense emerges first in the seventeenth century and is linked with the development of words and ideas associated with markets, money, buying, and selling. From its origin, then, the term "resource" is embedded in social considerations of money and capital. The definition also hints at the relational nature of resources; things are resources because they are linked to scarcity and desire.

Resources are socially constructed, which does not necessarily mean that humans make resources; oil and coal, for example, were made by eons of geologic processes. "Socially constructed" in this case means that a resource is a function of social, technical, and economic considerations. For centuries, oil was just a messy black substance that oozed from the surface of the earth. It only became a valuable resource with the creation of a carbon economy. The history and geography of resources are the unfolding tale of how "nature" becomes commodity, with all the social and political consequences involved in this valuation and subsequent revaluation.

The translation from inert material to resource occurs through technical change and commodification. "Commodification" means that the material is valued and traded, it has a price equivalent, and it enters the arena of things bought and sold. For things to become commodities, technical change is often required. The movement of oil from sticky liquid to valuable commodity requires the design and construction of a vast technical apparatus to transform the raw material of oil into fuel and to produce its valuable byproducts, such as plastics. Technical change and commodification are not external to each other but are inexorably interconnected. Technical developments occur through the increased valuation of the resource. Let us further consider the case of two primary resources, coal and oil.

THE CASE OF COAL

When the Romans first invaded what they called Britannia around two thousand years ago, coal was used as raw material for jewelry. When carved and polished, it adorned the bodies of affluent Britano-Romans. Some local tribes in South Wales

Box 5.1   THE HUBBERT CURVE

The Hubbert Curve is named after a geophysicist who first employed it in 1956 to predict the decline of US oil production. The curve, essentially a symmetrical bell-shaped curve, suggests that nonrenewable resource use rises quickly from zero to a peak and then falls off; at the top are peak production levels. Hubbert used it to predict that oil production in the continental United States would peak in 1965. The curve is perfectly bell-shaped; in reality, resource use is rarely so symmetrical. However, it raises the issue of immediate and rapid falloff from peak production. The curve has been used to model historical resource exploitation, such as coal production in the United Kingdom. It is also part of the considerable debate about the existence and timing of a global oil peak. The figure below shows the gradual tailing off of most sources of global oil production.

(Note: NGL stands for natural gas condensates).

References

Bardi, U. (2009) Peak Oil: The Four Stages of a New Idea. *Energy* 34: 322–326.

Gorelick, S. M. (2010) *Oil Panic and the Global Crisis: Predictions and Myths.* Chichester: Wiley-Blackwell.

Hemmingsen, E. (2010) At the Base of Hubbert's Peak: Grounding the Debate on Petroleum Scarcity. *Geoforum* 41: 531–540.

The Hubbert Curve: ideal

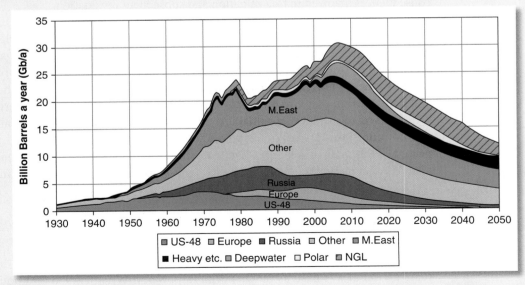

The Hubbert Curve: empirical

also used the material to cremate their dead leaders, but it was only in the twelfth century that people in Britain began using it as fuel. Before then, and for five centuries more, wood was the principal fuel for cooking and heating. As the population expanded, the forest reserves became depleted and, as so often happens in the history of resources, an alternative resource had to be exploited. Coal that was close to the surface was readily available, and soon there was a vigorous trade in coal mined in the northeast of England, in the area around Newcastle, then shipped to the large urban centers such as London. The burning of coal became such a common domestic practice by 1600 that there was rising concern with air quality. In 1661 John Evelyn described London as similar to an active volcano as smoke and noxious fumes belched out from the city's chimneys to create an unhealthy air quality. The smoke blocked out the sun, and sooty particles covered buildings. Despite its side effects, coal was preferred because wood was two to five times more expensive. And here we come to a second characteristic of resource use: the difference between private costs and benefits and social costs and benefits. For individual London households, it was cheaper to use coal than wood. As more households adopted this strategy to cope with private costs, they imposed social costs on their neighbors in terms of the declining quality of air in the city.

As the demand for coal increased, it became profitable to make larger outlays to dig deeper into the earth. There was a problem, however. The deeper the mines were sunk, the more vulnerable they were to flooding. Scientists and inventors tackled the problem with attempts to build a pumping machine using a piston action fueled by the steam from burning coal. It worked, but it used tremendous quantities of coal, which coal mines could easily access, but otherwise was not suitable for wider usage. James Watt devised an improvement to the pumping machine to make it more energy-efficient. He added a condenser that enabled the piston's cylinder to remain hot and thus able to pump more efficiently. His machine did not need such large quantities of coal; the innovation freed the machine from the coal mine. In 1776, Watt created two coal-driven, steam-powered engines, one to pump water from a coal mine, the other to power an iron foundry. It was a momentous year: the Industrial Revolution was inaugurated, Adam Smith published *The Wealth of Nations,* and the fledgling American Republic declared independence.

Coal powered the Industrial Revolution and would prove an important ingredient in the future manufacture of iron and steel. In 1830 Britain produced four-fifths of the world's coal, and by the middle of the nineteenth century, it was the world's leading industrial power and later the world's unrivalled superpower. Coal was not the only factor in the stunning national success, but it was an important ingredient. Coal mining was also at the center of a nexus of capital-labor relations. Coal-mining areas, with their large pools of workers living side by side, produced not only coal but also an organized force of working-class politics. Political radicalism as well as coal came from the coalfields of south Wales, northern England, and central Scotland.

By 1900, the United States was the world's largest coal producer, and, as in Britain, coal was a vital resource in the country's rise to industrial prominence. Coal powered the rising industrial nation and was an essential part in the subsequent creation of a mighty iron and steel industry. Emissions from coal-burning power plants also figured in the nation's history of environmental legislation. There is no simple path between growing environmental health hazards and resultant environmental legislation. Smoke-belching factories also implied economic growth, to such an extent that the political scientist Matthew Crenson writes of the "un-politics of air pollution" in many industrial cities in the United States. Factory chimneys were seen as a sign of progress and full employment, so that attempts to restrict emissions were often resisted and disputed. In many industrial cities, air quality did not become a political issue because smoking factories symbolized growth and jobs, and the problems of polluted air were downplayed. In 1970, however, the landmark Clean Air Act established new standards of air quality; it was just the opening salvo in the ongoing struggle to control and restrict air pollution. Coal producers and owners of coal-fired power stations continue to lobby to restrict further legislation. And here we come to another element in resource use: the producers always trumpet the benefits and try to ignore or downplay the costs.

5.1 Coal regions in the United States

The United States remains a major coal producer; it ranks second in the world after China (Figure 5.1). In 2010 the United States produced over one billion tons of

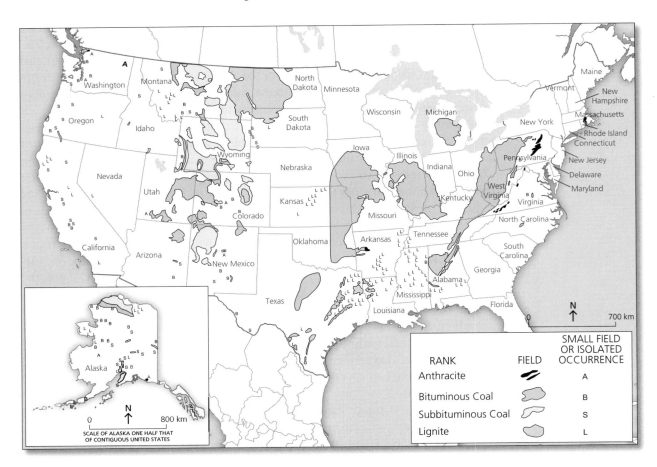

coal, almost 40 percent from the state of Wyoming and 12 percent from West Virginia. In the past thirty years, there has been a rapid growth in shallow mining (close to the surface), as opposed to deep mining, and more of this mining in the states west of the Mississippi, a rapid expansion caused by more efficient and powerful mechanical digging equipment and the need for lower-sulfur coal. In 1970 almost 70 percent of US coal came from Appalachia; now it is just 17 percent. Coalfields in the Illinois Basin in the central United States and the Powder River Basin in the western states are now the principal sources of US coal production. Coal is dug out close to the surface by giant machines and then transported by train. Day and night the coal trains move the fuel from the coal mines to the power plants. Almost 90 percent of coal produced in the United States is destined for power plants that generate electricity. The coal reserves of the United States are difficult to estimate with accuracy. While there may be 182 billion tons, largely in western states, probably only 10 percent of that is recoverable. The rest may be too expensive to mine in current economic circumstances. Resources only become recoverable resources when their exploitation is economically feasible.

In 2010 the top four coal producers in the world were, in order, China, the United States, India, and Australia. All four countries have experienced rapid increase in their production of coal as the demand for energy has followed an upward trajectory. Coal production in China, as in Britain and the United States before it, fuels, quite literally, the country's very rapid economic growth (Figure 5.2). In 2010 China produced over 3 billion tons of coal, three times more than the United States. Even this is not enough: China is also the second largest importer of coal, after Japan. China's substantial and accelerating industrial growth draws in imports from all over the world. Coal from the United States' Powder River Basin is now being sold to China, and the large US coal companies are seeking to build and expand more coal terminals in Washington and Oregon. Australia has experienced a commodity boom as it exports vast quantities of coal and iron ore to China.

Coal is responsible for 42 percent of the world's electricity. Every time we recharge our cell phone, plug a device into a socket, or turn on a light, a coal-fired generator probably produced the power. Coal production continues to increase. While the basic supply of coal is not yet an issue, the wider implications of its burning and exploitation remain problematic. There are proponents of clean coal, but that remains more a fantasy than an empirical fact. Coal has two major problems.

First, burning coal produces noxious fumes that pollute the skies and cause global climate change. Two particular gases, sulfur dioxide (SO_2) and carbon dioxide (CO_2), cause problems. SO_2 is a major byproduct of burning high-sulfur coal, the kind of coal that is found in the eastern United States and throughout much of China. It is the main ingredient in acid rain, as the SO_2 combines with elements in the atmosphere to become sulfuric acid. The term "acid rain" was first used in 1872 by an English inspector of chemical works, Robert Smith, who noticed how the poisonous fumes from British factories turned into acidic rain that eroded buildings and polluted the water. The term and the underlying process were little used or discussed apart from a paper published in 1955 by Eville Gorham that identified its significance in the Lake District of England. Then, as SO_2 levels mounted, a flood of

5.2 Air pollution in Shanghai. Burning coal produces airborne pollution. Chinese cities, despite massive cleanups, still have high levels of air pollution from coal-fired plants.

papers began to note its significance. A Swedish researcher, Svante Odén, noted its effects in Scandinavia in destroying forest and making lakes and rivers more acidic. Much of the acid smoke that fell as acid rain in Scandinavia came from coal burning in Britain and Germany. Airborne pollutants do not respect international boundaries. And here we come to another element in resource use: while the benefits may accrue to an individual company, region, or country, the costs are often borne by other companies, regions, and countries. There are social costs to private enterprise. While the benefits may be privatized, the costs are often socialized.

SO_2 became a major problem in the United States especially because of the burning of high-sulfur coals. In the upland areas of the Adirondacks, it was discovered that by the 1980s, 80 percent of lakes suffered from acidification that killed fish and microorganisms. Because of the region's geology, mainly igneous and metamorphic rocks with limited soil cover, there were few carbonate rocks or soils to buffer the effects. The small lakes at higher elevations were particularly vulnerable because they had less buffering soil; the higher elevation also created more rain and snow-melt, which led to more acid rain. The very small lakes with large runoff were being doused in acid baths that killed the fish stock. Things got so bad that lime was dumped into the lakes to counter the rising acidity. The Adirondack Lakes are far from the immediate polluting sources. The principal source was the power stations along the Ohio River, and in the wake of the Clean Air Act, they were forced to build taller chimneys to reduce the local impact of emissions. The increasing height of the chimneys did take the SO_2 from the immediate area but pushed it higher into the atmosphere, where it drifted westward and eventually fell as acid rain on the mountains of upstate New York. Resource use often has unforeseen consequences.

While acidity levels in some lakes remain high, SO_2 levels across the United States have decreased in the past twenty years. An Acid Rain Program was adapted in 1990 that required power plants to halve their SO_2 emissions by 2010. The process was aided by the greater use of low-sulfur coal from the western states. The net effect: SO_2 was much reduced. In China, by contrast, because it has lower pollution standards and uses sulfur-rich coal, the problems of acid rain continue to be a major side effect of the country's economic growth, poisoning the air, polluting water, and contaminating soils.

The burning of coal also produces CO_2. Coal burning around the world is responsible for one-third of all CO_2 emissions, and coal-fired power stations are the single biggest source of CO_2 in the earth's atmosphere. CO_2 is a "greenhouse" gas, so named because it produces a greenhouse effect of trapping heat in the atmosphere.

The link between CO_2 and global climate change is now well established. The steady rise of CO_2 in the atmosphere is recorded in the Keeling Curve, which plots the concentration of the gas in the atmosphere from 1958 to the present day (Figure 5.3).

5.3 The Keeling Curve

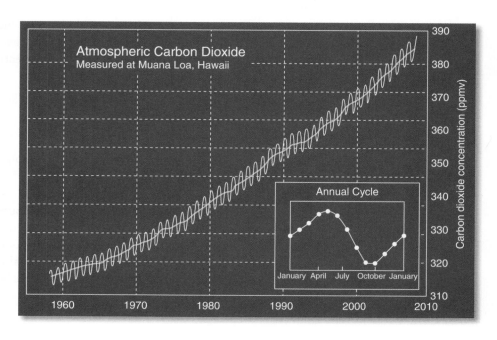

The curve is named after Charles David Keeling, who initiated the measuring from the Mauna Loa Observatory in Hawaii. This site, free from many local sources of pollution, is a good indicator of global patterns. The yearly variation occurs because more coal is burned in the northern hemisphere winter. The curve is on a seemingly inexorable upward swing. When James Watt invented the steam engine, CO_2 levels were roughly 280 parts per million (ppm). At the start of Keeling's measurements in 1959, the figure had risen to 315 ppm. Currently it is on track to soon pass 400 ppm. (The latest figure is available at http://co2now.org.) The level is accelerating. The consensus among most climate scientists is that climate change becomes significant at 350 ppm. In the United States, coal production is estimated to rise to 1.5 billion tons by 2025. And CO_2 levels are predicted to rise above 400 by 2015.

A second problem is that coal mining often involves environmental destruction as the land is poked and prodded, vegetation is destroyed, and waste material pollutes the soil and the air. One of the most environmentally damaging forms of coal mining in operation in the Appalachia region of the United States is mountaintop removal (MTR). The process involves removal of the mountaintop to gain access to the coal seams and dumping the material into the neighboring valleys. The negative environmental impacts include disruption of local ecosystems, loss of biodiversity, and polluted air, soil, and water. By 2010 over one million acres of MTR mining had occurred. A study by geographers Bard Woods and Jason Gordon showed that while the negative environmental consequences were obvious, the positive economic benefits to local communities, often touted by supporters of MTR, were less apparent. In 2011 the US Environmental Protection Agency issued new policy guidelines that restricted the permits allocated to surface mining operations on the grounds that they would pollute local water supplies.

In some cases reclamation is possible. Across the old industrial landscapes of Europe and North America, land reclamation projects are turning mining wasteland into recreational opportunities. In Leipzig, Germany, for example, a former coal mining area has been turned into a theme park; it opened in 2005, and by 2015 a recreational area of seventeen interlinked lakes will have been created. The old mining area is reimagined and remade as a place of recreation and pleasure rather than pollution and work.

LAWS OF RESOURCE USE

We can summarize some of the themes we have considered so far as five laws of resource use:

1. Resources become resources because previous resources become exhausted, unavailable, depleted, or too expensive. Coal was used in Britain because wood was becoming more expensive. Nuclear power was developed in countries such as Japan and France because they had few coal reserves or oil supplies. Wind and wave are being exploited as energy sources because of the rising cost of nonrenewable sources.

2. Resource use creates new geographies, whether it be in the eighteenth-century creation of plantation economies in the West Indies to feed the sugar habit of Europeans, the nineteenth-century creation of coalfield landscapes across Europe and North America, or the late twentieth and early twenty-first century creation of vast mining operations in Australia to feed China's demand for energy and raw materials.

3. All resource usage tends to have wider social and political consequences. Nineteenth-century coal production, for example, was also the setting for organized labor movements and political radicalism. The national competition for resources is an important element in the interactions between states. The United States' insatiable demand for oil makes it curry favor with oil-rich countries such as Saudi Arabia even though it has vastly different cultural and political values.

4. All resource use has implications for public spaces and the wider community as well as for private enterprises. The use of fossil fuels, for example, has many positive consequences but also pollutes the air we breathe and is a cause of climate change that affects us all. The greater use of fracking has the very real possibility of polluting public water supplies.

5. Initiatives to regulate and diminish the negative public consequences of resource use and exploitation always come up against powerful interests that firstly deny the problem and then minimize it. In 1980 the head of the US National Coal Association stated that the negative effects of acid rain were only in the imaginations of those who wanted to promote regulation. When major oil companies fund those who deny climate change, they are taking part in a long and constant story of resistance to regulation.

THE LIMITS TO GROWTH?

The relationship between population and resources, like the relationship between population and food, is dominated by the notion of limits. In the middle of the twentieth century, biological concepts such as carrying capacity were employed to indicate that perhaps we were coming up against the limits of growth. The basic idea was that the world could only carry so much population and sustain so much growth. There was a limit to the carrying capacity of the earth. For neo-Malthusians such as Garret Hardin and Paul Ehrlich, the limits had been reached by the 1970s; the only response was to severely limit population growth.

In 1972 an influential book entitled *The Limits to Growth* was published. Its central argument, summarized in its title, was that there were limits to continual economic growth. The supply of nonrenewable resources, such as iron and oil, was not infinite, and on current trends, the limits to supply would soon be reached

5.4 Oil derricks in Los Angeles. This oil field, like many in the United States and around the world, is coming to the end of its life.

(Figure 5.4). The book's argument was strengthened the next year when oil prices increased fourfold. However, the 1973 oil shock led to much more efficient use of oil resources and a renewed search for alternative sources of supply (Figures 5.5 and 5.6). The limits-to-growth argument also highlights another law of resource use: there is always the tendency to exaggerate the risks and preach a form of resource Armageddon.

The book was dismissed by critics for its neo-Malthusian pessimism compared to the reality of human ingenuity. Resources did not run out. Critics such as the economist J. L. Simon argued that as we come close to "limits," price changes stimulate new forms of resource use, alternative supplies, and new ways of doing things. Rather than simply walking over the edge of fixed supply, we negotiate an increasing price curve.

However, the book did stimulate a debate about longer-term prospects and strengthened the notion of sustainability. The arguments have shifted and morphed since the early 1970s. Rather than mechanistic limits to growth, there is an emerging notion of the desirability of more sustainable resource use.

While the idea of limits to growth has its weaknesses and major resource scarcities have yet to materialize, there is a more general point to be made. If there is a heavy reliance on one particular resource, then supply issues can become problematic. We will illuminate this with reference to the case of oil.

5.5 Nuclear power plant construction near Chinon, France. France, without oil reserves and with coal reserves long since depleted, relies heavily on nuclear power as a source of electricity. There are fifty nuclear power plants producing almost four-fifths of its electricity needs.

MAYBE PEAK OIL BUT DEFINITELY TOUGH OIL

From 1881 to 1973 the price of oil, in real terms, remained flat. Oil prices were low and, more importantly, stable. Economic growth in the first three-quarters of the twentieth century was quite literally lubricated by the steady supply of cheap, easily available oil. Adjusting for inflation, between 1881 and 1973 the price of a barrel of oil averaged under $20 (in 2008 prices). On October 16, 1973, the oil cartel Organization of Petroleum Exporting Countries (OPEC), dominated by Middle East oil producers such as Saudi Arabia, increased the price of oil by 70 percent to $5.11 a barrel (over $40 in 2008 terms). Oil was central to the economies of richer countries, and, since supply was limited and very largely controlled by the OPEC members, the oil-producing nations effectively used their power to increase the price of oil and hence increase their revenues. The result was dramatic. Between 1972 and 1977, as the current account balances of the world's rich countries increased only from $8 billion to $9 billion, those of OPEC countries increased from $1.5 billion to $7 billion. Non-oil-producing poor countries, meanwhile, increased their deficit from $5 billion to $36 billion. The oil price increase was one of the largest and quickest transfers of global wealth in the history of the world.

The 1973 oil shock had a number of rippling consequences. The era of cheap fuel was over, and energy had to be used more efficiently. Car companies, for

5.6 Windmills off the coast of Denmark. Denmark is a leader in wind power generation. Wind power from turbines such as these provide almost one-fifth of all electricity production in the country, which now has a technological lead in the provision of this alternative energy source. About half of all wind turbines used around the world are made in Denmark.

example, had to change to more fuel-efficient models. Car companies in Japan, where oil prices were always much higher, already had experience in fuel efficiency. In the United States, a generation of cheap oil meant that car companies had few fuel-efficient models and were slow to realize the seismic shift in oil prices and associated consumer demand. The long decline of the Detroit car industry began with the 1973 oil price shock.

The price increase also prompted oil companies to look for alternative sources of oil. They wanted an alternative to the oil supply from existing OPEC members, and especially the Middle East OPEC members. The supply of oil on the world market is still dominated by the Middle East. Saudi Arabia remains the largest single exporter of oil at 7.9 million barrels a day, followed by Russia (7.0 million), UAE (2.5 million), Norway (2.3 million), and Iran (2.3 million). The increase in the price of oil also meant that areas previously considered only marginally feasible now came into the possibility of profitability. The oil companies went long and they went deep in their search for oil.

The search for oil is prompted by the seemingly insatiable demand for oil. In 1970, across the globe, around 45 million barrels of oil were consumed every day. By 2010 it was closer to 85 million. Even with energy efficiencies, the raw demand keeps on growing. Rapid industrialization is based on oil. In 1970 China consumed only half a million barrels of oil a day. By 2010 it was close to 8.6 million.

While demand seems infinite, the supply is fixed. Estimating oil reserves is a difficult business. There is always the possibility of discovering reserves as yet unknown. And even the knowledge of existing reserves is more an estimation than a fine calibration. Yet the long-term prospect does not look good. In 2009 the total world supply was estimated at 1.33 trillion barrels of oil. It sounds like a lot—it is a lot—but with oil consumption rising and most of the world now surveyed for oil reserves, there is the possibility that oil supply may soon be peaking. The rate of extraction is now double that of new discoveries. The estimates of when oil supply will peak vary from 2010–2015, a view shared by US military intelligence, to a more optimistic 2050.

There is considerable debate about peak oil. There are those who focus on the narrow debate of estimating the precise date of the oil peak. This is a discussion that sheds more heat than light, since the oil supply business is one of estimates rather than solid empirical facts. Then there is the debate that widens out to look at the consequences of oil supply peaking sometime in the future. We can consider three of them.

Box 5.2 THE GEOPOLITICS OF OIL

Oil is a vital resource. The need for energy security, for assuring long-term and reliable sources of oil, is an increasingly vital consideration of national security. The need for oil creates a strong nexus of mutual interest between major oil importers and large oil companies. It also dictates foreign policy. US foreign policy, for example, has to take into account relations with major oil-producing nations, sometimes creating alliances with dictatorial and authoritarian regimes, other times being actively involved in regime change and direct military interventions. The crucial test is not that foreign oil suppliers treat their own people well, but that the oil keeps coming at a reasonable price. Securing oil supplies is a vital part of the operation of US global power.

China, as a leading oil importer, also tailors its foreign policy to its energy needs, but in the process may get dragged into regional disputes such as between Sudan and one of the newest countries in the world, South Sudan. As the minister of oil and mining in South Sudan said of the Chinese, "Their wish is to see the continuation of production and the flow of the crude [oil]. This is their concern" (Higgins 2011, pp. A1). China's need for

oil also makes it forge new alliances with old enemies. The new pipeline that takes oil from Russia to China represents a recent reversal of old enmities. Linking up the supply and demand for oil can turn centuries-old enemies into today's trading partners.

Large and powerful oil importers need to ensure the supply of oil. Treaties, interventions, wars, in some cases supporting regimes and in others undermining them, all become part of the changing tactics devised to meet the need for energy security. The geopolitics of oil links importers and exporters in complex, ever-changing relationships. The suppliers band together in cartels to regulate the supply the price, while the importers draw upon a wide variety of tactics and use their political, economic, and sometimes military power.

References

Higgins, A. (2011) Oil Interests Push China into Sudanese Quagmire. *The Washington Post*, December 25, pp. A1 and A20. Quote is from page A1.

Harvey. D. (2003) *The New Imperialism*. Oxford: Oxford University Press.

Yergin, D. (2011) *The Quest: Energy, Security, and The Remaking of The Modern World*. New York: Penguin.

The first is the search for alternative sources of supply, especially the search for renewable sources of supply such as biofuels, wind, waves, and solar. A list of biofuels is given in Table 5.1. Brazil, for example, even although it has huge oil supplies, also now uses half of its entire sugar cane crop to produce fuel ethanol. In regions across the world, the skyline is sprouting serried ranks of windmills that look like modernist mobiles. Solar panels are being installed in roofs in cities across the globe. In many cases, the costs of alternative energies are still high, yet as oil prices increase and more efficient renewable energy technologies are introduced, we may be at the cusp of a major shift in energy supply.

A second consequence is the long-term future for countries that derive most of their revenue from oil. In oil-based regimes such as Venezuela, with peak production

Crop	Fuel Source	Main Producing Countries
Sugar cane	Ethanol (from sugar)	Brazil, India, China, Thailand
Sugar beet	Ethanol (from sugar)	France, United States, Germany, Russia
Cassava	Ethanol (from starch)	Nigeria, Brazil, Thailand, Indonesia
Maize	Ethanol (from starch)	United States, China
Oil palm	Bio-diesel	Malaysia, Indonesia, Nigeria, Thailand
Rapeseed	Bio-diesel	China, Canada, India, Germany
Soybean	Bio-diesel	United States, Brazil, Argentina, China

Table 5.1 ■ BIOFUELS

in 1996, the decline of oil export revenue is the source of political conflict and social unrest. Saudi Arabia derives all of its wealth from oil exports, yet oil production peaked in 2005. When your major and almost only source of revenue begins to decline, national economic stability is put at risk. The possibility of moving past peak production into a world of possibly declining revenue raises issues of social stability and regime longevity. In places such as Dubai and Abu Dhabi, the frenetic pace of building and development are in part an attempt to build an alternative economic future before the oil runs out.

The third consequence is the implication for economies and socio-spatial assemblages that are predicated on cheap oil (Figure 5.7). In the United States, for

5.7 This tiny car in Florence, Italy, is ideal to manage the narrow streets of the old city. It also has the advantage of very high gas mileage, a necessity in a country with high oil prices.

example, much of its suburbanization is based on low and stable oil prices. All those low-density family homes, out-of-town shopping centers, and long-distance commutes arose at a time of dependably cheap gas prices. But as we move into rising and unstable oil prices, this suburbanization, with its heavy reliance on private automobiles, now looks like a landscape creation based on oil prices that will never return. The reliance of a built form precariously balanced on one fossil fuel with large and fluctuating costs raises issues of long-term sustainability. The suburbs were built on gas costs on the order of $27 a barrel (at 2007 prices). In one month in the summer of 2008, they reached over $140. In March 2009, in the middle of a huge recession, the price was $43 a barrel, with OPEC officials suggesting that an ideal price, for them, was between $60 and $70. Prices will remain deflated during recessions but will then tend to rise. There are few large oil reserves left, and the price will inevitably rise when the global economy ticks upwards. Where does that leave low-density suburban sprawl, which is so reliant on large-scale private car usage? The general answer: in a very precarious position. This same question was asked before. In 1984 I noted, in a section entitled "Will Suburbs Become a Thing of the Past?":

The growth of the suburbs was based upon a number of conditions which are now disappearing into recent history . . . If these changes are long term and large scale this may lead to lack of demand for suburban housing and a rapid fall off in the house prices of suburban districts. Those who live in the suburbs may find it difficult to either sell their houses or recoup their investment.

(SHORT, 1984, 23)

The long-term sustainability of low-density, energy-profligate, heavy-ecological footprint suburbs is now a matter of serious consideration.

Even if we take the most optimistic estimates and put the peaking of oil into the distant future, we are still in the era of tough oil. Most of the easy oil reserves close to the surface have been tapped. Many of the big fields are in steep decline. Mexico and Indonesia used to be major oil exporters but are now importers of oil. More than one-third of the world's oil comes from large fields of more than 5 million barrels a day. Discoveries of these fields declined from 130 in the 1960s to only 34 in the 2000s.

We have moved from an era of easy oil, one of large, shallow reserves that were easily exploitable, to an age of tough oil in which reserves are deeper, further offshore, and more expensive to exploit. The new fields are smaller and not as long-lasting; they peak fast, then decline sharply, so there is a continual search for new fields. Companies are persistently at the furthest extent of their experience and technical capabilities as they drill deeper in ever more inaccessible places. The days of essentially putting short wells into huge shallow reserves are over; more oil production takes the form of drilling deeper and further offshore.

The United States has a very heavy reliance on oil, yet a limited supply. Oil production in the United States peaked at 10.5 million barrels in 1985. In 2009 it was just over 7 million barrels. Consumption increased in the same period from 15.7 million to 19.6 million barrels. The United States has to import an increasing proportion of the oil it consumes in its automobiles and industries. Oil is quite literally an essential lubricant of economic growth in the United States. That means exploring alternative sources of oil, such as tar sands in Alberta, that require expensive and environmentally damaging production. The oil is extracted either through strip mining, which tears away the surface vegetation, releases heavy metals, and creates air pollution, or by large injections of water and solvents, which leads to water pollution. The oil predicament also makes the country susceptible to geopolitical as well as economic considerations. US foreign policy has to take into account the sensibilities of such oil-rich countries as Saudi Arabia while also positioning itself to secure access to oil. The desperate need for oil means sidling up to some dictatorships while undermining others. The one constant in US foreign policy in the Middle East is the need to secure long-term access to oil. The need for a steady supply of oil is an important shaper and determining factor in US foreign policy.

The oil crunch, the large and growing gap between the national supply and demand, has also led to a vigorous search for domestic oil reserves. All the easy shallow reserves in places like Pennsylvania and California have long dried up. Now the search looks to places that only decades before were considered too difficult or too expensive to extract oil from. The history of oil extraction in the Gulf of Mexico highlights the shift. Drilling first started in 1937, just off the Louisiana coast. The first well was located in 14 feet of water less than a mile from the shoreline. By 1993 approximately 12 percent of all oil produced was from deepwater wells, defined as 5,000 feet or deeper. Only 2.5 percent of new wells, forty in total, were deepwater. By 2009, 80 percent of oil came from deepwater wells and over a third of all new wells sunk were deepwater. Between 2006 and April 2010, the number of deepwater rigs grew by 43 percent. As they ventured further offshore and drilled deeper and deeper, oil companies were always at the ever-extending limits of their technical capabilities. Massive and potentially dangerous machinery has to be placed on small platforms far out to sea. At the deeper levels, the oil is subject to up to 10,000 pounds of pressure per square inch, making the safe and steady release of the oil a difficult proposition. It is easy to fracture the surrounding geologic formations. Oil is a hazardous, highly flammable liquid. Pumping millions of gallons of it at high pressure though a small pipe more than three miles down is a high-risk activity. On the ocean floor, where the wellheads are located, temperatures are low and visibility is hazy. Adjustments have to be made using remotely guided machinery. Blowout preventers on the ocean floor are connected to the surface platforms by long pipelines exposed to strong undersea currents. In summary, it is a difficult and dangerous operation to extract deep-sea oil from a small, floating platform so far above the wellhead. The very recent shift to deep offshore drilling, made urgent by the need for oil, means that the technology is continually evolving, which generates new risks and accidents. Between 1969 and 2009, there were seventy-nine reported cases of loss of well control and seepage of oil and gas in the Gulf. From 2001 to 2009, there were 1,550 injuries, 60 deaths, and 948 fires and explosions with

Box 5.3 COMMODITY CARTELS

OPEC is just one of a number of commodity cartels, organizations of primary producers who band together to ensure high prices for their resource. They often arise from national dissatisfaction with the private companies that control the trade. The oil trade used to be controlled by the large oil companies, the Seven Sisters as they were called. In 1959 they sought to decrease the price by 10 percent to stimulate demand. A rational move on their part, but for countries that relied on oil exports it was a major cut in revenue. Venezuela, a country where oil exports made up 90 percent of foreign earnings, held talks with other oil-producing countries to resist the price increase. In 1960 OPEC was formed; the initial members were Iraq, Iran, Kuwait, Saudi Arabia, and Venezuela. In 1973, with more members and control of over 70 percent of the global oil supply, the cartel raised the price of a barrel of oil from $2.48 a barrel to $11.65.

The success of OPEC in raising and controlling prices stimulated other commodity cartels, which were soon established: coffee (1973), bauxite (1974), bananas (1974), and iron ore (1975). Commodity cartels exercise greatest power when there are a small number of producers with shared value systems, demand for their commodities is high, substitution costs are prohibitive, and they control most of the world supply. Their strength also depends on the nature of the commodity. Oil can be kept in the ground and still retain its value. Bananas, in contrast, rot if kept, so the suppliers have limited power to keep their products off the market. OPEC is by far the most successful cartel. It has remained a very powerful organization in controlling world oil prices, as it controls such a large proportion of such a valuable commodity. OPEC members now hold 81 percent of the world reserve of crude oil. The other cartels proved short-lived, the coffee cartel ending in 1989 and the bauxite cartel in 1994, or if they did survive, like the natural rubber cartel, they have proved less influential in shaping world prices.

References

Alhaji, A. F. and Huettner, D. (2000) OPEC and Other Commodity Cartels: A Comparison. *Energy Policy* 28: 1151–1164.

Klan, R. (2011) In the Footsteps of the OPEC: Trends in Collective Bargaining over Natural Resources. *Strategic Analysis* 35: 162–168.

The OPEC website is a useful source of data http://www.opec.org/opec_web/en/

a workforce of only 35,000 people. On April 20, 2010, an explosion aboard the Deepwater Horizon drilling rig led to oil gushing uncontrollably from the underground reservoir. For almost two months, 53,000 barrels a day, 5 million gallons in all, gushed from the well into the Gulf of Mexico, poisoning the water, contaminating the beaches, and killing sea creatures and animal life.

Brazil has a similar story of hard-won oil. With its rapid economic growth, Brazil has a huge demand for oil. Reserves were discovered off the coast, and production increased from less than one million barrels of oil in 1990 to 2.7 million barrels by 2010. It is tough to extract, since the largest oil reserves lie 200 miles offshore at depths of three miles below the seabed. In November 2011, 3,000 barrels of oil leaked from a site in the Frade oilfield.

Even if the exact timing of global peak oil is difficult to assess accurately, it is easy to see that we are in an era of tough oil, not only in terms of the cost and risks of deep drilling into ever more dangerous places, but also in the search for immediate alternatives. The tar sands of Alberta are being exploited for their oil at the cost of large amounts of water and heat, elevated pollution rates as the tar sand oil produces between 5 to 15 percent more CO_2 emission than other oil, and the need for a 1,700-mile pipeline through much of North America. The reliance on fossil fuels in the United States is leading to the exploitation of natural gas locked up in shale deposits. The gas is released through hydraulic fracturing ("fracking")—high-pressure application of water, sand, and chemicals that essentially cracks the rock and releases the gas. Fracking pollutes the local water supply. We get cheap gas but polluted water. The ultimate law of resource use is that we pay a price for what we get. The cost can be shifted from private to public, from local to national, or from one country to another, but the world is a closed system. The cost and benefits are always exacted, although they may be shifted across space. There is no free lunch.

The initial limits-of-growth argument was misplaced. The real issue is not that supplies of resources will run out but that their continued supply may create other costs and negative consequences. We still have oil and natural gas, but the years of easy exploitation are over. In the era of tough oil, there is still oil. But what we have to ask is not "is it going to run out?" but "is continuing its supply worth the rising costs?"

Cited References

Almedia, P. D. and Silva, P. D. (2011) Timing and Future Consequences of the Peak of Oil Production. *Futures* 43: 1044–1055.

Bridge, G. and Wood, A. (eds) (2010) Geographies of Peak Oil: Special Issue. *Geoforum* 41: 523–605.

Crenson, M. A. (1971) *The Un-Politics of Air Pollution: A Study of Non-Decision Making.* Baltimore: Johns Hopkins University Press.

Gorham, E. (1955) On the Acidity and Salinity of Rain. *Geochimica et Cosmochimica Acta* 7: 231–239.

Jenkins, J., Roy, K., Driscoll, C., and Buerkett, C. (2007) *Acid Rain in the Adirondacks: An Environmental History.* Ithaca: Cornell University Press.

Meadows, D. H. (1972) *The Limits to Growth.* New York: Universe.

Odén, S. (1976) The Acidity Problem: An Outline of Concepts. *Water, Air and Soil Pollution* 6: 137–166.

Short, J. R. (1984) *An Introduction to Urban Geography.* Henley: Routledge.

Woods, B. R. and Gordon, J. S. (2011) Mountaintop Removal and Job Creation: Exploring the Relationship Using Spatial Regression. *Annals of the Association of American Geographers* 101: 806–815.

Select Guide to Further Reading

Burns, S. S. (2007) *Bringing Down the Mountains: The Impact of Mountaintop Removal on Southern West Virginia.* Morgantown: West Virginia University Press.

Freese, B. (2003) *Coal: A Human History.* Cambridge: Perseus.

Holzman, D. C. (2011) Mountaintop Removal Mining: Digging into Community Health Concerns. *Environmental Health Perspectives* 119: a476–a483. http://dx.doi.org/10.1289/ehp.119-a476

Klare, M. (2010) *Rising Powers, Shrinking Planet.* New York: Henry Holt.

Kolbert, E. (2006) *Field Notes from a Catastrophe: Man, Nature and Climate Change.* New York: Bloomsbury.

Zimmerer. K. S. (ed) (2011) Geographies of Energy: Special Issue. *Annals of Association of American Geographers* 101: 705–980.

Websites

Data on coal production is available at the website of the World Coal Association
http://www.worldcoal.org/resources/coal-statistics/

Data on global oil production and prices is available at
http://www.worldoil.com/industry_statistics_home.aspx
http://quotes.post1.org/historical-crude-oil-price-chart/

US oil figures can be obtained at
http://205.254.135.7/petroleum/

Check out the current CO_2 level at
http://co2now.org

6 People and the Environment

The environment is a source of economic opportunity, a repository of meaning, a sometime hazardous context and always the background to our individual and collective lives. Examining the relationship between people and environment (also referred to as society-nature) is at the heart of human geography. In this chapter I will look at three broad themes: the environment as a source of cultural meaning, the affect of environment on human feelings and activity, and the impacts of human activity on the environment.

ENVIRONMENT AND CULTURAL MEANING

We can make a distinction between three basic forms of social-spatial-economic relations: hunting-gathering, traditional agriculture, and urban-industrial systems. Each has overlapping but also distinct conceptions of environmental space. Respectively, they tend to inflate the importance of sacred space, productive space, and managed space.

Sacred Space

In hunting-gathering societies, people derive their individual and collective sustenance by hunting animals and gathering food. There was and often still is a gendered and age division of labor, with men responsible for hunting and women and younger children responsible for gathering other food. People need to be in tune with the seasonal rhythms of flora and fauna. Such close connection with the environment provides both the material basis of life and spiritual sustenance. The environment is not an inert container of resources but a living organism filled with beings, gods, and spirits that provide comfort and support as well as irritation and trials. Nature is the ground of being, powerful and present, and human-nature relations are not simply functional and economic but also filled with spiritual meaning and cosmological significance.

In Cherokee tradition the word for earth, *elohi*, also means history, culture, and religion. All living things and all places are bound up in a web of material and spiritual connections. Collective and individual identity is bound to specific places, plants, and animals. There is a kinship between animals and humans, a bond between the hunted and the hunter, planter and planted. A deep and profound religiosity imbues the economic relations of everyday life. Ritual and performance in dance and song, as well as material culture such as shelter, clothing, and decoration, link people, places, and living things in a tight nexus of material and spiritual connections.

The cosmologies of hunting-gathering societies are rooted in an animistic conception of the world. The essence of the animistic cosmologies of hunting-gathering societies is that the Earth is alive and nurturing. Nature is a spiritual resource as well as an economic entity, part of the fabric of connections between all things. Space is sacred, and territory is the fundamental source of meaning and identity. Consider the case of the indigenous peoples of the central Australian desert. Before the coming of the whites in the late nineteenth century, the total Arrernte pre-contact population is estimated to have been between 8,000 and 10,000. Food was scarce. The landscape was a complex system of land titles based on lineage and family ties. Responsibility for "managing" specific sites often lay in the hands of senior elders, both men and women (Figure 6.1). The complex, interlocking titles were less monopoly controls, as we understand private property under a capitalist system, and more relational and totemic, allowing individuals and groups a broad range of claims, responsibilities, and bargaining options that enabled long-term occupancy of a harsh environment with irregular water and variable food sources. The cosmology bound people to the land in intricate webs of meaning that also sustained long-term economic usage.

6.1 Sacred site in Alice Springs, Australia

The cosmologies of these early societies did not prevent major ecosystem transformation and species collapse. Calvin Martin looked at the effect of early contact with Europeans on the Micmac tribe in the Gaspe Peninsula. Prior to the arrival of Europeans, the beaver was hunted in a sustainable way; there were millions of beaver, and their hunting was bound by rules, regulations, and religious invocations that severely limited the hunting of "relatives in fur masks." With the coming of the French and the Dutch, a vigorous trade was promoted. Europeans wanted furs from the Micmac, and other tribal groups, for which they traded knives, axes, guns, and alcohol. The increasing competition for furs, the decline of traditional constraints caused by the deadly epidemics of the Columbian Encounter, and the waning influence of the traditional shaman led to a wholesale slaughter of beaver by Micmac hunters, who no longer hunted for immediate needs but in an unrestrained slaughter. The beaver was turned from a relative in a fur mask to a commodity.

Productive Space

Joseph Campbell made a distinction between the environmental cosmology of the hunting-gatherers, concerned more with the "way of animal powers," and that of agricultural peoples, concerned more with the "way of the seeded earth." It is a shift from the notion of sacred space to that of productive space. The distinction is perhaps too clear-cut. In reality, many traditional agriculture societies grew out of hunting-gathering groups and still retained elements of the earlier environmental beliefs. Along the Atlantic seaboard of what is now the United States, people hunted the mammoth, bison, and other megafauna, but as the climate warmed at the ending of the Ice Age, farming became more intensive. Hunting-gathering cosmologies, concerned with the relations with animals, were carried over into agricultural cosmologies concerned with the fertility of the land. Maize, beans, squash, tobacco, potatoes, and corn were grown throughout the central Atlantic region. The Iroquois referred to corn, beans, and squash as the "Three Sisters" or "Our Supporters." An annual cycle of festivals and rituals, especially at planting and harvesting times, respectively invoked continued agricultural plenty and gave thanks for it. Animal spirits were still respected. The panther was an animal of great spiritual significance for the traditional Iroquois.

The agriculturalists tended to stress more the sacrifice, symbolic and real, in order to promote and sustain fertility. Ensuring the fertility of the land is vital to agricultural societies and central to their belief systems. In some societies, such as the Aztec, the sacrifice took on a literal meaning as humans were offered up to the gods on altars in public displays. From its agricultural roots the practice grew to become an instrument of political coercion and control. More than 4,000 human sacrifices were made at a reconsecration of the Great Pyramid of Tenochtitlan in 1487. The idea of sacrifice continues to this day in contemporary religious practices. The Christian Eucharist, which signifies the body and blood of Christ, is an updated and particularized version of the older and more widespread sacrifice narrative of agricultural societies.

As we move towards more commodified forms of agriculture where we grow things for profit rather than to simply eat, we shift from the idea of land as a primary source of meaning and identity to land as a commodity, a vehicle to accumulate wealth. Today, modern agriculture relies on chemicals and fertilizers rather than ritual sacrifice.

Managed Space

The rise of cities and the development of industry create new environmental belief systems. On the one hand, there is a strengthening of the belief in technological mastery of the world. The success of urban industrialization in transforming our experience of the world suggested that nature could be managed and controlled rather than revered and respected. A technological triumphalism saw few limits and no constraints. Nature was less a living thing and more a resource to be exploited, a backdrop for human desires and social needs. As land was commodified, the particularities of place as spiritual significance were replaced by the generality of market space. Particular places had economic value but not cosmological significance. The environment was merely a calculus of economic costs and benefits, and nature was now a commodity to be bought, sold, and traded.

Yet, on the other hand, the environmental degradation caused by such an attitude did generate counterclaims and alternative visions. Romanticism was a reaction to the scientific rationalism of nature and the commodification of land. It saw nature as a source of profound aesthetic experiences and a perfect vehicle for a personal connection to the infinite. Because factories were being built and cities replacing fields, William Wordsworth was singing the praises of daffodils and Henry David Thoreau was espousing the virtues of the woods and lonely places. All kinds of public health measures and environmental movements grew up to contest the dominant narrative of nature simply as resource. In the United States, for example, because industrial growth was accelerating, John Muir was extolling the virtues of protecting wilderness. Rapid industrialization and urbanization generated resistances and new ideologies that stressed preservation and conservation. Scientific discourses such as ecology developed out of the concern to consider the links that bound all living things. Public policies such as wilderness preservation and land conservation were also developed. The promotion of sustained economic growth now competed with a belief in environmental protection.

Today we have competing claims. There are powerful forces that promote continued economic growth and tend to see nature primarily as a commodity to be developed and exploited. Arguments about jobs or economic growth are often used to trump "merely" environmental concerns. Yet we also have an increasingly powerful awareness of unrestrained growth's environmental consequences. The proponents of sustainability often draw upon the ideas of hunting-gathering belief systems. The "rediscovered" (invented?) traditions of indigenous peoples are touted often as a more sustainable and sustaining environmental ethic suitable for our present predicament. We live in a world where economic growth and global environmental impacts are unprecedented, but also in a time when a new environmental ethic, one shaped both by past belief systems and present practices, is taking shape; its main ideas include a greater awareness of our environmental impact, a less triumphalist optimism in technology, and a greater concern with long-term sustainability than short-term growth.

The link between economic growth and environmental quality is sometimes represented as a bell-shaped curve termed the environmental Kuznets curve (Figure 6.2). (The adjective is placed in front of the proper noun because there is another Kuznets curve that depicts a similar relationship between per capita income and inequality.) At the early stages of economic growth, when per capita

6.2 Kuznets curve

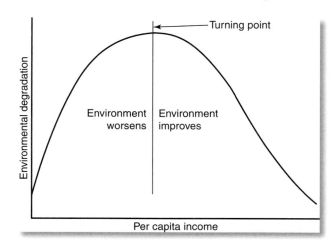

Box 6.1 ALTERNATIVE VISIONS

The Huichol Indians live in a mountain area in western Mexico. Their total numbers are around 25,000–50,000. Although deeply impacted by the Columbian Encounter, they still retain many of their traditional belief systems. Huichol is still spoken, and there are two local governments, one that answers to the local people while another represents the Mexican state.

The Huichol interact with the modern world. Their crafts cater to a tourist market. But they also practice a form of animism that imbues the area with primary spiritual significance. The landscape is a sacred geography whose protection is vital to the integrity of their worldview. The local mountains are not inert geological features but sacred portals to an understanding of the infinite, sites of cosmic significance. One mountain, Cerro del Quemado, known to the Huichol as Wirikuta, is considered the birthplace of the sun.

Two mining companies, Canada's First Majestic Silver and the Mexican Real Bonanza, have a very different conception of the area. They see it is as a place to extract silver. In 2009 they purchased mineral rights from the Mexican government and will most likely use cyanide in open pit mining.

This is a form of struggle witnessed throughout the world. On the one hand, a small group of people with indigenous beliefs and uncertain land rights; on the other hand, powerful international corporations looking to extract commodities. The Huichol have sought to resist the mining proposals, while the mining companies have sworn to protect the sacred sites, maintain international environmental standards, and employ local people. Many of the non-Huichol local people support the mining proposal for the jobs it will generate. Behind the conflict are very different and competing ideas of the environment, as a commodity to be exploited and as a scared space to be revered. As one Huichol said of the mountain,

> this is the center of the world. It is our church. The mining company has promised that the mountain will look the same. But it won't be the same if you take away its soul.

References

Booth, W. (2012) Where Cosmic and Commercial Collide. *The Washington Post,* February 14, pp. A1 and A11. Quote is from page A11.

Liffman, P. M. (2010) *Huichol Territory and the Mexican Nation: Indigenous Ritual, Land Conflict and Sovereignty Claims.* Tucson: University of Arizona Press.

income is still relatively low, the environment worsens as aggregate growth is pursued despite the environmental effects. Then, as incomes increase, more people place priority on environmental quality. Evidence can be found that both contests and confirms this dynamic between income and environment. In terms of counterargument, for example, levels of carbon emission continue to increase with rising per capita incomes. Moreover, richer regions and countries may export the negative environmental consequences of their high growth through shipping pollution waste or offshoring the more environmentally damaging economic practices. And poorer countries and regions may be able to affect environmental quality much earlier than the curve suggests as social movements and governments are made acutely aware of the damaging consequences and the false nature of the jobs-versus-environment slogan. Eco-communities in regions across China have promoted environmental improvement despite low per capita income.

In terms of environmental awareness and appropriate policy responses, there is now a wide variety of opinion. At one extreme is "deep ecology." The term was first used by the Norwegian philosopher Arne Næss to refer to a deep reverence for Nature that implies the radical restructuring of our current lifestyles to be more biocentric. At the other end of the continuum is an environmental sensitivity that suggests less radical change but a more pronounced commitment to alternative technologies, reducing pollution, and sustainable development. The deep ecologist questions the morality of growth, while the environmentalist/conservationist wants sustainable growth.

There is now a vigorous environmental debate with an increasing number of strands of social ecology, which link environmental issues more directly to political issues, and indeed sees the environment as a deeply political issue. For example, ecofeminism highlights the gendered nature of many environmental ideologies and practices and tries to engage feminist and ecological issues in a shared dialogue. What they all share is a questioning of the belief in unbridled economic growth and a commitment to a new relationship between humans and nature.

ENVIRONMENTAL IMPACTS ON SOCIETY

Recent geographical scholarship is developing the idea of "affect" to refer to the force that makes us feel, think, or act. At the level of individuals we also know that certain very local environments have an affect (an emotional effect). People recovering in hospital rooms that look out onto attractive scenes of nature get better more quickly than those whose views are only dismal walls. The affect of the micro-environment in influencing moods and behaviors is exploited by restaurants that play discordant music to stop people from lingering too long and by stores that play soothing music to make consumers shop longer. Placing mirrors in public spaces so that people can see themselves reduces vandalism. In public we act differently than when we are in more private spaces. Our mood and behavior are both affected by our environment. A group of Dutch researchers found that there was a very positive relationship between the amount of green space in the local environment and people's self-reported indicators of physical and mental health. The relationship was strongest for reports of anxiety. In other words, people said they felt less anxious if there was more green space in their local neighborhood. Local environments do play a role in people's sense of well-being.

There is also the bystander effect. It is a well-known finding that individuals often do not help people in distress, for example if they scream for help in a public place. The effect is more noticeable in dense urban areas than in rural areas. The difference is not due to rural dwellers being more caring, it is the result of more stimuli in urban environment, so that people may not hear or see the distress, and because there tend to be more people, so there is a wider diffusion of responsibility. The bystander effect is more pronounced in some environments rather than others because of the difference in environment, not because of a difference in people. Different environments not only exaggerate certain forms of behavior over others, they have specific forms of behavior encoded: our dress and demeanor at a job interview are different than if we are in a club with friends.

The context of place is important. People first meeting in stressful situations have greater attraction to each other than if they meet first in less stressful situations: same people, different context, and so different outcomes. The title of Sam Summers's book *Situations Matter* summarizes a very interesting body of work. Place matters in group creativity. Colleagues who work closer together, literally less than ten meters away, tend to do better work than when they are situated a kilometer or more apart. Small, flexible spaces are places where creativity between people can flourish, a point not lost on designers of buildings for creative industries, who work to ensure close contact and random encounters in everyday work life.

There is no simple answer to the question of what role the local environment plays in guiding human feelings and behaviors; there is a complex social construction of the environment as people and groups give meanings to space and place, which change over time.

The meaning of places changes over time. Consider the city of Tunis. While it was under French occupation, a major avenue was constructed to link the city to the port area (Figure 6.3). It was built to represent the French presence, a central boulevard surrounded by roads and bordered by wide pavement that specifically echoed the Champs-Élysées so that Tunis could be seen as a smaller version of Paris, both linked by their expression of French culture and power. French and local elites paraded along the street to show their embrace and display of modernity. It was built to make visible the connection between France and Tunisia, to show the rationality and technological superiority of France compared to medieval religiosity.

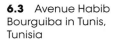

6.3 Avenue Habib Bourguiba in Tunis, Tunisia

After independence, the street was renamed after a revolutionary hero and was known as Avenue Habib Bourguiba, which came to represent a modern independent Tunisia and was the place for celebrations of national identity and solidarity. In late 2010 it became the scene of demonstrations against the regime of Zine El Abidine Ben Ali. As part of the Arab Spring, young people flooded into the street, gaining strength from each other's presence, hardening the resolve of the protestors, and highlighting the lack of support for the status quo: one street with multiple meanings and very different affects.

HUMAN IMPACTS AND ENVIRONMENTAL CHANGE

The relationship between society and nature can also be considered from the opposite direction by looking at the impacts of humans on the environment. There are two distinct approaches. The first is an accounting of human impacts on the environment. This has a long history. George Perkins Marsh (1801–1882) was one of the first to argue that deforestation could lead to desertification. His book *Man and Nature,* first published in 1864, indicates some of the connections between human actions and environmental impacts. A classic and foundational work by William Leroy Thomas, *Man's Role in Changing The Face of The Earth* (published 1955), deals with the rising dominance of nature by humans and looks at such issues as deforestation, urbanization, and the depletion of resources (Figures 6.4 and 6.5). This work has influenced generations of geographers. An updated edition of *The Earth as Transformed by Human Action* (1990), covers subsequent research. An important aim of this ongoing body of work is to examine and measure the major impacts of human action on the environment, including:

6.4 Land use change 1: creating sugar cane plantations from tropical rainforest in Queensland, Australia

1. destruction of habitats and loss of biodiversity

2. pollution of water and soil

3. land use changes (e.g., desertification, deforestation, loss of productive farmland urbanization)

4. global climate change.

6.5 Land use change 2: the urbanization of the rural landscape, Maryland

The best geographical research is not simply an accounting and mapping of impacts but a deeper consideration of the social and political effects and drivers behind these changes. We will consider just one of the very many examples: a study of land use changes in Colombia since 1500. The researchers identified seven periods of landscape change; these are listed in Table 6.1. From 1500 to 2000, there was marked long-term decline in forest cover. There was also a drastic reduction in the nomadic hunting-gathering in the savannas and a large increase in the amount of grazing on

Table 6.1 ■ LAND USE CHANGES IN COLOMBIA 1500–2000		
Era of landscape change	**Date**	**Main land use changes**
Pre-Spanish	Before 1500	80 percent nomadic hunting-gathering in savanna
Conquest	1500–1600	Reversion to forest due to demographic collapse
Colonial Period	1600–1800	Forest clearance
Independence and state formation (1800–1850)	1800–1850	Clearance of land for cattle grazing
International markets	1850–1920	Marked forest clearance for grazing
Early urbanization	1920–1970	Deforestation
Industrialization	1970–2000	Deforestation

Source: After Etter et al., 2008.

cleared land and natural grasslands. The periodization used in Table 6.1 references political and economic conditions such as conquest, colonialism, the development of the state, and the growth of international markets. These changes have an impact on land use (Figure 6.6). Land use change is linked to political and economic changes.

There is now a large body of work that looks specifically at the relationships between socioeconomic factors and environmental changes. One line of work is termed political ecology, since it highlights political as much as ecological issues. The term was first used in the 1930s but came to higher prominence in the 1980s. Piers Blaikie looked at soil erosion in developing countries. In his work on Nepal, he showed that rather than being the result of overpopulation or mismanagement, soil erosion resulted from marginalization and poverty. Soil erosion was not a function of peasant farmers' mismanagement but a reflection of their precarious position in commodity markets. In his 1983 book *Silent Violence: Food, Famine, and Peasantry in Northern Nigeria*, Michael Watts looked at the political context of household vulnerability to hunger. He built on Sen's work on the social construction of hunger and famine that we discussed in chapter 4, and in particular examined the role of colonialism and agrarian capitalism in subjecting the Hausa-speaking peasantry to food insecurity. Hunger was not the result of drought or resource scarcity but of political relations.

Political ecology looks at the struggle over resources, who controls them and how the costs and benefits are apportioned. Political ecology situates land use changes in their socioeconomic context and links strategies of corporate profitability to how households are made more or less vulnerable to environmental hazards such as deforestation, social erosion, or irregular food supply. The environment is not a neutral backdrop but the very field in which power is revealed, contested, and enforced.

While many of the early political ecology studies focused on developing societies and rural land use changes, more recent work widens the approach to look at the city. Urban political ecology is now a vibrant part of geographical research.

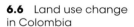

6.6 Land use change in Colombia

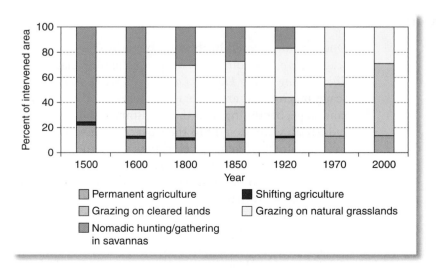

Climate Change

One of the most significant impacts of human activities on the environment is global climate change. There is now a large body of work that measures and seeks to explain climate change. Global warming, for example, is caused by many factors, but one important factor is the increasing amounts of carbon dioxide in the atmosphere, which creates the greenhouse effect to warm the surface of the earth. In broad outline, the effect includes an increase in global temperatures by about 1.5°F since 1880, a decrease in the amount of sea and land ice, and rising sea levels on an average of 3.19 mm per annum. Much of the basic data and some striking images are available at the NASA website (http://climate.nasa.gov/). Climate change produces a variety of different effects. The official federal site that collates data on the United States has a regional breakdown. In the southwest of the United States, key issues include decreasing water supplies, increasing forest wildfires, and flooding. In the southeast, major elements include significant sea level rise, higher seawater temperatures, and ocean acidification. In the northeast, changes include increased warming and poorer air quality, severe flooding due to sea level rise, and reductions in fish stocks, especially cod. Some of the complicated suite of impacts on the United States is illustrated in Figure 6.7.

A volume on climate change, edited by Richard Aspinall, gives a sense of the range of global dynamics; it contains articles examining glacier melt in the Andes and the effects on household vulnerability; increasing drought in Jamaica and the impact on local farmers; the "double exposure" of climate change and economic restructuring in California's Central Valley; and the renewed geopolitical rivalries in the Arctic because warming is leading to new shipping routes, easier access to natural resources, and the ability to project a military presence. The general conclusion to this exciting body of work is that climate change is enmeshed in social structures and economic processes at all levels from the households to the firm and the state. Climate change generates new household vulnerabilities and stimulates new coping strategies as well as changes in geopolitical relations.

Landscape

One line of research in the society-nature theme looks more specifically at landscapes as an embodiment of the people/nature relationship. In his classic 1955 study *The Making of the English Landscape*, W. G. Hoskins explored the English landscape much as an archeologist explores an excavation. The different levels in the landscape, beginning with the pre-Roman and continuing all the way through the industrial, were brought to the surface for inspection, cleaned of dust, and examined. In direct reference to Hoskins's work, the geographer Michael Conzen's 2010 book is entitled *The Making of the American Landscape*. The historical geographer Don Meinig also brought together a fascinating collection of essays that looks at the notion of ordinary landscapes. In his own essay in the collection, he highlights the various meanings of landscapes and how they can be viewed as nature, habitat, artifact, system, problem, wealth, ideology, history, place, and aesthetic.

Landscape is a complicated text, telling us who has power and how and why that power is wielded. Landscape studies are now infused by a critical engagement

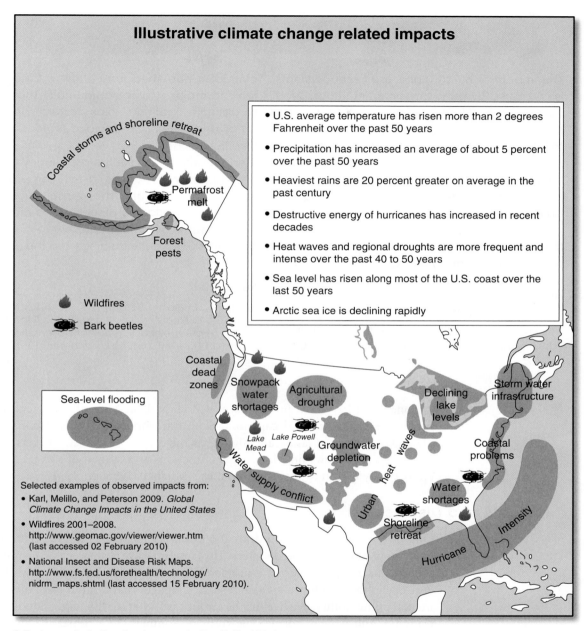

6.7 Impact of climate changes in the United States

with the social processes behind their making and their connection with deeper political relations. The influential cultural geographer Denis Cosgrove, for example, made a distinction between dominant and alternative cultures. Landscapes reflect the dominant culture, but have traces of alternative cultures. Cosgrove examined landscapes and performance in early modern Europe and landscape transformation in sixteenth-century Venice and twentieth-century Rome. In this more critical cultural geography, landscape is interrogated for its connection with capitalism,

Box 6.2   GROUND TRUTHING

The impact of human land use on ecosystems is measured by using traditional methods, such as map comparison, as well as remote sensing. If we use remotely sensed data, it is important to identify finer-grained processes in order to see the effects and impacts on households and their vulnerabilities and coping strategies. This is sometimes referred to as ground truthing. It is an evocative phrase that encapsulates the very nature of human geography. Geographers seek to identify the truth on the ground by utilizing different scales of analysis, from the telescope to the microscope, and by employing aggregate analysis as well as detailed interview techniques.

There is bias in much of ground truthing. Laura Martin and colleagues looked at the location of 2,573 terrestrial study sites that were the basis of studies published from 2004 to 2009 in the top ten major ecological journals. They found a distinct locational bias toward protected areas and temperate deciduous woodlands in wealthy countries. Even when studies considered urbanized and settled areas, they focused on fragments of "natural" areas. Large parts of the global south and the densely populated areas of the world, the places where most of us live and work, are underrepresented in ecological studies. Not quite truthing of all the ground.

References

Martin, L. J., Blossy, B., and Ellis, E. (2012) Mapping Where Ecologists Work: Biases in the Global Distribution of Terrestrial Ecological Observations. *Frontiers in Ecology and the Environment* 10: 195–201.

national identity, social justice, race, and class. Don Mitchell connects the making of the California landscape to agricultural workers and their labor processes. This labor history of landscape highlights the conflicts between workers and their employers and shows how landscape "functions as a system of social control and opportunity within capitalist economies" (Mitchell, 1996, pp. 199).

Hazards and Disasters

One of the most visible and dramatic examples of people/nature relations is the experience of hazards and disasters. The tsunami wave that sweeps away the coastal settlements, the storm surges that flood cities, and the flash flood that washes away entire neighborhoods are vivid and searing images that remind us of our environmental vulnerability. We live in a hazardous world of earthquakes, floods, volcanic eruption, and violent storms. The ruins of Pompeii are a constant reminder that we live in a world that can easily turn into a stage for destruction and disaster. Floods and storms are less unpredictable acts of God and more predictable events as science has replaced religion and accurate instrumentation notes and records even small-scale environmental changes. We have a better sense of the underlying dynamics and hence predictability of storms, floods, and eruptions. Our knowledge is not absolute. The earthquake that struck Haiti in 2010 and the tsunami that overwhelmed towns in Aceh were unforeseen events. We do know the location of fault zones, but precise plate shifts cannot be predicted within actionable certainty.

Box 6.3   A MODIFIED EARTH: A SOCIALLY CONSTRUCTED NATURE

A popular text that summarizes much of the research on people/nature themes is simply titled *The Human Impact on the Natural Environment*. It provides a good survey of material and case studies. But look again at the title. It assumes that people are impacting a "natural" environment. The increasing amount of human impact raises the question: is there such a thing as the natural environment, or have we as humans so transformed the earth that most of us now live in human modified environments? Bill McKibben, a popular writer on ecology, wrote a book with the suggestive title *The End of Nature*. More recently, in his book *Eaarth*, he argues that we have wrought such tremendous change that we need a new term—the title of his book. Think of it as Earth 2.0, an Earth so modified that it counts as a new form. He focuses on climate change to show that changes are creating permanent drought, rapid melting of the polar ice caps, an expansion of the tropical region by as much as two degrees of latitude north and south, and increased ocean acidity. This is not, he argues, some short-term change that will soon revert back to a more "natural" state. We live more and more in a world quite literally of our own making. It is also a world of our own writing. A number of scholars point to the social construction of nature, by which they mean that Nature is not just something out there; it is not only appropriated and used but also represented and understood by humans. The title of an edited book sums up the basic idea: *Social Nature*.

We are now in a new geological age, the Anthropocene, a name used to indicate the profound and fundamental restructuring caused by human agency. The term was first coined by the Nobel-prize winner Paul Crutzen. Erle Ellis and colleagues have mapped the world's *anthromes*, biological areas that are shaped by human impacts.

This profound transformation comes with costs and benefits. The loss of more natural ecosystems, while providing benefit in the short term, may have longer-term costs. A major report by the United Nations, *The Global Biodiversity Outlook*, suggests that some ecosystems are close to the tipping point at which they will become less useful to humans. One indicator of the changes is the decline in biodiversity. More than one in five of all mammal species and close to one in three of all amphibian species are close to extinction. And yet it is only recently that we have started to put a specific value on nature and develop an economic metric for measuring biodiversity.

There is also an emerging movement known as rewilding that aims to create landscapes and ecosystems similar to those that existed in Paleolithic times. This ecological strategy consists of the reintroduction of predators such as wolves and cougars into core reserves, with migratory corridors linking the cores. It is often summarized up as "cores, corridors, and carnivores." A 15,000-acre reserve in the center of the Netherlands known as Oostvaardersplassen was created in the 1980s and stocked with a variety of animals in an attempt to recreate a European wilderness at the end of the last Ice Age.

References

Castree, N. and Braun, B. (eds) (2001) *Social Nature: Theory, Practice, and Politics*. Malden and Oxford: Blackwell.

Crutzen, P. (2002) Geology of mankind. *Nature* 415: 23

Ellis, E. E., Goldewijk, K. K., Siebert, S., Lightman, D., and Ramankutty, N.(2010) Anthropogenic Transformation of the Biomes, 1700 to 2000. *Global Ecology and Biogeography*, 19: 589–606.

Box 6.3   CONTINUED

Foley, S. F. et al. (2013) The Palaeoanthropocene-The beginnings of anthropogenic environmental change. *Anthropocene* http://dx.doi.org/10.1016/j.ancene.2013.11.002

Global Diversity Outlook *http://www.cbd.int/gbo3/ebook/.* Accessed January 20, 2012.

Goudie, A. S. (2006) *The Human Impact on the Natural Environment: Past, Present and Future.* 6th ed. Oxford: Blackwell.

Kolbert, E. (2012) Recall of the Wild. *The New Yorker,* December 24 and 31, pp. 50–59.

McKibben, B. (2010) *Eaarth: Making a Life on a Tough New Planet.* New York: Time Books.

Meine, C., Soule, M., and Noss, R. F. (2006) "A Mission-Driven Discipline": The Growth of Conservation Biology. *Conservation Biology* 20: 631–651.

We need to be very careful in using the term "natural disasters," because they tend to be very social events in terms of who is affected most. Vulnerability to hazards magnifies as the population increases and more people live in marginal places. I use "marginal" in the double sense implied by "on the edge of things." First, places like the southern Atlantic seaboard of the United States are zones of hurricane activity. If we build houses and cities in hurricane zones, it should come as no surprise that someday storms will wash away beachfront property. Hazards become disasters when we build on fault lines and develop along hurricane coasts. Marginality also occurs when people are forced to inhabit places such as the squatter settlements on steep slopes or slums on floodable plains and thus are more vulnerable to environmental hazards. The poor are made more vulnerable because they are often forced to live in the more environmentally hazardous areas. "Natural" disasters are less acts of nature and more the result of human actions. It is important to consider the social context of vulnerability of hazards.

How hazards impact households or become disasters is mediated through the prism of social and economic power. Disasters do not affect everyone equally. Based on a sample of 141 countries, Neumayer and Plumper show that disasters killed more women than men and that the higher women's socioeconomic status, the smaller the gender gap in mortality. The most impacted were low-income women. "Natural" disasters, on closer inspection, are very social in their outcomes and effects.

Bear in mind the fault lines of power, class, and race revealed in these three brief examples:

1. In the Grand Cayman Islands, situated firmly in a zone of hurricane activity, there are two responses to the threat of hurricane. The very wealthy, with the warning provided by accurate forecasting, hop on a plane and simply fly away from the island to safety. The poorer inhabitants of the island, unable to flee, have to wait out the storm.

2. Rising temperatures brought about by global warming have different effects. Increasingly hot days have less impact on mortality in the United States because it is a relatively rich country with access to air-conditioning, either individually

BOX 6.4   THE TRAGEDY OF THE COMMONS?

In a paper published in 1968, Garret Hardin described the tragedy of the commons. The setting for the tragedy occurs, according to Hardin, when individuals use a collective resource. He gives the example of a common pasture used by individual herders. The tragedy happens because each individual, seeking to maximize their personal interest, tends to overuse the commons, and the result is deterioration of the common space. The solution lies either in some form of government regulation or a privatization of the common property.

The image invoked by Hardin's paper is compelling, yet problems remain with the concept. Hardin describes the case of open-access resources, whereas in many traditional societies the commons were, and sometimes still are, either a common pool resource or, more often, common property. The tragedy of the common occurs in traditional societies less frequently than Hardin suggests because they were regulated through collective property agreements.

In the most sustained examination of the issue, Nobel Prize winner Elinor Ostrom argues against the simple solution of either privatization or government regulations. She proposes a number of principles for common-pool resource management, including cheap and easy access to conflict resolution, community rights linked with higher levels of regulation, encouragement of collective decision-making, and effective exclusion of unentitled parties.

The environment can be considered as a common-pool resource that is susceptible to overuse and deterioration. The depletion of deep-sea ocean fisheries, for example, is a case where users, acting rationally to harvest as many fish as possible, collectively undermine the resource base. Global climate change, to take another example, results from the action of carbon polluters who do not pay the full cost of their actions. If we see the environment as a common-pool resource, a very valuable and fragile one, then we can imagine a range of policy responses along the line suggested by Ostrom.

References

Hardin. G. (1968) The Tragedy of the Commons. *Science* 162: 1243–1248.

Lant, C. L., Ruhl, J. B., and Kraft, S. E. (2008) The Tragedy of Ecosystem Services. *BioScience* 10: 969–974.

McWhinnie, S. F. (2009) The Tragedy of the Commons in International Fisheries: An Empirical Example. *Journal of Environmental Economics and Management* 57: 321–333.

Ostrom, E, (1990) *Governing the Commons: The Evolution of Institutions for Collective Action.* Cambridge: Cambridge University Press.

Ostrom, E. (2009) A Polycentric Approach for Coping with Climate Change. *Social Science Research Network.* http://papers.ssrn.com/sol3/papers.cfm?abstract_id=1934353

or collectively. In rural India, in contrast, an increase from 70 to 90 degrees increases mortality by more than 1 percent. The same hazard of global warming, but with very different outcomes, depending on who you are and where you are.

3.   The drowning of New Orleans in the wake of Hurricane Katrina in 2005 was anything but a natural disaster. The levees were overwhelmed because they were inadequately built and poorly maintained. The poor environmental management that allowed the erosion of the marshland and the construction of a navigation canal heightened the damaging impact of the storm surge.

The disaster was not a natural disaster caused by unforeseen, unpredictable events. It was the result of building a city in an area of environmental hazard, pursuing a destructive environmental management policy that enhanced risk, failing to build and maintain the necessary infrastructure to protect the city, and doing little to help the most vulnerable citizens of that city in the event of flooding.

The experience of environmental hazards and the way that hazards become disasters tell us as much about the human geography of class and power as they do about the physical geography of weather and landforms.

Cited References

Aspinall, R. (ed) (2010) Special Issue: Climate Change. *Annals of Association of American Geographers* 100: 715–1045.

Blaikie, P. M. (1985) *The Political Economy of Soil Erosion in Developing Countries.* London: Pearson.

Burgess, R., Deschenes, O., Donaldson, D., and Greenstone, M. (2009) Weather and Death in India. http://94.126.106.9/R4D/PDF/Outputs/IIG/E12-weather-and-death-in-india.pdf Accessed January 24, 2012.

Campbell, J. (1983) *Historical Atlas of Word Mythology.* San Francisco: Harper and Row.

Conzen, M. (ed) (2010) *The Making of the American Landscape.* New York: Routledge.

Cosgrove, D. (1984) *Social Formation and Symbolic Landscape.* London: Croom Helm.

Cosgrove, D. (2008) *Geography and Vision: Seeing, Imagining and Representing the World.* London: I. B. Tauris.

Etter, A., McAlpine, C., and Possingham, H. (2008) Historical Patterns and Drivers of Landscape Change in Colombia since 1500: A Regionalized Spatial Approach. *Annals of Association of American Geographers* 98: 2–23.

Hoskins, W. G. (1955) *The Making of the English Landscape.* London: Hodder and Stoughton.

Krech, S. (ed) (1981) *Indians, Animals, and the Fur Trade: A Critique of* Keepers of the Game. Athens: University of Georgia Press.

Lui, L. (2008) Sustainability Efforts in China: Reflections on the Environmental Kuznets Curve through a Locational Evaluation of "Eco-communities." *Annals of Association of American Geographers* 98: 604–629.

Martin, C. (1978) *Keepers of the Game; Indian-Animal Relations and the Fur Trade.* Berkeley: University of California Press.

Meinig, D. (ed) (1979) *The Interpretation of Ordinary Landscapes.* New York: Oxford University Press.

Maas, J. Verheij, J. R. A., Vries, S. de, Spreeuwenberg, P., Schellevis, F. G., and Groenewegen, P. P. (2009) Morbidity Is Related to a Green Living Environment. *Journal of Epidemiological Community Health* 63:967–973.

Mitchell, D. (1996) *The Lie of the Land: Migrant Workers and the California Landscape.* Minneapolis: University of Minnesota Press.

Neumayer, E. and Plumper, T. (2008) The Gendered Nature of Natural Disasters: The Impact of Catastrophic Events on the Gender Gap in Life Expectancy, 1981–2002. *Annals of Association of American Geographers* 97: 551–566.

Summers, S. (2011) *Situations Matter: Understanding How Context Transforms Your World.* New York: Riverhead.

Thomas, W. L. (ed) (1955) *Man's Role in Changing the Face of the Earth.* Chicago: University of Chicago Press.

Turner, B. L., Clark, W.C., Kates, R., Richards, J. F. Mathews, J. T., and Meyer, W. B. (eds) (1993) *The Earth as Transformed by Human Action.* Cambridge: Cambridge University Press.

Watts. M. J. (1983) *Silent Violence: Food, Famine and Peasantry in Northern Nigeria.* Berkeley: University of California Press.

Select Guide to Further Reading

Benton, L. M. and Short, J. R. (1999) *Environmental Discourse and Practice.* Oxford: Blackwell.

Benton, L. M. and Short, J. R. (2000) *Environmental Discourse and Practice: A Reader.* Oxford: Blackwell.

Hartman, C. and Squires, G. D. (eds) (2006) *There Is No Such Thing as a Natural Disaster: Race, Class, and Hurricane Katrina.* New York: Routledge.

Hecht, S. B. and Cockburn, A. (2011) *The Fate of the Forest: Developers, Destroyers, and Defenders of the Amazon.* Chicago: University of Chicago Press.

Howard, P., Thompson, I. H., and Waterton, E. (eds) (2012) *The Routledge Companion to Landscape Studies.* New York and London: Routedge.

Mitchell, D. (2012) *They Saved the Crops: Labor, Landscape, and the Struggle over Industrial Farming in Bracero-Era California.* Athens: University of Georgia Press.

Montz, B. E. and Tobin, G. A. (2011). Natural Hazards: An Evolving Tradition in Applied Geography. *Applied Geography* 3: 1–4.

Olwig, K. and Mitchell, D. (eds) (2008) *Justice, Power and The Political Landscape.* New York: Routledge.

Peet, R., Robbins, P., and Watts, R. (eds.) (2010) *Global Political Ecology.* New York: Routledge.

Wisner, B., Blaikie, P., Cannon, T., and Davis, I. (2004) *At Risk: Natural Hazards, People's Vulnerability and Disasters.* London; Routledge.

White, L., Jr. (1967) The Historical Roots of Our Ecological Crisis. *Science* 155: 1203–1207.

Websites

The Intergovernmental Panel on Climate Change
http://www.ipcc.ch/
NASA website on global climate change
http://climate.nasa.gov/
US climate change and impacts
http://www.globalchange.gov/
Measuring global diversity
http://www.teebweb.org/
NASA Earth observatory
http://earthobservatory.nasa.gov/
NASA land use changes
http://climate.nasa.gov/imagesVideo/imagesOfChange/
United Nations Environment Program
http://www.unep.org/

The Economic Organization of Space

The economic organization of space is the subject of Part 3. In chapter 7, we identify the economic geography of the primary, secondary, and tertiary sectors. In chapter 8, we take a different tack, looking at economic geography of the different scales of global and regional and the role of the state, consumers, labor, capital, and nongovernment agencies.

7 The Geography of Three Economic Sectors

Three distinct sectors of economic activity can be identified: primary, secondary, and tertiary. These are outlined in Figure 7.1. Some care should be taken with this division, because it suggests strong demarcation lines between the sectors, whereas, in reality, there is considerable interaction. Consider the case of a financial institution (tertiary sector) that lends money to a farmer to buy machinery to grow potatoes (primary) that are then transformed in a factory into potato chips (secondary). All three sectors are connected in complex arrangements, networks, and flows. In the rest of this chapter, we will explore some of the socio-spatial dimensions of each of these sectors separately but will be mindful of the flows and connections that link them together.

As economies grow and mature, the secondary and tertiary sectors tend to become more important. Table 7.1 highlights the changes in the sector mix in China. As the economy developed, the tertiary sector became an increasingly important element. The relative decline of the primary sector and rise of the secondary

7.1 Three sectors of the economy

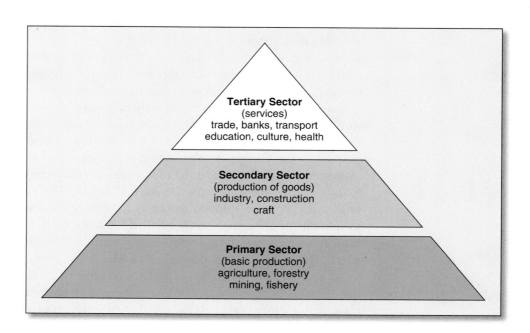

Table 7.1 ■ CHANGING SECTOR COMPOSITION IN CHINA, 1978–2012			
Year	**1978**	**1996**	**2012**
GDP	100	100	100
Primary	28.1	20.2	10.1
Secondary	48.2	49.0	46.8
Tertiary	23.7	30.8	43.1

Source: China Statistical Yearbooks.

and tertiary sectors in a national economy is linked to profound socio-spatial changes, including the commercialization of agriculture, high levels of rural to urban migration, and increasing levels of industrialization and urbanization.

THE PRIMARY SECTOR

The primary sector includes agriculture, forestry, mining, and fishing. The primary sector is very much influenced by geography. Mining is a function of mineral distribution, while fishing takes place beside rivers, lakes, and coasts. I will mainly focus on agriculture. The type of agriculture possible depends in large part on climate and weather, soils, and water availability. Natural rubber production, for example, takes place in tropical areas, especially in Thailand, Indonesia, Malaysia, India, and Vietnam. Wheat growing, in contrast, is concentrated in the temperate grasslands of the world. The wheat belt countries include Canada, Russia, and the United States in the northern hemisphere and Argentina and Australia in the southern hemisphere.

Geography obviously plays an important role in the distribution of primary activities. But it would be incorrect to see the primary sector only as the outcome of locational opportunities and constraints. Take the case of sugar. Traditionally, it was a tropical plant that could only be grown in the hot, humid areas of the world. By the seventeenth century, a market for sugar had developed in Europe to such an extent that the search for sugar-growing areas constituted an important element in the European colonization and annexation of Caribbean islands. The work was brutally hard, and the indigenous people were soon killed off. The need for labor fueled the slave trade. Between 1700 and 1786, almost three-quarters of a million slaves were shipped to Jamaica to work on the plantations. The move shifted the racial balance. In Grenada in 1700, the white/black ratio was 1:2, but by 1783 it was 1:25. European countries without tropical colonies were at a huge disadvantage, having to pay others for an expensive good. It is not incidental that sugar beet was developed in Germany, a country with no tropical possessions. By the early 1800s, the first beet sugar factory opened in Germany. Sugar beet is a plant with a tuber that contains a high concentration of sucrose. The plant can be

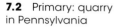

7.2 Primary: quarry in Pennsylvania

grown in colder climates, and so the tropical source became less important. As beet sugar production increased, the sugar plantation economies of the Caribbean dramatically declined.

The von Thünen Model

Markets play an important part in affecting agricultural production. In 1826 the wealthy German landowner Johann Heinrich von Thünen (1783–1850) proposed a model of land use around a city (Figure 7.3). His model was highly idealized in order to identify the independent role of location. The "isolated" city of his model was situated on a flat plain with homogenous fertility and unvarying transportation costs. The city was the main market for famers. Since farmers closer to the city paid less for transport, they could bid more for land, which resulted in higher land costs closer to the city. Only farmers growing the more intensive crops, with high returns, could thus afford the land closer to the city. The net result, according to von Thünen, was a concentric ring pattern with more expensive land and thus more intensive agriculture closer to the city. At the time he was writing, market gardening and firewood production were intensive land uses, while livestock farming was more extensive.

While the von Thünen model operates on the assumption of a flat plain with unvarying fertility, conditions that are rarely met with in the real world, it has been useful as a platform for subsequent studies. The von Thünen model is useful to explain historical developments. The environmental historian William Cronon, in his 1991 book *Nature's Metropolis,* examines the relationship between Chicago and its

7.3 The von Thünen model

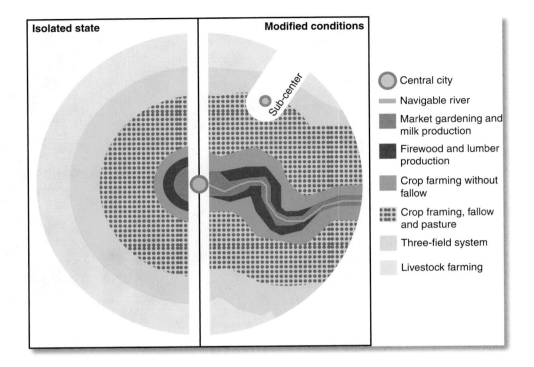

hinterland from 1850 to 1890. He shows how the physical world was turned into a commodified human landscape as grain, lumber, and meat production transformed prairies and woodlands into the physical basis for the city's growth and development. More detailed analyses of contemporary conditions look at the rural-urban fringe of cities. In capitalist land markets, the ring of land closest to the city is often underutilized, in contrast to von Thünen's predictions, because of the heavy shadow of possible future land use conversion. With rural-to-urban conversions a very real possibility, landowners make few investments in agricultural production. The land use planning system that directs which areas are available for rural-to-urban conversion will clearly affect the simple linear-distance model proposed by von Thünen.

In the case of Megalopolis, as the urbanized seaboard of the United States is often called, there is empirical evidence of the validity of the von Thünen model. Land closer to the cities is much more expensive than land on the periphery of Megalopolis. If farmers do locate in areas closer to the city, they need to engage in intensive high-yield farming, such as the market gardening of fruit and vegetables. In some cases, it is not so much distance as time of transportation that is important. Large cities require quick and immediate supplies of fruit and vegetables and other specialized agricultural products. Restaurants, for example, require daily supplies for their diners. Proximity to the city provides swift access, but at the price of high land values, which in turn means that only intensive farming with high yields makes economic sense. Organic fruits and vegetables is another emerging market that yields a high dollar return per acre. Affluent consumers are willing to bear the greater costs associated with these products. High-yield counties are located around

New York City, Philadelphia, and Boston. There are other areas of relatively high yield such as New Jersey (giving credence to the nickname Garden State), Rhode Island, and southern Connecticut. Agricultural land is being lost as the suburban spread flows across the landscape, but the remaining farmland that is safe from urban development, even temporarily, and close to the city has become so expensive that very intensive forms of farming are required, including nurseries, greenhouse crops, and higher-value specialty products.

There are now many case studies of land use change that draw upon the von Thünen model, including tropical forest degradation close to Dar es Salaam in Tanzania and crop production outside of Yaoundé in Cameroon. In their study of land use changes in forest areas of Indonesia, Miet Maertens and her colleagues used satellite imagery, GIS data, and survey techniques. The von Thünen model, while useful, did not explain all the variation in this Indonesian forest frontier area. Not just distance to markets was important, so were population levels, access to technology, and individual household characteristics.

The Agrarian Transition and the Commercialization of Agriculture

The agrarian transition occurs as agriculture shifts from subsistence to commercial and moves from meeting local market demands to provisioning national and global food supply chains. It involves changes to agriculture, including intensification and expansion, market integration, and environmental change.

The extension and intensification of agriculture are pronounced (see Figure 7.4). There is a global expansion of arable land, an expansion of irrigated surfaces,

7.4 San Joaquin Valley, California

Box 7.1   FOOD SUPPLY CHAINS

The supply and demand for food are linked through food supply chains, which have become longer and more complex. There are three interrelated reasons. First, with urbanization more people live in towns and cities. This growing urban population needs to be supplied with food produced elsewhere. Long and complex transportation links connect urban consumers with rural providers. Second, there is also dietary transition. As household incomes grow, so does the consumption of dairy, meat, and fish. Bennett's Law states that the consumption of starch staples declines as household income increases. In China, for example, economic growth and the development of a middle class has led to increased consumption of meat and dairy products. Third, there is the increased globalization of trade in foodstuffs. Food supply chains are increasingly multinational and global. The longest chains are often associated with very large retailers, such as supermarkets that are large enough to have substantial economies of scale. One study that looked at exports of horticultural products from sub-Saharan Africa to Europe found important positive welfare effects as rural providers were able to make more money and have a more dependable source of income.

There are least four types of food supply chains. In *buyer-driven chains*, a small number of retailers consolidate their supply around a few suppliers, although there are opportunities for smallholders where crops need intensive care, as in Peru's asparagus sector. In *producer-driven chains*, such as coffee, cocoa, and tomatoes, producers can establish cartels. In *bilateral oligopolies*, such as bananas and pineapples, large-scale producers combine with large-scale retailers. In *traditional markets*, smallholders cater to domestic and local markets.

Consumers, especially more affluent food consumers, can access different types of food chains, shopping at supermarkets as well as at local organic markets and buying food from distant international food supply chains as well as from local producers.

References

Lee, J., Gereffi, G., and Beauvais, J. (2012) Global Value Chains and Agrifood Standards: Challenges and Possibilities for Small Holders in Developing Countries. *Proceedings of the National Academy of Sciences* 109: 12326–12331.

Maertens, M., Minten, B., and Swinnen, J. (2012) Modern Food Supply Chains and Development: Evidence from Horticulture Export Sectors in Sub-Saharan Africa. *Development Policy Review* 30: 473–497.

and the development of intensive mixed farming systems in dense population areas. In developed countries, there is large-scale mechanization, biological selection, and increasing use of chemicals to boost yields. In some developing countries, there is a marked commercialization of agriculture and integration into global food supply chains.

Market integration takes two main forms. On the one hand, there is the commercialization of the peasantry, as subsistence smallholders become commercial farmers. Geographer Sarah Turner looked at the contemporary process among

Hmong farmers in the upland areas of northern Vietnam. She conducted more than 200 interviews and measured the expansion of rice paddies as a replacement for opium cultivation, which was banned by the government.

There are enormous barriers to this process, as smallholders and subsistence farmers often lack access to capital and technology. There are many cases, however, where traditional peasant societies respond creatively to the new commercial realities despite the barriers. Small-scale farmers can, for example, market their ecological sensitivity to sophisticated consumers, as in the case of smallholding organic coffee growers in Costa Rica. The growth of fair-trade initiatives, for example, often links ethical consumers with small-scale producers.

There is also evidence of a land grab as peasant farmers are displaced in the wake of the forced commodification of land with the resultant commercialization of agriculture. This has a long history. In England, for example, the Enclosure Movement privatized the common land of fields, marshes, heaths, and woodlands. Between 1760 and 1820, almost 20 percent of England's total acreage was enclosed and the English peasantry was destroyed. A system of traditional rights and obligations was replaced with the cash nexus of agrarian capitalism.

Similar processes are occurring now throughout the world, reinforced by a growing commercialism of agriculture. Across the globe, the land of indigenous peoples is still being appropriated as companies and governments enclose commons and dispossess the peasantry in a global land grab. The process is fueled by the commercialization of agriculture as food production in many regions becomes more linked to global markets and the growing demand for biofuels. When agricultural land becomes more valuable as a commodity, rich and powerful interests seek to possess the land. This often involves the dispossession of local communities with long-established links to particular parcels of land. The land grab is particularly pronounced when the peasantry is of a minority ethnicity compared to the ruling elites. Often marginalized by political structures and denied full access to political power, peasants struggle to maintain their land rights. Peasant societies struggle against well-connected corporations and powerful state bureaucracies. The Mapuche tribal group was restricted to land reserves by the Chilean government in 1883. Even this "reserved" land is now subject to state and private appropriation as hydroelectric dams are built, logging companies move in, and plantations are created to grow sugar and soya.

The market for biofuels and food for exports is generating a mass enclosure of traditional lands and the dispossession of peasant societies. In many countries, legal land rights are uncertain. The traditional claims to land often do not hold up in modern legal frameworks more concerned with adjudicating private property rights than communal rights. In the Philippines, for example, only 3.5 million out of a total of 12 million hectares are in private property. The rest of the land has uncertain formal legal status, making it more susceptible to a land grab.

There are also instances where peasant communities resist the land grab. The Bajo Aguán region in Honduras has been a scene of intense conflict over the last two decades. In the 1990s, large landowners purchased land from farmer cooperatives to harvest palm oil for export. Local activists complained that the deals were unfair and people were not made aware that they were signing away land rights. One company, owned by a member of the very wealthy Honduran elite, amassed one-fifth of all the land in the region. In 2009 peasants invaded and occupied company land. Troops were sent in, people were evicted, and more than forty people were killed. The peasants resisted, and the bad publicity led to one German bank withdrawing loans to some of the large companies. In 2011 the Honduran government passed a law that allowed peasant farmers in Bajo Aguán to purchase 4,000 hectares at favorable interest rates. This particular story has all the elements of the global land grab: marginalized peasants, rich landowners, and a growing market for food exports and biofuels. In this case, however, the peasants resisted and forced a change in the government attitude.

The commercialization of agriculture involves greater capital investment in machinery and biotechnology, which leads to greater productivity. To take just one example: the average American farm produced 40 bushels of grain per acre in 1900. A hundred years later, the same acre was producing 100 bushels (see Table 7.2). This enormous increase in productivity is the result of increased use of pesticides, genetically engineered crops, and heavy doses of fertilizers. All of these come at a price.

Pesticides, for example, increase productivity by reducing the negative impacts of insects on crop yields. The negative environmental consequences of heavy pesticide use were first popularized by Rachel Carson in her 1962 book *Silent Spring*. The title of the book describes a spring devoid of birdsong after pesticides have decimated songbirds. Almost 3 billion kilograms of pesticides are used around the world each year. In the United States alone, the Figure is 500 million kilograms. One study looked at the impact on public health, the development of pesticide resistance in pests, honeybee and bird losses, and groundwater contamination, estimating the total costs in the United States in 2002 at $10 billion. The costs are probably much higher in countries with less stringent environmental protection legislation and enforcement.

Table 7.2 ■ CORN PRODUCTION IN THE UNITED STATES			
Year	Yield (bushels per acre)	Hours required for 100 bushels	Equipment used
1850	40	75–90	Plow
1900	40	35–40	Gangplow, disk, harrow, 2-row planter
1950	50	10–14	Tractor, 3-bottom plow, disk, harrow, 4-row planter, 2-row picker
2000	100	2.5	Tractor, 5-bottom plow, 25 ft. tandem disk, planter, 25 ft. herbicide applicator, 15 ft. self-propelled combine, trucks

Source: American Farm Bureau.

Increased use of fertilizer, especially nitrogen, also has deleterious effects on groundwater contamination and air quality through emission of nitrous oxides. Runoff from fertilized fields finds its way into streams, rivers, and seas, creating super nutrient-enriched environments in which algae and plants grow so much that they can reduce the oxygen to such low levels that dead zones occur. Eutrophication is the name given to the process of the enrichment of ecosystems with chemical nutrients, which creates algal blooms that result in dead zones. Nutrient enrichment also causes new patterns of disease for humans and wildlife. In Caribbean wetlands, for example, increased nutrient runoff creates lusher vegetation that provides a home for malarial mosquito larvae.

The issue of genetically modified (GMO) crops is controversial. Crops are genetically modified to make them more resistant to disease and predators and to produce higher yields. While the proponents of GMO highlight the advantages of cheaper food, critics point to the risk of unintended health effects on consumers and the risk of contamination between GMO and non-GMO crop varieties, with unknown consequences. The risks and full costs of GMO agriculture have yet to be fully assessed.

The most sustained commercialization of agriculture in the developing world that involved large inputs of biotechnology was the Green Revolution, the name given to a series of innovations and transfer, especially marked from the late 1940s to the 1970s, that increased agriculture prediction through new high-yielding varieties of crops, irrigation, and liberal helpings of pesticides and fertilizers. It began in Mexico and was then implemented in India, Philippines, and selected African countries. The Green Revolution did improve yields, but at the cost of environmental damage and increased negative health impacts on local communities. It is now seen as a deeply flawed experiment with some positive consequences, such as increased crop production and cheaper food for consumers. We need a real green revolution, one that is sensitive to environmental impacts, community concerns, and translating sustainable and safe practices into mainstream agriculture.

THE SECONDARY SECTOR

The manufacturing of goods constitutes the bulk of the secondary sector. While craft industries have existed for centuries—glass making in Venice, for example, dates from the fourteenth century—the large-scale manufacturing of goods as a major component of an economy is a comparatively recent phenomenon associated with the Industrial Revolution.

The Industrial Revolution is one of several long waves of production based on the clustering of innovations. The Soviet economist Nikolai Kondratieff first identified these long, fifty-year cycles in the 1920s. Kondratieff made a distinction between inventions and innovations. Inventions are new ways of doing things; they occur almost randomly, but tend to be adopted into production techniques in waves of innovation. The basic nature of these Kondratieff cycles is noted in

Box 7.2   THE INDUSTRIAL REVOLUTION

The Industrial Revolution occurred around 1800 and was centered in Britain. At its core, the Industrial Revolution was a new way of making things. Production capacities were increased by mechanization. Steam power released capacities beyond the limits of even the most strenuous human exertion. Textile production was increased tenfold by mechanization. Once started, the Industrial Revolution took off in an upward cycle of increased growth and expansion as inventions were turned into innovations that improved, increased, and streamlined the making of things. The Industrial Revolution was also an institutional revolution, as economic transactions shifted from one based on patronage and personal contact to a greater reliance on anonymous markets, performance measurements, and impersonal exchange.

Britain was the first industrial nation. A number of reasons lay behind its transformation. Britain was a relatively small, politically stable, densely populated country. Colonial expansion assured cheap imports and secured export markets. Because of high wages, British companies were forced to introduce labor-saving techniques. It is also important to note the role of London. In 1800 the city had a population of almost one million, almost double the size of any other European city. The city's population growth provided a huge, growing, and secure market for food producers and manufacturers, and this effective demand was the basis for further investment in agricultural and industrial production.

The very early Industrial Revolution was centered in Manchester. One compelling reason is the importance of the culture of innovation: between 1600 and 1800, a proto-industrialization system of economic organization was established, there was a capacity for continuous innovation, and there was a large middle class of small capitalists able to employ a range of entrepreneurial talent, social networks, and local cultures that allowed a constant improvement in products and processes. The city's location was important: it was close to the coal that provided the raw power that animated the incessant spinning and weaving machines. But other places were also close to coalfields, so this single locational factor has limited explanatory power. Manchester became the first industrial city because it was the first truly innovative city.

References

Allen, R. C. (2009) *The British Industrial Revolution in Global Perspective*. Cambridge: Cambridge University Press.

Allen, D. W. (2011) *The Institutional Revolution: Measurement and the Economic Emergence of the Modern World*. Chicago: University of Chicago Press.

Hall, P. G. (1998) *Cities in Civilization*. New York: Pantheon Books.

Table 7.3. Four cycles are commonly noted: textiles, iron and steel, mass production, and high-tech. Each Kondratieff cycle is associated with key innovations that structure society and space. The first two, from 1785 to 1895, are associated with the development of factories, the emergence of industrial districts, and the growth of towns and cities.

The first Kondratieff cycle, from 1787 to 1845, is associated with textile manufacturing and saw its full flowering in Manchester. In 1750, Manchester in England

Table 7.3 ■ THE FOUR KONDRATIEFF CYCLES			
	Textiles	Iron and steel	Mass production	High tech
	1787–1845	1846–1895	1896–1947	1948–2000 (?)
Key innovation	power loom	steel-making	electric light, automobile	transistor, computer
Key industry	cotton, iron	steel	cars, chemicals	electronics
Industrial organization	small factories	large factories	giant factories	large and small factories
Labor	machine minders	craft labor	deskilled	segmented
Geography	towns	towns	conurbations	new industrial regions

was just one of hundreds of textile towns located all over Europe. What made it the first industrial city was developments in technology, new sources of supply and demand, and social networks that fostered innovation and risk taking. In the 1760s, new steam-powered machines increased production levels. In 1774 the population of Manchester was only 41,032; by 1831 it was 270,901. Mills were working day and night. Other ancillary industries also developed. Railways links were built to transport its goods, and by 1840 the city was served by six railway lines and was a center of locomotive construction.

The second and third cycles were also experienced in other parts of the developed world, especially Germany and the United States. New industrial regions were established in North America and Europe. The city of Paterson in New Jersey was a center of textile production and then the making of locomotive engines (see Figures 7.5 and 7.6). Pittsburgh in Pennsylvania was surrounded by bituminous coal; the state produced almost a quarter of the nation's total coal production, over 10 billion tons in 200 years. By the mid-nineteenth century, there were over a thousand factories using coal as their power source. There were at least sixty-five glass factories. During the Civil War, the city became a center for armaments manufacturing. The Scottish-born industrialist Andrew Carnegie founded the first steelworks in 1873, and by 1910 the city was producing a third of the nation's steel. Aluminum was first made in Pittsburgh in 1888. The city grew from a population of only around 46,000 with a metropolitan population of 100,000 to a city population in 1920 of almost 600,000 with a metro population of almost 1.5 million. Pittsburgh was the epicenter of US industrialization, and even today major employers include Alcoa, U.S. Steel, and Wheeling-Pittsburgh Steel. As the economy matured, the city of Pittsburgh was only the central point in a wider suburbanization of people and jobs throughout a wider urban region. With the creation of large integrated industrial establishments such as large-scale steel works, industry, jobs, and people were widely distributed throughout a forty-mile radius from downtown Pittsburgh. As firms increased in size, the plants grew larger. The result was a complex suburbanized metropolitan economy. The rapid and heavy industrialization also created unhealthy pollution.

7.5 Paterson, New Jersey, was a site of textile production in the US industrial revolution.

7.6 Paterson was also a site of locomotive engineering.

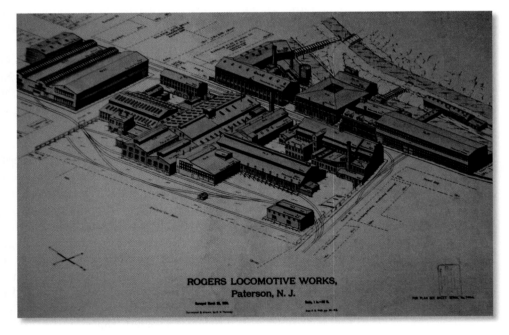

The third Kondratieff cycle was based on automobile manufacturing, giant factories, and standardized deskilled manufacturing processes. The exemplar city was Detroit as it became home to car manufacturing and new forms of industrial production. At the beginning of the twentieth century, cars were luxury items, handcrafted and designed for the wealthy. Detroit was only one of many car-making

7.7 Secondary: steel-making plant in Baltimore

7.8 Secondary: metalworks in Amsterdam

cities. Even before the coming of car production, Detroit had been a manufacturing center; by 1900 it had almost a thousand machine shops making ships, stoves, engines, and mining machinery. There was a pool of skilled labor and a network of local financiers. Detroit was soon producing two-fifths of the nation's car output, concentrating on the cheaper end of the market.

Henry Ford transformed the manufacturing of cars. He was born in 1861 and grew up close to Detroit. In 1879 he went to work for the Michigan Car Company, which was building ten cars a day. In 1899 he formed the Detroit Automobile Company, but it was not a success. Ford was too much of a perfectionist and had yet to hone his market sensibilities. Fine-tune them he did, however, when he founded the Ford Motor Company in 1903 with twelve shareholders, all from Detroit. In 1908 the first Model T appeared on the market. It was a simple yet robust model that went through numerous design improvements to become one of the first mass-produced cars. Assembly lines and mass production had been developed over the previous century in a range of manufacturing industries, including bicycles and watches as well as the Chicago meat processing and packing industry. Ford did not invent mass production, but he refined and improved it. Car production became standardized, precise, and continuous. Mass production allowed reduction in the final price: the cost of a Model T in 1908 was $805, but by 1924 it was down to $290. With each price decrease, new markets were created, and so mass production not only met demand but created new demand. Cars became less a luxury item and more a regular purchase, especially in the rural hinterland, where farmers used them for a variety of purposes. By 1920 every second car in the world was a Model T Ford. In order to reduce labor turnover, Ford also paid high wages for the time. A well-paid industrial workforce was essential to decreasing labor turnover and maintaining worker allegiance. Ford was instrumental in creating the highly paid blue-collar sector of the new industrial city.

Detroit was the forerunner of a form of production named after Henry Ford. Fordist production is controlled by a small number of very large companies operating under oligopolistic conditions. Fordist production is mechanized and repetitive, with long production lines. Under Fordism there were outbreaks of labor unrest when the business cycle softened demand and management implemented layoffs and wage cuts. But, by and large, a stable system of capital-labor relations was established as a relatively affluent working class was created. The high point of this wave lasted from 1945 to the mid-1970s.

The fourth Kondratieff cycle is associated with the development of high-tech information technology (IT) industries. The Kondratieff distinction between inventions and innovations is apparent in this fourth cycle. The inventions associated with the IT sector occured in a steady stream throughout the twentieth century but only become a wave of high-tech innovation that transformed the economy and society by the very end of the twentieth century (Table 7.4). The IT wave took over a century to turn inventions into the wave of innovations that occurred from 1980

Table 7.4 ■ INVENTIONS IN COMPUTER TECHNOLOGY	
Approximate date	**Inventions**
1890	punch cards and mechanical calculating machines
1939	vacuum tubes and electromechanical calculating
1952	transistors and electronics
1964	mainframe computing
1971	microprocessors
1981	personal computers
1994	the Internet

onwards. By 1994 the World Wide Web had become a powerful information portal to business and personal computer users.

Each of the waves has an exemplar city or region: Manchester, Pittsburgh, and Detroit. For the fourth wave it is Silicon Valley, a high-tech cluster centered on Palo Alto in California (see Figure 7.9) where personal computing was developed for mass markets. Nearby Stanford University played a major role as a source of smart computer scientists and as the force behind the establishment of Stanford Industrial Park, where Hewlett-Packard was established by two Stanford graduates in 1953. Technological innovation was funded by a steady stream of government defense contracts and facilitated by corporate initiatives, such as Xerox's Palo Alto Research Center. Over time, the area became home to legal firms and venture capitalist firms that facilitated and funded the start-up and establishment of innovative companies. By 2013, major computing companies, such as Adobe, Apple, Cisco,

7.9 Silicon Valley

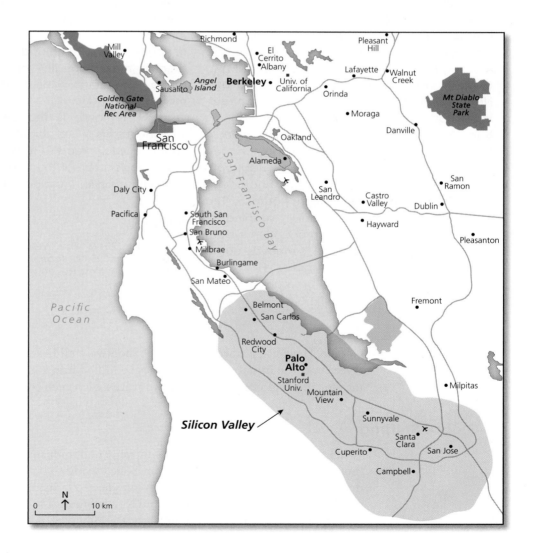

Box 7.3 GLOBAL PRODUCTION CHAINS AND REGIONAL COMPLEXES

The geography of manufacturing is complex, with global supply chains linking iron ore fields in Australia to steel plants in China to fabrication sites throughout Asia, Europe, and North America. Factories are now linked into a dense circuitry of connections as products designed in one country are assembled in another, with parts drawn from suppliers in many other countries.

As an example of one production chain, consider the manufacturing of clothes for retailers in the United States and Europe. One clothing retailer, Hennes and Mauritz (H&M), a Swedish company with stores in Europe and North America, keeps its prices low by contracting in low-wage areas of the world, such as Bangladesh, where four million people work in the 5,000 textile factories, most of them women paid around $38 a month to work. H&M contracts with 900 factories worldwide to produce a constantly changing design portfolio. The company has been successful in keeping inventory low; the just-in-time production system ensures that goods are made to meet demand. Stores often receive daily supplies. High turnover means that profits can be made through selling many items rather than one; hence the price of individual items can be reduced, which in turn aids turnover. Workers, however, toil for low wages in often-poor working conditions. Between 2005 and 2013, more than 1,800 workers died in Bangladesh in factory fires and building collapses in the textile sector. One building collapse in 2013 killed 1,127 workers.

While supply chains are global, there are also regional manufacturing clusters such as the garment factories in Dhaka. The small town of Poole in Dorset, England, is home to the two biggest makers of tiny electric motors that rotate on bearings made of gas molecules. The motors are used to make printed circuit boards. Warsaw, Indiana, is the center of medical implant makers. While global supply chains highlight the wide spread of a globalized economy, these clusters reveal the importance of spatial agglomeration for the regional economy.

References

Marsh, P. (2012) *The New Industrial Revolution: Consumers, Globalization and the End of Mass Production*. New Haven and London: Yale University Press.

Google, Hewlett-Packard, Intel, and Yahoo were all headquartered in the region. Over time, the initial early advantages solidified into a major competitive advantage for this region as a center for innovative high-tech computing.

Global Shifting

"Global shift" is used to describe the movement of industrial employment from the industrial regions and cities of the developed world to the cities and regions of the developing world. Since the 1970s there has been a redistribution of manufacturing employment from Western Europe and North America to Asia, Latin America, and other parts of the world that involves the deindustrialization of the advanced economies and a rapid industrialization in selected cities in a small group of developing countries, including China, Singapore, Taiwan, and South Korea.

Smooth global transport networks reduce the cost of transporting goods around the world, and the development of routine manufacturing processes allows manufacturing to become established in areas of unskilled labor. Economic globalization allows companies to search for cheap labor outside their national borders. Economic globalization allows corporations to relocate in order to minimize wage costs. There is a deterritorialization of corporations. The old adage that what is good for General Motors is good for America no longer applies, as General Motors makes cars in China and Europe. Although listed as a US company, Nike's interests do not necessarily parallel US interests. What is good for Nike shareholders is good for Nike shareholders. Whether it is good for US workers is beside the point. The low cost of international transport and the growing ease of international trade, crucial requirements of economic globalization, have allowed capital to be more easily disassociated from national interests and local community concerns. Capital is free to roam the world in search of lower and lower wages. Globalization has liberated capital from territory, citizens, and communities.

Global shift is moving up the manufacturing chain. In the early 1990s, China's economic growth was dominated by traditional labor-intensive manufacturing sectors such as textiles, clothing, and footwear. More recently, however, growth has been more noticeable in the capital-intensive, high-tech sectors such as machinery and electronics.

The global shift in manufacturing employment was most pronounced from the 1970s to the 2000s. Since 2010 there has been a further redistribution as some manufacturing jobs relocate back to the United States. From 2010 to 2012, 525,000 manufacturing jobs were added, and 50,000 of those arose from overseas firms moving operations to the United States. The reason: the narrowing wage gap between China and United States as wages increase in China and decline in the United States. The gap in wage cost in the respective countries is shrinking from $20 per hour in 2000 to an estimated $7 per hour in 2015. Rising productivity and increasing innovation are making manufacturing in the United States a more attractive proposition. We may be at the beginning of a global reshifting, especially for the advanced manufacturing sector. The more unskilled routine manufacturing will still continue to shift to areas with lower labor costs.

THE TERTIARY SECTOR

In mature economies there is a shift from manufacturing to services. In the United States, for example, service employment now accounts for one in every three US workers and almost 30 percent of GNP. Services are defined as selling, assistance, and expertise rather than making a tangible product. In some cases, the distinction is clear; when you buy a car you are buying a good, whereas when you hire someone to clean your house you are buying a service. At other times, the distinction is fuzzy; the classic example is a restaurant, where you buy food but also a service. The term "services" is best considered a loose and hazy one, with slippage at the edges. The term also covers a wide range of activities, from health care and financial consultancy to computer information companies. The sector includes a range of wildly differing job experiences. At one end are the high-paying Wall Street brokers working in high finance and international currency dealing, all making good wages and lucrative annual bonuses that fuel the local housing markets (Figure 7.10). At the other end are nighttime contract cleaners of the offices that house these executives.

One particularly dynamic sector of services is the knowledge-based industries, so-called producer services such as advertising, banking services, financial services, business consultancies, and information technology. Together these sectors constitute the dynamic edge of mature capitalist economy. Since 1980, in the developed world, a region's success rests less on manufacturing employment and more on the extent to which it can generate, retain, and attract knowledge-based employment.

In the nineteenth and early twentieth century, the factory contained both the assembly line and the offices that administered the whole process of buying raw material, hiring workers, and selling finished products. The business service sector has become more prominent as these services sectors have been hived off into separate divisions and into separate companies. We can think of a simple model of contemporary multinational manufacturing business. At the base is the routine assembly plant that needs all those things noted in the standard location models of industry, such as cheap labor and low taxes. As economic globalization has created a flatter world these plants can be located in a range of countries around the world. Another level of the company that has separated out from the production plants is the research and development sector that tests new products. This sector needs to be

7.10 Tertiary: Wall Street is a center of financial services

close to pools of highly skilled labor, knowledge pools and the amenity-rich locations that attract such workers. Then there is the company headquarters, which needs a metropolitan location in order to maximize face-to-face business contacts and be close to business services such as advertising, financing, legal services, and other important services and decision-makers. Consider the case of Boeing, a company with almost 156,000 workers around the world, almost 66,000 of them in the state of Washington. In 2001 the company moved its headquarters from Seattle to Chicago and separated its corporate headquarters from its production base. According to the company, the move was made in order to secure ready access to global markets and easier access to financial markets. It was also lubricated by subsidies of over $60 million from the state of Illinois and the city of Chicago, which was in competition with Denver and Dallas-Fort Worth.

The growth of the service sector also produces a more polarized job market with, on the one hand, high-paying jobs with full benefits and, on the other, minimum-wage employment with few benefits. At the core of the new service economy are highly paid knowledge-based professionals, symbolic analysts such as business consultants, and investment bankers. Paid generously, they have employment security, good working conditions, and generous benefits. They often work long hours with brutal deadlines, but they are firmly located in the middle to upper-middle class, and they can assure their children's similar economic success by being able to buy good private education or by being able to make the right residential choices to ensure the best public education. At the very upper levels of this sector is a world of affluence. It is the world of the corporate jet and the million-dollar-plus stock options that provide a deep financial cushioning from the vagaries of life. Outside of this core group, there are two peripheries. A semi-periphery consists of full-time workers with less income, status, and prestige. Their jobs are less secure, and too often they are only able to hang on to middle-class status if more than one person in the household is working. A periphery comprises people on short-term or part-time contracts. They may work from home on their computer and relish the flexibility of such work or may be picked up on a daily basis at the street corner by landscape gardeners to manicure the lawns of the wealthy.

The shift from a manufacturing-based economy to a service-based economy has profound effects on income distribution. A strong manufacturing base allows low-skilled workers to obtain relatively good wages. The service economy, in contrast, provides high-paying jobs for those with marketable skills, but more limited opportunities for low-skilled workers. For those lacking high educational attainment, the opportunities shrink to the low-waged service sector.

The shift from manufacturing to a more service orientated economy also goes hand in hand with an increase in female employment. In the United States in 1950, the female participation rate in the formal economy was only 30 percent, but by 2012 it had increased to almost 58 percent. By 2012, out of a total employed labor force of 155 million, 72.6 million were women. The workforce has been feminized in the shift to a more service-based economy.

From the early 1970s, global shift affected mostly the manufacturing sectors. In more recent years, there has been a significant increase in the global shift in service

Box 7.4   THE CULTURAL-CREATIVE ECONOMY

An important and growing sector of the economy is the cultural industry sector, which includes the artistic industries of music, dance, theatre, literature, the visual arts, crafts, and many newer forms of practice such as video art, performance art, and computer and multimedia art. There are also the "cultural-products sectors," which include high fashion, furniture, news media, jewelry, advertising, and architecture.

The work of creative artists enhances the design, production, and marketing of products and services in other sectors. Cultural industries concentrate in world cities and other large cities. Indeed, they contribute immensely to the economies of cities like Los Angeles and Paris. The concept of "path dependence" can be used to analyze cultural production as well as technological innovation. Path-dependent theories claim that small historic events or locational advantages can affect macroeconomic consequences that privilege certain paths to development and limit others. This idea sheds light on the prestigious success that Paris enjoys in high fashion, New York in advertising, and Los Angeles in motion picture entertainment. Their leading roles in these industries have long enjoyed wide recognition, and their advantages over potential competitors relate not only to the quality of their products, but also to the "symbolic images"—such as authenticity and reputation—that those products carry.

Creative talent drives economic development. Richard Florida argues for a new social class, the creative class, which leads the new creative economy. The creative class divides into two groups of people. The first makes up the "super-creative core," a broad and diverse group including scientists, engineers, university professors, poets, novelists, artists, entertainers, actors, designers, and architects, as well as nonfiction writers, editors, cultural figures, think-tank researchers, analysts, and other opinion-makers. The other group consists of "creative professionals" who work in a wide range of knowledge-intensive industries such as high-tech sectors, financial services, the legal and health care professions, and business management. The former group produces new forms or designs that are readily transferable and widely useful, while the latter group engages in creative problem solving.

There is a vigorous debate about the rise of the so-called creative class, its contingency and flexibility, its scalability from a few well-known case studies, and its ideological underpinnings as a form of urban economic policy. A convincing argument could be made that the poor are the real creative class, because of their ingenuity and resourcefulness in the face of limited income and restricted employment opportunities.

References

Currid, E. (2007) *The Warhol Economy: How Fashion, Art, and Music Drive New York*. Princeton: Princeton University Press.

Florida, R. (2002) *The Rise of the Creative Class: And How It's Transforming Work, Leisure, Community, and Everyday Life*. New York: Basic Books.

Hutton, T. (2014) *Cities and The Cultural Economy*. New York: Routledge.

Peck, J. (2005) Struggling with the Creative Class. *International Journal of Urban Regional Research* 29:740–770.

Scott, A. J. (2008). *Social Economy of the Metropolis: Cognitive-Cultural Capitalism and the Global Resurgence of Cities*. Oxford: Oxford University Press.

Scott, A. J. (2012). *A World in Emergence: Cities and Regions in the 21st Century*. Edward Elgar Publishing.

Kim, Y-H. and Short, J. R. (2008) *Cities and Economies*. New York: Routledge.

employment. A new round of economic globalization, made possible by changes in technology, is sending a range of service employment overseas from the developed world to the developing world. Back offices in Bangalore, India, now process home loans for US mortgage companies, while many insurance claims made in the United States are routinely processed in offices situated in New Delhi. The economics are simple. Software designers in the United States cost $7,000 a month, while experienced designers in India cost only $1,000 a month. US companies now routinely outsource work previously done at home. In the 1970s and 1980s, engineers would come to the United States and Europe; now the jobs come to them.

Selected cities in developing countries are developing as centers of service employment. In part they develop as hubs of corporate national headquartering, which generate service employment. In China, for example, Beijing and Shanghai are the favored sites for headquarters of foreign companies. In China corporate companies are attracted to Beijing because of the closer proximity to key decision-makers, an important criterion in order to work effectively in a centrally planned economy. However, even in the secondary city of Shanghai there has been a shift from manufacturing to service employment. In 2000, for the first time, tertiary employment became more important than secondary employment. There has been a shift from manufacturing to service. In 1995 there were almost 400,000 people employed in manufacturing and 300,000 in service employment. By 2002 manufacturing employment had shrunk to 288,000, while service had slightly increased to 313,000. While only in one four jobs in China are classified as service, almost one in two in Shanghai are in services. By 2003 the financial service sectors accounted alone accounted for 10 percent of the city's GDP.

As service employment increases, there is the danger of what is called "Baumol's disease" after the economist William Baumol, who first noted that while innovation and efficiency occur rapidly in the manufacturing sector, leading to price reduction, they are less pronounced in the service sector. You can make a car quicker and more efficiently, but it still takes a string quartet the same time to play a Beethoven quartet. As an economy becomes more dominated by the service sector, it is subject to rising costs. While prices for goods decline due to efficiencies in manufacturing, the costs of services keep rising in absolute and relative terms. In his book *The Cost Disease*, Baumol suggests that while we can work to reduce service costs, they are the price of a successful economy.

SUMMARY

A global trend is evident for each of the three sectors. There is an increasing intensification and commercialization of agriculture. Manufacturing is becoming more automated and also relocating toward a select group of developing economies. In much of the developed world, there is a decline of manufacturing employment and a rise in service employment. Around the world, the more dynamic economies are shifting from agriculture to manufacturing and from manufacturing to services.

Cited References

Ahrends, A., Burgess, N. D., Milledge, S. A., Bulling, M. T., Fisher, B., Smart, J. C., and Lewis, S. L. (2010) Predictable Waves of Sequential Forest Degradation and Biodiversity Loss Spreading from an African City. *Proceedings of the National Academy of Sciences* 107: 14556–14561.

Baumol, W. (2012) *The Cost Disease: Why Computers Get Cheaper and Health Care Doesn't*. New Haven and London: Yale University Press.

Folefack. A. J. J. and Adamowski, J. F. (2012) Application of the Von Thünen Model in Determining Optimal Locations to Transport Compost for Crop Production Outside of Yaoundé, Cameroon. *Journal of Human Ecology* 39: 125–143.

Maertens, M., Zeller, M. and Briner, R. (2011) Agriculture Land-Use in Forest Frontier Areas: Theory and Evidence from Indonesia. *Environmental Research Journal* 5: 505–522.

Turner, S. (2012) "Forever Hmong": Ethnic Minority Livelihoods and Agrarian Transition in Upland Northern Vietnam. *The Professional Geographer* 64: 540–553.

Select Guide to Further Reading

Borras, J. and Franco, J. (2010) Towards a Broader View of the Politics of Global Land Grab: Rethinking Land Issues, Reframing Resistance. *Initiatives in Critical Agrarian Studies Working Paper 001.* http://www.tni.org/paper/towards-broader-view-politics-global-land-grabbing Accessed January 19, 2012.

Evenson, R. E. and Gollin, D. (2003) Assessing the Impact of the Green Revolution, 1960–2000. *Science* 300: 758–762.

Hall, T. (2010) *Earth into Property: Colonization, Decolonization, and Capitalism.* Montreal: McGill-Queens University Press.

Harris, C. (2003) *Making Native Space: Colonialism, Resistance and Reserves in British Columbia.* Vancouver: University of British Columbia Press.

Horlings, L. G. and Marsden, T. K. (2011) Towards the Real Green Revolution? Exploring the Conceptual Dimensions of a New Ecological Modernization of Agriculture that Could "Feed the World." *Global Environmental Change* 21: 441–452.

Knudsen, M. T., Halberg, N., Olesen, J. E., Byrne, J., Iyer, V., and Toly, N. (2006) Global Trends in Agriculture and Food Systems. In Niels Halberg (ed), *Global Development of Organic Agriculture: Challenges and Promises.* Wallingford: CABI Publishing, 1–48.

Pearce, F. (2012) *The Land Grabbers: The New Fight Over Who Owns the Earth.* Boston: Beacon.

Pimentel, D. (2005) Economic and Environmental Costs of the Application of Pesticides Primarily in the United States. *Environment, Development and Sustainability* 7: 229–252.

Scholtz, C. S. (2006) *Negotiating Claims: The Emergence of Indigenous Land Claim Negotiation Policies in Australia, Canada, New Zealand, and the United States.* New York: Routledge.

Sinclair, R. (1967) Von Thünen and Urban Sprawl. *Annals of Association of American Geographers* 57: 72–87.

Lyon, S., Aranda Bezaury, J., and Mutersbaugh, T. (2010). Gender Equity in Fairtrade–Organic Coffee Producer Organizations: Cases from Mesoamerica. *Geoforum, 41*(1), 93–103.

Morgan, K., Marsden, T., and Murdoch, J. (2006) *Worlds of Food: Place, Power and Provenance in the Food Chain*. New York: Oxford University Press.

Sen, D., & Majumder, S. (2011). Fair Trade and Fair Trade Certification of Food and Agricultural Commodities: Promises, Pitfalls, and Possibilities. *Environment and Society: Advances in Research* 2 (1), 29–47.

Websites

For the US economy see

Federal Reserve Bank of Richmond – economic indicators
http://www.richmondfed.org/research/national_economy/national_economic_indicators

U.S. Department of Commerce, Bureau of Economic Analysis
http://www.bea.gov

U.S. Department of Labor, Bureau of Labor Statistics
http://www.bls.gov/eag/eag.us.htm

U.S. Department of Commerce, Center for Economic Studies
http://www.census.gov/ces/dataproducts/economicdata.html

U.S. Department of Commerce, Economics and Statistics Administration
http://www.esa.doc.gov/about-economic-indicators

For the international economy see

http://www.internationaleconomics.net/data.html
http://data.worldbank.org
http://www.imf.org/external/data.htm
http://libguides.princeton.edu/internationalecon
http://www.newyorkfed.org/research/global_economy/globalindicators.html

8

The Economic Geography of Different Scales and Various Agents

In this chapter, we will look at the economic organization of space at different scales. Then we will examine five important agents that shape these economic geographies: capital, consumers, government, nongovernmental organizations, and labor.

GLOBAL DIFFERENCES

Across the surface of the globe, there is an uneven development of economic activity that results in marked disparities in living standards and quality of life. Table 8.1 highlights data from three countries, Brazil, Cameroon, and the United States. In Cameroon, many people do not live past their mid-fifties, while in the United States people regularly live into their seventies and beyond.

To explain these differences, some, such as Jared Diamond, take a very long-term view, 13,000 years to be precise, and focus on how initial geographical advantages were turned into economic advantages. Geography plays a part in shaping the global economic order of marked disparities, but it is rarely pivotal. Japan, with few natural resources, has reached a high level of economic development and good living standards, while much of tropical Africa, despite a bounty of resources and minerals, remains poor.

The patterns not only vary over space, they change over time. In the fifteenth century, China was far ahead of Europe, and had enough scientific and technical knowledge to inaugurate an industrial revolution. This did not happen, and China focused inwards. In contrast, technologically backward Europe became the center of massive economic change as the Industrial Revolution, centered on Britain, transformed the old patterns into a new global order in which manufacturing and economic vitality became the monopoly of the West. In recent years, even this order has changed with the global shift of manufacturing and the rise of new industrial powers such as Brazil, China, and India. The global economy is dynamic and ever-changing.

The American economist Walt Rostow identified different stages of economic development (see Figure 8.1). In traditional society, stage 1, the majority of people are employed in the primary sector, with very few in the secondary and tertiary sectors, much like Cameroon. In the transitional stage 2, there is some specialization

Table 8.1 ■ GLOBAL DIFFERENCES	Cameroon	Brazil	USA
GDP per capita $	2,300	12,000	49,800
% labor force in agriculture	70	20	0.7
% labor force in manufacturing	13	14	20
% labor force in services	17	66	79
Life expectancy from years at birth	54	72	78

Source: CIA World Factbook.

8.1 The Rostow model

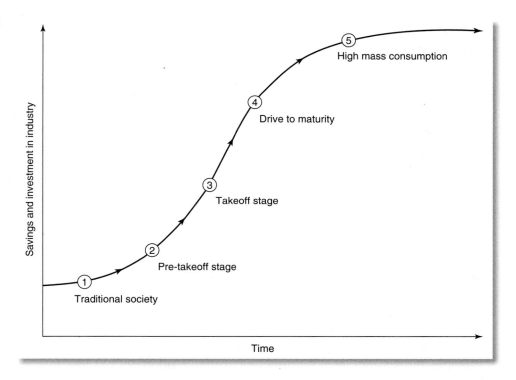

and a more developed infrastructure. Stage 3 is termed "takeoff" and refers to rapid industrialization. The takeoff period is different for different countries: for the United Kingdom from 1783 to 1802, for the United States from 1843 to 1850 and for China since 1990. Stage 4 is the drive to maturity, involving diversification and innovation with less reliance on imports. In stage 5, high mass consumption, the domestic demand of consumers is a major economic engine and the service sector is dominant.

The stages are less an explanatory model than a historical sequence with, at its heart, the notion that through time and encouragement of private investment,

Box 8.1 DIFFERENT ECONOMIES

We can distinguish between different types of economy. Employment in the **formal economy** involves the sale of labor in the marketplace, formally recorded in government and official statistics. The **informal economy** is the unrecorded sector where few, if any, taxes are paid. The informal sector is a response to the lack of formal employment opportunities. This sector is just as complex as the formal sector. Based on his work in Latin American cities, Ray Bromley identifies different sectors, including retail distribution, small-scale transport, personal services, security services, gambling services, and recycling enterprises. Work conditions vary from short-term wage-work to precarious self-employment. The workers in this sector may be disguised wage-workers (they are paid a wage but it is not recorded), workers on short-term wage-work, dependent workers who may lease a personal transport vehicle from an employer, and the self-employed. In his research on the city of Cali, Colombia, Bromley found that 40 to 45 percent of people who worked in the street were in precarious self-employment, 39 to 43 percent were disguised wage-workers, 12 to 15 percent were dependent workers, and only 3 percent were short-term wage-workers.

The divisions between the formal and informal sectors fluctuate according to circumstance. When and where the formal economy provides many employment opportunities, the informal sector becomes less significant. However, if the formal sector provides few jobs or only jobs with low wages, then the informal sector is a sophisticated coping strategy as people use a variety of tactics to make a living.

The **illegal economy** is the shadowy world of prostitution, selling illegal drugs, racketeering, and the like. The previously cited work by Bromley noted the importance of prostitution, begging, and property crimes involving illegal appropriation through stealth (theft), the threat or use of violence (robbery), or deception (conning). It is difficult to estimate the sector's full extent. Much of the global illegal sector consists of the production and distribution of goods and services for which there is a demand even though they are illegal. The demarcation of legal-illegal varies: alcohol is not illegal in the United States but cocaine is; prostitution is legal and regulated in both Germany and the Netherlands but is illegal in most of the United States; one can buy marijuana in Amsterdam without breaking the law, but the same transaction in New York would be considered criminal. The line between legal and illegal is constantly being crossed: police who take bribes; chemical companies that illegally dump waste; corporations that form illegal cartels to charge high prices to the federal government. The distinction between the three sectors, formal, informal, and illegal, is at times fuzzy. Rather than look at the differences, a more rewarding strategy may be to look at how transactions transgress the lines.

A **social economy** consists of not-for-profit activities; it is also sometimes referred to as the "third sector." It includes cooperatives, charities, voluntary groups, trusts, and religious organizations. This sphere of economic activity, somewhere between the market and the state, plays an important role in certain parts of the economy as both funding source and employer.

The **communal economy** involves the cashless exchange of goods and services. It is common in neighborhoods and extended family systems. If someone wants a babysitter for an evening, they have a number of possibilities: they can hire someone and record the transaction and pay taxes (the formal economy); they can hire a teenager and pay them an agreed

Box 8.1 CONTINUED

sum without informing the authorities (the informal sector); or they can ask a neighbor, with the often unspoken understanding that they will return the favor. The last, and often the most common, response is an example of the communal economy in action. It can range from reciprocal favors, such as babysitting, grass-cutting and garbage removal, to a host of household chores, from building maintenance to carpooling.

The **domestic economy** is the amount, type, and division of labor within the home. A hundred years ago, there was much greater use of paid domestic labor for middle- and upper-income groups. The increasing cost of labor has meant the decline of mass domestic labor, though it still persists amongst the wealthy, and

in rich countries foreign, vulnerable, and illegal workers do a high proportion of such work. The division of labor is a source of change, conflict, and negotiation within the households. As more women have joined the formal labor force, they feel the double demand of work and home because they carry much of the domestic load. The division of domestic labor is not simply an apportionment of necessary work, it involves questions and representations of femininity, masculinity, and the family.

References

Bromley, R. (1997) Working in the Streets of Cali, Colombia: Survival Strategy, Necessity or Unavoidable Evil? *Cities in the Developing World: Issues, Theory and Policy*, 124–138.

countries can achieve economic growth. The assumption is that every economy can be like the United States if it follows the same path of encouraging private investment and ensuring returns to investors. Global inequalities and differences are thus a function of time, with some countries more advanced along the trajectory than others. That raises the questions: why are some countries where they are on this historical trajectory, and why are some countries rich and some so poor? The answer, according to some, lies in the differential ability to adopt economic opportunity and harness technological possibilities. Cultures that promote innovation and openness tend to do better than others. Small differences over time became sources of major divergences. When the Ottoman sultan forbade the establishment of a printing press in 1485, it reduced the opportunities for a spread of learning and an increase in technical proficiency. Institutions, especially institutions that secure property rights and allow broad economic and political participation, play a significant role in economic growth. The Industrial Revolution in Britain was due to many factors, but there were important institutional shifts, including the creation of an efficient banking system to connect savings to investment and the establishment of a mass education system to train people for work and industrial employment.

The global economy has winners and losers not just as a historical accident but as part of the very process of economic development. Some countries are rich not because they are further along the Rostow trajectory or have a more innovative culture, but because other countries are poor. The initial advantage of some countries was reinforced by colonialism and economic imperialism, which led to the differential distribution of wealth and poverty. Countries are not just located at different stages in time, they are part of a spatially connected order, a world system comprising core, periphery, and semi-periphery. For two hundred years the core was in Western Europe and later in North America. Economic transactions are marked by an unequal exchange of cheap raw materials from the periphery to the core and the export of manufactured goods from the core to the periphery. This essential dynamic explains the colonial expansion of core countries as they sought to establish monopoly control over regions that were then transformed into colonial peripheries used to feed and sustain the core economies by supplying cheap raw materials and purchasing manufactured goods. Britain was a core country that incorporated much of India into commercial domination and political control. Raw cotton grown in India was shipped to Britain, processed into cloth in Lancashire cotton mills, and then exported abroad. The indigenous cotton manufacturing industry in India was destroyed, while the domestic cotton industry in Britain was a leading force in the Industrial Revolution, which propelled national economic growth.

This core-periphery model allows us to globalize such issues as the Industrial Revolution, presenting them less as unique national experiences and more as part of a global drama. The model is dynamic. The category of semi-periphery is something of a transitional condition situated somewhere between the dominance of the core and the relative weakness of the periphery. Some countries can move from the periphery toward the core. In the past fifty years, China, South Korea, and others have undergone marked industrialization to place them closer to the core. And even some strategic raw primary producers, such as the oil-producing countries of OPEC or mineral-rich Australia, can use their collective interests and combined power to increase prices and force redistribution in global wealth. The core-periphery model has the enormous advantage of globalizing historical events and adding a much-needed dose of political economy to standard historical narratives while being flexible enough to explain the moves of some national economies from periphery to semi-periphery, with the possibility of core membership changing and shuffling. From their initial advantages, the core countries became richer.

REGIONAL DIFFERENCES

Economic disparities are also evident at the regional level. Consider the case of China. China's economy, like most national economies, is a patchwork quilt of very different regional economies, some growing faster than others, some more industrialized than others. Figure 8.2 shows the marked regional variation in income levels. The fastest-growing coastal regions, where the bulk of export-oriented manufacturing takes place, are wealthier than the more distant inland regions with much less manufacturing activity. These differences are the principal reason behind the large-scale internal migration from inland provinces to the coastal regions of the country.

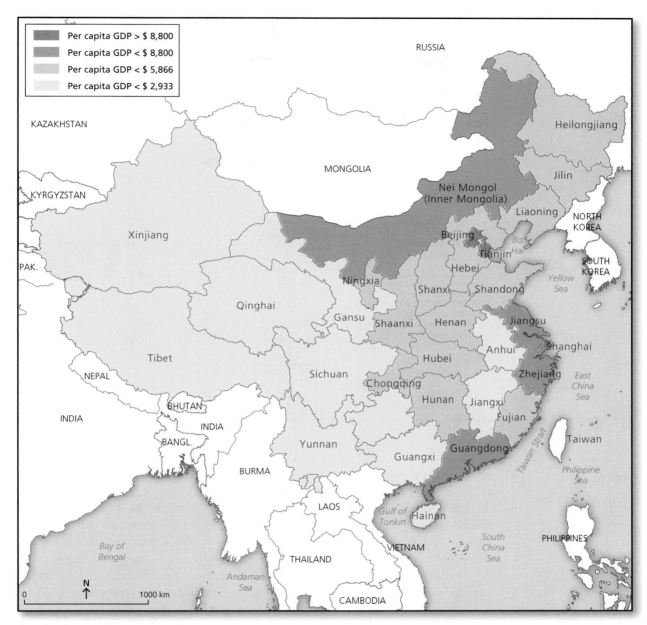

8.2 Regional differences in China

Regional disparities are best understood with reference to models of regional economic growth. The process of cumulative causation occurs when growth feeds on itself. Growth in a leading region spreads out into other lagging regions through diffusion of innovations and providing markets (Figure 8.3). There are also backwash effects that include the flow of capital and labor from the lagging to the leading regions. In the United Kingdom, the backwash effects are clearly more

8.3 Cumulative causation. Diagram courtesy of Barcelona Field Studies Centre.

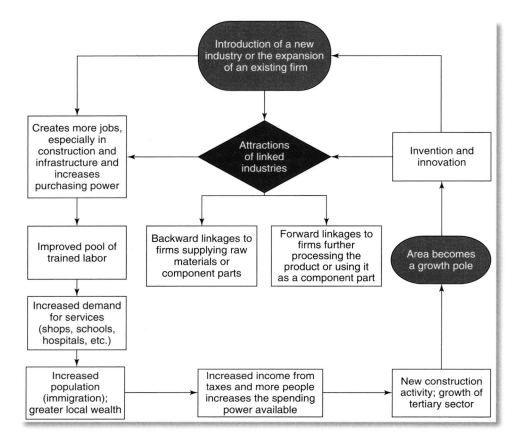

pronounced than the spread effects, with growth concentrated in London and the southeast part of the country, which attracts more labor and capital that in turn through cumulative causation generate even more growth. The flow of capital and skilled labor from the peripheral regions, such as Scotland, limits economic growth and ultimately leads to pronounced regional disparities. As Figure 8.4 shows, Britain has the widest regional disparities among the larger economies.

Uneven regional development is not a temporary condition that will be ironed out though time but is absolutely essential to a capitalist mode of production. Waves of investment are uneven across space, making some regions more developed than others. These investments are spatially fixed and form the basis for subsequent rounds of capital investment. Some regions are then bypassed by subsequent waves of investment as capital searches for areas of greatest profit. The result is the constant production of uneven development.

There is a distinct clustering of similar economic activities at the regional scale. Four factors are important:

- locational pull of resources such as proximity to transport links or energy sources;

8.4 Regional disparities

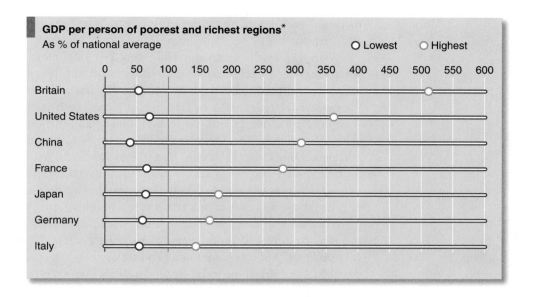

GDP per person of poorest and richest regions*
As % of national average

- the concentration of firms and workers, which provides a pool of specialized labor that benefits both labor and companies;
- subsidiary trades and service that are attracted to the core industries;
- the spillover of innovative ideas from firm to firm.

Regional economic complexes emerge because of the locational pull of reduced transaction costs. However, these are maintained by the tight social networks between firms that require interpersonal trust, proximity, and regular face-to-face contact. These social networks are particularly important in highly specialized sectors. Even in the information age, the spatial clustering of activities, firms, and workers provides the efficient means of communication that help solve problems and facilitate mutual cooperation.

Regional economic clusters provide a "thick market" (a large pool of labor and specialized firms), market access, and savings in public goods provision. In effect, economic agglomerations, because they concentrate things in the same place, make markets more efficient. There are efficiency gains from the scale effects. And in turn this spatial ensemble of benefits, through cumulative causation, creates path-dependent development. Once the movie industry was established in the Los Angeles area, for example, it continued to attract capital and skilled labor, which made it even more attractive to make movies in that location.

There are also countervailing forces at work. The more firms cluster in one specific region, the more land and labor costs go up and congestion costs increase. These centrifugal forces can disrupt the clustering of routine production but are less compelling for specialized sectors such as entertainment, financial services, or cultural-creative industries. The high-tech sector is still concentrated in Silicon Valley despite the high cost of land and labor. Industrial clustering is also found in the small-craft-based industries of Northern Italy that specialize in clothing, design, and furniture.

Manuel Castells and Peter Hall identify contemporary industrial complexes, which they term technopoles, established around high-technology industry. They include semi-planned territorial complexes such as Silicon Valley in the United States, science cities such as Daejeon in Korea, technology parks such as Sophia Antipolis in France, twenty-six technopoles spread through Japan, and large metro areas around the globe, including more established ones such as London and Tokyo and newer ones such as Seville, Spain, and Adelaide, Australia. They identify four foundational elements: a determined administration; liminal individuals at the edge of different worlds, such as the business and academic worlds; an environment of innovation; and easy access to venture capital.

We can also consider regional economic dynamics from the perspective of stage of product and profit cycles. A product cycle is the development of a brand new product. At early stages of a product cycle, when new products are just being created, it is important to be close to research and development. Sales, shown in red in Figure 8.5, go through a steep rise during the growth and maturity phases and then drop off. Profits, shown in the shallower curve, are negative until the growth period. Innovation occurs in the more specialized regions, but as the products became more standardized the crucial locational component is less closeness to innovation and more reducing labor costs. Consider the case of typewriters, for example, which were introduced in the early twentieth century but then declined by the end of the century as computers replaced them. Typewriting manufacturing shifted from the early specialized centers where labor was expensive, such as Syracuse, New York, to closer but cheaper labor areas such as Cortland, New York, to extremely cheap labor areas in Mexico before finally becoming obsolete. Similarly, today, while new computer technologies are generated in Silicon Valley, the production of actual computer chips can occur in newly industrializing regions with good infrastructure and cheap labor, such as Thailand. In the early stages of product development, when super profits can be made, new firms are attracted

8.5 Product and profit cycles

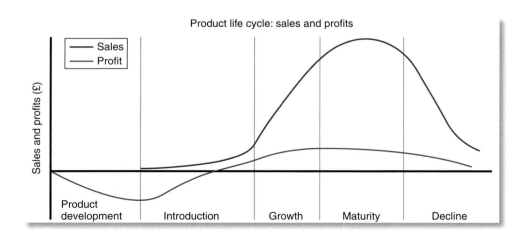

Box 8.2 TRANSNATIONAL CORPORATIONS

There are four ideal types of transnational corporations (TNCs):

- *multinational*, with decentralized organizational structure that operates as a series of semi-independent entities;
- *international*, controlled from one central headquarters with overseas operations as appendages;
- *global*, in which a centralized hub implements parent-company strategies to reach a global market;
- *integrated network* of complex, globally integrated operations.

We can get some idea of the range by considering three TNCs: Nike, Starbucks, and Toyota. Nike is a sportswear and equipment company that exhibits characteristics of the integrated network. In 2011 its revenue was $20.6 billion. Nike does not make any goods directly. There are no Nike factories. The company buys goods from factory owners and then sells them to consumers. In the early years of the company, the factories were in Japan; then, as labor costs increased in Japan, by the early 1980s most Nike shoes were made in South Korea, and the city of Pusan became the capital of Asian shoe manufacturing. Since then Nike has further reduced its costs by having shoes made in China, Indonesia, and Vietnam, where labor costs per worker were only $100 a month. Indonesia is now one of the largest suppliers of Nike shoes: seventeen factories employ 90,000 workers, producing around 7 million pairs of shoes. In South China, the center of shoe manufacturing is the city of Guangzhou. Just outside the city, one shoe factory, used by Nike, makes 35,000 shoes a day.

Toyota is an automotive company headquartered in Japan but with factories around the world and a global workforce of over 300,000. It strongly exhibits characteristics of the international and integrated network. Toyota emerged in the 1930s and produced its first car in 1935. It made cars in Japan but wanted to sell them abroad. The problem was that many countries, especially those with their own auto industries, put up tariff walls to protect domestic producers. In order to jump these tariff walls, Toyota established manufacturing plants in selected countries. It became a multinational company headquartered in Japan but with manufacturing plants around the world. Unlike Nike, it retained direct control of the factories producing its products. Over the years they established a reputation for reliable, well-made cars that ranged from budget to luxury. A successful global brand was established, and in 2008 it became the world's largest automaker and the fifth largest company in the world, with significant market shares in North America, Asia, and Africa and smaller shares in Europe. It makes around 8 million vehicles a year, with manufacturing and assembly plants in twenty-seven different countries. Toyota has five major plants in the United States. Although a global company, Toyota is still anchored in Japan. The company is headquartered there, and the very senior management tends to be Japanese. As late as 2008, almost 5.1 million of the 8.5 million vehicles were produced in Japan. The explicit desire to become the world's number one automaker was an ambitious one. This drive to global dominance is, according to many analysts, the root of its recall problems in 2009–2010, when over 8.3 million vehicles were recalled for either accelerator or braking problems or both. The rapid increase in production perhaps outstripped quality control and the ability of engineers and managers to carefully scrutinize new

Box 8.2   CONTINUED

model developments for design problems and associated safety issues. The problems were widely reported. A global company also gets global publicity when things go wrong.

The first Starbucks opened in 1971 with a small storefront cafe in Seattle. Its globalization is relatively recent. The first store outside the United States opened in Tokyo in 1996. By 2010, Starbucks had 16,858 stores in fifty-two countries and a global workforce of over 130,000. Starbucks cafes have remarkable similarity around the world. There are few nods to local particularity or national differences. In some cases, the generic nature creates backlash. There was early difficulty breaking into European markets, and Italy is still a holdout—a country with thousands of coffee bars, but no Starbucks.

What Starbucks has done is less to meet a demand than to create a demand. Starbucks now embodies a global coffee culture, sometimes building on existing cultural traditions, in other places creating them anew. It has become a third place between home and workplace where socializing and telecommuting, as much as coffee drinking, occur—a meeting place as much as a selling place. While in some places it signifies US cultural dominance, in others it is perceived as a symbol of modernity.

References

Dicken, P. (2011) *Global Shift: Mapping the Changing Contours of the World Economy*. 6th ed. New York: Guildford.

to the location of the initial innovation, but as more firms enter the markets new spatial forces are at work and firms may relocate closer to markets or away from higher-wage areas in order to maintain and increase profitability.

As an example of regional differences, we can consider the new geography of employment in the United States. Enrico Moretti identifies a divergence from around the mid-1980s, when selected cities with propulsive economic sectors kept attracting more growth and generating higher-wage jobs. Meanwhile, certain urban regions failed to attract new growth and were unable to replace the jobs lost by deindustrialization. In these declining urban regions, wage levels dropped and the more mobile and higher-skilled workers left. For urban regional economies to be successful, they need to constantly push up the steep slope of innovation adoption, which requires expertise, education, and knowledge. The more the national economy shifts towards a knowledge-based economy, the more the differences became marked between those regions that attract and those that fail to attract these sectors. There are now three types of economic regions in the United States:

* the brain hubs of a well-educated labor force, higher wages, and innovation;
* dying manufacturing hubs of deindustrializing cities;
* city regions in the middle that could go either way.

THE STATE

Economic globalization is creating a more integrated global economy, but even in this new world of interconnections and transactions that span the globe, the state still remains important. Many firms operate within national markets, and national regulations play an important role in shaping the economic decision-making context.

The state is not a singular organization but a collection of different institutions and agencies. Sometimes their interests coincide, other times they collide. The US Department of Defense, for example, wants to maintain a large and expensive military presence funded by the government. The US Treasury, in contrast, is concerned with controlling government expenditure. The clashes are resolved through the political process.

The state shapes economic geographies. Within the nation's borders, the state has fiscal powers of taxation and spending, currency control, fixing exchange rates, and setting interest rates. Increasing interest rates, for example, slows down industries such as house building that rely on long lines of credit. Lowering interest rates in turn can stimulate such industries.

The state sets the regulatory framework, which affects economic activity. The economic geographer Jamie Peck examines the political economy of workfare, the welfare-to-work initiatives that have developed since the 1990s. He traces the development of workfare policies in Canada, the United States, and the United Kingdom and shows that workfare is not so much concerned with creating jobs as with deterring welfare claims and facilitating the acceptance of low-paying jobs.

The state also has a role in shaping the connection between national economies and the global economy. At one extreme are the closed economies that limit trade and economic connection with the outside world; examples include Cambodia under the Khmer Rouge and present-day North Korea. Such instances are rare, because global trade is the lifeblood of most national economies. At the other extreme are more loosely regulated economies that facilitate penetration by foreign capital. Most countries fall somewhere between the two.

The governments of developing countries, seeking to support the industrialization of the national economy, follow either an import substitution strategy in which they protect local industry or an export-oriented form of industrialization. The former is associated with protectionism, while the latter is linked to the ideology of free trade. One dominant view is that countries develop through the adoption of free-trade policies. In a provocative argument, Ha-Joon Chang argues for protectionism rather than free trade. He claims that promotion of a free-trade strategy works against the development interests of national economies. Protectionism allows local firms to grow and prosper by borrowing ideas and techniques from more efficient producers. Since the rise of Britain, most countries, even successful one such as the United States, have competed initially with forms of protectionism for local industries. More recently, the spectacular success of countries such as South Korea has been based on protecting local industries before they became internationally competitive.

The empirical evidence suggests that more open trade leads to rising per capita income. However, per capita income is a crude measure that does not measure the distribution of income, merely the average. The evidence on income distribution is inconclusive. There are examples of countries where income inequality actually increased in the wake of trade liberalization: Argentina, Chile, Colombia, Costa Rica, and Uruguay all saw increasing inequality. In the United States, the declining incomes of the middle class are commonly linked to open trade policies.

The development state is the name given to countries that have successfully crafted their economic policies to move from the periphery of the global economy closer to the core. The term implies a state that is focused on economic development. Examples include Japan, South Korea, and China. While they adopted a variety of different measures, they all pursued strong government control that aided specific industries, protection of domestic industries in the early years, infrastructure enhancement, spending on education, and a strong commitment to export-led growth.

The most dramatic and recent example is China. The China model, which consists of directing public spending to foster infrastructure improvement and educational attainment, while lacking democratic accountability, was spectacularly successful in raising 600 million people from chronic poverty in less than two decades.

The development state was primarily an East Asian phenomenon, and that raises the question whether it is transferable. Francis Fukuyama argues that there are limits to this transferability, as the model is culturally specific to Confucian societies with a meritocracy in public service, a heavy emphasis on education, and a deference to authority. His argument would seem to be undermined by the relative success of countries like Brazil that have different traditions from East Asian societies but are still achieving economic growth.

Does the development state have to be authoritarian? In the early years of industrialization, this tends to be the case, and modernization does not necessarily lead to democratization but may make democratization more possible. The more developed and richer a country becomes, with wealth widely spread, the more it tends to move further to the democratic end of the political spectrum.

The development state can achieve spectacular success as public and private interests are focused on the same goal of achieving rapid growth. However, the reliance on export-led growth makes the economies vulnerable to global shocks.

CONSUMERS

We can make a distinction between different types of capitalist economy. In the nineteenth and early twentieth century, capitalist economies were based on the production of commodities and the majority of people were relatively poor. Beginning in the United States, in the 1920s, a new economy emerged based on the mass production and mass consumption of goods. In societies of high mass consumption, the consumer emerges as an important element in the making of economic

Box 8.3 THE PROMISE AND REALITY OF NEOLIBERALISM

One set of economic ideas has circulated widely around the world. Neoliberalism is an economic ideology that promotes deregulation, minimal or small government, low taxation, and free trade. It has a number of strands, a long history, and now pervasive adoption by governments and economic elites all around the world. Classical economists of the eighteenth century, such as Adam Smith, believed in the invisible hand of the market to make things work. More recently, it is part of a broader shift in economic ideologies away from the New Deal Keynesianism that dominated from the 1930s to the late 1970s. Theorists of neoliberalism included Friedrich Hayek (1899–1992), who, in his 1944 book *The Road to Serfdom*, argued against centralized government planning. Milton Friedman (1912–2006), a Nobel Prize–winning economist, also lauded the virtues of free markets and small, limited governments. His book, *Free to Choose*, published in 1980, linked individual freedoms with functioning markets and restrained governments. In this restated neoliberalism, unregulated markets were the solution and governments were the problem.

The neoliberal promotes an agenda of privatization of public goods and services, of reduced taxes especially for the wealthy, of reduced governmental commitment to the welfare of its ordinary citizens, and of emphasis on enhancing corporate profitability and improving business competitiveness. This agenda's core proposition is that deregulated markets will increase economic growth and raise living standards. Neoliberalism as a political theory has the benefits of being simple, easily understood, and even easier to articulate. As a political practice, however, its greatest difficulty lies in implementation when it comes up against the brute realities of mature markets dominated by powerful sectional interests. These interests promote free trade when it meets their needs but not when it

undercuts their power and market share. The tenets of neoliberalism are breached regularly in the face of political realities. Elaborate subsidies and tariff barriers, for example, maintain agricultural producers in the developed world. While efficient Japanese carmakers want free trade, inefficient Japanese rice farmers do not. The US financial services sector wants to penetrate foreign markets, yet the US agricultural lobby funds the erection of import-blocking tariffs.

The neoliberal agenda is promoted by global systems of governance. Both the International Monetary Fund and the World Trade Organization, for example, promote neoliberal economic policies. Around its central ideological core, there are subsidiary ideas about accountability, choice, competition, incentives, and performance. Neoliberalism is also a political process that recasts citizens as consumers, reimagines states less as providers of public services and more as promoters of private growth, and shifts governance issues from citizen entitlements to consumer choices. In full-blown neoliberalism, markets trump the state, capital wins out over organized labor, consumers replace citizens, and market choice replaces citizen rights. The private market and the accompanying individual consumerism are enthroned as the means and measure of success.

There are sites of resistance and narratives of dissent. There has been the development of a global discourse of human rights, environmental protection, and shared projects of poverty reduction. An alternative global vision to neoliberalism is emerging.

References

Dumenil, G. and Levy, D. (2011) *The Crisis of Neoliberalism*. Cambridge, MA: Harvard University Press

Harvery, D. (2007) *A Brief History of Neoliberalism*. New York: Oxford University Press.

Steger, M. and Roy, R. K. (2010) *Neoliberalism: A Very Short Introduction*. New York: Oxford University Press.

geographies. Consumer spending in the United States is now responsible for two-thirds of all economic activity. There are many implications in the enthronement of the consumer. I will discuss only five.

First, as consumer spending shifts from meeting basic requirements to discretionary spending, desire rather than need becomes a more important driver of consumption. Consumers have to be persuaded to buy things, and this basic fact is the reason behind the growth and emergence of advertising and promotion of goods. While we may want clothes, we have to be persuaded to buy particular brands. Consumption is now tied to the creation of identities and the pursuit of lifestyles. To buy a pair of sunglasses is to shield your eyes form the sun, but to buy a pair of Ray-Bans is to evoke other images and make other claims. Consumption is now tied to aspirations, images, and desires as much as to basic needs and requirements.

Second, forms of consumption are markers of social status and social difference. People are not only distinguished by how much they have but by what they have and how they use it. Forms of consumption mark different levels of society. While all middle-income groups can have a beach holiday, only the richer can afford a Caribbean vacation, and only the very rich can rent a villa in St. Bart's. Luxury fever can filter down the income scale as the consumption trends of the very rich become embedded in popular consciousness.

Third, the full flowering of a society of high mass consumption is predicated upon access to credit so that consumers can buy big-ticket items. The rise of credit to lubricate mass consumption has its upside, as it enables purchase before the full price is saved. It also has its downsides, as it makes the economy vulnerable to credit squeezes. That is what happened after the 2008 meltdown as many housing consumers in the United States had extended credit on homes that were depreciating in value. Unable to gain access to any more credit, the economy spluttered and declined as demand fell. The more consumer spending is reliant on credit, the more the economy is vulnerable to credit crises.

Fourth, the economic geography of places is shaped by the places of consumption. As shopping becomes an increasingly important social and economic activity, the the retail sites become bigger. The typical mall has increased in size and scope. The mall is the cathedral of consumerism, an alternative retail environment where consumers are enticed, entertained, and encased in a totalizing retail space.

Retail establishments are clustered together. We can understand this phenomenon with reference to Hotelling's Law, named after the economist Harold Hotelling and his classic paper, first published in 1929. The law states that it is rational for producers to make products similar to their competitors. If we substitute retailers for producers, then the law explains the clustering of retail distributions. Assume a straight street. If there is only one coffee shop, the owner is indifferent to location anywhere along the street. But if there are two or more coffee shops, it is more rational for them to be together at the center of the street, drawing upon 50 percent of the street's coffee drinkers. Retail establishments cluster together because it makes rational economic sense even for providers of the same product, because otherwise they might lose customers (see Figure 8.6). That is why a Burger King and a McDonald's are often close together when you turn off the highway. Even retailers with different merchandise cluster, because they get the extra advantage of possible market capture of consumers of other producers. That is why you often find a Starbucks clustered with the two hamburger sellers.

Finally, there is the growing dominance of retailers over producers. Traditionally, manufacturers made things, and then sold them to retailers who sold them to customers. Retailers were simply in the middle, buying goods from producers and then selling them to customers. But with the rise of the big-box retailer and a more flexible production system, with many small companies producing small runs of goods relatively quickly, power shifts from the large number of small manufacturers to the small number of larger retailers. The very large retailers have such enormous power that they can force producers to compete with each other to meet strict cost limits. Manufacturers are willing to do this because access to a big retailer assures a large customer base. The lower price per item is offset by the higher turnover of items. Take the case of Wal-Mart, which in 2012 had 10,130 stores in over fifteen countries. Wal-Mart uses its enormous leverage to drive down the prices of the manufacturers who supply these stores. Wal-Mart reduced the price of goods by relying on producers from low-wage countries, thus pushing North American producers to reduce their costs. A number of North American producers have offshored their production to reduce costs in order to sell to Wal-Mart. Wal-Mart and stores like it are a major cause for the shift in manufacturing to lower-wage regions.

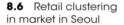

8.6 Retail clustering in market in Seoul

Wal-Mart uses its market power to reduce costs, leading to more offshoring and more imported goods from cheap-labor regions, which in turn leads to fewer jobs and lower incomes in the formerly richer regions and consequently lower wages, forcing more people to seek deals at Wal-Mart. While big-box retailers reduce costs and increase productivity, there is also the associated downward spiral of job loss and wage reduction.

LABOR

An important, though often neglected, element of economic geography is labor. The capital-labor relationship is crucial to the modern economy. Capital seeks to keep the costs of labor down and uses its influence over the state to ensure legislation that minimizes the costs and power of labor. Labor in turn seeks to organize in order to have bargaining power to raise wages and improve working conditions (see Figure 8.7). Changes in economic geography can in part be understood in relation to capital-labor relations. The suburbanization of industry was a response to the growing power of labor within cities. The shift of car manufacturers from Detroit and Michigan to the southern states was a move by capital to reduce the costs and power of labor. More recently, the global shift in manufacturing is in part a move to cheaper regions of the world with less organized labor, such as China.

8.7 This poster in Sydney, Australia, is a reminder that work on this construction site is only possible with a union card.

There is a geography of labor that includes the importance of the geography of labor legislation, the political geography of union organizing, and the power of place. The geographer Andy Herod, for example, provides examples of how organized labor impacts and influences the geography of capitalism with reference to selected case studies of garment workers, steel workers, and dockworkers.

The overall nature of the capital-labor relationship has shifted. From the 1930s to the 1980s, organized labor in the Europe and North America was powerful and played an important role in creating public policies that guaranteed relatively high levels of social welfare. Skilled labor was in short supply and so could use its bargaining power to increase both wages and what is termed the social wage, the range of social benefits provided by the state. There were national variations in the affluent West, with social welfare levels significantly higher in the Scandinavian democracies than in the United States. Since the 1980s, the power of labor has been weakened by global shift and mechanization. The deindustrialization of the economies has led to a weakening of organized labor and a resultant shift in capital-labor relations, with wages stagnating and welfare provisions being cut back.

The basic geographic difference that strengthens capital and weakens labor is differential mobility. Capital is freer to roam the globe in the search for profitable investments. Labor, in contrast, is more fixed in place, unable to freely move across national borders. Mobile capital has more power in a globalizing economy than a labor force more fixed in space.

And here we come to a paradox. Even as firms and companies seek to minimize labor costs, the high-mass-consumption economies need consumers to have enough disposable income to buy goods and services. This is the Wal-Mart economy, where companies pay low wages but then have to provide cheaper goods. The goods are cheap because the wages of the producers are low.

Labor is not just an economic entity. It is embodied in people. An important element of the new economic geography considers how social differences are reinforced, undermined, and contested in the workplace. Who works in what jobs and how much they are paid is not a simple labor market process but a wider economic and social differentiator. There is considerable work on ethnicity, for example, that examines ethnic economies, where workers in one sector or trade share common ethnicity, and the geography of ethnic networks and the connection between ethnic networks and accelerating economic globalization. Geraldine Pratt explores the geography of Filipina domestic workers in Vancouver, Canada. Women from a variety of occupations were restricted through immigration laws, that did not recognize their national qualifications, to the domestic service sector.

There has also been a fruitful infusion of feminist perspectives into economic geography. Gender relations intertwine with uneven development, globalization, locational strategies, and employment practices. Issues such as the feminization of poverty, the dominance of young women in the factories of coastal China, the feminization of domestic service, and the double bind that affects many women as they work both outside and inside the home all highlight the close connections between

8.8 Informal employment in Panama

gender, work, and the economy. The workplace is structured with distinct sexualized and gendered scripts. Gender relations are created and contested in the workplace.

Households get by through use of the different sectors of the economy. The getting-by strategies available to a household will depend on the resources. A household with a large income from the formal economy will not have to sell cigarettes on the street corner. A household with few formal opportunities, in contrast, has to look at alternative sources. Households with few formal opportunities either from the market or the state have to rely on the informal economy.

At the very bottom are the poor, who have to be creative in their survival strategies (see Figure 8.8). Around 40 percent of the world's population lives on less than $2 a day. One billion people live on less than $1.25 per day. Lacking income, they are trapped in extreme poverty. One proposed solution is the use of microcredit—lending small amounts to people to provide them the financial means to become more self-reliant. Muhammad Yunus pioneered the use of microloans in Bangladesh. One study looked at the detailed diaries of 250 households in Bangladesh, India, and South Africa. It was clear that the problem is not only the meager income but the unpredictable and irregular nature of that income, which makes saving and planning very difficult. One proposal is to shift emphasis from the encouragement of microfinance toward easier access to savings opportunities.

CAPITAL

"Capital" has a number of meanings. In the standard literature, it is used to refer to real assets such as factories, property, and machinery, or financial assets such as bonds, securities, and stocks. But this is only the physical expression; capital is also a social relationship.

The mobility of capital has been reinforced by changes in production. In the Fordist model, plants were huge, fixed capital investments. Bargaining between capital and labor thus took place against a fixed location. More recently, a more flexible form of production has been introduced. Nike, for example, has no shoe factories and no Nike workers. Nike's shoes are made under contract by a range of shoe manufactures. Factories compete to obtain Nike orders and are then licensed by Nike if they are capable of making shoes to cost and design specifications. The old model of manufacturers making things and retailers simply selling them has been replaced by the power of retailers and brands. Now retailers tell the manufacturers what to produce. Contracts are for short-run lines rather than long-run batches. This just-in-time production system ensures that goods are made to meet demand. Just-in-time, flexible production allows low prices and high turnover. It also means a marked change in capital-labor relations. Capital is now hypermobile. Workers in one factory cannot bargain in the same effective way that the workers of the old Ford system could. Capital is no longer fixed in place. Retailers can move their production contracts to another factory in another country. While capital can roam the world, labor is fixed in place. The result is an uneven bargaining arrangement.

Capitalism is a dynamic, crisis-laden economic system with tremendous vitality. Perhaps the most sustained geographical analysis of capital as a social relationship is the work of David Harvey, who since 1973 has been developing a historical geography of capitalism. In his 2010 book *The Enigma of Capital,* he considers the global circulation of capital. In particular, he outlines the recurring crises of capitalism. In order for the system to continue, money needs to be mobilized and invested, technology employed, nature exploited, labor assembled, and credit made available. At any of these stages, problems may occur; there may be lack of money to make suitable investments, technological innovation may undermine profitability, labor may become too powerful and demand too much in wages, environmental costs may restrict growth, or access to credit may dry up. A profit squeeze or credit crisis can cause blockages in the smooth functioning of the system. In fact, smooth functioning is rare. Capitalism is capable of amazing growth and innovating, but it is subject to recurring crises and continual turmoil as the crisis solved in one area became a crisis in another area. The globalization of capitalism has kept the system going but widened the opportunity for recurring crises across the globe.

NONGOVERNMENT AGENCIES

Certain nongovernment agencies are important actors in the global economy. Three in particular have great influence: the International Monetary Fund (IMF), the World Bank, and the World Trade Organization (WTO). The IMF was initially set up to provide monetary and currency stability so as to enhance world trade. By 2012 the IMF had 188 members. Each member country contributes a certain sum of money as a credit deposit. Collectively, these deposits provide a pool of money from which members may draw. The IMF acts like an international credit union for states. A country's deposits determine how much it can draw upon, known as "special drawing rights," and its voting power. The rich countries dominate the IMF, as they contribute most of the funds and set the agenda through their voting power. The IMF wields its power through its surveillance system and the strings it attaches to lending. Surveillance (the term used by the IMF) involves monitoring of a member's economic policies and evaluation of their economy. One example: South Korea asked for IMF assistance on 21 November 1997 in the wake of depleted

Box 8.4   THE CHANGING CONCERNS OF ECONOMIC GEOGRAPHY

The subdiscipline of economic geography has undergone important shifts as economic geographers look at the economy in different ways. Early work, produced at time of industrial growth, focused on theories of industrial location. One of the earliest studies was Alfred Marshall's *Principle of Economics,* which first appeared in 1891. A strong German contribution is embodied in Albert Weber's *Theory of the Location of Industries* (1909) and August Losch's *The Economics of Location* (1939). By the middle of the twentieth century, a body of work sought to explain the location of industry through looking at the various factors of production from the standpoint of the individual enterprises. Estall and Buchanan (1961) discuss the role of various factors, including materials, markets and transfer costs, energy sources, labor and capital, technological change, and the role of government. In their case study of iron and steel, for example, they point to the pull effects of coal (declining) iron ore, material assembly, market, capital, and labor as well as the importance of inertia.

Critics of standard industrial location theory pointed to the assumption of perfect economic rationality. Decision-makers, in the models at least, had all the necessary information and were blessed with perfect rationality. Scholars pointed to the need to incorporate suboptimal decision-making and satisfying rather than maximizing behavior. Critics also pointed to the emphasis on single-plant, single-product establishments and raised the need for a fuller understanding of agglomerations, corporate context, and multinational transactions. An institutional approach emerged that stressed the interaction between firms rather than the behaviors of individual firms and showed that location was the result of complex negotiation and bargaining with a variety of other agents in a wider social and political context.

The concerns of economic geographers have also widened. Some economic geographers have utilized evolutionary economics to refine location and relocation theories. A Marxist political economy approach is often invoked to explain how uneven development is an essential part of capitalist economies. A new economic geography now locates economic processes in deeper social, cultural, and political contexts in the exploration of themes such as commodity chains, technology and agglomeration, commodification of the environment, and the role of knowledge-based economies and creativity in regional and city development.

References

Boschma, R. and Frenken, K. (2011) The Emerging Empirics of Evolutionary Economic Geography. *Journal of Economic Geography* 11: 295–307.

Barnes, T. J., Peck, J., and Sheppard. E. (eds) (2012) *The Wiley-Blackwell Companion to Economic Geography.* Oxford: Wiley-Blackwell.

Estall, R. C. and Buchanan, R. O. (1961) *Industrial Activity and Economic Geography,* London: Hutchinson.

Krugman, P. (2011) The New Economic Geography, Now Middle-Aged. *Regional Studies* 45: 1–7.

foreign reserves and rising short-term loans. The IMF agreed to lend $56 billion and in exchange asked for an economic adjustment package that depressed economic growth, caused unemployment, cut government spending, led to a decline in living standards, and allowed more access for foreign financial institutions. The IMF imposed market principles and freer international trade on Korean society. The IMF's argument was that South Korea's problems were due to lack of transparency in financial dealings, a bloated public sector, and a job market that ensured jobs rather than productivity.

The World Bank was created in 1944. Its initial name, the International Bank for Reconstruction and Development (IBRD), describes its role. It was a fund established to aid the reconstruction of Europe, and its first loan was $250 million to a war-damaged France. Once Europe got back on its feet, the Bank widened its remit. The first loan to a developing country was $13.5 million given to Chile in 1948 for a hydroelectric scheme.

The World Bank now has almost universal membership. Like the IMF, it was and still is dominated by the rich countries. In response to criticism, both internal and external, from both the developing and developed world, from both private investors angry at delays and administrative snafus and aid workers upset at corruption and inefficiency, the World Bank in 1989 shifted its emphasis to eradicating world poverty with more carefully assessed and monitored development schemes.

The World Trade Organization (WTO) is the latest version of what was originally called the General Agreement on Tariffs and Trade (GATT), established in 1948 as a forum for stimulating world trade by reducing customs duties and lowering trade barriers. GATT was a forum for getting rid of protectionism. The first round of multilateral discussions, held between 1948 and 1967, led to some tariff reductions. The long-drawn-out nature of the discussions led many commentators to suggest that the acronym stood for General Agreement to Talk and Talk. The most decisive round was the Uruguay round, 1986 to 1994, which established new rules for trade in services and intellectual property, new forms of dispute settlement, and trade policy reviews, as well as the creation of the WTO in 1995. The Doha round began in 2001 and is not yet concluded. WTO now has 159 members which together account for 97 percent of the world's trade. China became a full member in 2000. Membership in the WTO is vital to countries seeking access to global markets. But this access comes at a price. For the stronger economies, free trade can mean access to new markets, especially for banking and cultural economies, but it can also mean the decline of traditional industries. For the weaker economies, membership signifies access to the large consumer markets of the rich world, but can mean an inability to control the fate of traditionally protected industries. Membership in WTO implies a willingness to shape national economic policy around the principle of free global trade.

Cited References

Hall, P. and Castells, M. (1994) *Technopoles of the World: The Making of 21st Century Industrial Complexes.* New York: Routledge.

Chang, H.-J. (2007) *Bad Samarians: The Myth of Free Trade and the Secret History of Capitalism.* London: Bloomsbury Press.

Daryl, C., Morduch, J., Rutherford, S., and Ruthven, O. (2009) *Portfolios of the Poor: How the World's Poor Live on $2 a Day.* Princeton: Princeton University Press.

Diamond, J. M. (1998) *Guns, Germs and Steel: A Short History of Everybody for the Last 13,000 Years.* New York: Vintage.

Fukuyama, F. (2012) The Future of History. *Foreign Affairs,* January-February, pp. 53–61.

Harvey, D. (2010) *The Enigma of Capital and the Crises of Capitalism.* London: Profile.

Herod, A. (1998) *Labor Geographies: Workers and the Landscapes of Capitalism.* New York: Guilford Press.

Hotelling, H. (1929) Stability in Competition. *Economic Journal* 39: 41–57.

Moretti, E. (2012) *The New Geography of Jobs.* Boston: Houghton Mifflin.

Pratt, G. (1999) From Registered Nurse to Registered Nanny: Discursive Geographies of Filipina Domestic Workers in Vancouver, BC. *Economic Geography* 75: 215–236.

Peck, J. (2001) *Workfare States.* New York: Guilford Press.

Rostow, W. W. (1990) *The Stages of Economic Growth: A Non-Communist Manifesto.* 3rd ed. Cambridge, UK, and New York: Cambridge University Press.

Select Guide to Further Reading

Allen, R. C. (2011) *Global Economic History: A Very Short Introduction.* Oxford: Oxford University Press.

Acemoglu, D. and Robinson, J. (2012) *Why Nations Fail: The Origins of Power, Prosperity, and Poverty.* New York: Crown.

Chant, S. (ed) (2010) *The International Handbook of Gender and Poverty: Concepts, Research, Policy.* Cheltenham, UK: Edward Elgar.

Escobar, A. (2011) *Encountering Development: The Making and Unmaking of the Third World.* Princeton, NJ: Princeton University Press.

Frank, A. G. (1966) *The Development of Underdevelopment.* New England Free Press.

Inglehart, R. and Welzel, C. (2005) *Modernization, Cultural Change, and Democracy: The Human Development Sequence.* Cambridge, UK, and New York: Cambridge University Press.

Jessop, B. and Sum, N.-G. (2006) *Beyond The Regulation Approach: Putting Capitalist Economies in Place.* Cheltenham, UK: Edward Elgar.

Landes, D. S. (1999) *The Wealth and Poverty of Nations: Why Some Are So Rich and Some So Poor.* New York: Norton.

Leyshon, A., Lee, R., McDowell, L., and Sunley, P. (eds.) (2011) *The SAGE Handbook of Economic Geography.* London: Sage.

Smith, N. (2008) *Uneven Development: Nature, Capital and the Production of Space.* 3rd ed. Athens: University of Georgia Press.

Wood, A. and Roberts, S. M. (2011) *Economic Geography: Places, Networks and Flows.* London: Routledge.

On economic and historical discussions of the core-periphery model, see

Krugman, P. (1991) Increasing Returns and Economic Geography. *Journal of Political Economy* 99: 483–499.

Wallerstein, I. (1974) *The Modern World System.* Vol. 1. New York: Academic Press.

Wallerstein, I. (1980) *The Modern World System.* Vol. 2. New York: Academic Press.

Wallerstein, I. (1989) *The Modern World System.* Vol. 3. San Diego: Academic Press.

Websites

International Institute for Environment and Development
http://www.iied.org
The International Labor Office
http://www.ilo.org/global/lang--en/index.htm
The IMF
http://www.imf.org/external/index.htm
The World Bank
http://www.worldbank.org
The World Trade Organization
http://www.wto.org

PART 4

The Global Organization of Space

In this section, we will look at the emergence of a global society through the global flows of economic transactions and cultural interactions. Chapter 9 considers the rise of the global economy, explores the idea of space-time convergence, and considers the pace and geography of economic globalization. Chapter 10 examines the formation of global and local cultures in the transmission of language, architecture, and religion.

9

Creating a Global Economy

In this chapter, we focus on the creation of a global economy. In many of the current discussions of globalization, one common assumption is that it is a recent phenomenon. In this reading, globalization goes hand in hand with the construction of the modern world. However, while its pace has increased, globalization is long established as a continuing process of the human occupancy of the globe. Our focus in this chapter is the growing economic interaction between peoples and societies spread around the globe. We will consider this interaction through three related topics: space-time convergence, waves of globalization, and the question "how flat is the world?"

SPACE-TIME CONVERGENCE

Space-time convergence is a collapse in the time it takes to cover distance. This convergence, both cause and effect of widening economic transactions, reduces the cost of transporting goods and people and pulls places closer together. A series of space-time convergences caused by new developments in transportation effectively brought the world closer together. The very first was the invention of the wheel, which allowed more goods to be effectively transported. The wheel was invented around five thousand years ago, appearing at a number of sites in the Middle East and Europe around the same time. The earliest wheeled vehicles had to move over rough surfaces that made movement slow and difficult. The full flowering of the advantages of the wheel had to await the creation of smoother transport surfaces.

For centuries, the easiest way to move people and goods long distance was across water. Natural wind could power sailing ships. Initially, most seaborne trade was limited by navigational knowledge. The development of the compass around 1280 enabled sailors to plot their direction more accurately, thus reducing the time and therefore the cost of long-distance sea travel. Equipped with a compass, sailors could now venture out more confidently from the enclosed seas of the Baltic and the Mediterranean to travel across the wider oceans. There were geopolitical consequences. The Roman Empire, for example, was essentially restricted to the extended basin of the Mediterranean because it had limited ability to sail across the wider seas. But, equipped with a compass, the early modern traders of Europe could venture across the Atlantic and round the Horn of Africa. Maritime empires such as the Spanish, Portuguese, and British were established and developed because the compass made it easier to move across the distant seas and expansive oceans.

Improvements in navigation made it quicker, safer, and hence cheaper to sail across the oceans. Sea travel also avoided the frictions of distance imposed by traveling through different societies, separate countries, and competing empires. The neutrality of the open sea aided long-distance trade and commerce. Because most long-distance trade for the past five hundred years occurred by sea, economic activity is still concentrated in coastal regions and in (current and former) port cities. London and New York, for example, grew as major cities in part because their economies were invigorated by their port status. Amsterdam grew from a small watery town to a major city as the Dutch commercial empire spread tentacles across the globe. Port cities also took on a more cosmopolitan feel, filled as they were with exotic goods and foreign peoples. The big commercial ports connected with a world wider than their immediate hinterlands; they had an openness to the wider world. When Peter the Great wanted to modernize Russia, he created, in 1703, the new city of St. Petersburg, located on the Baltic and therefore more open to foreign influences and international trade. He moved the capital from the interior city of Moscow to create a window on Europe.

The earliest cargo of long-distance maritime global trade was limited to luxury goods and prized items. When transport is costly, it is only economically feasible to concentrate on high-priced items. Early trade between Europe and East Asia, for example, focused on such expensive goods as spices, highly prized for their ability to season food in an era before refrigeration. In the seventeenth century, a pound of nutmeg purchased in the Spice Islands of Southeast Asia cost 60,000 times more when sold in a London market. The spice islands of Banda and Run became vital resources fought over by Portugal, Holland, and England; they also become significant features of European maps of the region. Figure 9.1 is from a map of Southeast Asia in a 1636 Mercator-Hondius atlas. The Spice Islands are disproportionately large, a reflection of their economic importance at the time.

When the age of steam replaced the age of sail in maritime transport, there was an extra tug on the shrinking net of space-time. Around 1890, steamships moved more tonnage than sailing ships. The increasing use of steam allowed bigger ships to carry more goods more quickly and more cheaply. In 1850 it took between eighteen and twenty-four days to sail from Liverpool to Gibraltar. A steamship could make the same journey in between seven and nine days. Not only was steam quicker, it was more reliable, less dependent on the vagaries of the wind. Steam meant faster, more reliable, and more predictable transport times. Highly prized goods and commodities no longer dominated international trade as the declining transport cost per unit "smoothed out" the globe as a transportation surface for ever-cheaper goods and commodities.

Transport developments created new geographies that made the operation of comparative advantage more feasible. Comparative advantage refers to the ability of a region or country to produce goods at lower cost than other areas. Comparative advantage works best when the unit costs of transport are low. With a smoother transportation surface and cheaper transport costs, the mechanisms of global comparative advantage generate new economic geographies. It thus became

9.1 The Spice Islands

more efficient in the late nineteenth century to grow wheat in the United States than in Britain, because the cost of land in particular, and in some cases labor, was so much less. Steamships made it profitable for grain grown in the United States and other distant places, such as Australia, to be shipped to meet demand in Europe.

Before the railways, inland canals were an important transport artery for reducing overland transport costs. Take the case of the Erie Canal, begun in 1817 and completed in 1825: it cut a straight, watery line through the 363 miles between Buffalo and Albany and connected the Great Lakes with New York City (Figure 9.2). The canal compressed space-time. Before the Canal opened, it could take up to twenty days to travel between Buffalo and New York City. After the canal opened, it took less than four days. The cost of moving a ton of freight plummeted from $100 a ton to $5 a ton. Twenty miles either side of the canal, the equivalent of a day's wagon ride, the local economy was transformed. Along the path of the canal, villages turned into towns and towns into cities as local economies were now linked to larger national and global markets. Goods, people, and ideas flowed along the route of the canal. But just as the canal was creating its greatest impact, a new form of transportation compressed space and time even more. The coming of the railways reduced travel time from Buffalo to New York City still more. Goods moved along the canal at around fifty-five miles a day; the railway covered that distance in an hour. The railway could also travel year-round, whereas the canal froze over in wintry upstate New York. By 1850 more freight was being carried on rail than on the canal. The canal soon became obsolete, replaced as a major means of transport by the railroads, and towns along the canal soon withered. Some towns, such as Syracuse, which were located on both the canal and the railway line, grafted new railway-connected growth onto canal-based growth and thus continued to thrive.

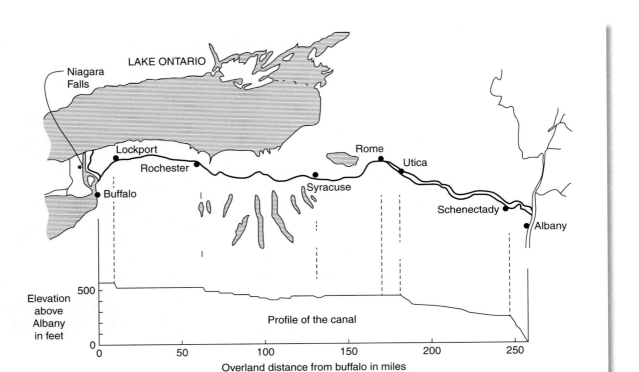

9.2 The Erie Canal

9.3 Space-time convergence between Boston and New York

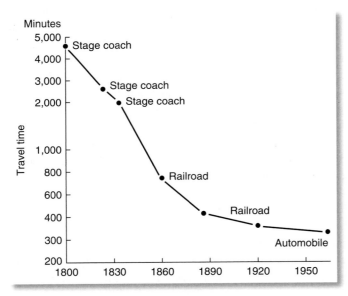

Railways annihilated distance, brought cities closer together, and made interaction easier and cheaper. The geographer Donald Janelle plotted the travel times between Boston and New York. Figure 9.3 shows the declining travel time between the cities with the introduction of new transport modes and their subsequent improvement. Over time, Boston and New York came closer together, making the movement of people, goods, and ideas between them easier and quicker.

Space-time convergences can bend physical space. London's space-time map is shown in Figure 9.4. Consider the case of the connection between Stranraer and London. Because of the lack of plane connections, the relatively poor railway connections, and the lack of motorways, it can take up to nine hours to travel between the two places. The result is that a space-time map warps the physical distance. London is closer in space-time terms to Paris than it is to Stranraer.

Space-time compression continues apace. Arnold Horner measured convergence of rail times between cities in Europe over the period

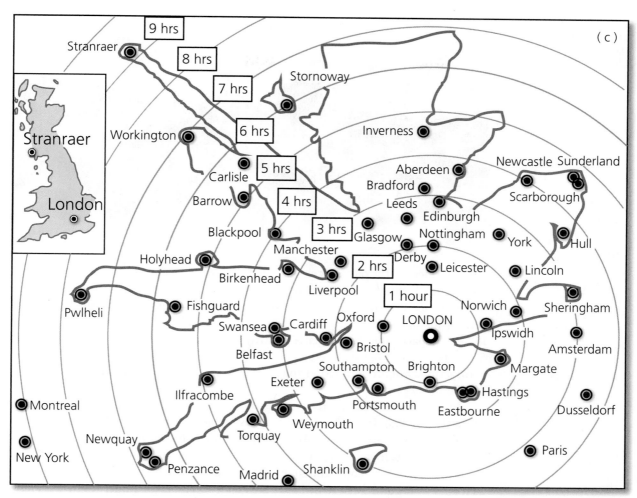

9.4 Space-time connections of London

1964 to 1999. More recently, David Banister argues that the desire to move faster further is ultimately unsustainable because of its energy costs. Rather than reducing travel times and increasing distance, he promotes alternative plans that reduce travel distances.

Space-time convergence continues. Developments in maritime trade include the increasing size of ships and the growing use of containers to pack the goods. The large box containers allow for easier loading on and off the ships; hence the unit cost of transport declines as more goods are shipped more quickly. As the size of the ships increases, new types of port facilities are required. The modern container ships could not, unlike the older smaller ships, sail up narrow shallow rivers. Port facilities migrated from the more urban locations to deepwater locations. The result was that by the 1970s many port cities across the world could no longer handle the big container ships. Shipping moved seawards to deepwater ports. The result was an

9.5 Space-time convergence: cheap air travel shrinks the globe. Baltimore-Washington International Airport.

abandonment of the old dock sites located upstream. In places as varied as London's Docklands, Baltimore's Inner Harbor, and Sydney's Inner Harbor, these sites—large areas of vacant land at the heart of metropolitan regions—sometimes became the setting for new postindustrial development of residential and commercial activity. Each space-time convergence destroys old geographies and creates new ones. Space-time convergence effectively shrinks and reshapes the globe as economic transactions are brought closer together. The world is flattened and distorted as it is shrunk.

In recent years, the increasing use of air transport has shrunk the globe even more (Figure 9.5). In 1873 a novel by Jules Verne depicted rapid travel around the world. The book was entitled *Around the World in Eighty Days*. Today, with good air connections, it could now take less than forty hours. Air transport is still more suitable for moving people and high-value goods. High-value perishable items, such as fresh flowers and fresh fruits, are particularly suitable for transport by air. Flowers grown in Colombia are transported by air to flower markets in North America because the cost of the final item makes the relatively high air freight an affordable cost. There is a distinct seasonality, as fresh fruit grown in the southern hemisphere is shipped to northern markets in winter. Airfreight allows a never-ending supply of seasonal produce. The growing trade in horticultural produce between Kenya and British supermarkets, for example, was possible because produce with a limited life span was shipped through Nairobi airport. Airfreight allows for quick travel along the path of global food chains; however, unstable fuel prices may make airfreight vulnerable to rapid price changes.

As an economy matures, the transfer and exchange of information become as important as the movement of goods. And here we come to the importance of cost rather than time. Once the telephone was invented, messages could be transmitted very quickly. The most important variable now becomes not space-time but time-cost compression. In 1919 it cost almost $300 (in 2004 prices) to make a ten-minute call between New York and Los Angeles. Ninety years later the cost is negligible. Calling long distance is no longer an expensive proposition. The same process occurs with Internet connections. As the real cost of communication falls, there is an extra tug pulling closer the net of space-time-cost. Each successive wave of space-time-cost convergence creates new markets and new economic geographies.

THREE WAVES OF GLOBALIZATION

Space-time convergences do not occur either randomly or regularly. They tend to be bunched together as distinct waves of globalization. We can identify three distinct waves of globalization.

The First Wave

The first modern wave followed the Columbian Encounter of 1492; it inaugurated a truly global economy. Before, the world was largely a system of regional empires and separate hemispheric ecologies. There was a substantial distinction between the east and west hemispheres, what are often called the Old and New Worlds. After 1492, a global system took shape.

A major consequence of the encounter between the Old and New Worlds after 1492 was the demographic holocaust that we discussed in chapter 3. The population estimates of the New World around 1490 range from 54 million to 112 million. By 1650 that population had fallen to just over 5 million. The cause was the introduction of new diseases from the Old World for which the indigenous people had no immunity.

The demographic holocaust was just one consequence of the Columbian Encounter. Others followed. The decline of the local populations led to the need for imported labor to dig in the mines and tend the estates. The slave trade shipped close to 20 million people from Africa to the New World. Then there was the biotic exchange. New World crops such as corn and potatoes enriched the diets of the whole world, leading to population increases in Europe. Turkeys, tomatoes, sunflowers, and peanuts were transplanted from the western to the eastern hemisphere, while horses, hens, cattle, pigs, sugarcane, and wheat moved in the opposite direction. Major environmental changes were wrought as a variety of plants and animals were dispersed around the world. When we pick tomatoes in Europe, or ride horses in America, we are participating in a globalization process that began when Christopher Columbus landed in the New World. The Columbian Encounter bridged the hemispheric divide in a series of transactions and exchanges of people, plants, viruses, and animals that activated a global world.

The Second Wave

A second wave of globalization took place from approximately 1865 to 1970. From 1865 to 1914, economic globalization was facilitated by low tariffs, an international labor market, and relatively free capital mobility. Critics of the time called it "British internationalism." British overseas investments were twice those of France

Box 9.1   THE FLOW OF CAPITAL

There are distinct phases of global capital mobility. First, there was a period of marked upswing from 1880 to 1914, when there were few restrictions on the movement of capital. Much of the capital flowed from London markets to developing economies around the world. The First World War ended this period. Then a brief period of resurgence from 1925 to 1930 was followed by the Depression and the collapse of international capital markets. Second, a period of stability emerged after the Second World War. Capital flows were relatively small and regulated. The system ended in 1971 and ushered in the present period of increased capital mobility. Financial deregulation promoted global capital flows. The amount of direct foreign investment has increased in most countries. Four qualifying points need to be made:

1. The level of foreign direct investment is highly variable at the aggregate and national levels. Capital outflows constituted over 20 percent of world GDP in 2007, but this figure rapidly fell in the wake of the 2008 collapse to under 5 percent.

2. The bulk of foreign investment occurs between already rich countries. It is a form of diversified investment rather than development investment. That more investment goes to capital-rich rather than capital-poor countries is termed the Lucas Paradox. The disparity from classic theory, which says that capital should flow to places that need it, is the result of institutional structures, heightened sense of risk, and asymmetric information. Many developing economies are considered too much of a risk. The paradox is that the places that need most foreign investment may be getting less of it.

3. Be careful of what you wish for. Increased capital mobility makes it easy to attract investment but comes with the danger that it may lead to rapid and destabilizing capital flows. A smooth surface for capital flows means that a highly mobile capital can undermine national economic planning. Consider the case of Argentina, where the government racked up deficits to reduce unemployment. Investor confidence was shaken, and capital outflows increased. As the currency depreciated, even more capital flowed outwards, creating capital shortages and the potential for runs on the bank. The government introduced capital controls and forced companies to repatriate foreign profits.

4. Even when capital flows into developing economies, it comes at a price. Consider the case of an economy with an important commodity that attracts a lot of capital from overseas. Carmen and Vincent Reinhart looked at capital bonanzas in 181 countries from 1980 to 2007. They found that bonanzas have become more frequent because of fewer restrictions on capital mobility and are associated in medium- and lower-income countries with higher incidence of banking, currency, and inflation crises. As they note, "a bonanza is not to be confused with a blessing."

References

Lucas, R. (1990) Why Doesn't Capital Flow from Rich to Poor Countries? *American Economic Review* 80: 92–96.

Reinhart, C. M. and Reinhart, V. (2008) Capital Flows Bonanzas: An Encompassing View of the Past and Present. National Bureau of Economic Research Working Paper 14321. http://www.nber.org/papers/w14321.pdf

and five times those of the United States. It was an economic globalization centered in London. Other countries, such as France, Germany, and the United States, were also involved through their smaller trading empires. The global system was neither fair nor equitable. It was a system dominated by merchants, manufacturers, and investors in the rich countries seeking raw materials, markets, and investment opportunities.

This second wave of globalization was associated with major shifts in space-time convergences triggered by the appearance of the railways, the telegraph, and the steamship. It took less time to travel large distances. People, ideas, and messages could move more quickly. News of events was more quickly transmitted across the globe, in effect shrinking the globe to a more compressed space.

Railways had been introduced before 1865 but were limited to partial networks in only a few countries. After 1865, there is a widening and deepening of the railway network around the world. In 1870 there were only 125,000 miles of track in the world; by 1911 this had increased to 657,000 miles. Far away from the railroad track, life may have remained unchanged, but the whistle of the train announced that the world had sped up.

Ocean distances were reduced by the construction and enlargement of canals. The Suez Canal reduced the time it took to sail from Western Europe to

9.6 Panama Canal

East Asia by linking the Mediterranean with the Red Sea. This "highway to India" was completed in 1869. The British invasion of Egypt in 1882 was in large part an attempt to control the canal, so vital for maintaining British links with their colony in India. But as ships increased in size and the region was susceptible to political instability, the Suez Canal became a less important transit site. On the other side of the world, the Panama Canal was cut through a narrow isthmus to reduce the distance between the Atlantic and Pacific (Figure 9.6). After unsuccessful attempts by the French, the United States built the Panama Canal, and it opened to traffic in 1914. In order to control the canal, the United States appropriated property along its route. The Canal Zone became a source of friction between the United States and an increasingly more independent-minded Panama. In 1999 the Panama Canal Zone reverted to Panamanian control. As the container ships got bigger, more traffic was diverted away from the canal. The growing trade between the United States and East Asia, for example, was occurring through the ports on the west coast of the United States. Almost a third of the world's container ships are too large to pass through the existing canal. Larger locks that can handle bigger ships are due to open in 2015.

The period from 1865 to 1914 marked a widening and deepening of economic integration around the world. London was the pivot of the international trading system, the sun of the trading universe. The formation of a world economy involved the economic and often political incorporation of larger areas of the world. Large parts of Africa and Asia, and even faraway islands in the South Pacific, were annexed to a global economic order. Overseas territories provided cheap raw materials, secure markets for manufactured goods, sources of national prestige, and pawns in the great game of global geopolitics. The period from 1865 to 1914 was also an age of imperialism, as a neo-mercantilist doctrine emerged that argued for protection of home industries and for the possession of overseas colonies to ensure cheap raw materials and a secure market and to deny access to competitors.

This second wave of globalization has a major disjuncture, the modern "Thirty Years War" from 1914 to 1945, marked by two world wars and a worldwide economic depression. It was a time of dislocation and economic disintegration, but the experience of world war led many countries to seek the basis for a renewed integration. The charter of the United Nations was first drawn up in 1945 to provide a forum for international dialogue. The Council of Europe in 1949 was followed by the European Coal and Steel Community in 1952, the European Economic Community in 1958, and then the European Community in 1967. From the ashes of the war there was a conscious attempt to create a unified Europe. In the new postwar world, rules and organizations were established to stop the world economy from slipping into the downward spiral caused by the national economic protectionism that occurred during the Great Depression. Delegates from forty-four countries met in 1944 in Bretton Woods, New Hampshire, to establish a new economic order that stressed free trade and created the World Bank and the International Monetary Fund (IMF) in order to integrate national economies into a global system. The United Nations, IMF, and World Bank were systems of international regulation that provided the backbone of a globalized world, a world now centered more on the United States. While the UN is headquartered in New York, the IMF and the World Bank are only a few blocks from the White House in Washington, DC.

The Third Wave

A third wave of globalization emerged after 1970. It is associated with an even more marked space-time-cost compression, global production chains, and a deregulated global financial system, creating a "flatter" world with easier and hence quicker economic links across the globe. The icon of the flat world is the shipping container (Figure 9.7). First developed in 1956, the container allows the easy and cheap transportation around the world of trailer-sized loads from ships to trains and trucks without breaking bulk. It is not the shipping container that created economic globalization, but globalization that created the container. The container both flattened the world and emerged from this flattening. A series of decisions from 1968 to 1970 by the International Organization of Standardization created global standards

Box 9.2   THE FLOW OF REMITTANCES

Remittances are the money that temporary and permanent migrants send back to their home country. As both international migration and capital mobility have increased, so has the level of remittances. As it becomes easier, and much cheaper, to send relatively small amounts of money back home, modest remittances are added to the global flow of money.

By 2010, close to $300 billion in total was sent from one country to another. The biggest exporter was the United States, with close to $48 billion in remittances. The next largest was Saudi Arabia, with $26 billion. The largest importers include India ($55 billion) and China ($51 billion). However vast these sums are, they constitute less than 5 percent of each country's GDP. Table 9.1 lists a sample of the countries where remittances constitute a relatively large proportion of GDP. What are some of the main characteristics of this subset of countries?

In the case of El Salvador, for example, out-migration increased substantially from the late 1970s as bloody civil war racked the country. Millions fled, and many of them sent money back to their families, villages, and neighborhoods. In 1978 traditional agricultural exports were responsible for most of the hard currency in the country; remittances were responsible for only 8 percent. By the first decade of the twenty-first century, remittances made up 70 percent and traditional exports only 12 percent. In many small counties, as well as regions and villages in large countries, remittances are a vital source of much-needed cash and capital,

Table 9.1 ■ INFLOWS OF REMITTANCES, 2010	
Country	**Remittances as percentage share of GDP**
Bangladesh	11.8
Bosnia	12.7
El Salvador	15.7
Guyana	17.3
Haiti	15.4
Honduras	19.3
Jamaica	13.8
Jordan	15.6
Lesotho	24.8
Moldova	23.1
Nepal	22.9
Tajikistan	35.1
Tonga	27.7

Source: Based on data from World Bank and IMF.

Box 9.2 CONTINUED

fueling local housing construction and paying for education and the provision of social services.

In some cases, remittances are an integral part of international economic relations. Almost 8 million Mexicans, 15 percent of the entire Mexican-born workforce, are now working in the United States. Many of these migrants send significant parts of their earnings back in the form of remittances. By 2010, the flow of total remittances was close to $25 billion. The flow varies over time. Economic downturns reduce immigration and hence the flow of remittances. The longer migrants stay in a country or bring their own families or start their own families, the more the flow tends to drop off. In counties such as Saudi Arabia, where economic migrants are not encouraged to stay yet are vital to the economic functioning of the country, the level of remittances remains steadily high.

References

See a web anthology of migration and resources: http://essays.ssrc.org/remittances_anthology/home/

of size, markings, and corner fittings. The result was a truly global form of cheap transportation. In 2012 close to 20 million containers made over 200 million journeys per year.

The steep fall in transport costs now makes available everyday things from around the world. It is the flattening of the world as low transport costs enable relatively cheap products to be made in one country and then sold in another halfway around the world. Blueberries grown in Chile, T-shirts manufactured in Vietnam, cheap plastic toys made in China, and white wines bottled in New Zealand can all be purchased in the same store in Syracuse, New York. The global trade in goods is an important part of our everyday lives. And global trade now has the power to influence, affect, and even destroy local and national economies.

9.7 Box containers sit on a wharf in Bermuda.

Distance and transport costs are no longer the barrier they once were. A flatter world is a smaller world.

There is a pronounced global shift of manufacturing employment from the rich industrial countries in North America and Western Europe to newly industrializing regions of the world. As manufacturing jobs are routinized and deskilled, they are capable of being offshored. Production is being prized away from the pools of skilled and higher-paid labor in traditional manufacturing regions. This shift has two consequences. The first is the rise of a new working class in the newly created industrial regions. A female working class emerges as young women fill many of the new jobs in the maquiladoras along the US/Mexican border or in the industrial cities of coastal China. The second consequence is the decline in the economic and political strength of the organized working class of the old industrial regions of Europe and North America.

The big-box retailers reinforce the world's flattening by forcing the global shift in manufacturing. Traditionally, manufacturers made things and then sold them to retailers, who sold them to customers. Retailers were simply in the middle, buying goods from producers and then selling goods to customers. With the rise of the big-box retailer and a more flexible production system, with many small companies producing small runs of goods relatively quickly, power shifted from the large number of small manufacturers to the small number of larger retailers. The very large retailers have such enormous power that they can force producers to compete with each other to meet strict cost limits. Manufacturers are willing to do this because access to a big retailer assures a large customer base. The lower price per item is offset by the higher turnover of items.

Production chains now stretch and snake their way across the globe looking for competitive advantage. The process is driven by competition. At one end, consumers seek greater value, and retailers, competing with one another to provide the best value, force producers into cheaper labor areas and more efficient production zones. At the other end of the chain, producers need to keep finding ways to reduce costs, improve techniques, and hire cheaper labor. As distance shrinks, relocation to ever-cheaper labor areas continues to flatten the world.

The waves of globalization have left a legacy. Just as waves sweeping onto a shore affect the topography of the beach, which in turn shapes the flow of subsequent waves, so the tides of globalization have impacted places, and the character of places has in turn affected the subsequent flows of global contact. We can imagine the world as a series of places in a continual process of globalization and reglobalization.

A FLAT WORLD?

The journalist Thomas Friedman wrote an influential book with the provocative title *The World Is Flat*. But is the world really flat? Is the smoothing of the differences enough to justify using the term "flat world"? Two counterarguments can be made. The first is the simple fact that only some of the world is flat, and by "flat" I mean a smoothing of the tyranny of economic distance and a lessening of the friction of national economic differences. Production chains only snake their way into selected countries. Nike athletic shoes are made from components in some countries, including China, Indonesia, and Vietnam, but not in Myanmar, Pakistan, Somalia, or Zimbabwe or most other developing and poor countries. Starbucks has few stores in sub-Saharan Africa. There are limits to economic globalization. The cheapness of labor is not the only issue for a mobile capital. Decent, reliable infrastructure, cheap transport links, the rule of law, and a stable political system are all prerequisites for long-term global shift, and much of the developing world lacks one or many of these elements. The world is not completely flat, but parts of it are, where distance is almost frictionless and economic transactions are easily connected to other parts of the world. In other parts, however, distance is only overcome at great transactional costs. We live in a misshapen world, parts of which are flat, others curved, and yet others pockmarked by disconnected ravines and inaccessible peaks.

The world's topography is more varied than flat. At the international level, there are still many countries only loosely connected to global flows of investment or global shifts in manufacturing. And even within the more connected, flatter countries, there is often a marked demarcation between the more inaccessible rural areas and the metropolitan regions where most of the global economic activity is concentrated. Many of the rural areas of the developing world are far from markets and lack the necessary infrastructure to ensure easy and cheap transportation, the hallmark of a flat world. The flat areas, where much of the world's global economic activities take place, are like landing strips in the middle of rugged terrain, often constituting small parts of larger countries and, in total, only a tiny part of the earth's economic surface.

The second point is that economic globalization is about creating hierarchies as well as flat surfaces; it generates spatial difference as well as homogeneity. Economic globalization is not just the product of a consumerist culture and a competitive capitalism continually seeking to squeeze costs. Since the 1970s, there has also been a globalization of finance. Capital now flows in larger and more viscous currents across the world. In this case, the flattening of the world is also tied to the networking of the world. Flat surfaces are ideal to move goods cheaply and quickly, but in order to do business you need nodes of concentrated activity. A global system of cities, connected by flows of capital, ideas, information, and skilled personnel, "landscapes" the world into concentrated nodes of heightened connectivity and accumulated control. We will discuss this topic more in a later chapter.

In summary, while there has been a flattening of the world, a flat world is not yet a reality.

The differential flattening that does occur has redistributional consequences. Globalization has different effects on capital and labor and on different sectors of labor. While capital is freer to move across the surface of the globe, labor is much more restricted. The low cost of international transport and the growing ease of international trade, crucial requirements of economic globalization, have allowed capital to be more easily disassociated from national interests and local community

Box 9.3 THE DIFFUSION OF DISEASES

Space-time convergence, the shrinking of the time taken to cover distance, has an effect on the diffusion of disease. The travel time between India and Fiji during the time of sailing ships was longer than the lifespan of the measles virus. The virus was thus not imported when Indian laborers were shipped to the islands as cheap labor for the plantations. People infected with measles when they left India had enough time to recover from the disease before they docked in Fiji. But travel times during the age of steamships decreased to within the incubation period of measles. Measles contracted in India was then imported into Fiji, with devastating results.

In the case of Iceland, with increasing connection to the outside world, waves of measles outbreaks became more frequent. The coming of the railway in the United States made it easier for cholera epidemics to sweep across the country. In our globalized world, there is a greater possibility of global pandemics. The influenza pandemic of 1918 killed between 3 and 5 percent of the worlds' population, with total death estimates ranging from 50 to 100 million.

The collapse of distance brought about by recent transport improvements, such as jet travel, has increased the ease and frequency of the transfer of communicable diseases. The swine flu epidemic of 2009, similar to the 1918 pandemic in that it was an H1N1 influenza virus, infected one-fifth of the population and more than half of all children in nineteen countries; it killed more than 200,000 people around the world. Although very contagious, it was not very lethal, killing fewer than 2 in every 10,000 infected. An equally contagious but more lethal virus will generate the kind of global death rate last seen more than a hundred years ago. If a contagious deadly virus does emerge, it will move quickly and inexorably across the globe.

References

Cliff, A. and Haggett. P. (2004) Time, Travel and Infection. *British Medical Bulletin* 69: 87–99.

Cliff, A. D., Haggett, P., and Raynor, M. S. (2004) *World Atlas of Epidemic Diseases*. London: Hodder Arnold.

Kerkhove, M. D., Hirve, S., Koukounari, A., and Mounts, A. W. (2013) Estimating Age-Specific Cumulative Incidence for the 2009 Influenza Pandemic: A Meta-Analysis of A(H1N1)pdm09 Serological Studies from 19 Countries. *Influenza and Other Respiratory Viruses* 7(5): 872–886.

http://onlinelibrary.wiley.com/doi/10.1111/irv.12074/abstract

concerns. Capital is free to roam the space of the world in search of lower wages and higher returns, while labor is more immobile. Retailers can move their production contracts to another factory in another country, but organized labor is more fixed in place. The result is an uneven bargaining arrangement. Globalization has liberated capital but largely restricted workers to national markets.

There are different levels in the flows of globalization that lead to different geographies of globalization. At the top level of the flat world, capital flows with fewer and fewer restrictions. Here are the global rich and the highly skilled, especially in the business of global business. At the bottom are the unskilled and those without capital, whose movements are much more circumscribed; they live in a more rugged topography.

Long ago, distance severely restricted economic interaction. The cost and difficulty of movement meant that most contact was between peoples and areas close together. The world that people inhabited was shaped more by the local than the global. The geographic-historical long view would perceive a world gradually coming together, not as a continuous process but in a series of fits and starts with some areas now pulled together, now pulled apart. World historical geography is in large part the story of global space-time convergence and successive waves of globalization.

Cited References

Banister, D. (2011) The Trilogy of Distance, Speed and Time. *Journal of Transport Geography* 19: 950–959.

Barrett. H., Wilbery, B., Brown, A., and Binns, T. (1999) Globalization and the Changing Networks of Food Supply: The Importation of Fresh Horticultural Produce from Kenya into the UK. *Transactions Institute of British Geographers* 24: 159–174

Friedman, T. (2006) *The World Is Flat: A Brief History of the Twenty-First Century.* New York: Farrar Straus and Giroux.

Horner, A. (2000) Changing Rail Travel Times and Time-Space Adjustments in Europe. *Geography* 85: 55–68.

Janelle, D. (1968) Central Place Development in a Space-Time Framework. *Professional Geographer* 20: 5–10.

Select Guide to Further Reading

Crosby, A. A. (1972) *The Columbian Exchange: Biological and Cultural Consequences of 1492.* Westport, CT: Greenwood.

Dicken, P. (2011) *Global Shift: Mapping the Changing Contours of the World Economy.* 6th ed. New York: Guildford.

Engel, C. and Wang, J. (2011) International Trade in Durable Goods: Understanding Volatility, Cyclicality, and Elasticities. *Journal of International Economics* 83: 37–52. http://www.ifw-kiel.de/konfer/staff-seminar/paper/2009/engel.pdf

Knwoles, R. D. (2006) Transport Shaping Space: Differential Collapse in Time-Space. *Journal of Transport Geography* 14: 407–425.

Mann, C. C. (2006) *1491: New Revelations of the Americas before Columbus.* New York: Knopf.

Mann, C. C. (2011) *1493: Uncovering the New World Columbus Created.* New York: Knopf.

Sheriff, C. (1997) *The Artificial River: The Erie Canal and the Paradox of Progress.* New York: Hill and Wang.

Short, J. R. (2001) *Global Dimensions: Space, Place and the Contemporary World.* London: Reaktion Books.

Short, J. R. (2004) *Global Metropolitan: Globalizing Cities in a Capitalist World.* London: Routledge.

Sobel, D. (1995) *Longitude: The True Story of a Lone Genius Who Solved the Greatest Scientific Problem of His Time.* New York: Walker.

Websites

Bank for International Settlements' International Financial Statistics
http://www.bis.org/statistics/about_banking_stats.htm
International Trade Centre's Trade Map
http://www.trademap.org
United Nations Comtrade Yearbook (2011)
http://comtrade.un.org/pb
World Bank Trade Indicators. http://web.worldbank.org/WBSITE/EXTERNAL/TOP-ICS/TRADE/0,,contentMDK:22421950~pagePK:148956~piPK:216618~theSit ePK:239071,00.html

10 | The Global Geography of Culture

Culture is a tricky concept. It is used to cover things in the material world as well as systems of belief, ideas, and practices. The word historically implies the notion of cultivation, of tending to something. This is an important point, because it reminds us that culture is not an a priori set of characteristics; it is something that is produced and cultivated as a response to specific circumstances. Culture is always more provisional, more elastic, more something in a continual process of being made than most people imagine.

Until the late eighteenth century, the word "culture" was often used interchangeably with "civilization," referencing a belief in the Enlightenment ideology of human mastery over nature. Yet at the end of the eighteenth century, thinkers such as the German philosopher Johann Gottfried Herder (1744–1803) wrote of the need to conceive of a plurality of cultures. There were entire cultural worlds below the privileged life of the court and beyond the refined manners of the elite. Local peoples also had culture. This view was reinforced in the nineteenth century through a self-conscious creation of "national" and "folk" cultures. Take a single example: in the nineteenth century, the Czech National Revival was a broad-based cultural and political movement in which a Czech identity was crafted in music, arts, and literature. Czech composers such as Bedřich Smetana and Antonín Dvořák drew upon folk motifs in their chamber music and operas. It was an attempt to forge a distinctive national culture at a time when the ruling elite spoke and wrote in German, and globalization, according to some, was sweeping away nationally distinct and uniquely local cultures. The defense of culture involves the invention of culture. Wherever and whenever a "culture" is perceived as weakened by contact with either a specific foreign other or a generic global other, local cultures are not only preserved and defended, they are also created and expanded in a complex dance between the local, the national, and the global. Whenever a wave of globalization sweeps around the world, there is a corresponding revival of the local and the national. Resistances to globalization often take the form of more explicit concern and promotion of national and local cultures as a way for groups to forge, redefine, or reestablish a place in the world. Culture is both a resistance to and an accommodation with wider social forces.

Traditional cultural geography highlighted the connection to the local. Emphasis was on vernacular building forms, local ways of doing things, and the construction of specific landscapes. More recently, the field has been enlivened by an awareness that culture is shaped not only by people's connection to the local, but also by their interaction with the national and the global. There are three dynamically linked sources of production of culture: the connection with the local, the relationship with the national, and the interaction with the global. In this chapter, we will focus on the connections between the global and the local. In chapter 12 we will explore the role of the national.

Cultures are never static, fixed in time and place. A subtler view of cultures sees them as resulting from ongoing interactions between the local, the global, and the national. The processes that shape local and national cultures are not one-way interactions but are rather dynamic and multifaceted, so that hybrids of the "newly arrived" and the "previously there" are constantly reconfigured and remobilized in and through global flows of people, ideas, and beliefs. Culture is not just passive audiences watching imported television programs or eating fast food from global chains. Culture is an active process; one definition of culture is tending, husbanding resources, with the same root as "cultivation." A culture is not just consuming things; it is the production of a worldview, an aesthetic sensibility, the active creation of a history and geography, the working out of a place in the world. Culture is the active use of global flows of ideas and practices by local and national groups adapting, adopting, or rejecting these flows into their own specific worldviews, which in turn become part of further flows of culture used and adapted, rejected and resisted by others in turn.

Global flows of culture are continually shaping and reshaping the world. Arjun Appadurai identifies flows of people, technologies, capital, media images, and the political configurations of such ideas as freedom, welfare, rights, sovereignty, representation, and democracy. Flows circulate globally and become reexpressed through and in local contexts.

THE (RE- AND DE-) TERRITORIALIZATION OF CULTURE

When we think of culture, we often think of distinctive songs, dances, foods—all those things that comprise collective memories and group identities. In much of our understanding, these are all tied to place: Mexican food, Indian music, Italian design, the Armenian language. The term "territorialization of culture" signifies this connection between culture and specific places. However, it is also important to consider the process of the deterritorialization of culture, in which cultures are lifted from particular places, and the reterritorialization of culture, whereby cultural practices are transplanted and transformed.

The widespread global diffusion of flows of people and ideas has broken the simple, unproblematic connection between culture and place. On closer inspection, the connection between culture and place is always complex and problematic. "Mexican" food, for example, is a mixture of Spanish and indigenous cuisines that evolved in different parts of the world in different ways for almost five hundred years. When Spaniards came to the New World and enslaved Africans were shipped across the ocean, they combined with indigenous people to create a New World cuisine that was creolized and hybridized right from the beginning. There is no unchanging Mexican cuisine; it is and always was a changing hybrid.

Cultures are always in the process of deterritorialization and reterritorialization, particularly marked during waves of globalization and reinforced by rapid space-time convergence. We can consider four examples of the reterritorialization of culture as revealed by population movement, language, architecture, and religion.

POPULATION MOVEMENT

People are always on the move, tracing complicated paths through space-time. There are the daily rituals of journeying to and from school and work, the weekly movements to places of recreation, the seasonal and annual trips and outings. There are also the more radical ruptures when we change houses, jobs, or even countries. As people change places, cultures are transformed, both de- and reterritorialized.

The reterritorialization of culture occurs through long-distance and especially international migration, when people leave one country to settle, either permanently or temporarily, in another. There are powerful push-and-pull factors at work as people search for better living conditions or religious and political freedoms. The level of migration depends on the range of factors pushing and pulling migrants as well as the regulatory regime that controls migration. Countries vary in the severity of their immigration regimes, which can be defined as the set of rules that govern the entry, settlement, and assimilation of foreign migrants. Regimes tend to be more severe during economic downturns and relaxed when economic growth creates labor shortages. In the late nineteenth century, for example, the United States had an open-door policy that encouraged immigrants from Europe but severely restricted immigration from China. Today, most countries try to control the level of immigration. Regimes vary from the more open, such as the Australian and Canadian, to the more closed and restricted, such as the South Korean.

Migration affects both origin and destination countries. Origin countries may lose some of the most talented population but receive remittances. Destination countries may receive skilled migrants, but there may be a depression of wage levels in sectors where the often cheaper immigrant labor force predominates.

International migration tends to increase during periods of increased globalization, such as in the late nineteenth and early twentieth century and over the past thirty years. Figure 10.1 plots the immigration history of the United States. High absolute and relative numbers of immigrants were recorded from 1890 to 1930. During this period, there were few restrictions on immigration from Europe. People came from Ireland and Italy, Russia and Scandinavia in the hundreds of thousands, changing the religious and ethnic composition of the country and leaving a permanent legacy. This period of large-scale immigration ended after 1930 as the Depression inaugurated tighter immigration controls. The number of foreign-born declined in absolute numbers and as a proportion of the total population. Between 1930 and 1960, the previous waves of immigrants were incorporated into the mainstream of US society. When the controls were lifted in the mid-1960s,

10.1 Foreign-born population in the United States, 1860 to 2009

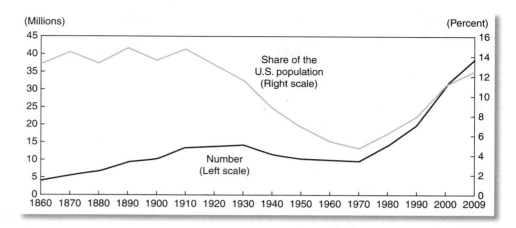

a new wave of increased immigration ensued. The absolute and relative levels of the foreign-born rose to levels not seen for over a hundred years. This second, more recent, large wave of immigration has a wider source than the first, including Africa and Asia as well as Europe and Latin America, and gives a new and different feel to the United States, making it more Hispanic, more Asian, and more cosmopolitan. While many immigrants in the first wave arrived in cities, in the second wave there has been a wider spread throughout metropolitan regions.

Across the world, 190 million people now reside in a country outside their country of birth, around 3 percent of the world's population. Half of all international migrants are women. If we include illegal and undocumented workers, the level of international migration across the globe is even higher. The current wave of international immigration is now substantial. In the United States, for example, 8 million immigrants entered between 2000 and 2005, the largest five-year total in the nation's history.

While the movement of capital is encouraged, the movement of people tends to be more problematic as resistance in destination countries is generated from perceptions of depression of living standards for native-born workers and feelings of local and national cultures being swamped by the foreign others. In the United States, for example, there is the added sense that between 12 million and 25 million people are in the country illegally. The description of this group is itself a battleground, with terms such as "illegals," which references the illegality of the people's permanent residence, competing with the term "undocumented," which suggests an administrative mix-up that can be easily sorted out.

There are now many countries that are significant sites of foreign immigration. The Gulf States, for example, with their combination of wealth, small population, and large demand for labor, have some of the highest percentage rates of foreign-born, including Qatar (75.9 percent), United Arab Emirates (71.4 percent), and Kuwait (62.4 percent). Among the larger developed nations, the highest rates are found in Australia (19.9 percent) and Canada (18.7 percent). In all these countries, the percentage of foreign-born has increased in the past thirty years, a result

Box 10.1 POPULATION MOVEMENT

The most dominant form of movement is rural-to-urban migration. This movement is particularly pronounced during periods of rapid industrialization and urbanization. In contemporary China, for example, there are approximately 150 million rural migrants in coastal cities, almost 11 percent of the total population. Around the world, and especially in developing countries, large cities are often fringed with the settlements of rural migrants searching for economic opportunities and a better way of life for their children.

Sometime this shift takes place within one country, as in the case of China. In other cases, people move from rural areas in one country to cities in another country. Rural migrants from Mexico move to cities in the United States as well as to cities inside Mexico.

Urban-to-urban migration also occurs, as people move from declining urban economies to expanding ones.

International migration is now an important form of population movement. Almost 192 million people live outside the country of their birth, around 3 percent of the total world population. These immigrants are either temporary migrants, perhaps sending money back in the form of remittances, or permanent migrants making a life in a new country. International migrants are the raw material of cultural globalization as they bring their culture with them, adding a new cultural dimension to their destination. It is rare that cultures are mechanistically transported; there is creative reworking as cultural forms are adapted and changed.

E. G. Ravenstein (1834–1913) was born in Germany but moved to Britain, eventually becoming a professor of geography. He arrived at a time of intense population movement associated with rapid urbanization and industrialization.

Spurred by a comment that the migration process was random, he analyzed UK census data in 1871 and 1881 to propose a number of laws of migration. These included:

1. Most migrants move only a short distance, toward the nearest city.
2. Growing cities attract migrants from nearby rural areas that depopulate rapidly; in turn, migrants from more distant areas fill the "gaps" left in the rural population. Migration is stepped.
3. Each main current of migration produces a compensating countercurrent.
4. Long-distance migrants tend to move to major cities.
5. Rural people have a higher propensity to migrate than urban people.
6. Women have a higher propensity to migrate than men within countries, but more men tend to move in international migration.
7. Migration is driven in largest part by economic forces.

These laws are not physical laws but generalizations made at a particular time in a specific context. While some of them stand up in many different circumstances—3, 4, and 7—the others can vary depending on the context. There are more female than male Filipina international immigrants, undermining law 6. In the United States, more than one-third of all Filipino migrants live in just three metro areas, tending to support law 4.

There are gravity models that suggest that population movement between two areas is a direct function of their population size, and an inverse function of the distance and intervening opportunities between them. There are also less formal models that explain migration with reverence to specific push and pull forces

Box 10.1 CONTINUED

between origins and destinations. Typical push forces include limited economic opportunities, social unrest, and political instability, while pull factors include readily available employment opportunities, presence of friends and family, and social and political stability. Once migration links are established, a chain of migration is established between people in the origin and destination areas.

References

Cordey-Hayes, M. (2012) Migration and the Dynamics of Multiregional Population Systems. *Environment and Planning A* 7: 793–814.

King, R. and Skeldon, R. (2010) 'Mind the Gap!': Integrating Approaches to Internal and International Migration. *Journal of Ethnic and Migration Studies* 36: 1619–1646.

Ravenstein, E. G. (1885) The Laws of Migration. *Journal of the Statistical Society of London* 48: 167–235.

of increasing flows of migrant labor. In the United Kingdom, the percentage of foreign-born increased from 5.8 percent in 1971 to 11.6 percent in 2011. In absolute terms, the number has increased from over 3 million to just over 7 million. In the United States, the percentage of foreign-born has increased from 4.7 percent in 1970 to 12.9 percent in 2010.

We should also note that there is also a wide range of countries with very low numbers of foreign-born. They include poor countries such as Sudan (1.7 percent), Eastern European countries such as Poland (1.8 percent), authoritarian regimes such as China (0.29 percent), and South American countries such as Colombia (0.26 percent). A mixture of limited economic opportunities, more attractive alternatives, and restrictive immigration policies limits the number of foreign-born in these countries.

There are multiple migrant experiences. Take the case of Dubai, where there are two very different streams of migrants. There is the encouragement of investors, technical experts, and those associated with "flight capital," which is seeking a safe and opaque site for money made elsewhere. Then there are the building worker migrants, often coming from rural communities in Pakistan and Bangladesh, who live many to a room and have tough working conditions. Their entry is tightly controlled and monitored. Luxury homes and migrant camps, foreign investors and building laborers, welcome guests and barely tolerated foreign workers: these are the extremes of divergent migrant experiences. There are also the expatriate communities of technical workers and experts—English financial specialists in Singapore, Scottish engineers in Saudi Arabia, European aid workers in Nairobi, Indian doctors in the United States. And there are the unskilled and often exploited workers—the female Filipino domestic servants in Hong Kong, the Mexican gardeners in California, and the vast armies of undocumented and illegal workers in shadow urban economies around the world.

International migration channels are often routed very largely, although not exclusively, through major metropolitan areas. In cities around the world,

10.2 Ethnic homogeneity in Seoul, South Korea

the number of the foreign-born has increased. In the United States, for example, a third of all the foreign-born in 2010 are located in the five largest metropolitan areas. Marie Price and Lisa Benton-Short identify immigrant gateway cities around the world. They include

- established gateways such as Amsterdam, Birmingham (UK), New York, Sydney, and Toronto;
- emerging gateways such as Dublin, Johannesburg, Singapore, and Washington, DC;
- exceptional gateways such as Riyadh and Tel Aviv.

Global and globalizing cities are now places of minority populations, diasporic communities, and hybrid identities. The metropolis is now the place of the Other, who, with their distinctive languages, cuisines, and cultures, now add to the cosmopolitan mix of the big cities. There is undeniable global mixing in the large metropolitan regions, but not in all big cities. In countries with restrictive regimes of tight regulations on the entry of foreign-born immigrants, even very large cities may remain remarkably homogenous. Seoul, in South Korea, has a population of more than 10 million, but less than 1 percent of them are foreign-born. Seoul is a closed gateway city (Figure 10.2).

Immigrant places are where otherness is renewed and celebrated, performed and remembered in creative acts of representation and memory. And this representation adds to the cosmopolitan mix of the city.

Otherness is also created and maintained by acts of power. Kay Anderson provides a fascinating case study of the evolution of Chinatown in Vancouver, British Columbia. She shows how the racial category of Chinese was constructed and maintained by white politicians and local elites. As she notes,

. . ."Chinatown" was a shared characterization—one constructed and distributed by and for Europeans, who, in arbitrarily conferring outsider status on these pioneers to British Columbia, were affirming their own identity and privilege. That they directed that purpose in large part through the medium of Chinatown attests to the importance of place in the making of a system of racial classification.

(ANDERSON 1987, P. 594)

Chinatown in Vancouver, like other Chinatowns in cities around the world, has evolved from a place of compulsion and restriction of ethnic difference to what is now a setting for performance and celebration of ethnic difference.

Migrant communities throughout the world are important networks of information flows, capital flows, and economic exchanges. Just as chains of migration are routed through families and friends, so business deals are conducted among family members dispersed through the world. Economic globalization is intimately linked to this particular form of global population dispersal. Businesses are culturally embedded. A flattening world is linked to the deepening economic interactions of far-flung communities, with shared family ties, ethnicity, and race also functioning as conduits of international trade and commerce.

International migration shapes the culture of both destination and origin areas. When migrant communities are established, they bring their culture with them. Sometimes it is frozen in the time of departure and lasts longer than it does at home. Yet cultures always have enough plasticity to adapt to the new and the foreign. Both home and away, origin and destination are constantly changing in response to these continual interactions and flows.

Globalization, it has often argued, undermines local identities. However, an alternative case can be made that globalization has both deterritorialized and strengthened local cultures. In the nineteenth century, there was a massive immigration to the United States from many European countries. Italians, Germans, Poles, and Irish all moved in the millions to the United States. Their connection with home was always limited, separated as they were by rudimentary communication links. Letters could take weeks. New identities were created. People from different parts of what is now Italy became "Italians" in the United States: a kind of Italian nationality was achieved in the United States even before there was an Italian nation-state. New identities were shaped. Irish Americans took on the mythic elements of Irish nationalism. Folk memories did not die; indeed, in many cases they became both strengthened and stuck in time. Irish Americans, unlike the Irish in Ireland, could scarcely "remember" anything other than the famine. In more recent years, however, immigrants to the United States and other destination countries have been able to stay in closer connection with their families back home. Cheaper travel, ease of transmitting money, and ease of communications all allow diasporic communities to remain in touch, to influence their new surroundings, and to be subtly transformed in the process of being diasporic. All those easier communication systems of a globalized world allow groups to be more in touch with their home areas.

LANGUAGE

Language is an important part of culture. Until space-time convergence became such a pronounced characteristic of the modern world, there was a richer variety of different languages spread widely around the world. Language was originally connected to specific places. Indigenous peoples of the northern latitudes had a rich variety of words for snow. Igor Krupnik and colleagues at the Smithsonian studied the vocabulary of ten Inuit and Yupik dialects. They found that Inuit speakers in Canada's Nunavik region have fifty-three words for different types of snow, including a word for wet snow that can be used to ice sled runners. Speakers of a local dialect around Wales in Alaska have seventy different terms for sea ice. When life is firmly based on local conditions, language has to become a fine filter of understanding. The Sami people have 180 words related to snow and ice and a thousand separate words to describe reindeer. Indigenous languages are rooted in place and highly sensitive to the nuances of the local environment.

Local places provide the context and setting for a multitude of languages. Yet language also embodies spatial flow as well as place. The spread of empires, for example, diffused language use around the world. The Roman Empire created the first pan-European language of Latin, the language of the dominant elites, which became the accepted linguistic current of the expanding empire. As the empire declined, flow and spread was then replaced by place and stasis. Local variations became more important, and we can make a broad distinction between the Romance languages at the center of the empire and the languages not descended from Latin, such as Old Norse, German, and English, that emerged at the periphery. We retain this linguistic legacy in the names of the days of the week. The Romance languages have names—e.g., *jeudi* (French), *jueves* (Spanish), and *giovedì* (Italian)—that derive from the name of the Roman god Jupiter. In contrast, English still draws on the Old Norse name of Thor to designate the fifth day of the week as Thursday. The day is similarly named *torsdag* in Danish, Norwegian, and Swedish. The closer to the heart of the empire, the stronger the linguistic legacy of Latin; the further away, the weaker the linguistic impact.

Three trends in the geography of language are apparent. First, there is the emergence of distinct linguistic geographies as languages grow and develop in specific communities in particular places. Before marked space-time convergence, there were many more languages spread widely across the surface of the habitable globe. Figure 10.3 depicts the complex linguistic map of languages of the Pacific Northwest. Notice the mosaic of many language families across one single region. Localization is apparent not only in specific languages but also in the existence of particular dialects. In Scotland, for example, the accent of Glasgow has much harder consonants than the softer, sing-song dialect of the Highlands.

Second, there is the interaction and sometimes replacement of local variants with outside languages because of population movement, social change, and the operation of political power. National identity is created, maintained, and reproduced in language. Graham Robb, in his wonderfully descriptive account of the historical geography of France, outlines the process whereby the national language of French finally replaced a myriad of different language and dialects. France encompasses at least five major languages, Catalan, Franco-Provençal, Gallo-Italian, Langue d'Oc, and Langue d'Oïl (now considered standard French) with at least ninety distinct dialects. At the time of the French Revolution, French, as we know it today, was only spoken in Paris and the surrounding area. Creating a national language was a major goal of successive republican governments. Even as late

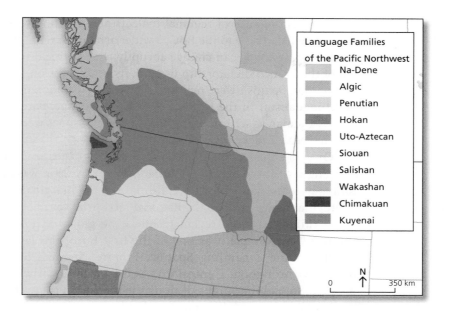

10.3 Indigenous languages of the Pacific Northwest

as the mid-nineteenth century, most of the people living south of the Loire did not speak French, and in Brittany most spoke Breton. The national education system fostered the exclusive use of French, so that French became the national language of France, a process heightened by the space-time convergence that Robb (2007, p. 248) describes as the "contraction of space and the gravitational pull of Paris." But even today local variants persist, a testimony to the continuing connection between language and locality. Almost two million people speak Occitan, one and a half million Alsatian, and a half million Breton. Local dialects persist, although the higher up the socioeconomic hierarchy, the more the everyday usage of "proper" French.

Place and socioeconomic status combine to produce social geographies of language. In many national societies, such as those of France and England, the higher socioeconomic groups speak a similar national language despite their various locations, while further down the socioeconomic hierarchy, the national language can vary by distinct regional dialects.

While the spoken word varies, the written word is more standardized. National written languages emerge with national education systems and shared print cultures of books and newspapers that create a national readership. There is a complex relationship between language and national identity.

Throughout the nineteenth and much of the twentieth century, the emphasis was on the construction of both written and spoken national languages. As a young boy growing up in Scotland, when I listened to the national radio or television I never heard anyone who sounded like me, my family, or any of my friends and neighbors. A more formalized English was spoken, called "received pronunciation." Scots' accents were definitely restricted to the periphery and the marginal and denied expression in the national media. More recently, however, there has been conscious acceptance of regional dialects and different forms of spoken English. When you listen now to the BBC, a wider array of accents can be heard.

Language usage can change abruptly with political ruptures. In Spain, at the fall of the Franco dictatorship in 1975, its centralization of power and promotion of Castilian Spanish were replaced by not only democratization but also a greater multilingualism. In the region of Catalonia around Barcelona, public signs now display Catalan as well as Spanish words. The Basques were also given greater freedom to speak and write in Basque.

On closer inspection, many "national" languages arose from the promotion of one language at the expense of others. The promotion was aided by national education systems, national print cultures, and the marginalization and suppression of other languages within the national territorial space.

A third and more recent trend is the globalization of certain languages. Spanish, for example, was one of the first European languages to be exported as part of the expanding Spanish Empire. Spanish became the language of the elites throughout Central and South America. The emigration of Chinese speakers spread the language along the migration routes to diasporic communities across the world. The most global language is English, now the hegemonic language of the contemporary world. Waves of globalization centering in the United Kingdom and United States, the extensive impact of the British Empire during the colonial period and the dominance of the American economy, culture, science, technology, and politics in the contemporary world have all led to the dominance of English. It is now the lingua franca of global interaction. Most scientific, technological, and academic information in the world is expressed in English, and over 80 percent of all information stored in electronic retrieval systems is in English. English has become the language of international entertainment, popular music, movies, and advertising.

Over seventy-five countries officially recognize English as a primary or secondary language. They include Botswana and Cameroon, India and Liberia, Rwanda and Sudan. The number of people who speak English as a first or second language is estimated at 573 million. A further 670 million may have native-like fluency in the language. Even nonspeakers are exposed to the language on a daily basis through advertising, government functions, or interpersonal communication. David Crystal describes them as members of an expanding circle who have, via the dynamic processes of globalization, been exposed to the usage of English on many informal levels. Almost 1.6 billion people, over a fifth of the world's population, exhibit some reasonable competence in the language.

Growing global English competency has accelerated the rate of cultural globalization by facilitating the movement of ideas and information. The growing use of English around the world, however, is not simply the result of diffusion outward from a dominant center. There is a conscious adoption of English around the world. People in non-English-speaking countries are trying to learn English to more fully participate in international activities. English is required in order to be competitive in global markets. Many countries around the world have adopted English as a second language and emphasize it as an important subject in their schools. In the early days of the People's Republic of China (PRC), English was labeled as an "imperialist language" and suppressed. After the break with the Soviet Union, teaching Russian was abandoned and the teaching of English was revived and relabeled as "the instrument for struggles in the international stage." In the contemporary PRC, there is a great increase in the use of English, fueled by the increasing number of students educated in English-speaking countries, especially the United States, and an increase in the demand for English-language skills among professionals and workers in the booming international trade sector. English-language teaching is now an important industry.

For individuals in many countries, English skills are an invaluable asset in the job market. English is a form of cultural capital as national governments seek to produce a globally competitive workforce and individuals seek to achieve more employment opportunities in a globalizing world.

Not only has English expanded to become the dominant worldwide medium of communicative practice, it has also undergone considerable reinvention by non-native-speaking communities, many of whom are speaking English in their own ways. English, as a global medium of communication, is being reterritorialized within particular communities. Instead of adopting a standard form of English, non-native speakers are reshaping the language to best suit their purposes. The sub-title of David Crystal's survey of global English is "One Language, Many Voices." While the introduction of English represents a deterritorialization of the language, its modification or creolization represents the ensuing reterritorialization of the language as local communities adapt the language to local needs. Robert McCrum writes of "Globish" as the new spoken international language, primarily used in economic transactions. It joins the list of other hybrid languages, such as Spanglish (Spanish-English). One colleague from Copenhagen assures me that she speaks fluent Danglish (Danish-English).

The complex history of English as a language of both the colonizer and the colonized is summarized in the recent history of India, which was an important part of the British Empire. In order to govern this vast and populous land, the colonial authorities created an English-speaking Indian intellectual elite to help in the efficient running of the empire. The English-speaking elite became the leaders of the independence movement. In 1950 the constitution of the newly independent India was written in English. And the languages of the colonized were incorporated into English. Words like *nirvana*, *bungalow*, and *jungle* are now part of Standard English.

English is both spoken and written. While spoken English is a much more flexible form of communication—it is legitimate to speak of global Englishes, including Spanglish—written English, in contrast, is more rule-bound, programmatic, and slow to change. While we can think of a reterritorialization of spoken English, a reterritorialization of written English is less apparent. The use of English as a written global form of communication is particularly visible in the communities of knowledge. English has become the language of global intellectual discourse and the dominant language of intellectual communities involved in the production, reproduction, and circulation of knowledge. English dominates the global epistemic community.

We lose something if we only use one language to describe the world. Languages are not just reflectors of the external world; they embody it. How we describe the world is crucially dependent on where we are and how we speak and write. The creation of a monolingual geography raises issues about what we are losing in terms of the range and subtlety of languages used to describe the world. Daniel Nettle and Suzanne Romaine drew attention to the extinction of language in their evocatively named book *Vanishing Voices*. And K. D. Harrison made a similar point with his book *When Languages Die*. They estimate that at least half of the world's languages will disappear in this century. We are losing linguistic diversity. In a world dominated by fewer languages, we gain global communication but lose diversity, linguistic subtlety, and something that is almost impossible to resuscitate. Linguistic variety, like ecological diversity, is a sign of health and vitality. There is a strong correlation between areas of biodiversity and linguistic diversity at numerous scales of analysis. A loss of biodiversity is associated with a decline in linguistic variety. The loss of biodiversity and language diversity impoverishes our world.

ARCHITECTURE

For the great German polymath Goethe (1749–1832), architecture is "silent music." Two of the dominant melodies of this music are the vernacular and the global. Vernacular architecture uses local resources and traditions in the design and construction of buildings. The materials draw on local sources, whether they are wood and clay, ice or rock, and architectural design is a calibrated response to local conditions of weather and topography. Classic examples would be the Inuit igloo, built of local ice, or the Swedish Lutheran church, built of local birch.

There are also transnational architectural styles that transcend particular places. Consider the classical architecture of Greece and Rome, so admired that they have been copied and recopied all over the world (Figure 10.4). Neoclassical architecture,

10.4 The Parthenon, Athens. Work began on this building in 447 BCE. It was dedicated to the Goddess Athena.

Box 10.2 THE TOURIST GAZE

Tourism is an important industry. There are almost one billion international tourist visits each year to a vast array of tourist landscapes: Florida beaches, the tourist resorts along Spain's Mediterranean coastline, the small Caribbean islands of Dominica and Barbados, and even remoter islands such as the Maldives and Fiji. It is a significant economic sector in large countries. Countries with the largest tourist arrivals are France, the United States, and China, while the countries with the largest receipts from tourism are the United States, Spain, France, and China.

Tourism used to be the preserve of wealthy English aristocrats taking the Grand Tour, visiting classical Mediterranean countries, often purchasing artwork to add culture and class to their residences back home. With space-time convergence, mass tourism became possible and brought more of the world into easier and quicker tourist access. The tourist market is now finely graded, from cheap mass tourism to exclusive and expensive tourist experiences. As tourist sites became more popular, there is constant demand for a more restricted experience, away from the crowds.

There are a variety of tourisms, including sun-and-sand holidays by the beach, ecotourism, heritage tourism, culinary tourism, and even slum tourism, in places such as the favelas of Brazil. In the wake of Hurricane Katrina, disaster tourists visited New Orleans to see the aftermath of the storm.

John Urry describes what he terms the "tourist gaze." When people go on holiday, they look upon different landscapes, settings, and peoples. This gaze is socially organized and systematized. He highlights how the tourist gaze—"gazes" would be more accurate—has changed for different groups and places over the years. There are stock images such as Paris as romantic, South East Asia as exotic, English villages as representing an unchanging organic order. The gaze is not an innocent seeing but a perception guided and shaped and freighted with subtle and not so subtle messages about history and geography. The cultural geographer Patrick McGreevy explores the changing meaning of visiting Niagara Falls. He shows how the perception of the place is bound up with themes of remoteness, death, nature, and the future. The experience itself has changed over the years from an almost sacred pilgrimage, part of a romanticism of nature, into a more commodified tourist package.

References

McGreevy, P. (1994) *Imagining Niagara: The Meaning and Making of Niagara.* Amherst: University of Massachusetts Press.
Urry, J. (2002) *The Tourist Gaze.* 2nd ed. London: Sage.

the style that echoes the classic architecture of Rome and Greece, became popular in the mid-eighteenth century and soon was used in countries and cities worldwide. Here we come to a complex connection between place and culture. Neoclassicism meant different things in different places. In the United States, it was associated with democratic values and republican virtues (Figures 10.5). In Nazi Germany, it was associated with the attempt to build a thousand-year Reich based on racist belief, the use of "timeless" classical imagery reinforcing the political agenda of Nazi ideology.

From the 1950s to the 1980s, architectural designs around the world were associated with modernist designs. Modernist architecture was concerned with form

10.5 The neoclassical design of the Lincoln Memorial, Washington, DC. Construction commenced in 1914.

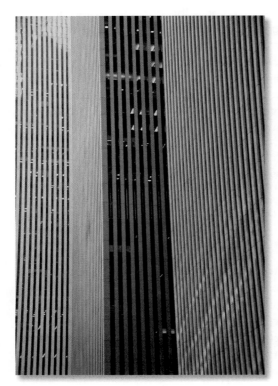

10.6 Modernist buildings along Sixth Avenue, New York

following function, truth to material, and a revulsion against bourgeois decoration. It preferred clean-cut lines and soon became serialized into tall, flat-topped buildings constructed in towns and cities all over the world, so specifically meant for global usage that it was designated "The International Style." And it truly was international: Communist headquarters in Eastern Europe, corporate offices in New York, government buildings in Brasilia, and public housing projects in London and Chicago all used it (Figure 10.6). Despite the differences in place, the buildings all looked the same. In the West, international modernist architecture soon reached dominance and then was so ubiquitous to become boring. The modernist mantra of "less is more" turned into "less is a bore."

Since the 1980s, there has been a reaction to modernism, usually called postmodernism. It less a distinct style and more a conscious distancing from the austere, flat-topped straight line of modernist design; it includes historical referencing, ornamentation, and playfulness with material and design. Office buildings with Georgian facades, museums with Renaissance decoration, and neoclassical houses now became popular. Variants include deconstructivism, which involves use of nonrectilinear surfaces (Figure 10.7). In the highly competitive world of global cities, not to have a postmodernist building is to be out of date, too far from the cusp of the future.

10.7 A postmodern building in New York City, designed by Frank Gehry and completed in 2007.

This hyper-brief history of architectural styles is just a small indication of the way that buildings and cities reflect transnational forms and styles.

RELIGION

There are many connections between religion and space. We have already noted, in chapter 6, that the very first religions were animist, firmly based in place, with sacredness located in specific sites. Some of these belief systems grew into more universal religions that effectively lifted the religious gaze above particular peoples and places to an all-seeing, all-knowing, single God on high. The monotheistic religions depicted a sky-centered, universal God looking down over the entire world. The brutal defeat of the Canaanites by the Israelites, mentioned at various points in the Bible, is one of the first descriptions we have of the destruction of an earth-based polytheism by a monotheistic religion. The basis of this holy war, for the Israelites, was the fundamentalist religious doctrine that people should worship only one God. The Canaanites were depicted as corrupt and evil, and their fertility-based polytheism was replaced by the stringent demands of adherence to a single universal God. The war between the Canaanites and the Israelites played out again and again across time and over space as monotheistic religions displaced the more local, place-based belief systems, whether it was in the destruction of local religious traditions in South America by the Catholic Church or the marginalization of indigenous Native American beliefs by Christian missionaries in North America. Across the world, it is a similar tale of sky-based monotheistic religions displacing more earth-based polytheistic beliefs. Barbara Ehrenreich makes a convincing case that many religions began as more festive events, ceremonies filled with music and dance, what she terms "ecstatic worship." As the religions became connected with establishment power, the authorities sought to control and reduce these forms of ecstatic worship. From medieval times, Christian worship was made more formal. When Christian missionaries arrived in the wake of imperialism and colonization, they similarly devalued the ecstatic forms of worship that they encountered.

Organized religions, with their gods and priests and rituals to make sense of the mysteries of life, also grew out of the need to justify and legitimize the social hierarchy in the early city-states. When these empires expanded and came into contact with other urban empires, there was both creative and destructive cultural collision. Karen Armstrong updates the idea of a pivotal "axial age" that lasted from 900 to 200 BCE, during which the great religious traditions of the world came into being across the globe—Confucianism and Daoism in China, Hinduism and Buddhism in India, monotheism in Israel, and philosophical rationalism in Greece. Their universal messages of empathy and compassion grew out of the collective experience of living in cities as well as their awareness of people in other cities and regions.

Two main hearth areas can be identified in this axial age. The Indic region of northern India, centered on the Indus Valley, is the hearth source for Jainism, Buddhism, Hinduism, and Sikhism. The Semitic region of the Middle East, especially around present-day Israel and Saudi Arabia, is the primary hearth for the three more recent "religions of the book," Judaism, Christianity, and Islam. From these primary hearth areas, some of the religions diffused more widely along trade routes and were carried along in, and as, waves of globalization. Buddhism, for example, spread along the trade route of the Silk Road, finding expression and acceptance in China, Korea, and Japan. Christianity spread out across the trade routes of the Roman Empire. It was initially suppressed, and Christians were persecuted because their religious faith undermined civic responsibilities. Yet when the Roman emperor Constantine converted to Christianity in 312 CE, it had the backing of political power and became the dominant religion throughout Europe. It built upon the older more place-based religions, often using their sacred sites as locations for places of Christian worship. Many important cathedrals in Europe were sited on pre-Christian sacred sites. Christianity was then exported around the world as part of European colonialism and imperialism. The Spanish took their Catholicism with them when they invaded the New World. The British settler societies of North America and Australia brought their Protestant religion with them, self-consciously believing in its superiority over local religious beliefs and practices. Christianity was one of the more expansionist religions, associated as it was with the powerful expansionist forces of the day. In some countries, it was resisted. British control in India and the Middle East did little to change the religious beliefs of the majority of the colonized people. In others, it was incorporated into complex blends of the old and new. In parts of South America, the old gods still appear, suitably modified in Catholic worship; in Haiti, for example, Catholic rituals are part of ceremonies that also draw upon older African practices brought by slaves.

Box 10.3 ORIENTALISM, ORNAMENTALISM, AND OCCIDENTALISM

There is a hierarchy to the production of geographical knowledge. The world is always described by certain people from certain places. It is a legacy of the British Empire that to this day Iran and Iraq are described as the Middle East. It is only Middle East if you are describing it from London. The cultural critic Edward Said described Orientalism as the writing and description of these places by those in the West. The term is not innocent of political meaning and the operation of military power. To be described and portrayed is to be discursively captured. The geographer Derek Gregory explores the contemporary operation of Orientalism.

Riffing on this idea, the historian David Cannadine describes an Ornamentalism that he defines as the importance of class and status as much as race and ethnicity, especially for the British Empire. He stresses the construction of affinities between different elites in the encounter between East and West. Cannadine's assertion is that class as much as, if not more than, race and ethnicity was a key factor in the social distinctions in the imperial experience.

There is also an Occidentalism as well as an Orientalism. While Orientalism is a much-studied phenomenon, Occidentalism receives rather less attention. The West is also understood and imagined by its enemies. Ian Buruma and Avishai Margalit trace the roots of anti-Western ideas. These two authors point to the important role of the sinful Western city in this ideology. Purifying the evil city is a major trope. The United States and especially its cities are often projected as a "rootless, cosmopolitan, superficial, trivial, materialistic, racially mixed, fashion-addicted civilization" (Buruma and Margalit 2004, p. 8).

References

Buruma, I. and Margalit, A. (2004) *Occidentalism: The West in the Eyes of Its Enemies*. New York: Penguin.

Cannadine, D. (2001) *Ornamentalism: How the British Saw Their Empire*. Harmondsworth: Allen Lane.

Gregory, D. (2004) *The Colonial Present: Afghanistan, Palestine, and Iraq*. Malden, MA: Blackwell.

Said, E. (1979) *Orientalism*. New York: Vintage.

Sharp, J. (2009) *Geographies of Postcolonialism: Spaces of Power and Representation*. London: Sage.

In still others, it was enthusiastically adopted. In late nineteenth- and early twentieth-century Korea, Christianity gave meaning and purpose to the lives of ordinary people denied both in a very hierarchical and feudal Confucian system.

There is a profound relationship between religion and space. Three themes are important. First, there is the notion of sacred sites. In place-based animist beliefs, the landscape was filled with spiritual significance. In the more universal religions, there is a more marked categorization of sacred and profane space. Most of the world was profane, a word whose etymological meaning is "in front of (i.e., outside) the temple." A small number of places were considered sacred sites, birthplaces of prophets, scenes of revelations, centers of religious authority and worship—places where the veil between the material and spiritual world was only lightly drawn. Jerusalem, for example, is a sacred site for the three religions of the book: Christianity, Judaism, and Islam. The sharing of this sacred space by different religions is part of the political tension in the city. Some sites become places of pilgrimage. One of the principal duties of every devout Muslim is to make a pilgrimage to Mecca at least once in their life. Catholics in medieval Europe made pilgrimages to the tomb of St. James in Santiago de Compostela in Spain. Pilgrims continue to follow these trails across the Pyrenees and through northern Spain.

Different sects of even the same religion have their own sacred sites. Catholics visit the shrine at Lourdes in search of cures for illness. The profane treatment of sacred sites can become sources of friction. In 1984 Indian troops attacked militants hiding out in the Golden Temple in Amritsar, one of the holiest places for Sikhs. The damage incensed the Sikh community and led to sectarian violence and the assassination of the prime minister who ordered the attack. Sectarian rivalry is expressed most vividly in the destruction of these special sites. In 2004, when terrorists exploded a bomb near the golden-domed mosque in Karbala in Iraq, they desecrated one of the most revered sites for Shia Muslims. The explosion triggered a bitter round of sectarian violence in Iraq between Shia and Sunni.

Second, there is the religious organization of space. In societies dominated by one religion, there is a conjoining of public and private space, a centrality of religious space in social and spatial organization. In medieval Europe, the tallest and most central buildings were the churches and cathedrals. They towered over the surrounding city as a constant symbol of both religious expression and the central importance of religiosity in organizing human affairs. There are also the territorial administrative units of religion. The Catholic Church, with its center in Rome, is divided into archdioceses, dioceses, and parishes (Figure 10.8). In more

10.8 St. Peter's in Rome is an important center for Roman Catholicism.

multicultural societies, the spatial organizing role of religion may be more opaque. An eruv is a Jewish ritual enclosure that marks out a space in which Jews observing the Sabbath can carry things and move between public and private space without transgressing Orthodox beliefs. In the Upper West Side of Manhattan, an area of 200 city blocks was separated out using existing walls and fences and specially made cord and wire. Figure 10.9 shows the map of another eruv in New Rochelle,

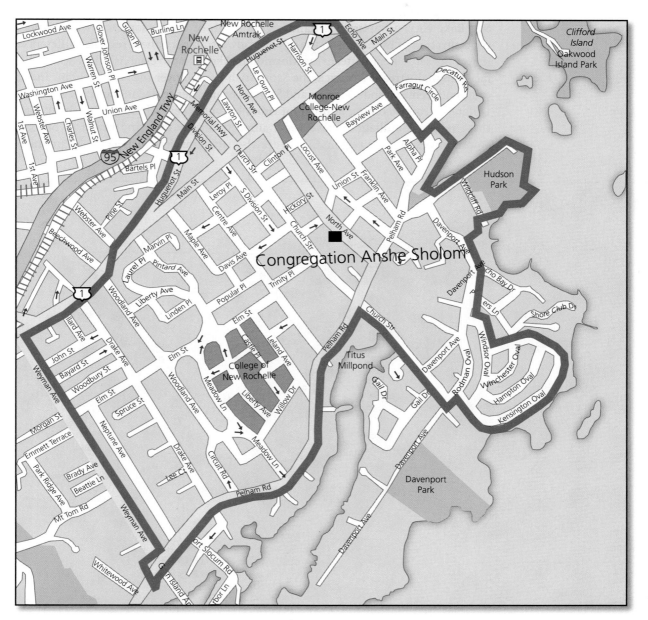

10.9   An eruv in New Rochelle, New York

New York, centered around the Congregation Anshe Sholom. An eruv is a silent presence, a marker for only some members of the community. The connection between religion and space also varies by gender. Gender relations are often encoded in religious beliefs through the demarcation of public and private space, with differential access afforded to men and women.

Third, there is the spatial expression of religion beliefs and practices. Figure 10.10 plots the majority church affiliation in every county in the United States. Distinct regional groupings are evident: Mormons in the mountain west, grouped around Salt Lake City; a Baptist heartland region south of the Mason-Dixon Line; and a concentration of Lutherans in the upper Midwest. In part, these regional differences reflect the settlement patterns, as Mormon trekked west to establish their way of life far from mainstream America, the Scots-Irish poured over the Appalachians in the eighteenth century, and Germans and Scandinavians later settled in the upper Midwest. Different groups coming at different times brought their religions with them. And these religious affiliations have wider impacts on the tone and practices of local communities in these regions. There are also small outliers such as the Mennonites

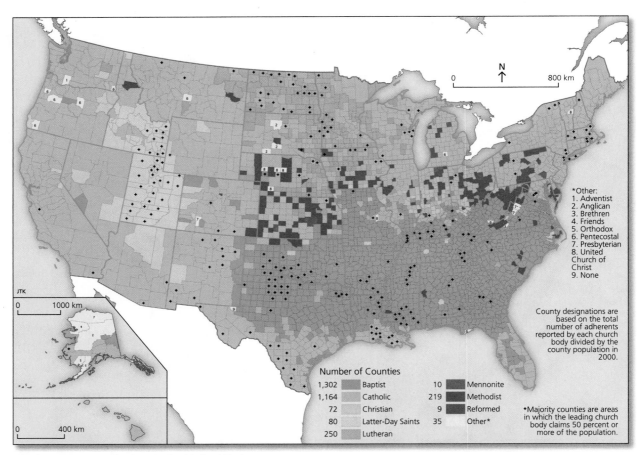

10.10 Religious affiliation in the United States

in selected rural counties. The geographer John Bauer, using a slightly different religious classification, looked at regional changes in religious affiliation from 1980 to 2000. While there was great stability, there were also some marked changes as the strength of Catholic region deepened and extended in the West, a trend associated with increasing size of the Hispanic population.

The traditional maps that plot the distribution for the major religions are now inadequate to convey the complexity of religious devotion in this latest wave of globalization. When there are mosques in Detroit and ashrams in Memphis, the spatial geography of religion is more complex than can be summarized in simple maps that shade in entire areas with a single category of religious belief. This very diversity is also an important generator of religious fundamentalism. At a more global scale, we are now in an era of both religious fundamentalism and religious diversity. The recent wave of globalization has spread and diffused different religions around the world.

Religious beliefs are part of cultural identity, for some people the principal source of their identity. So when they feel their beliefs are under attack or threat, from secularism or other religions, the political backlash can be profound. We are in an interesting time with powerful competing forces. On the one hand, we are in the middle of a major wave of cultural globalization and the expression of religious diversity in shared national spaces; on the other, we are also witnessing a rise of religious fundamentalism, whether in a fundamentalist Islam that promotes sharia law based on the Koran, a Hindu fundamentalism strongly associated with Indian nationalism, Jewish fundamentalism that sees occupation of the West Bank as part of God's covenant, or Christian fundamentalists arguing for the Ten Commandments as the guiding light of civil law. For many, religious belief provides a simple message in a complex world, an articulation of fixed primary identity when cultural change is everywhere, a platform and vehicle for political mobilization, and an anchor of meaning and relevance in a society of ever-accelerating transformation.

THE COMMODIFICATION OF CULTURE

Globalization has not disrupted the long connection between culture and place, but it has added some new wrinkles. The commodification of selected cultural forms has transformed some local cultures into globalized forms. Hollywood movies, for example, are now more international, dealing with broader themes than simply US concerns. Indian restaurants serve food that is only ever found in Indian restaurants around the world rather than replicating dishes from India. Sushi restaurants are found not only in Japan but in cities all over the world and have become an important signifier of coolness.

In some cases, cultural globalization is aided by the nature of national cultures. Big-budget Hollywood movies tend to draw upon US themes to provide narrative drive and meaning. But what exactly is this America that is being represented? It is an America that has to appeal to a heterogeneous experience even within the United States. In order for things to sell well in the United States, they already need to have a level of smoothing in order for them to succeed throughout the country. Much of the warp and weft of life in specific parts of the United States is filtered through the need to reach a more general national market. A case can be made that American culture has been so successful in achieving global penetration because it is already been partly globalized just in order to reach a wide US audience. The country is so diverse and heterogeneous that successful US cultural products have to be smoothed out in order to succeed, and that makes them already primed for global dispersal.

National and local cultures in turn also influence global cultural forms. As more and more US films are sold abroad, US filmmakers have to make allowances for foreign markets. The particularities of US life are replaced in expensive Hollywood movies by images, plots, and characters that are instantly recognizable in foreign markets.

The commodification of culture does lead to a certain similarity in the cultural mix available to audiences around the world. But the more astute companies tailor their cultural products for specific audiences. Akio Morita, the legendary head of Sony, first coined the term "glocalization," which represented a business strategy to create worldwide operations that were attuned to local markets and conditions. Two waves of Coca-Cola globalization can be identified. The first and earliest involved the marketing and sale of Coca-Cola. The second and more recent involves the sale of Coca-Cola alongside the sale and marketing of "local" brands. In Brazil, soft drinks are often marketed by Coca-Cola as rainforest drinks with "forest" tastes and plant sources.

Culture is not divorced from commerce. Fredric Jameson notes that in the latest stage of capitalism, symbolic meanings and associations increasingly determine the economic value of goods. Imposing symbolism, meanings, values, and emotions onto goods blurs the boundary between the image of those products and their concrete reality. There is now an intrinsic link between economics and culture. There is even a range of cultural industries that includes music, dance, theatre, literature, the visual arts, crafts, and many newer forms of practice, such as video art, performance art, computer art, and multimedia art. The economic geographer Allen Scott introduces a broader list of "cultural-products sectors," which includes high fashion, furniture design, news media, jewelry, advertising, and architecture.

THE MYTH OF HOMOGENEITY

Debates on cultural globalization often polarize into whether the recent surge of cultural flows and global consciousness has increased or decreased sameness between people and places around the world. One popular argument is that the world is becoming more alike as more of the world is drinking Coca-Cola, eating at McDonald's, and watching Disney movies. It is a compelling image that captures some if not all of the complexity. The facts that people across the globe are watching CNN and MTV, that McDonald's restaurants are opening throughout

10.11 Fast food in Shanghai

the world, and that Hollywood films dominate the world film market are taken as indisputable evidences of the homogenization and Americanization of the world (Figure 10.11). The homogenization thesis assumes that the same things are consumed in the same ways.

An alternative argument is that, while particular television programs, sport spectacles, network news, advertisements, and films may rapidly encircle the globe, this does not mean that the responses of those viewing and listening will be uniform. Goods, ideas, and symbols may be diffused globally, but they are consumed within national and local cultures. Ideas, symbols, and goods that circulate around the world are consumed in national contexts and in local circumstances. Similar goods mean different things in different places. There is enough variation to suggest that there is little prospect of a unified global culture; rather, there are a variety of global cultures. Specific cultural backgrounds are not just empty containers for the receipt of global messages, they are critical to how messages are received and consumed. People in the contemporary world have become increasingly familiar with the presence of different cultures, rather than being sucked into a single cultural orbit. To be sure, more people around the world can draw upon a similar range of flows, but there is still a wide variety of cultural formations. In fact, cultural globalization has led to a more explicit concern with more local cultures as certain groups seek to redefine or reestablish their place in the world.

We can replace the popular image of local cultures under assault from a global culture with a more complex picture of local cultures being generated and recreated in response to globalization. The sense of a pervasive globalization has not so much overwhelmed local cultures as helped create them. The search for authenticity in "pure" local cultures (which are in fact mixtures) has helped in the creation of world music, ethnic cuisine, and indigenous culture. Religious fundamentalism is less a return to a pure theocratic ideology and more the self-conscious recreation of religious beliefs in the face of secularization and globalization. Cultural authenticity is less an excavation of the pure and more a contemporary representation of the contrived.

Cited References

Anderson, K. J. (1987) The Idea of Chinatown: The Power of Place and Institutional Practice in the Making of a Racial Category. *Annals of Association of American Geographers* 77: 580–598.

Appadurai, A. (1996) *Modernity at Large: Cultural Dimensions of Globalization* Minneapolis: University of Minnesota Press.

Armstrong. K. (2006) *The Great Transformation: The Beginning of Our Religious Traditions.* New York: Knopf.

Bauer, J. T. (2012) U.S. Religious Regions Revisited. *The Professional Geographer* 64: 521–539.

Crystal, D. (2003) *English as a Global Language.* 2nd ed. Cambridge: Cambridge University Press.

Crystal, D. (2010) *Evolving English: One Language, Many Voices.* London: British Library.

Ehrenreich, B. (2006) *Dancing in The Streets.* New York: Metropolitan.

Gorenflo, L. J., Romaine, S., Mittermeier, R. A., and Walker-Painemilla, K. (2012) Co-occurrence of Linguistic and Biological Diversity in Biodiversity Hotspots and High Biodiversity Wilderness Areas. *Proceedings of National Academy of Sciences* 109: 8032–8037.

Harrison, K. D. (2007) *When Languages Die: The Extinction of the World's Languages and the Erosion of Human Knowledge.* New York: Oxford University Press.

Jameson. F. (1991) *Postmodernism, or, The Cultural Logic of Late Capitalism.* Durham: Duke University Press.

Krupnik, I. (2011) How Many Eskimo Words for Ice? Collecting Inuit Sea Ice Terminologies in the International Polar Year 2007–2008. *The Canadian Geographer* 55: 56–68.

McCrum, R. (2010) *Globish.* New York: Norton

Nettle, D. and Romaine, S. (2000) *Vanishing Voices: The Extinction of the World's Languages.* New York: Oxford University Press.

Price, M. and Benton-Short, L. (eds) (2008) *Migrants to the Metropolis.* Syracuse, NY: Syracuse University Press.

Robb, G. (2007) *The Discovery of France: A Historical Geography from the Revolution to the First World War.* New York: W.W. Norton.

Select Guide to Further Reading

Collins-Kreiner, N. (2010) The Geography of Pilgrimage and Tourism: Transformations and Implications for Applied Geography. *Applied Geography* 30:153–164.

Eira, I. M. G., Jaedicke, C., Magga, O. H., Maynard, N. G., Vikhamar-Schuler, D., and Mathiesen, S. D. (2013) Traditional Sámi Snow Terminology and Physical Snow Classification—Two Ways of Knowing. *Cold Regions Science and Technology* 85: 117–130.

Morin, K. M. and Guelke, J. K. (eds) (2007) *Women, Religion and Space.* Syracuse, NY: Syracuse University Press.

Jones, R. C. (2008) *Immigrants outside Megalopolis: Ethnic Transformation in the Heartland.* Lanham, MD: Rowman & Littlefield.

Knox, P. (2011) *Cities and Design.* New York and London: Routledge.

Lees, L. (2001) Towards a Critical Geography of Architecture: The Case of an Ersatz Colosseum. *Cultural Geographies* 8: 51–86.

Robson, D. (2012) Chilly Words: How Eskimos Really Say "Snow." *New Scientist* 216: 2896–2897.

Shelton, T., Zook, M., and Graham, M. (2012) The Technology of Religion: Mapping Religious Cyberscapes. *The Professional Geographer* 64: 602–617.

Short, J. R., Boniche, A., Kim, Y., and Li, P. (2001) Cultural Globalization, Global English and Geography Journals. *Professional Geographer* 53: 1–11.

Stump, R. W. (2008) *The Geography of Religion*. Lanham, MD: Rowman & Littlefield.

Watson, S. (2005) Symbolic Spaces of Difference: Contesting the Eruv in Barnet, London and Tenafly, New Jersey. *Environment and Planning D: Society and Space* 23:597–613.

Websites

Alice Statler Library – travel and tourism industry statistics
    http://www.ccsf.edu/Library/alice/hospitality/travelstats.html

International Organization for Migration
    http://www.iom.int/cms/en/sites/iom/home/about-migration/facts—Figures-1.html

OECD International Migration Statistics
    http://www.oecd-ilibrary.org/social-issues-migration-health/data/oecd-international-migration-statistics_mig-data-en

World Bank – tourism statistics
    http://data.worldbank.org/indicator/ST.INT.ARVL

World Tourism Organization Yearbook 2012
    http://www2.unwto.org/en/publication/yearbook-tourism-statistics-data-2006-2010-2012-edition

UN migration issues
    http://unstats.un.org/unsd/demographic/sconcerns/migration

PART 5

The Political Organization of Space

There are many relationships between space and politics. There are the various organizations of political space, such as empires, states, and administrative units. Politics also revolves around issues of space and place, such as when neighboring states have boundary disputes or when a city government tries to locate a new incinerator. Finally, many political processes take place in space, as in the geography of elections. In this part we will look at some of these themes. Chapter 11 will focus on empires, and chapter 12 will consider the nation-state.

11 Empires

The very earliest form of human society was small groups of extended families that, over time, merged into larger social units, eventually creating such diverse socio-spatial entities as empires, city-states, and nation-states. In this chapter we will look at empires as a spatial unit of political organization.

EARLY EMPIRES

Some of the earliest empires were city-states in Mesopotamia. The city of Uruk emerged around six thousand years ago in the southern part of Mesopotamia. Settled agriculture, sophisticated irrigation, and a marked division of labor propelled Uruk's growth. The city broadened its influence, referred to as the "Uruk expansion," through a wider net of control in the upper reaches of Mesopotamia, between the Euphrates and Tigris Rivers. Surrounding peoples were brought into the cultural and economic control of Uruk. The city's elites developed more expensive tastes, and the search for more exotic goods and materials to meet this demand drove the expansion. Eventually, expansion reached its peak and then turned into decline. In a process that is repeated over and over again, the empire collapsed, local traditions reemerged in regions formerly controlled by Uruk, and in the main city, invaders razed the monumental buildings of the temple.

There are a number of themes in this empire's brief story that figure in later imperial experiences: empires emerge, extend their reach, and then collapse from external pressures and internal conflicts. Across time and over space, the same process is repeated. What is different is the increasing territorial extent of the empires and the enduring consequences of imperial incorporation. Subsequent imperial history is of powers becoming larger and their territorial reach more extensive as space-convergence improvements extend the effective imperial range. In the Middle East, after Uruk came the Hittites, the Assyrians, and the Persians. The Persian Empire peaked from around 559 BCE to 331 BCE (Figure 11.1), its spatial expansion aided by the greater use of more mobile cavalry and better roads. At its greatest extent it covered a vast area, from the Indus Valley in the east to Greece in the west and from Central Asia in the north to southern Egypt on the southern reaches.

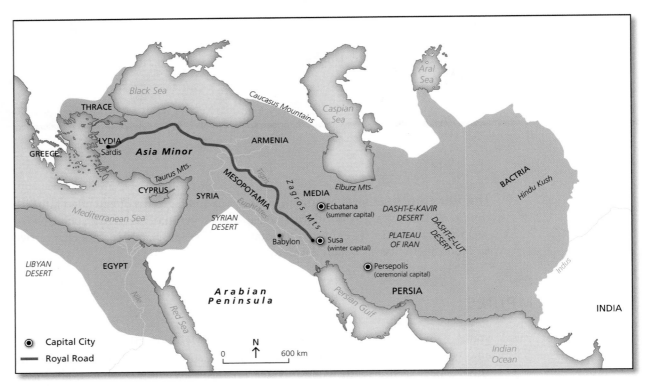

11.1 The Persian Empire

We can make some generalization about the geography of empire. Through time, empires grow in size as they are more able to overcome the tyranny of distance. While the Uruk expansion was limited to the Tigris and Euphrates river basins, the Persian Empire stretched from the Mediterranean Sea to the Indus River. Better transport and improved road networks enable empires to extend their spatial reach. Yet empires, no matter how vast, have territorial limits to their power. As they expand further from the core, their ability to wield effective and overpowering force tends to weaken. There is a distance decay effect in their military power and political reach. Far from the empire's center, borders are vulnerable. The early empires relied on force whose effectiveness declined markedly with distance from the imperial center. The further an early empire stretched, the more difficult it was to control the ever-more-distant periphery. There were limits on early imperial expansion because of the marked "distance decay" effect of military reach and political control.

The historical geography of the world is filled with the rise and fall of empires and the spatial spread of imperial influences. Alexander the Great reversed the flow of Persian influence by extending Greek influence throughout Eurasia, taking over much of the remnants of the Persian Empire. The Roman Empire turned the Mediterranean into a Roman lake. These and other empires, such as the Mali in West Africa and the Mayan, Aztec, and Inca in the Americas, were also cohering spatial units that in many cases created a more homogenous political surface that aided cultural mixing, economic ties, and religious dispersals which diffused creeds and beliefs across space. Empires pulled peoples and region together in shared experiences of (often forced and brutal) spatial convergence. Empires promoted global integration.

MODERN EMPIRES

The more recent the empire, the greater its enduring consequences. English is spoken around the world because of the wide sphere of influence of the British Empire. The experience of empire is one of the most important global phenomena of the past five hundred years. I will discuss three spatial elements: global integration, imperial overstretch, and imperial disintegration.

GLOBAL INTEGRATION

The global integration of space is the defining feature of early modernity. Charles Parker argues that in the period 1400 to 1800, empire building across the globe (including the Chinese, Ottoman, Mughal, and Safavid as well as the Spanish and British) created international markets and global exchange networks. These global empires encouraged, forced, and facilitated the movement of people, the spread of new technologies, the diffusion of cultures, and the transmission of religion and scientific practices. The result was a tighter integration of global space. Increasing contact between different cultures led to cross-cultural borrowings. Portugal's trade with Africa, Asia, and South America in the sixteenth and seventeenth centuries resulted in a complex aesthetic blending and technological borrowing: West African wooden and ivory sculpture that incorporated Portuguese figures, precious objects produced in Goa using Christian iconography for the market in Portugal, Japanese paintings that depicted Portuguese merchants, and the introduction of European firearms and maps into Japan.

Whether in intellectual discourses and practices, such as cartography and mapmaking, or in sports, language, religion, and forms of government, modern empires have integrated much of the world: Spanish-speaking South America, cricket playing in India and rugby in Fiji, Catholicism in Goa, and British-inspired representative government in Australia and Canada are just some of the many consequences of the globally integrating effects of modern empires.

Empire was not undertaken just for the opportunity of cross-cultural integration. There was a hard material core. Empires provided access to resources. The push to empire in the modern world was largely driven by economics. Spain and Portugal laid claims to vast territory in the New World, Africa, and Asia to provide gold, silver, spices, and raw materials for the home countries. The British-based East India Company, and subsequently the British Crown, created a commercial empire on the Indian subcontinent because it provided a rich source of raw materials for British industry as well as a captive market for goods produced in Britain. The Dutch East India Company, and subsequently the Dutch state, annexed land in South America and islands in the Caribbean (Figure 11.2).

It is possible to identify a core-periphery spatial structure to the global political economy that emerged from this imperial relationship. The core consisted of the imperial centers in Europe, with a vast periphery of regions throughout the world under their control. The success of the core was predicated upon the exploitation of the periphery.

From the sixteenth to the twentieth century, much of the world was incorporated by these core powers. Incorporation was achieved through a variety of means, including colonization, informal control, and direct imperial annexation. The British Empire, for example, colonized North America and Australia, had informal control in South America, and annexed much of the Indian subcontinent. Empire could be costly—much better to have economic control without political responsibilities. British economic interests were vigorously pursued in South America without formal annexation. Latin America was the real success story of British commercial empire, because there was market penetration without enacting the responsibilities of formal empire. Direct imperial annexation was, in a sense, a sign of failure to achieve economic ends without direct political intervention. Formal annexation became more common in the late nineteenth century because of increasing imperial rivalries between core countries. Formal imperialism also resulted when the ruling elites of peripheral countries refused to go along with business arrangements.

11.2 The Dutch Empire in the New World. Willemstad, Curaçao, retains its Dutch architectural heritage. The Dutch controlled the island from 1634. It was a center of the slave trade.

Box 11.1   THE CARIBBEAN AS IMPERIAL SHATTER ZONE

The shifting balance of imperial victory and defeat is evident in the changing ownership of islands in the Caribbean. From 1492, the Spanish expanded their imperial control to the large islands of the Caribbean and most of the mainland in the search for gold, precious minerals, and land. It was difficult to retain effective control over the scatter of islands in the Caribbean. They were too many and too widely scattered to police effectively. From 1600 to 1800, other European powers moved into the Caribbean to establish sugar plantations. They were able to annex various groups of islands and the more remote slices of the mainland. The Dutch for example, gained control of slivers of land in South America as well as of the smaller islands of Aruba, Bonaire, and Curaçao. The French gained control of various islands, some of which remain part of France to this day. In 1657 the Danish West India Company established the town of St. Thomas, in what is now the US Virgin Islands, as the center of a sugar plantation economy based on slave labor.

The need for labor to work the mines and plantations and the decline of the indigenous population led to the slave trade, in which almost 20 million people were captured in Africa and shipped to the New World. The Caribbean was transformed in the process as millions of African slaves became a vital part of the economic geography of the region, an important cultural element, and a nascent political force. The sugar colonies were the scenes of constant eruptions as slaves continually revolted against the appalling living and working conditions. Effective control was always difficult to maintain. These islands were far from the core countries. And after emancipation, the former slaves sought both economic freedom and political independence.

The competition and shifting alliances between European powers were often embodied in changes of territorial control. Consider the island of Dominica, which was under French control from 1632 to 1761, then British control, then French control again from 1778 to 1783, and then British again until it achieved independence in 1978. Most of the small island nations of the Caribbean have similarly complex histories. Trinidad was under Spanish control from 1532 to 1797, when it became a British territory until achieving independence in 1962. St. Lucia was held nine different times by France and six different times by the British, including the last colonial period of 1803 to 1979, when it finally became independent. The French legacy can be heard in the language of the locals.

The imperial legacy lives on. France still controls St. Bart's, Martinique, and Guadeloupe, the latter two being departments of France (equivalent to states in the United States). Montserrat remains a British territory, as do the British Virgin Islands. The Dutch have effective control over Aruba, Curaçao, and Bonaire and share control of the small island of St. Maarten/St. Martin with the French. In 1898 the United States invaded Puerto Rico, and in 1904 it acquired land along what was to be the Panama Canal. In 1917 the United States bought the Virgin Islands from Denmark, less an economic move (as the sugar economy had slumped) and more part of a geopolitical strategy of maintaining a more visible military position in the region and to protect its interests in the Panama Canal.

Colonization involved a rewriting of space to show who was in control and who was controlled. Timothy Mitchell identifies three broad strategies for the framing of colonial states: producing a plan of urban segmentation that includes racial segregation, creating a fixed distinction between inside and outside, and constructing central spaces of observation to keep an eye on things and to show the presence of colonial power. Under British rule in Accra, now the capital of Ghana, new areas of European settlement were created that were sharply demarcated from the "native" areas. Laws barred "natives" from living in areas reserved for whites. Further north, Tunis came under French rule in 1881. The French built neoclassical buildings and created straight boulevards and symmetrical squares as a direct response to the tight and convoluted street pattern of the old Arab town: Gallic "rationalism" counterpoised to Islamic "chaos."

A key concept is that of the ruling elites, the groups that have power in a country or region. Collaborative elites reproduce the imperial center. This was the case of Anglo-Americans in North America before the American Revolution and the British colonial settlers in Australia and New Zealand. Collaborative elites can also encourage imperial incorporation. Throughout much of Africa and India, for example, the British authorities used indirect rule, working through local rulers who were rewarded for their efforts. Local leaders and existing hierarchies were employed to secure colonial rule. If and when the collaborative elite lost legitimacy and their grip on power, then the colonial powers often had to intervene.

The spatial structure of core-periphery, in which the periphery is used as a source of raw materials and as a market for goods produced in the core, laid the basis for subsequent economic development. The core industrialized while the periphery remained a cheap resource base and a secure market for manufactured goods. The industrial revolution in core countries was built on the foundation of unequal exchange between the core and the periphery. The poverty of much of the developing world is a direct result of the core-periphery structure.

The late nineteenth century also saw the "age of imperialism." From around 1880 to 1918, there was a scramble for territory as old and new European powers struggled to incorporate more of the periphery. A map of Africa in 1880 shows the limited range of European influence on the continent. But by 1914, most of the continent had been annexed by European powers, large and small (Figures 11.3 and 11.4). The age of imperialism resulted from growing competition between core powers, a belief that national economic development was made easier by possessing colonial territory, and the feeling that each significant power had to do something in order to not to be left out of the "spoils." Even tiny Belgium laid claim to a vast territory in the middle of the African continent.

By the second half of the twentieth century, the struggle for global supremacy was fought out between the United States and the USSR. Each had long histories of territorial annexation. The United States expanded out from a narrow sliver along the eastern seaboard through treaties, purchase, and conquest to become a continental power. In the late nineteenth century, it also began overseas expansion,

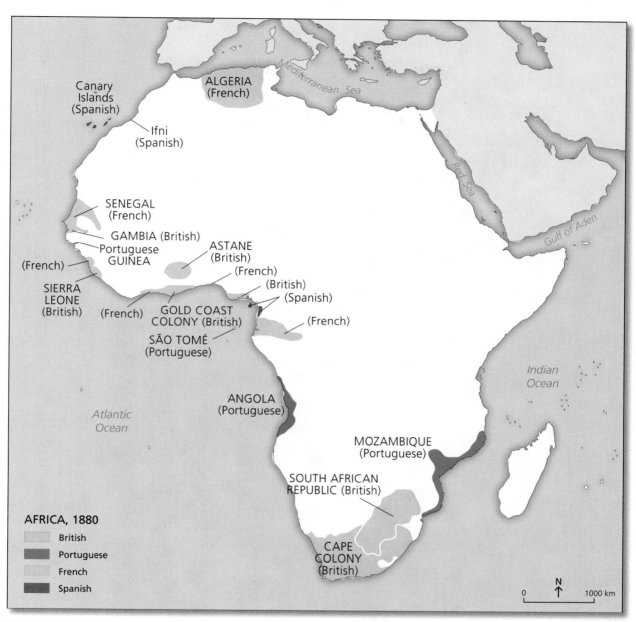

11.3 Africa, 1880

purchasing Alaska from the Russians in 1867 and picking up territories from a declining Spanish Empire, such as Puerto Rico and the Philippines. Hawaii was annexed in 1888. We have an interesting record of this imperial expansion in a popular children's book of the time, *The Navy Alphabet*, which was first printed in 1900 and was written by Frank Baum, who also wrote *The Wizard of Oz*. An illustration

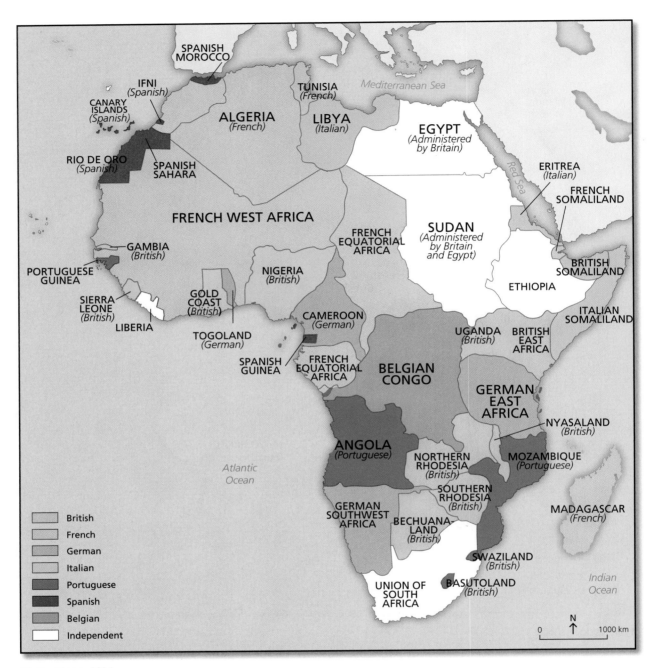

11.4 Africa, 1914

that accompanies the text clearly shows the imperial nature of the United States, with explicit use of the term "colonies" (Figure 11.5).

The Russian Empire grew from a tiny area centered on Moscow to become a vast continental power stretching from the Baltic to the Pacific and from the Arctic to

11.5 Teaching the US Empire, 1900

the subtropics. In 1462 Muscovy was a small isolated region. From this tiny enclave a Russian empire was created through annexation of territory. There was an early move east, drawn in part by the lure of the fur trade. By 1639 the Russians claimed land all the way to the Pacific. The empire was also extended to the west and south. In the north and west, territory was obtained in war with Sweden and Poland. In 1703 St. Petersburg was built by Peter the Great as a major port and as a "window on the west." In the south, the Russians annexed territory from the Tatars and other Turkic peoples, and in 1794 Odessa became the principal Russian port for trade through the Black Sea and Mediterranean. A small landlocked territory had expanded to become a major continental power. When the Bolsheviks grabbed power in 1917, the Russian Empire became the Soviet Empire.

The struggle between the United States and the USSR, called the Cold War, went through several phases. The chilliest period was from 1947 to 1964, as the USSR laid effective claim to most of European Europe by installing and maintaining communist regimes. In 1947 the Truman Doctrine announced that the United States would adopt a global posture against the USSR. Both countries established bases all over the world, formed alliances, and built up their military capabilities. Direct conflict did not occur, and a period of détente (less overt conflict) from 1964 to 1979 (when the USSR invaded Afghanistan) marked a warming of the interactions between the two superpowers. The military buildups and geopolitical maneuverings around the world continued, however, while, like two chess players with the world as their board, they moved pieces to gain advantage. Local elites remained in power with imperial backing if they tied their existence to imperial imperatives. Throughout much of the Cold War, for example, local elites in countries around the world, such as the Philippines under Marcos, maintained their grip on power by reminding the United States of their anti-communist credentials or, in the case of Cuba, informing the Soviet Union of their anti-capitalist policies.

A new cold war emerged in 1980 with a significant rise in military buildup. As each side responded to the other's military increases, there was steady escalation, and the dialogue of détente was replaced by the rhetoric of confrontation. The gradual decline of the USSR and its eventual collapse in 1991 meant the end of the bipolar structure of global geopolitics. The United States remains as the world's only superpower with a global reach.

The United States is not an empire in the old sense of colonial possessions. However, the US Empire is now a sprawling archipelago of military bases around the world, a vast military-industrial-security complex backing a pervasive worldview dominated by visions of global hegemony. There are now at least 700 bases with half a million US personnel spread around the world in at least 130 countries. The United States is the most powerful military state, with the ability to assert global reach. The contemporary US Empire is not like previous empires that annexed territory and peoples into a singular political orbit. The earlier fragments of US Empire, such as Hawaii and Puerto Rico, have long since been incorporated. The US Empire is less about annexing territory and subjugating peoples and more about orchestrating a global order to extend and maintain global economic connectivity.

IMPERIAL OVERSTRETCH

The rise and fall of empires is an enduring metaphor for the cyclical nature of success and failure as well as a constant reminder of the spatial limits of territorial expansion. What lies behind the fall of global empires? Paul Kennedy identifies "imperial overstretch," the tendency for empires to expand beyond their ability to maintain economic dominance and military power. The tendency to initiate and expand military commitments tends to undercut the economic ability to pay for them. In other words, the hubris of empire tends to lead to entanglements that gnaw away at the economic foundation of empire. The collapse of the Soviet Union, for example, was in part due to the inability of the state to maintain its expensive military posture as its economy was disintegrating. The United States is currently facing a fiscal crisis as it tries to pay for expensive social programs as well as the escalating cost of empire.

There are numerous limits to empire. The first is information overload. The bigger the empire, the more the information that needs to be analyzed and turned into convincing narratives. The second and most important is the fiscal limit, as imperial overstretch bumps up against the ability to pay for all the commitments. The possibilities for involvement are infinite, while the ability to pay for them is finite, especially at times of economic distress and declining relative economic power. Third, there are the strategic limits. As strategies and forces are continually restructured according to the demands of the last conflict, there is always the possibility that these will be unable to deal with new conflicts. Thus, in 2001, the US military was very well able to fight against another superpower, but unable to conduct an asymmetric war against small bands of transnational terrorists or undertake the nation-building necessary after the invasion of Afghanistan and Iraq. Big military powers have long reaction times that in a quick-changing world make them vulnerable to outdated assumptions, failed strategies, and incorrect tactics. Fourth, there is also the possibility of a "legitimation crisis," which can be defined as a major loss of public support for military involvements. These are more

Box 11.2 THE GLOBAL PRODUCTION OF SPACE

The production of global space has two distinct meanings, the creation of an understanding of the world's geography and the representation of this geography in cartographic forms. A traditional view sees both things simply as a Eurocentric process in which European powers incorporated the world into a global discourse and created new, more modern forms of cartographic representation. It is the story of how Europe explored, discovered, and mapped the world, displacing older, indigenous cartographies with more scientific mappings. Cartographic modernity in this rendering is exported from Europe to the rest of the world. There is now an exciting body of work that points to the creation of new knowledge in the process of interactions and encounters between colonial and colonized, the imperial center and the periphery, the modern and the indigenous. Knowledge was not so much imposed from one region of the world but created and circulated in a complex series of interactions in many different regions of the world. Modernity was created in the space of encounters, continually imported, transformed, and modified and then re-exported in a continual and ongoing global circulation of ideas and practices.

Kapil Raj describes the integration in the circulation of knowledge between South Asia and Europe between 1650 and 1900. Raj undermines the traditional view that science was exported from the European core to the colonial periphery. He shows that there was an intercultural knowledge encounter that produced new knowledge. In particular, the case of the geographical exploration of British India in the late eighteenth and early nineteenth centuries provides a good illustration of the way in which British and Indian practitioners and skills met around specific projects, how they were reshaped, and how the modern map and its uses co-emerged in India and Britain through the colonial encounter.

References

Raj, K. (2007) *Relocating Modern Science: Circulation and the Construction of Knowledge in South Asia and Europe, 1650–1900*. New York: Palgrave.

Short, J. R. (2012) *Korea; A Cartographic History*. Chicago: University of Chicago Press.

pronounced in more democratic societies, as the public can more easily voice its disapproval. Quick and successful troop deployments are easy to justify. The stunning success of the Gulf War in 1991 was, for many in the United States, a source of national pride, this single campaign erasing many of the wounds of Vietnam as the US military was applauded and honored rather than shunned and vilified. Fast-forward twelve years, and as the invasion of Iraq soon turned into a quagmire, with the mounting carnage shown nightly on television, public enthusiasm for the war faltered and waned. When empire involves seemingly ceaseless, costly campaigns, public opinion comes into play. The visible costs of empire can provoke a crisis of legitimation if wars and military engagements are too onerous for too long.

IMPERIAL DISINTEGRATION

Empires come and go, but their going is rarely easy. After the end of the Second World War, there was a wave of decolonization as imperial powers either left or were effectively kicked out of their colonial possessions. From 1945 to 1954, the wave was felt most intensely in Asia. The Dutch fought off independence struggles in Indonesia, but the persistent resistance finally led to the country becoming independent in 1949. The French had control over what was called French Indo-China, consisting of what is today Cambodia, Laos, and Vietnam, but here the independence struggle against French colonialism was interpreted by the United States as communist insurgency. An anti-colonial nationalist struggle was entangled by a superpower's geopolitical strategy as the Vietnamese fight for independence became the Vietnam War.

The decolonization of Africa came in the second wave, with independence for Sudan (1956), Ghana (1957), and Kenya (1963). In some cases, the struggle was intense. British authority in Kenya was contested especially by the members of the Kikuyu tribe, who mounted a guerilla campaign in pursuit of their goal of independence. The British responded by not only waging a counterinsurgency but also setting up a system of detention camps where up to 1.5 million people were rounded up and imprisoned. In a detailed study, the historian Caroline Elkins came to the conclusion that "there was in late colonial Kenya a murderous campaign to eliminate Kikuyu people, a campaign that left tens of thousands, perhaps hundreds of thousands, dead" (Elkins 2005, p. xvi).

With few "national" borders before colonization, many of the independence movements in Africa existed within the boundaries drawn up in arbitrary divisions of spoils by imperial cartographers. The result was that the national boundaries of post-independence Africa emerged from this cartographic legacy. These national boundaries, drawn initially for colonial convenience and compromise, cut across centuries-old tribal and ethnic differences that in some cases reemerged in the wake of decolonization. Compare Figure 11.4 with the contemporary political map of Africa in Figure 11.6 to see the enduring legacy of colonial borders and boundaries on present-day African nation-states. A major problem for the newly independent states was how to create national unity and national identity from such a variegated base. In some cases, the new nations are continually split apart by the resurfacing of tribal and ethnic differences.

The fall of the Soviet Union in 1991 is just the latest in a long line of imperial collapses. When popular uprisings took hold in East Germany in 1989, the Soviet leadership did not send in the troops—something they had done in Hungary in 1956 and in Czechoslovakia in 1968 to snuff out the popular uprising known as the Prague Spring. The system was economically and politically bankrupt, with the more astute leaders able to see the limits to the Soviet Empire. The unpopularity of the Soviet-dominated Communist system in Eastern Europe fueled public discontent. The people, when given an opportunity, showed a profound lack of support for the regime and a strong desire to be rid of the old leadership and scrap the Communist system. Events moved quickly. In June 1989 the popular political

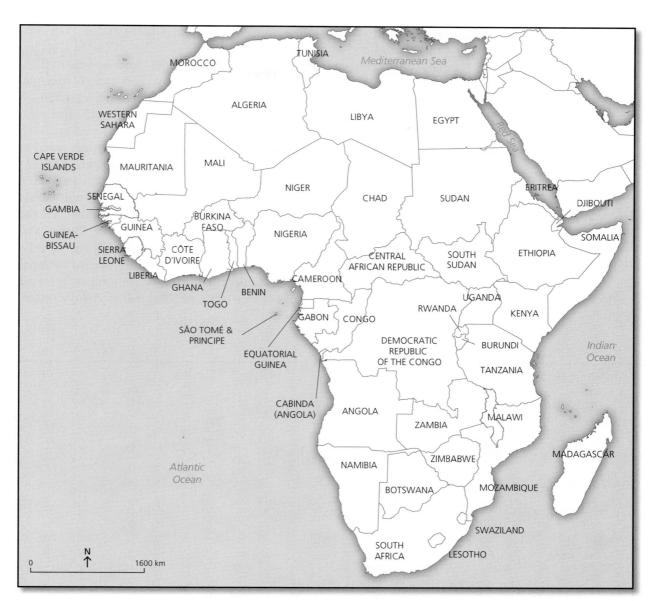

11.6 Political map of contemporary Africa

movement in Poland, Solidarity, won the first free election held for two generations. In September the Hungarians set a date for free elections. On November 9,
the Berlin Wall ceased to be a meaningful barrier as East Germans scrambled
freely over it, and Berliners, from both East and West, delighted in demolishing
the symbol of partition and Communist control. Later that year the Communist
leadership in Bulgaria, Czechoslovakia, East Germany, and Romania was overthrown by popular uprisings. The corrupt system collapsed as more and more
people voiced their disapproval. It was one of the rare examples of imperial decline

brought about by popular uprising and bottom-up resistance rather than top-down regime change.

New countries emerged from the break-up of the Soviet empire. Some of them had mature identities, such as the Baltic republics of Estonia, Latvia, and Lithuania, which had been swallowed whole by Soviet expansion. Others were broken off from larger national units, such as East Germany, a break that was healed with reunification with West Germany. Some were multiethnic agglomerations, such as Yugoslavia, which quickly began to break up over regional and ethnic tensions after 1989. In yet others, new states emerged in the post-imperial context. The political geographer Nick Megoran tells the story of Kyrgyzstan and Uzbekistan. Before 1924, these countries did not exist. The whole area was a complex, multiethnic place. It was annexed by the expanding Russian Empire in 1876, and in 1924 the now Soviet empire created the administrative structure of separate Kyrgyz and Uzbek units. This division helped forge separate identities, although not separate economic units. The collapse of the Soviet system in 1989 gave space for national emergence. In 1991 the two former regions of the USSR became separate states. Figure 11.7 outlines the borders of the new state of Kyrgyzstan. An uncertain,

11.7 Kyrgyzstan: Soviet imperial disintegration leads to new international boundaries in Central Asia.

Box 11.3 THE CLASH OF CIVILIZATIONS

In 1993 the political scientist Samuel Huntington wrote an essay with the provocative title "The Clash of Civilizations." He argued that people were divided along cultural lines drawn by religion, history, and geography. He identified nine different types of cultures, including Western, Islamic, Orthodox, Latin American, and Confucian. It is an odd mixture of the religious, such as Islamic and Confucian, and the purely geographical, such as Latin American and African. The most contentious conflict was between the West, characterized as societies founded on principles of pluralism, democracy, and individualism, and the Islamic, characterized as less tolerant of difference and authoritarian, with a primary commitment to religion and not to the nation-state.

Several criticisms are made of this argument. First, the categories are very large, homogeneous spatial blocs, whereas the real world is more fractured, with religious and cultural groups more widely dispersed and the spatial units more often heterogeneous than homogeneous. Flows and heterogeneity rather than closed boundaries and homogeneity mark a globalizing world. Second, the historical record of contact between Islam and the West reveals shared human values, commercial trading, and cultural exchange, interaction and penetration. Third, as the Arab Spring of 2011 revealed, the characteristics that Huntington asserted for the Islamic world were not eternal verities but the product of specific regimes and particular times. The demand for democratic inclusiveness is also a very important strain in parts of the Islamic world.

Huntington's ideas were given a wider play in the wake of 9/11. The idea of a clash of civilizations between the West and the Islamic world is also central to the ideologies of Islamic terrorist groups such as Al Qaeda. But despite the ongoing terrorist threat, the contemporary world is a more complex place than the broad cultural categories proposed by Huntington can encompass and more marked by civilization exchange and dialogue than outright clashes.

References

Huntingdon, S. P. (1993) The Clash of Civilizations. *Foreign Affairs* 72: 22–49.

Tolan, J. V., Veinstein, G., and Laurens, H. (2012) *Europe and the Islamic World*. Princeton: Princeton University Press.

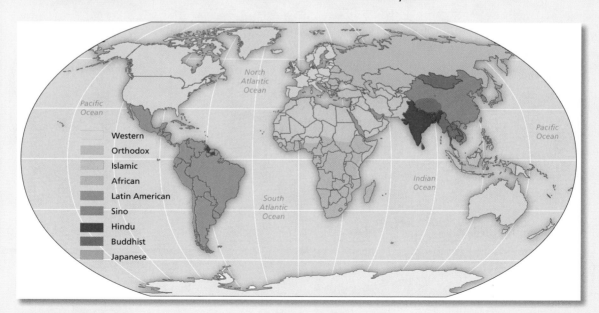

Clash of Civilizations

Box 11.4 THE PENTAGON'S VIEW OF THE WORLD

After the ending of the Cold War and the disintegration of the Soviet bloc, the United States remained as the world's sole superpower. With bases all over the world, a military budget that dwarfed those of all other countries, and the strategic capability of global reach, it was the most important military power on the planet. How does it see the world? It depends, of course, on the events, but Thomas Barnett provided a possible map of the Pentagon's general worldview. The world is divided into a functioning core marked by relative stability, rule of law, and integration into the global economy. Then there is a non-integrating gap marked by political instability, social unrest, and lack of integration into the global economy. Here is where the United States is involved in direct combat, shows of force, peacekeeping, anti-insurgency, and, at the extreme, drone strikes.

While very revealing, the map hides as much as it reveals. The non-integrating gap is shown as a solid surface, whereas in reality it contains islands of stability and places of connectivity. And in the core-functioning areas there are also areas of instability and insurgency. The map depicts solid homogenous surfaces, whereas the reality is a much more varied mosaic of difference. The map is an ideological rendering of a world divided into safe and unsafe areas by Pentagon strategists, rather than an accurate geographical rendering of global difference.

References

Barnett, T. (2004) *The Pentagon's New Map*. New York: Berkeley.

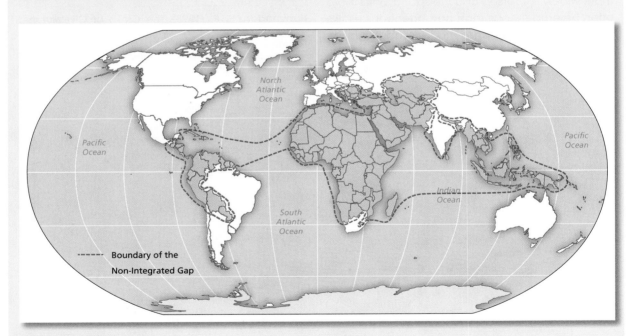

The Pentagon's world map

arbitrary, and hazy distinction now became codified into two separate states sharing an international boundary. Tensions between the two states erupted in 1998 and resulted in the closing of the border. The invented borders of the Soviet era moved from acts of imagination to lines of national conflict.

Cited References

Elkins, C. (2005) *Imperial Reckoning: The Untold Story of Britain's Gulag in Kenya.* New York: Henry Holt.

Kennedy, P. (1987) *The Rise and Fall of the Great Powers.* New York: Random House.

Megoran, N. (2012) Rethinking the Study of International Boundaries: A Biography of the Kyrgyzstan–Uzbekistan Boundary. *Annals of Association of American Geographers* 102: 464–481.

Mitchell, T. (1988) *Colonizing Egypt.* Berkeley and Los Angeles: University of California Press.

Parker, C. (2010) *Global Interactions in the Modern Age (1400–1800).* Cambridge: Cambridge University Press.

Select Guide to Further Reading

Alcock, S. E. (2001) *Empires.* Cambridge: Cambridge University Press.

Applebaum, A. (2012) *Iron Curtain: The Crushing of Eastern Europe, 1944–1956.* New York: Doubleday.

Brzezinski, Z. (2012) Balancing the East, Upgrading the West: U.S. Grand Strategy in an Age of Upheaval. *Foreign Affairs* 91: 97–104.

Burbank, J. and Cooper, F. (2010) *Empires in World History: Power and the Politics of Difference.* Princeton: Princeton University Press.

Darwin, J. (2010) *After Tamerlane: The Rise and Fall of Global Empires, 1400–2000.* London: Bloomsbury Press.

Levenson, J. A. (ed) (2007) *Encompassing the Globe: Portugal and the World in the 16th and 17th Centuries.* Washington, DC: Sackler Gallery, Smithsonian Institution.

Pagden, A. (2008) *Worlds at War: The 2,500-Year Struggle Between East and West.* New York: Random House.

Parker, G. (1998) *The Grand Strategy of Philip II.* New Haven: Yale University Press.

Parsons, T. H. (2010) *The Rule of Empires: Those Who Built Them, Those Who Endured Them, and Why They Always Fail.* Oxford: Oxford University Press.

Short, J. R. (2013) *Stress Testing the USA.* New York: Palgrave Macmillan.

Websites

A fascinating exhibition on Portugal and the world in the 16th and 17th centuries
http://www.asia.si.edu/encompassingtheglobe/

Empires through history
http://empires.findthedata.org

12 The Nation-State

The state is an important building block of the political organization of space. In this chapter we will consider the range of different types of states and introduce the notion of the nation-state as a spatial entity.

THE RANGE OF STATES

The land surface of the world is divided up into states, separate units of political authority (Figure 12.1). There is a steady rise in the number of states. In 1900 there were 57 independent countries, 70 by 1930, and 160 by 1990. There are now 193 member states in the United Nations. The increase in the past hundred years is due to decolonization, whereby former colonies such as Kenya, India, and Vietnam achieved independence, and break-ups, as formerly large empires and states fractured into separate national units. The break-up of the Austro-Hungarian empire after the First World War led to the creation of a large number of smaller units, including all or parts of Austria, Bosnia, Croatia, the Czech Republic, Hungary, Italy, Montenegro, Romania, Serbia, Slovakia, and Ukraine. Some of these states were reassembled as part of larger units such as the Soviet Union or Yugoslavia. The fall of the Soviet Union in 1991 in turn led to the creation of fifteen new states. The break-up of Yugoslavia after 1989 resulted, eventually, in six new independent countries. The fracturing continues: in 2008 Kosovo seceded unilaterally from Serbia, and in 2011 South Sudan seceded from Sudan.

At a time of increasing global integration, it is a seeming paradox that the creation of new states continues apace. But global integration allows smaller states to break off from difficult "marriages" as they find it easier to negotiate their place in the world, even as a small diminished state.

Not all states are equal. Along the dimension of power, we can distinguish between superpowers, major powers, and minor powers. Superpowers have the ability to influence events around the world. Successive superpowers have risen and fallen. In the late sixteenth and early seventeenth century, Spain was the first global power with possessions spread across the world. By the nineteenth century, Britain emerged after years of struggle with France to emerge as the world's superpower, its influence embodied not only by its territorial annexation but also by its naval power, which enabled it to influence events all over the world.

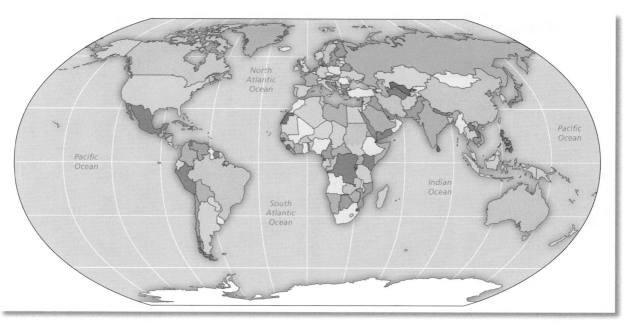

12.1   Political map of world

Britain's success encouraged emulation. Today the United States remains as the single largest superpower with the ability to achieve global military reach and project its power and influence around the world. This ability is due to the large distribution of bases spread around the world, a large military power, and commitment to high levels of government spending on the military. Table 12.1 lists the fifteen largest military spenders. The United States is clearly dominant, and it is responsible for over 40 percent of the world's total military spending, more than the next fourteen biggest spenders combined. Military spending is a function of wealth and size. The richer countries, such as Australia, Canada, France, Saudi Arabia, and the United Kingdom, are able to devote some of their considerable national wealth to the military, while the larger countries, such as China, Russia, and India, are able to mobilize their vast resources. These fifteen countries are responsible for more than 80 percent of all military spending in the world. Only a few countries have the military ability to project national power. While the United States is the superpower, the remaining fourteen countries are major powers able to exert some national power beyond their boundaries. The Chinese, for example, are building up their navy enough to back up substantial territorial claims in the South China Sea. Not all states are equal, with the more powerful able to exert an outsize role in world affairs. There is marked asymmetry in global affairs, with only very few countries having the military strength to impose their will across space.

A distinction can be made between soft and hard power. Hard power is the ability to coerce others through the superiority of military forces. Soft power is the ability to co-opt others to your point of view without the use of force. The United

Table 12.1 ■ MILITARY SPENDING, 2011				
Rank	Country	Spending ($ Bn.)	% of GDP	World Share (%)
	World Total	**1,630**	**2.6**	**100**
1	United States	711.0	4.7	41
2	China	143.0	2.0	8.2
3	Russia	71.9	3.9	4.1
4	United Kingdom	62.7	2.6	3.6
5	France	62.5	2.3	3.6
6	Japan	59.3	1.0	3.4
7	Saudi Arabia	48.2	8.7	2.8
8	India	46.8	2.5	2.7
9	Germany	46.7	1.3	2.7
10	Brazil	35.4	1.5	2.0
11	Italy	34.5	1.6	2.0
12	South Korea	30.8	2.7	1.8
13	Australia	26.7	1.8	1.5
14	Canada	24.7	1.4	1.4
15	Turkey	17.9	2.3	1.0

Source: Adapted from data from Stockholm International Peace Research Institute SIPRI Yearbook 2011: 15 countries with the highest military expenditure in 2011.

States has hard power through its military superiority, but also elements of soft power through wide dispersal of its cultural forms. The political scientist Joseph Nye, who drew the distinction, argues for the use of smart power, which combines hard and soft power in successful strategies.

States also vary along the dimension of economic wealth. There are a number of different methods used to classify national economies. The World Bank, for example, uses gross national income per capita to produce a fourfold classification of high, upper middle, lower middle, and low. Table 12.2 lists examples. Notice that there are substantial variations across the world, with the average gross national income of high-income Switzerland 134 times that of low-income countries. We live in an unequal world with national concentrations of wealth and vast areas of poverty. These income figures are more than just abstract statistics; they are a measure of the quality of life, as higher national incomes translate into better jobs, better housing, and better health care. There is a chance element to the lives we lead. Born into poverty in a poor country, your life chances are more limited and

Table 12.2 ■ INCOME CATEGORIES, 2010		
Income Category	**Country**	**GNI/per capita**
Low		$530
	Bangladesh	$700
	Mali	$600
Lower-middle		$1,623
	India	$1,270
	Ukraine	$3,000
Upper-middle		$5,886
	China	$4,270
	Peru	$4,270
High		$40,197
	Switzerland	$71,520
	USA	$47,520

Source: World Bank (http://worldbank.org)

circumscribed than if you are born the son or daughter of affluent Swiss parents where private affluence is reinforced by public bounty. While we may imagine the character of our lives is self-constructed, it is in large part based on where we were born. Geography in this particular case is destiny. The Economist Intelligence Unit estimates an index for eighty countries based on the number and quality of opportunities for citizens to lead a healthy and prosperous life. The top five countries are Switzerland, Australia, Norway, Sweden, and Denmark. The United States ranks sixteenth and the United Kingdom twenty-seventh. The bottom five are Angola, Bangladesh, Ukraine, Kenya, and Nigeria. You are luckier if you are born in Australia or Switzerland than Angola or Nigeria.

Table 12.2 also lists two examples from each of the four categories. There is substantial variation within each category. Ukraine, for example, has more than three times the average income of its upper-middle companion, India.

Assessing and comparing national wealth is an exercise fraught with many dangers. A UN report issued in 2012 took up this difficult task. The report's authors measured three kinds of assets: physical capital (buildings, infrastructure, etc.), human capital (including the educational skill levels of the population), and natural capital (land, forest resources, etc,). The United States was the richest country, with over $117. 8 trillion of wealth compared to Japan ($55.1 trillion), China ($20.0 trillion), and Germany ($19.5 trillion). When wealth per person was measured, the rankings changed to Japan, United States, Canada, Norway, and Australia. These are rough

Box 12.1 DEPICTING COUNTRIES IN RELATIVE SPACE

You are perhaps familiar with the standard atlas that shows countries of the world. Most depict nation-states in absolute space. All map projections are distortions, so, depending on the map projection, some areas are exaggerated while others are minimized. In the Mercator projection, for example, the size of countries in more northerly and southerly locations is exaggerated, while the size of countries in the tropical zone is minimized.

It is also useful to compare the relative size and comparative size of countries in relative space. At one website (http://www.worldmapper.org/), the size of a country is shown not in relation to land area but in relation to the data under consideration. The maps are in fact cartograms. In the world cartogram of total population, China and India "expand" in size because of their large populations. In the map of gross domestic product, in contrast, the United States, European countries, and Japan enlarge dramatically. In the world map of poverty, shown in the figure below, the size of a country is a function of the proportion of the world's poor living in that country. Notice the small sizes of North America, Europe, and Japan compared to the inflated sizes of Africa and countries in the Indian subcontinent. These maps provide revealing pictures of world geography.

References

http://www.worldmapper.org/
Dorling, D., Newman, M., and Barford, A. (2010) *The Atlas of the Real World*. Rev. ed. London: Thames and Hudson.

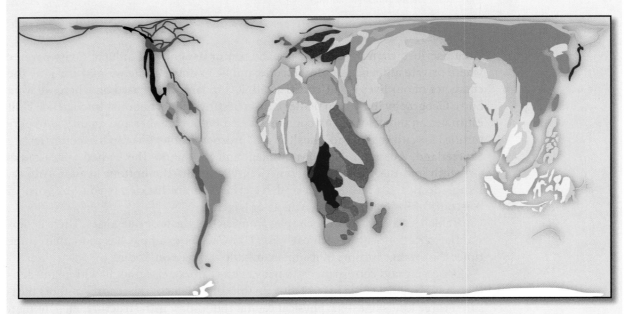

The world's poor

and ready measures, but they begin the process of identifying national wealth and widening the definition of national assets.

The data in Table 12.2 only refer to a national average; there are wider variations within countries, with some regions wealthier than other. In China, for example, there are substantial differences between the poor rural interior and the wealthier urban industrial coastal cities. The average income figure also masks substantial variation between households within one country. The level of income inequality is an important indicator of how income is spread across the national population. The CIA produces a ranking of inequality using the Gini index, which measures the spread of wealth across the population. The values range from the most unequal, Namibia, at 70 to Sweden at 23. The most unequal states are low- and middle-income countries such as Haiti and Chile. The most equal societies are small, affluent countries such as Sweden, Finland, Hungary, and Norway. However, a very poor country such as Bangladesh has a more equal income distribution than India, China, and Peru. It is even more equal than the United States. This reinforces, to some extent, the bell-shaped Kuznets curve, which depicts inequality increasing with rapid urbanization and industrialization. The general pattern is outlined in Figure 12.2. So in the case of China the inequality is to some extent a measure of recent industrialization and the growing economic differences between the interior rural areas and the faster growing industrial coastal urban regions. But notice how the United States, a country that has long since moved from a mainly agricultural to an industrial and service economy, once more has a relatively high level of inequality. The economist James K. Galbraith has produced an amended Kuznets curve to suggest that in some higher-income countries rising inequality is created when high tech and finance become larger parts of the economy. The large wealth amassed by owners and top earners in these sectors skews the national figure towards increased inequality. The smooth bell shape of the original Kuznets curve then starts to trend upwards (see Figure 12.3). The United States is situated after this inflexion in the curve.

The CIA collects data on national income inequality because it is a useful predictor of political stability. More equal societies tend to be more peaceful, less riven by conflict. Even societies that are unequal but have been so for some time have

12.2 The Kuznets Curve

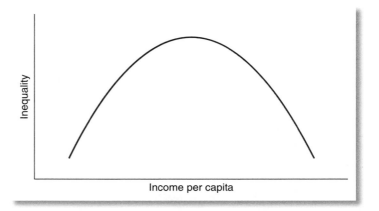

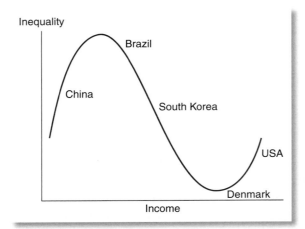

12.3 The Modified Kuznets Curve

a measure of stability. But societies where the rate of change in inequality is marked and sudden can become unstable as social movements emerge to resist and contest the sudden and marked concentration of wealth in just a few hands. The Arab Spring of 2011, for example, trailed in the wake of sudden increases in inequality due to globalization, privatization, and the adoption of neoliberal policies. Rapid growth that brings a quick increase in inequality can provide the basis for social stress and social upheaval. Even for more stable and affluent societies, the level of inequality is an important indicator of well-being. Richard Wilkinson and Kate Pickett found that in certain states of the United States and in the twenty richest countries, where there was a big gap between the incomes of rich and poor, there was more mental illness, drug and alcohol abuse, obesity, teenage pregnancy, and homicide. The more unequal a society, the shorter is the life expectancy and the poorer is children's educational performance. Scandinavian countries and Japan consistently do well on a range of such social indicators; they have the smallest differences between higher and lower incomes and the best levels of overall physical and mental health. Obesity is twice as common in the United Kingdom as in the more equal societies of Sweden and Norway, and six times more common in the United States than in Japan. It is not just that the lives of the poor are worse; the lives of everyone in the society are made worse. Life expectancy even among the rich is lower in more unequal societies. The United States is wealthier and spends more on health care than any other country, yet a baby born in Greece, at least before the current economic crisis, where average income levels are about half that of the United States, has a lower risk of infant mortality and longer life expectancy than an American baby. It is not only the wealth of society that structures health outcomes and social performances; so does the level of inequality.

Even within one country there are profound differences. National averages mask racial and ethnic differences. The infant mortality rate for the United States, for example, varies by race. For non-Hispanic blacks it is 13.1 per 1,000 live births, for non-Hispanic whites it is 5.6. In other words, black babies born in the United States are 2.3 times more likely to die than white babies. The black infant mortality rate in the United States is higher than the national average in Costa Rica (9.8), Sri Lanka (12.4), or Thailand (12.4).

States vary along a host of different dimensions, some easier than others to quantify. There are the hard statistics that measure military power, income levels, and inequality. There are also fuzzier measures that give an indication of political regime and quality of life. In terms of political organization, three main regimes can be identified: *totalitarian* systems, in which the government has control over wide and deep swathes of social, political, and economic life; *authoritarian* regimes, where power is concentrated but not so deeply entrenched as in the totalitarian regimes; and *democracies,* where political power arises from the majority will of

Box 12.2 MEASURING RISK

Countries can be ranked on their vulnerability to crisis and collapse. The Fund for Peace's Failed States Index, the Center for Systemic Peace's State Fragility Index, the Economist Intelligence Unit's Political Instability Index, and the PRS Group's International Country Risk Guide (ICRG) all measure risk and state fragility. The ICRG, for example, publishes monthly rankings for 140 countries measured along twelve factors, including socioeconomic conditions, internal conflict corruption, and ethnic tensions. There is also the Political Instability Task Force's global model, which focuses on political structures and relationships via four independent variables: regime type, infant mortality, conflict-ridden neighborhoods, and state-led discrimination.

The figure below shows the map produced by the Fund for Peace.

References

Goldstone, J.A., Bates, R.H., Epstein, D.L., Gurr, T.R., Lustik, M.B., Marshall, M.G., Ulfelder, J., and Woodward, M. (2010) A Global Model for Forecasting Political Instability. *American Journal of Political Science* 54: 190–208.

Economist Intelligence Unit's Political Instability Index http://www.eiu.com/

PRS Group's International Country Risk Guide http://www.prsgroup.com/icrg.aspx

The Fund for Peace's Failed States Index http://www.fundforpeace.org/global/?q=fsi

Center for Systemic Peace's State Fragility Index http://www.systemicpeace.org/

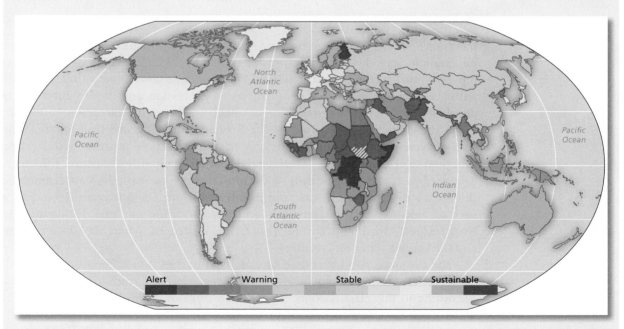

A risky world

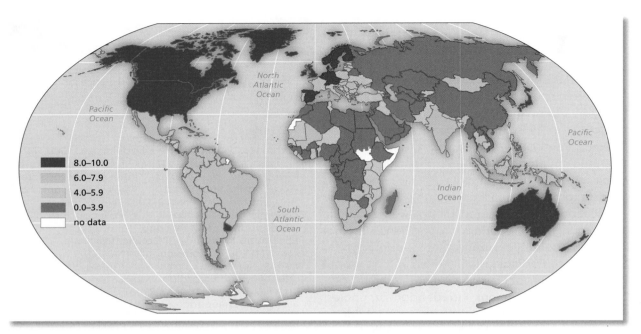

12.4 The Democracy Index

the people. There is some variation within these broad categories. Democracies, for example, include monarchies, such as United Kingdom and Sweden, as well as republics, such as the United States and France. While power may ultimately reside with the people, even in full democracies its expression and implementation are deeply influenced by the distribution of wealth and power in the society.

A democracy index is used by the Economist Intelligence Unit to gauge the level of democracy using sixty indicators related to electoral process, civil liberties, functioning of government, political participation, and political culture. The index, produced each year, ranges from 10, the most democratic, to 0, the least democratic (Figure 12.4). The most democratic countries include Scandinavian democracies such as Norway, Iceland, Denmark, and Sweden, while the least democratic are North Korea, Chad, and Turkmenistan. The United Kingdom stands eighteenth and the United States nineteenth.

The democracy index is used to classify countries into different regimes: full democracies, flawed democracies, hybrid regimes, and authoritarian regimes. According to this classification, more than a third of the world's population lives under the duress of authoritarianism (see Table 12.3). The democracy index is a function of the variables employed. Changes the mix of variables, and different results may emerge at the margins. But whatever variables are used, some countries, such as North Korea, will always come out as deeply undemocratic. At this extreme end, there are such depressing categories as kleptocracies, states geared to the enrichment of the tiny political elite. Some of the greediest include former Indonesian

Table 12.3 ■ POLITICAL REGIMES AND DEMOCRACY SCORES			
Category	Score	Percent of world's pop.	Examples
Full democracies	8–10	11.3	Canada, United States, United Kingdom
Flawed democracies	6–7.9	37.1	Argentina, Serbia, Philippines
Hybrid regimes	4–5.9	14.0	Armenia, Bolivia, Malawi
Authoritarian	0–3.9	37.6	Myanmar, Russia, Kuwait

Source: Based on data in http://upload.wikimedia.org/wikipedia/commons/thumb/e/ee/Democracy_Index_2011.png/800px-Democracy_Index_2011.png

president Suharto, who reputedly took between $15 billion and $35 billion; former president of the Philippines Ferdinand Marcos ($5 billion–$10 billion); and former Zairian president Mobutu ($5 billion), who plundered the country and pauperized the population. Current kleptocracies include Equatorial Guinea, where Teodoro Obiang Nguema, president since 1979, has amassed a personal fortune estimated at around $700 million. He has personal control over the nation's treasury and works well with foreign oil companies eager to drill for oil. Despite the fact that Equatorial Guinea is one of the world's poorest countries, the president lives a life of unrivaled opulence.

Classifications are snapshots in time. Popular movements and internal regime changes can alter them. Marcos was overthrown by a popular uprising, and Philippines is now classified as a flawed democracy, flawed no doubt but more democratic than in the Marcos era. Indonesia is also now in the same category. Myanmar, after years of authoritarian military control, seems to be moving toward something approaching greater democracy. Congo, formerly Zaire, remains in the authoritarian category.

States vary by quality of life as well as political system. A standard economic argument is that rising income levels create a greater a sense of well-being. More income, so the argument goes, creates happier people. The Easterlin Paradox, based on the work of the economist Richard Easterlin, suggests that once basic needs are met, however, there is little difference in reported happiness with increasing incomes. In other words, the paradox is that increasing income in a country, once a certain base level of income is reached, may not necessarily increase the level of happiness in the country. The debate continues. Including variables such as life expectancy, hours worked, and unemployment confirms the paradox. More recent papers highlight the finding that people in rich countries with more progressive taxation tend to report higher levels of happiness than those with lower and more regressive tax policies. Perhaps we need to measure gross national happiness as well as gross national income. What variables would you include? One of the few countries to measure happiness is Bhutan. However, their index does not capture the fears and anxieties of the ethnic Nepali minority in the south of the country, many of whom have fled to neighboring Nepal since the 1990s.

THE RISE AND FALL OF STATES

States vary enormously along a variety of dimensions, including military might, economic wealth, and political freedom. What is also worthy of note is the rapid rate of change, with poor countries sometimes becoming richer and authoritarian systems becoming more democratic. To be sure, there are opposing trends, as some countries become poorer and governments slide into authoritarianism. The system of nation-states is a dynamic jigsaw, constantly changing, sometimes slowly and at other times dramatically quickly. Perhaps we need maps of changing status to get a firmer sense of this dynamism.

The openness of a state is defined as the extent and ease to which people, ideas, information, goods, and services flow across its borders. Very closed societies such as North Korea are very stable. But once such a closed society becomes more open, there is a risk of political instability. That is why the rulers of closed states strive so hard to keep the lid on; it keeps them in power. The position of some individual states is difficult to assess. China, for example, encourages the free movement of capital and goods but keeps a firmer control over ideas that come over the Internet. It is open to the globalization of goods for its consumers, less open to the globalization of ideas and information for its citizens.

The political geography of states is complex and dynamic. States rise and fall, expand and contract. The United States, for example started off as thirteen colonial states pinned up against the eastern seaboard, but through annexation, invasion, purchase, and treaties it extended to continental proportions. The historian Norman Davies relates the fascinating story of states and kingdoms in Europe that no longer exist. He recounts the rise and fall of, among others, Byzantium (330–1453), Rosenau (1826–1918), Tsernagora (1910–1918), and the Soviet Union (1924–1989). States, despite their power and seeming permanence are, in the long-term, fragile organisms.

Their fragility results from the variety of crises that can beset them. Following on and developing the work of the German sociologist Jürgen Habermas, we can identify three contemporary and interlinked crises; fiscal, legitimation, and rationality. A fiscal crisis is when a state has more expenditure than revenue. Military and social spending, either singly or together, can outmatch the revenue from taxes and tariffs. In the short term the state can borrow money, and the biggest economies can borrow more, but ultimately a fiscal crisis turns into a political crisis as debts have to be repaid and unpopular cuts in spending have to be made. Fiscal crisis is an endemic feature of poor countries but is increasingly a problem for richer countries as well, because either they spend a lot on social welfare and the military (the United States) or they spend a lot on social welfare (Western European countries) or they have a low tax base and/or rampant tax evasion (e.g., Bulgaria, Italy). The shadow economy, in which people pay no taxes, constitutes 32 percent of the Bulgarian GDP, 21 percent of the Italian economy, but only 7 percent of the US economy. Fiscal crises prompt political crises.

A legitimation crisis is when the state loses its popular appeal and its ability to govern. When it loses the support of an increasing part of the population, its legitimacy is at risk. During the Arab Spring, for example, the governing elites of Egypt, Libya, and Tunisia no longer had the support of the majority of the population. In Syria, the Assad regime lost the support of the majority of the Sunni population. Declining living standards, a sense of injustice, and a feeling of profound alienation between the government and the governed prompt a legitimation crisis. The crisis can take a shallow form when the party in power is highly unpopular, or can be deeper when the entire system or regime is unpopular and wholesale change is demanded.

A rationality crisis occurs when the state makes enough poor decisions that other crises emerge. The US decision to invade Iraq in 2003 was based on faulty assumptions and led to the death of almost 100,000 Iraqis, the displacement of millions more, and the loss of over 4,000 US troops. In another case, in 2008 the Irish government guaranteed the losses of Irish banks. The banks received almost $4.5 billion each. By 2010, government support for the banks constituted almost a third of the country's entire GDP. The ruling party at the time of the bank bailouts, Fianna Fáil, the largest party since 1932, lost the 2011 election in a landslide defeat. It received only 17 percent of the votes. These examples show the interlinked nature of fiscal, legitimation, and rationality crises.

THE SPATIAL NATURE OF THE STATE

A state is a self-governing political unit. For it to be legitimate, it has to be recognized by other states and by the majority of its population. It has monopoly control over a territory and has boundaries with other states. There are currently almost 200 states in the world that cover the surface of the Earth and make claims on the surrounding and adjacent seas and oceans. States are spatial entities.

States vary in their spatial characteristics. There are large and small states. Size can be measured by territory and by population. Table 12.4 lists the top ten

Table 12.4 ■ THE TOP TEN "BIG" COUNTRIES	
By Area	**By Population**
Russia	China
Canada	India
China	US
US	Indonesia
Brazil	Brazil
Australia	Pakistan
India	Nigeria
Argentina	Bangladesh
Kazakhstan	Russia
Algeria	Japan

countries by area and population. Some countries, such as Australia and Canada, have a large territory but relatively small population. Some are small in area but large in population, such as Bangladesh. Some countries are big in both respects. Besides the United States, four other countries make both top tens: Brazil, Russia, India, and China. These big four are often grouped together—termed the BRICs, after the first letter of each country's name—because they all combine large size with developing economies. Their combined population of 2.8 billion constitutes just over 40 percent of the total world population. Indonesia is also a possible future member of the BRICs; its population is 237 million. Although perhaps poised to become a more dynamic economy, in part fueled by a demographic dividend, problems of poor infrastructure, corruption, underemployment, and poverty may limit its future growth. Despite the hurdles faced by each of the countries, they have the necessary size and rate of growth so that their combined growth potential represents a possible shift in geopolitical and geoeconomic power away from the core of rich countries. Their potential is in part based on their territorial sizes, which include large amounts of natural resources, such as in Brazil and Russia, as well as the potential for growth through the demographic dividend, especially pronounced in Brazil, India, and Indonesia. Size does matter.

One way that smaller countries try to offset their limited size is through organizations with other states. There are the economic unions that try to extend the size of the market. The European Union, for example, grew from the perceived need of European countries to avoid further conflict in the wake of two world wars, but also to provide a large enough economic entity to compete with the United States. It began as the European Economic Community of six countries formed by the Treaty of Rome in 1957. It was renamed as the European Union and expanded to include twenty-seven countries with a single market. The recent fiscal crisis, highlighted by the debt problems of Greece but also the very real potential for similar crises in Portugal, Italy, and Spain, reveals that unions do not solve all economic problems. States also come together for specific economic interests. We already noted the important role that OPEC plays in regulating the global supply and price of oil. There are looser economic organizations like NAFTA (North American Free Trade Agreement) between Canada, Mexico, and the United States. There are also security groupings and mutual defense organizations. The African Union consists of all fifty-four countries in the continent except Morocco. This organization provides troops in certain instances. African Union troops were involved in recent military-policing interventions in Darfur (7,000 troops) and Somalia (8,000 troops).

States also vary by location. One significant feature is access to sea transport, which in general tends to be far cheaper than overland or air transport. Landlocked states have to ship goods overland through another state, which increases costs and tariffs, in order to access global markets. There is no simple relationship between level of economic development and being landlocked. On a variety of different measures, Switzerland is one of the richest countries in the world, with many inhabitants enjoying high per capita income and a full range of quality

BOX 12.3 NATIONAL ENVIRONMENTAL IDEOLOGIES

Nations occupy territory. National identity is bound up with attachment to territory and its creative representation. National environmental ideologies build on myths of wilderness, countryside, and city. These myths often have bipolar quality. Consider wilderness. Its defeat is part of many national histories. In the United States, for example, the defeat of the wilderness in the nineteenth and early twentieth centuries was an important element in the sense of national identity, and the moving frontier gave a sense of an expansive national trajectory. Slowly an alternative began to emerge, that of preserving the remaining wilderness. As wilderness disappears, its survival can also become a national project. The National Park Movement in the United States took as its guiding principle the defense of remaining wilderness areas. The wilderness and its point of contact with the civilized world, the frontier, are the background to one of the essential US texts, the western movie. Countryside can also be idealized, especially in a rapidly industrializing and urbanizing country. An idealized representation of countryside is still at the core of English environmental ideology. The idea of the city can range from Jerusalem, a place of social uplift, the "city on the hill" of the early Puritans in North America, to Babylon, the place of vice and debauchery populated by the foreign Other. In the United States, there is a long anti-urban tradition that extols the virtue of the small town and rural life.

Environmental ideologies are expressed in painting, novels, and cinema. Australian landscape painting, for example, depicts the changing idea of the outback; many English novels deal with the tension of modernity in an idealized countryside; and the United States western provides mythic depictions of the frontier between the settled and the wild.

While the general categories of wilderness, countryside, and city are used in varying ways to construct and challenge national environmental ideologies, more specific features are also employed. In a fascinating study, Tricia Cusack tells the story of how five rivers became part of national identity. She tells the story of the Hudson as an icon of American nationalism, the Thames as embodying ideas of monarchy, empire, and commerce in England and Britain, the Seine and consumer culture in France following the War of 1870, the Volga and its role in Russian romantic nationalism, and the Shannon and its connection with Celtic Irish cultural identity. Rivers are more than just hydro-geomorphic features. They are texts that are used to generate and sometime unify diverse narratives and competing claims on national identity. The forests, mountains, rivers, coasts, valleys, and other features of the landscape become elements of a national landscape. National identity in the United States, for example, was shaped by the forests. The seemingly endless supply created a throwaway culture that did not build to last. Only when the forest cover was threatened was a conservation movement initiated. Trees shaped American identity just as Americans transformed the forest.

A "national" landscape is crafted and represented from the raw materials of the environment into texts of historic meaning and political significance.

References

Cusak, T. (2010) *Riverscapes and National Identity*. Syracuse: Syracuse University Press.

Rutkow, E. (2012) *American Canopy: Trees, Forests, and the Making of a Nation*. New York: Scribner.

Short, J. R. (2005) *Imagined Country*. Reprint with new introduction; first published 1991. Syracuse: Syracuse University Press.

public services. However, for many poor countries such as Bolivia, Chad, Mali, Mongolia, Niger, and Paraguay, landlocked status makes economic growth all that more difficult.

As spatial units, states can be lucky or unlucky in their territorial endowment. States that have rich oil reserves, for example, can wield effective political power because their resource endowment provides huge revenues. The Saudi government's oil revenues pay for its projection of soft power through the promotion of fundamentalism Islam around the world. In some cases, rich resources provide welcome revenues. In 2011 revenues from oil and gas accounted for one-half of Russia's federal budget, and raw materials constituted 80 percent of exports. However, a generous resource endowment, while it may provide short- and medium-term riches, can, over the longer term, lead to problems. The easy reliance on nature's bounty may hamper and restrict the innovation necessary for long-term economic growth. This is the so-called Dutch Disease, based on that country's experience with oil revenues that created a huge trade surplus and large currency reserves, which led to overvalued domestic industries that were uncompetitive in global markets. Resources prices are also very volatile, so that revenues may vary from one year to the next. In high-price years, governments may spend to shore up popular support, but that support may vanish when prices fall and spending has to be curtailed. Commodity price volatility is one manifestation of the "resource curse," sometimes known as the paradox of plenty. While valuable resources can create short-term booms, they may depress long-term economic growth. In less democratic countries, wealth from resources is easily diverted, stolen, and misspent.

NATION, STATE, AND MINORITIES

A distinction can make between a state and nation. A state is a political organization that controls a particular territory. A nation is a community of people with a common identity, shared cultural values, and a commitment and attachment to a particular area. In some cases, there is congruence between nation and state. In the case of the small landlocked country of Swaziland, the nation and the state are almost identical, with the great majority of the population composed of ethnic Swazi. Such instances are rare, especially with international migration creating more complex patterns.

The incongruence between nation and state takes two main forms. First, there are nations that lack a state. The traditional homeland of the Kurds is in the Near East. After the fall of the Ottoman Empire, just after the end of the First World War, the territory was divided by western powers that drew boundaries to suit their geopolitical interests rather than to honor national differences. The Kurdish homeland was divided among separate states, including Turkey, Syria, Iran, and Iraq. One nation was divided among a variety of states, with Kurds as vulnerable minorities (see Figure 12.5). In some cases the Kurds have been successful in creating regions of relative autonomy. After the US invasion of Iraq, the Kurdish region in northern Iraq achieved a large measure of autonomy. However, the Kurdish region in eastern

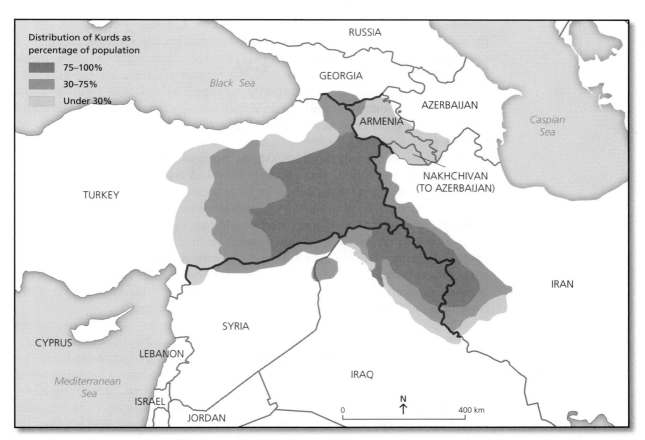

12.5 Distribution of Kurds in the Middle East

Turkey is still a scene of ongoing conflict between the Turkish government and Kurdish separatists.

There are also states with more than one nation. In Belgium, for example, the centuries-old rift between the Dutch-speaking north and the French-speaking south, despite their shared Catholic religion and rising living standards, remains always just below the surface and always capable of breaking out into explicit calls for separation. In some cases, rifts widen to civil war. Sudan was a colonial possession of the United Kingdom. It consisted of two different regions, a northern part centered on Khartoum in which most people are African-Arab and Muslim and a southern one where most people are black Africans and either animist or Christian. When the country achieved independence in 1956, the two parts were joined in one state. It was never a happy marriage. Power was retained in the north, and the south languished. Decades of civil war caused casualties and created famine. More than 2 million people died, and millions more were displaced. The south was able to secede only after years of war and famine. The state of South Sudan came into existence on July 9, 2011.

The population of a state is rarely homogenous. Differences in religion, ethnicity, and language, if they have distinct spatial expression, can create tensions in the internal coherence of the state. Minority groups are often targeted when economic difficulties provoke social unrest. In Indonesia, for example, there is a significant ethnic Chinese population, located in specific neighborhoods of cities and towns. Out of a total population of 240 million, more than 2 million are estimated to be ethnic Chinese. Their experience has not been a happy one. There is a long history of anti-Chinese feeling. In 1740, economic unrest led to demonstrations and mass killings. Ethnic Chinese could only travel with special permits. After independence from the Dutch in 1949, the ruling junta regularly provoked anti-Chinese feeling. In 1998, anti-Chinese rioting in the capital city of Jakarta erupted in violence and damage to Chinese-Indonesian communities. Minorities can often become scapegoats for wider economic issues. When economic conditions decline, the Other is often blamed.

In many states, there is some measure of tolerance for people different from one another. In others, however, the differences remain, often exacerbated and embodied in years of struggle. In Northern Ireland, for example, the latest era of struggles between the Catholic and Protestant communities lasted for almost forty years, from 1970 until a power-sharing administration began in 2007.

The protection of minority rights is a fundamental part of the Charter of the United Nations and is now an important element of the global discourse of international politics. However, the cases of Bosnia, Darfur, and Rwanda indicate that the human rights of minorities can still be violated. When a state is committed to harming minority groups within its borders, the international community has to overcome distance, time, and political inertia in order to stop states killing their own citizens. International involvement is slow, costly, and difficult to organize.

THE TERRITORIAL INTEGRITY OF THE STATE

A distinction can be made between government, state, and national territory. The government is the political expression of power. "State" is a wider term that covers the more embedded power structures, such as the army, the police, and the educational system. In some cases, a "deep state" of entrenched power operates despite changes of government. In more authoritarian regimes, government and state are more interconnected, while in more democratic states there is space between the government and the state.

We can identify centripetal forces that unify the state's power across space and centrifugal forces that disrupt it. Centripetal forces include external aggression, which may stimulate national bonding against a common enemy; federal structures that allow the safe expression of regional and other subnational differences; and national mass media and education, which create a shared culture and language. In some cases a measure of regional autonomy can blunt separatist claims. In Spain, for example, under the Franco regime (1936–1975) power was centered in Madrid and used to suppress both Basque and Catalan autonomy. Support for the soccer team of Barcelona was and still is a vigorous expression of Catalan identity. Since the fall of the Franco dictatorship, there has been a more pronounced commitment to power sharing. In other cases, separatist movements may lie dormant but then erupt. Scotland joined with England in 1707, and for three centuries Scottish nationalism in lowland Scotland was little more than a whisper, although many in the Highlands resisted vigorously in 1715 and 1745; recent years, however, have seen more vocal calls for separation.

Centrifugal forces include political and economic inequality. One reason behind a resurgence of Scottish nationalism is the large gap in living standards between Scotland and the southeast of England, the center of power and home of the elites. Despite the homogenizing abilities of the state, religious, ethnic, and language differences can persist and survive attempts at their eradication. In Spain, the Basque language is still a principal vehicle and embodiment of Basque identity and difference from Castilian Spain.

The state's responses to separatist movements within its national boundaries can range from repression to some form of accommodation. Many states began with repression. When the British state defeated the Highland rebels at the battle of Culloden in 1746, it made it illegal to wear tartan, play the bagpipes, or speak Gaelic. The territorial expansion of both the United States and Canada involved the defeat and removal of many indigenous nations.

A state has a monopoly of legitimate physical force. But in some instances, the rule of the state does not extend to all of its territory. A territorial crisis occurs when the state cannot rule effectively over all its territory. In some cases, the territorial divisions erupt into civil war. The US Civil War (1861–1865) was fought between northern and southern states, with the South declaring itself independent from the United States. It was a bloody war. By 1865 over 620,000 Americans had died as a direct result of the war, more than all Americans killed in twentieth-century conflicts. On one day, September 17, 1862, at the battle of Antietam in Maryland, more than 4,000 men were killed and 17,000 more were wounded.

The territorial control of the state varies along a continuum. At one extreme are states that wield undisputed monopoly power over their territory. At the other extremes are dysfunctional states with limited territorial control. In Somalia, for example, the government's control barely extends beyond the government compound in Mogadishu. In Afghanistan, the president of the country is known as the Mayor of Kabul to emphasize his limited power range. In Colombia, a fifty-year civil war was fought between the central government and an insurgency. In the 1950s, in the remote mountain areas, communist guerillas and members of the Liberal Party started to organize against the army and the Conservative Party. It was a struggle over control of land and political dominance. More than 200,000 were killed. In 1964, FARC (Revolutionary Armed Forces of Colombia) came into existence and waged a forty-year war against the central government. The rebels were funded through their proceeds from the drug trade, while the government received aid from the United States. Only in 2012 were negotiations leading to a possible end to the decades-old conflict.

The internal territorial integrity of the state is more assured where there is a homogenous population. But when there are marked differences overlaid by economic inequality and profound cultural differences, there are pressures on the integrity of state control over national space. When states cannot control the national territory, they become dysfunctional. Piracy developed along the coast of Somalia because of the power vacuum created by a dysfunctional state. The pirates were only halted with the intervention of outside powers.

BOUNDARIES AND FRONTIERS

States have edges, and these boundaries create both tensions that can lead to conflict and sites for cooperation with other states. Political geographers used to make a distinction between artificial and natural borders. People made artificial borders, while natural borders were coastline, mountain ranges, rivers, and the like. The limits of the United States are shaped in the east and west by the natural borders of oceanic coastlines but are more artificial in the north and south. More recent work tends to view borders as social constructions, the result of bordering practices rather than the embodiment of "natural" differences.

Viewing borders as social-spatial constructions focuses attention on their origin and evolution and interprets them as stages for the performance of national identity. Borders arise, shift, and change shape over time, their changing configuration embodying competition for territorial space. Consider the case of Hungary. During the Austro-Hungarian Empire (1867–1918), Hungary was joined with Austria in ruling over a large empire in central Europe. The break-up of its empire after the First World War reduced Austria to a small German-speaking state and started the process of reduction in the size of Hungary. In the Treaty of Trianon (1920), Hungary lost Vojvodina, Croatia, and Slavonia to the new state that became Yugoslavia, and forfeited its coastline. In the north, Hungary lost what is now Slovakia to newly formed Czechoslovakia. In the east, Hungary had to cede Transylvania and the Banat to Romania. To the west, Hungary lost Burgenland to Austria. In all, Hungary forfeited two-thirds of its former area.

The borders of many countries are complex texts that tell of the country's history. Poland, located in central Europe, has a more complicated history than most. Poland's current boundary encompasses territory that once belonged to Russia, Hungary, and Germany, while formerly Polish territory can be found in Belarus, the Czech Republic, Germany, Russia, and Ukraine. One Polish city, Wrocław, was a municipality of the Habsburg Empire, of the Kingdom of Prussia, of the German Empire, and then of Poland. Its name changed in the process from Vratislavia to Breslau to Wrocław. Over the longer term, boundaries are fluid and changeable.

Boundaries are used to define and contain. The Great Wall of China, a centuries-old building project first begun 2,500 years ago, was built to keep out marauders from the steppe. During the Cold War, the boundary between East and West Germany was used to define the limits of effective power but also to limit mobility and movement. Boundaries can be used to constrain the movement of people and goods, but in a globalized, interconnected world, it is increasingly difficult to limit the flow of information. But states try. The newest "border construction" in China is the government's control over Internet traffic.

A distinction can be made in the porosity of boundaries. Hard, impervious boundaries are created and maintained by the state as a display of power, a performance of national identity. The increasingly fenced boundary between the United States and Mexico, for example, is a form of border theater to display US intentions against illegal immigration and cross-border drug trade. The boundary between Canada and the United States is more porous than the boundary with Mexico. We can thus make a distinction between hard and soft borders, porous and nonporous boundaries. The boundary between the United States and its two neighbors provide example of hard, nonporous borders and soft, porous boundaries, although in reality they are both more porous than official pronouncements would suggest.

Along the edge of boundaries, frontier regions may develop. There are the landscapes of hard boundaries: the barbed wire, the border patrols, and the checkpoints. Between North and South Korea, the boundary is made visible on either side by a demilitarized zone of unpopulated territory filled with landmines. Figure 12.6 depicts this hard, nonporous boundary. Frontier zones in such cases may develop as liminal spaces lacking investment and development.

Boundaries can be places of conflict, especially where territorial sovereignty is disputed. Around the world, boundaries are often neither settled nor agreed upon. Let us consider one example in Southeast Asia.

French cartographers created the boundary between Thailand and Cambodia in 1907, when France was the colonial power in the region. An area around the ancient Khmer temple in Preah Vihear was given to Cambodia. Thailand occupied this area when the French withdrew in 1953, but the International Court of Justice confirmed Cambodian sovereignty in 1962. In 2008 Cambodia submitted an application to have

12.6 Boundary between North and South Korea

Box 12.4 IMAGINED COMMUNITIES

The construction of national identity is an important subject of recent writings. In an argument of great subtlety, Benedict Anderson argued that nations are not so much facts of race or ethnicity; rather, they are what he terms imagined communities. Anderson paid particular attention to the role of print capitalism in creating a national discourse. In a later elaboration, Anderson identified three institutions of power: the *census*, the *map*, and the *museum*, which together allow the state to imagine the people under its dominance, the geographic territory under its control, and the nature of historical legitimacy.

National imaginaries are rarely coherent, consistent, or stable. The dominant national imaginary in Australia has shifted from celebration as an Anglo-Celtic colonial outpost to the more uncertain embrace of a postcolonial, multicultural society. A major element in this shift is the changing role assigned to indigenous peoples.

There are national histories and national geographies, national characteristics and national claims to greatness. "National" events are enacted and reenacted; "national" stories are told and retold. National identities are also created through commemorative activities. Exhibitions, fairs, and sites of historical memory and commemoration are common vehicles for celebrations and claims of national identity. In the centennial celebrations of the United States (1876) and Australia (1888), the indigenous peoples were excluded. Fast-forward a hundred years and ritual and symbol were mobilized once again. Both bicentennial celebrations, of 1976 and 1988, praised political liberties and economic prosperity, yet the fundamental belief in the forward march of progress had weakened over the course of the intervening century. Now cultural diversity was celebrated rather than ignored. The indigenous peoples were given a more central role; in Australia, this emerged mainly as a result of Aboriginal protest at the concept and the practice of the celebrations.

References

Anderson. B. (2006) *Imagined Communities: Reflections on The Origin and Spread of Nationalism*. Rev. ed. London: Verso.
Spillman, L. (1997) *Nation and Commemoration*. Cambridge: Cambridge University Press.

the temple listed as a World Heritage site. Nationalist political parties in both countries fanned the controversy to inflame public opinion for their own political agendas. In 2008 troops from both countries exchanged fire. There were sporadic exchanges until April–May 2011, when more sustained conflict occurred. In a ten-day skirmish, Cambodia claimed that Thai forces fired 50,000 shells along the border. A ceasefire was brokered on May 4, 2011. The area around the temple remains in dispute.

National boundaries extend beyond the country's territory. International boundary disputes also involve islands and control over the sea. Japan and South Korea, for example, dispute the small island of Dokdo, which the Japanese refer to as Takeshima. Maritime sovereignty disputes are likely to grow as the search for valuable minerals and resources extends into the sea.

Boundaries can also be sites of cooperation. The opening of formerly closed boundaries and the easing of movement along formerly nonporous boundaries are often highly symbolic markers of regime change and interstate cooperation. The fall of the Berlin Wall in 1989 marked the end of the Cold War in Europe. When Berliners chipped away at the Wall, they were demolishing not only a concrete wall but also a political regime. A hard, nonporous boundary was replaced by the free flow of national unification.

The political geography of borders is now a lively area of geographical scholarship. The current emphasis is on the social construction of borders, practices of bordering, and the narration of borders as important parts of national identity. Vladimir Kolossov and John O'Loughlin tell the story of state and nation building in Ukraine through its shifting border, and Reece Jones recounts the bordering between India and Bangladesh. Jones begins his interesting paper with a description of Moushumi, a domestic worker in Bangladesh who crosses the border into India to visit her son. Prior to 1947, the trip would not have been a border crossing, as both areas were part of the same space of colonial British control. After 1947, however, the partition of the continent created an international border. It took a while for the border to become bordered. A map was drawn in 1947, but the border was not properly surveyed until 1952, and only in the 1960s were border security forces deployed. The Indian government has now fenced more than three-quarters of the 4,000-kilometer border. This hard border is now "a key site for the state to establish the binaries of power that frame the world as citizen–alien, national–foreign, here–there, and we–they" (Jones 2012, p. 691). Despite this hardening, cross-boundary flows still occur. The paper is interesting because it tells the story of the border as a place where the performances of state power are played out in conspicuous acts of security theater, but also highlights the limits to and often ragged nature of state territorial control. Borders are transgressed by smugglers and illegal immigrants and in unrecorded economic transactions. Borders are sites of performance of territorial control as well as examples of resistance, refusal, and transgression.

GEOGRAPHY OF ELECTIONS

States maintain their popular legitimacy through the performances of elections. There is a geography to these elections. Three distinct elements can be identified: the geography of voting, the geography of representation, and the geography of electoral systems.

The geography of voting examines the distribution in votes cast for different parties and candidates. Consider the voting for presidential candidates in Nigeria in 2011 (see Figure 12.7). The three candidates appealed to different parts of the country. One candidate won most of the northern region, another won the south, while a third candidate's support was very localized in one state. The differences reflect tribal and ethnic differences. The northern states are predominantly made up of Muslim and Hausa-Fulani tribes, while the south is Christian and dominated by Yoruba and Igbo tribal members.

There are national and regional cleavages in voting. In the 1968 US presidential election, there were three candidates. While the Republican, Richard Nixon, won

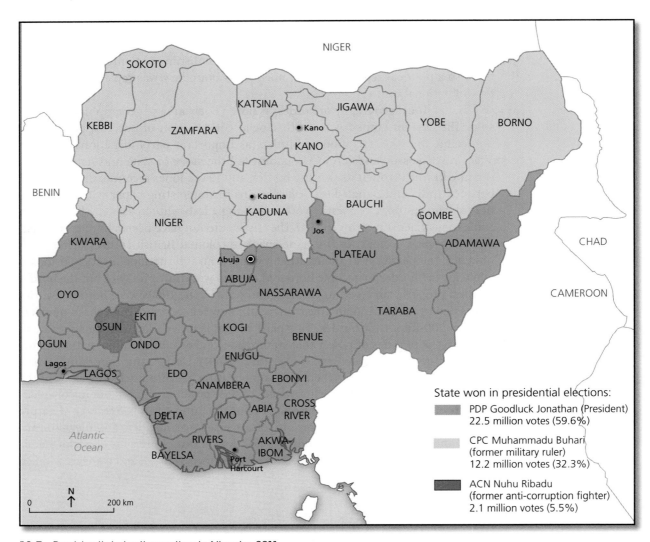

12.7 Presidential election voting in Nigeria, 2011

State won in presidential elections:

PDP Goodluck Jonathan (President)
22.5 million votes (59.6%)

CPC Muhammadu Buhari
(former military ruler)
12.2 million votes (32.3%)

ACN Nuhu Ribadu
(former anti-corruption fighter)
2.1 million votes (5.5%)

most of the country, the Democratic candidate, Hubert Humphrey, won most of the northeastern states as well as his home state of Minnesota. The third-party candidate, George Wallace, who pledged to maintain racial segregation, only won states in the Deep South.

There is also an even more local effect, known as the neighborhood effect. This refers to the fact that neighborhood can trump traditional allegiance. Democratic-leaning voters in a predominantly Republican neighborhood will vote for Republicans, and vice versa. We have detailed empirical demonstration for this neighborhood effect in voting outcomes. The precise causal factors are difficult to disentangle. Does the neighborhood cause the shift, or do people predisposed to the shift mark their intentions by moving to the neighborhood in the first place?

The geography of voting is influenced by distribution of income and racial and ethnic differences, but also by local factors such as neighborhood and the effect of friends and neighbors.

National territories are divided up into political constituencies. The geography of this representation has an impact on the results. Malapportionment refers to the imbalance between the number of voters and the population in each constituency. In some cases, numerical malapportionment is accepted, indeed codified into the legislative framework. In the United States, for example, each state receives two seats in the Senate, yet in 2012, while California and North Dakota each had two senators, California had a population of 37.7 million versus North Dakota's 683,000. This disparity was accepted by the Founding Fathers as the price to be paid to create a union of fiercely independent states. Malapportionment is a function of political power. Those who gain from the existing system rarely want to change the system.

There is also gerrymandering, which refers to the manipulation of voting boundaries to engineer specific political outcomes. The term originated in the activities of Elbridge Gerry, who in 1810 as governor of Massachusetts signed a bill that demarcated boundaries that favored his party (Democratic-Republican). The system was so "gerrymandered" that while the Democratic-Republicans won only 50,164 of the votes compared to the 51,766 gained by the Federalists, they won twenty-nine of the forty seats. Gerrymandering is a recurring feature of political boundary making. It is an ongoing reality of congressional boundaries in US states.

The US Constitution requires each state to establish new congressional districts every ten years to reflect the population changes measured by the census. This congressional redistricting is freighted with partisan political interests. In Utah, the results of the 2010 census revealed enough population increase to justify another congressional district, increasing the number from three to four. The political geography of Utah consists of the more Democratic-leaning metro area of Salt Lake City and the Republican-dominated rural areas. The Republicans control the state legislature and thus the redistricting. If the metro area was one congressional district, it could possibly ensure a Democratic victory. To avoid this possibility, the redistricting plan, produced by a Republican-dominated state legislature, ensured that the metro area was dismembered into three separate districts. The Democratic vote was spread and diluted in more rural districts. In Democratic-controlled Maryland, the post-2010 redistricting proposals ensured that Republican support was diffused to favor Democratic voters. A new District 6 was drawn up so that the more Republican voters in rural counties were lumped together but swamped by the more populous Democratic-voting suburban areas. District 3, the least compact congressional seat in the country, was the result of drawing boundaries to ensure a Democratic victory (Figure 12.8). The redistricting plan was placed on the November 2012 general election ballot; it passed.

States vary in the geography of their electoral systems. The biggest distinction is between the "first past the post" method, one of what are called plurality voting systems, that ensures that the politician with the majority of votes in a district wins that district. This dominates the electoral scene in Canada, the United Kingdom, and the United States. The system is simple and easy to understand, but it tends

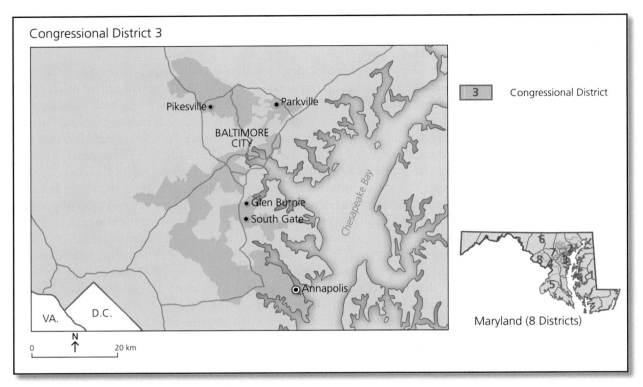

12.8 Congressional boundary redistricting in Maryland, 2011

Table 12.5 GENERAL ELECTION RESULTS IN THE UNITED KINGDOM, 2010		
Party	**Percent of votes**	**Percent of seats**
Conservative	36.1	47.0
Labour	29.0	39.6
Liberal Democrat	23.0	8.7

to solidify the political representation of large nationwide parties and marginalize third and fourth parties with wide, but not necessarily nationwide, depth of support. Table 12.5 provides the results of the 2010 general election in the United Kingdom for the three main parties. Notice how the Liberal Democrat Party won almost a quarter of all votes but managed to gain less than 10 percent of the seats. Smaller parties with wide support, but not deep enough to win particular seats, are penalized by the first-past-the-post system. When the Liberal Democrats joined with the Conservatives in a coalition government, their price was the promise of electoral reform.

A large number of countries, Ireland for example, now have a system of proportional representation that translates votes into seats in a more equitable manner.

Box 12.5 GEOPOLITICS

Geopolitics is the study of the power relations between empires and states. Early proponents include Rear Admiral A. T. Mahan of the US Navy, who wrote in 1890 about the influence of sea power, and the Englishman Sir Halford Mackinder, who provided a geopolitical strategy for the British Empire. Mackinder's 1919 book *Democratic Ideals and Reality* is concerned with geopolitical strategies in the immediate aftermath of the First World War.

More recent contributions include George Kennan, writing during the Cold War of the need for a US policy of containment of the USSR. Even more recently, popular writers such as Robert Kaplan have argued that a nation's position on the world map is a primary determinant of conflict. The world is viewed as a series of states competing over space, with emphasis on the notion of geographic pivots.

Since the 1990s, a more critical form of geopolitics has emerged that looks at the social construction of political spaces, exposes the material interests involved in the narratives used to explain this space, and explores the spatial construction of social identity. It also interrogates the ideological underpinning of standard geopolitics. Thus Gerry Kearns reexamines the imperial context of Mackinder's life, works, and geopolitical ideas. There is also a popular geopolitics that looks at the role of popular culture and mass media in structuring national identities and popular geographical understandings of the world. There is also a reworking of the spatial nature of war and conflict. Derek Gregory, for example, looks at the geographical dimension of contemporary war through an examination of three global borderlands: Afghanistan-Pakistan, US-Mexico, and cyberspace.

Geopolitics—traditional, popular, and critical—explores the meaning, contestation, construction, and maintenance of the political organization of space.

References

Dodds, K., Kuus, M., and Sharp, J. (eds.) (2013) *The Ashgate Research Companion to Critical Geopolitics.* Farnham, UK: Ashgate,

Dittmer, J. (2010) *Popular Culture, Geopolitics, and Identity.* Lanham, MD: Rowman & Littlefield.

Gregory, D. (2011) The Everywhere War. *Geographical Journal* 177: 238–250.

Kaplan, R. (2012) *The Revenge of Geography: What the Map Tells Us about Coming Conflicts and the Battle Against Fate.* New York: Random House.

Kearns, G. (2009) *Geopolitics and Empire: The Legacy of Halford Mackinder.* Oxford: Oxford University Press.

Mackinder, H. J. (1919) *Democratic Ideals and Reality: A Study in the Politics of Reconstruction.* London: Constable.

This can be done through giving seats in proportion to the votes cast. Some countries have a mix of seats allocated by first-past-the-post and then some by proportional representation methods. Under a single transferable vote system, electors rank candidates in order of preference. If their preferred candidate does not gain enough votes, the votes are given to the second ranked candidate. There are also preferential systems. In an alternative vote system, voters have an opportunity to express their second choice, as happens in Australia, or as in French presidential elections in a second round of voting if no candidate has an absolute majority in the first round. Each system has a mix of advantages and disadvantages. The first-past-the-post system ensures one party has a majority, but small and minority parties are underrepresented. In the proportional and preferential system, the legislature reflects voting preferences more closely, but the large number of parties can make for fragile and unstable coalition governments.

Political outcomes in part depend on geography. The geography of voting, the geography of representation, and the geography of electoral systems all play an important part in turning votes into representation.

Cited References

Davies, N. (2012) *Vanished Kingdoms: The Rise and Fall of States and Nations*. New York: Viking.

Easterlin, R. (1974) Does Economic Growth Improve the Human Lot? Some Empirical Evidence. In Paul A. David and Melvin W. Reder, eds., *Nations and Households in Economic Growth: Essays in Honor of Moses Abramovitz*, New York: Academic Press, pp. 89–125.

Galbraith, J. K. (2011) Inequality and Economic and Political Change: A Comparative Perspective. *Cambridge Journal of Regions, Economy and Society* 4: 13–27.

Habermas, J. (1975) *Legitimation Crisis*. Boston: Beacon Press.

Jones, R. (2012) Spaces of Refusal: Rethinking Sovereign Power and Resistance at the Border. *Annals of Association of American Geographers* 102: 685–699.

Kolossov, V. and O'Loughlin, J. (1998) New Borders for New World Orders: Territorialities at the Fin-de-siecle. *GeoJournal* 44: 259–273.

Nye, J. (2004) *Soft Power: The Means to Success in World Politics*. New York: Public Affairs.

Wilkinson, R. and Pickett, K. (2009) *The Spirit Level: Why More Equal Societies Almost Always Do Better*. London: Allen Lane.

Select Guide to Further Reading

Davies, N. and Moorhouse, R. (2003) *Microcosm: Portrait of a Central European City*. London: Pimlico.

Bremmer, I. (2006) *The J Curve: A New Way to Understand Why Nations Rise and Fall*. New York: Simon and Schuster.

Brooks, K. (2011) Is Indonesia Bound for the BRICs? *Foreign Affairs*, November–December, pp. 109–117.

Diener, A. C. and Hagen, J. (2012) *Borders: A Very Short Introduction*. New York: Oxford University Press.

Fikins, D. (2012) The Deep State. *The New Yorker*, March 12.
http://www.newyorker.com/reporting/2012/03/12/120312fa_fact_filkins

Megoran, N. (2012) Rethinking the Study of International Boundaries: A Biography of the Kyrgyzstan–Uzbekistan Boundary. *Annals of Association of American Geographers* 102: 464–481.

Popescu, G. (2012) *Bordering and Ordering the Twenty-First Century*. Lanham, MD: Rowman & Littlefield.

Richardson, T. (ed) (2013) Special Issue on Borders and Mobilities. *Mobilities* 8: 1–165.

Scuzzarello, S. and Kinnvall, C. (2013) Rebordering France and Denmark: Narratives and Practices of Border Construction in Two European Countries. *Mobilities* 8: 90–106.

Stevenson, B. and Wolfers, J. (2008) *Economic Growth and Subjective Well-Being: Reassessing the Easterlin Paradox.* NBER Working Paper No. 1482. http://www.nber.org/papers/w1482

Wrong, M. (2001) *In the Footsteps of Mr. Kurtz: Living on the Brink of Disaster in Mobuto's Congo.* New York: HarperCollins.

Websites

UN report on national wealth
www.ihdp.unu/edu/article/iwr

National comparative data
http://www.MyCountryRankings.org/
https://www.cia.gov/library/publications/the-world-factbook/
http://data.worldbank.org/
http://en.wikipedia.org/wiki/Democracy_Index#2011_rankings.
http://www.prsgroup.com/icrg.aspx
http://www.worldmapper.org/

Gross National Happiness
http://www.grossnationalhappiness.com/

Freedom House
http://www.freedomhouse.org/

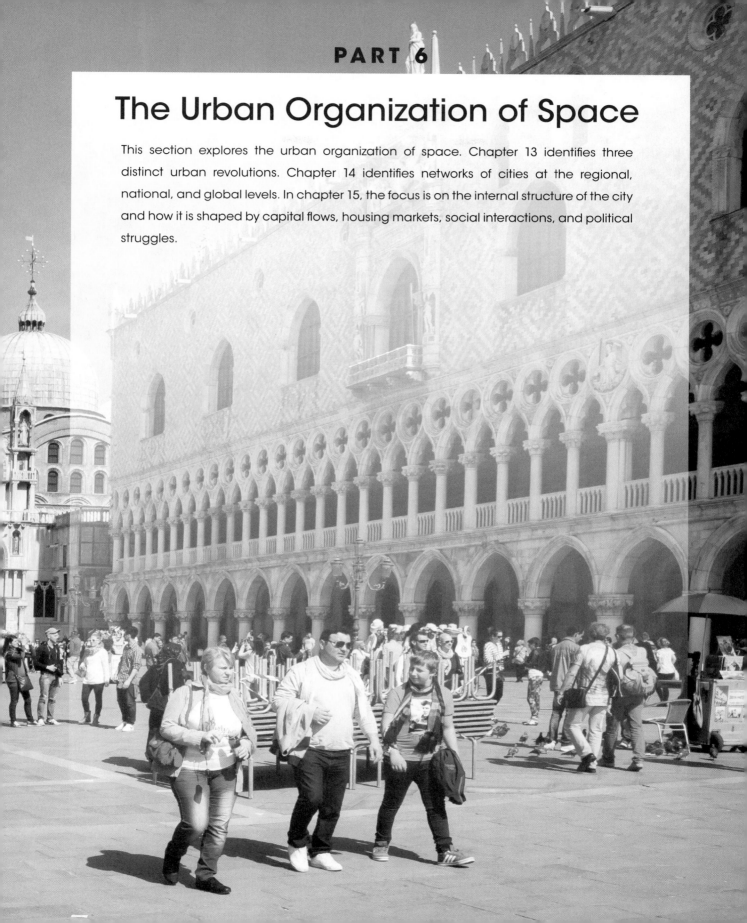

PART 6

The Urban Organization of Space

This section explores the urban organization of space. Chapter 13 identifies three distinct urban revolutions. Chapter 14 identifies networks of cities at the regional, national, and global levels. In chapter 15, the focus is on the internal structure of the city and how it is shaped by capital flows, housing markets, social interactions, and political struggles.

13 The Urban Transformation

A majority of the world's population now lives in urban areas. This shift constitutes a major change, because for most of the human occupancy of the earth, more people lived in rural areas. In this chapter we will consider the rise of cities and the nature of this urban transformation. We can identify three distinct urban revolutions.

THE FIRST URBAN REVOLUTION

The very first cities emerged between 11,000 and 5,000 years ago. They developed alongside settled agriculture, the domestication of animals, and the creation of complex irrigation systems. A traditional argument claims that the urban revolution was predicated upon the agricultural revolution: it was agricultural surplus that created cities. Most commentators now reverse the direction of the causal arrow. It was cities, or at least permanent settlements, that created agriculture. An 11,000-year-old complex of megaliths in Turkey, called Göbekli Tepe, provides some insights. The monuments were built by hunter-gatherers apparently in an act of religious devotion. The need for large numbers of people to stay in one place and cooperate to build these monuments created a demand for a stable and secure food supply; hence the invention of agriculture. It was a solution that allowed early societies to remain in place to build monuments. Cities caused the development of agriculture because they generated enough demand in one place to stimulate new sources of food production.

The development of agriculture and the creation of cities are often depicted as an upward trajectory of increasing civilization. However, the hunting-gathering societies that preceded this revolution spent less time working than agricultural societies; they are what one commentator terms the "original affluent society." In other words, preurban, preagricultural societies had more disposable time and more freedom. Even today, the Bushmen of the Kalahari spend only around 1,000 hours a year hunting and gathering food. And that is in a harsh environment; hunting-gatherers who lived in more hospitable climes would probably spend much less time. The rest of the time is spent entertaining, relaxing, and spending time with friends and families. Rice farmers in southern China, in contrast, spend around 3,000 hours a year tending to their rice crop.

The shift from hunting-gathering to settled agriculture involved more work. Mortality increased, and food intake declined to such a narrow range of foods that it led to an increase in anemia and vitamin deficiencies. The supply of food did not keep pace with the increasing population, so more farming land was needed, creating the constant growth that was an essential feature of the early urban empires. Agriculture and cities were a mixed blessing that, in the short term, meant declining living standards for the majority of the population while an elite prospered.

The urban-agricultural revolution, for the vast majority, marked a loss of freedom, greater work discipline, and more time devoted to the drudgery of work and the compulsion of social order. It was a social order that had to be imposed. An example: there are remains of an important urban culture in the desert Southwest of the United States known as the Anasazi. This independent urban civilization was centered on Chaco Canyon, New Mexico. The traditional rendition goes like this: between the tenth and twelfth centuries, the Anasazi culture, based on efficient agriculture, flowered into cities of vast cliff dwellings and major feats of engineering, architecture, and art. Brilliant pottery, sophisticated irrigation systems, and keen solar and astronomical observations round out a picture of an urban civilization that follows the old precept that cities equal civilization. Yet there is another interpretation of the Anasazi, a darker side suggesting that the Anasazi culture developed from the Toltec Empire, which lasted from the ninth to the twelfth century in central Mexico. This was an empire centered on human sacrifice and cannibalism. Thugs from the Toltec empire moved north into what is now New Mexico and found a pliant population of docile farmers whom they terrorized into a theocratic society. Social control was maintained through acts of cannibalistic terror. The Anasazi culture, so long admired, was one in which the bad and powerful controlled the weak and the vulnerable. The great feats of art and astronomy, road building and city formation were less sparks of human ingenuity and more the mark of organized social terrorism.

There was a distinct pattern to the spatial layout of the first cities. At the city center were the political elite and sites of religious devotion, the temples and altars that forged a direct link between the sacred and profane (see Figure 13.1). The city was like a map of the cosmos. Elites were located in the center of the city, with the poor at the periphery. The homology between cosmos and city was a way to legitimize the social hierarchy. The city not only housed people, it was a text that explained and justified the social world and embodied the wider cosmos.

The early cities were also vulnerable to ecological collapse. Over 4,000 years ago, the cities of Mesopotamia, including Ur, Uruk, and Umma, were brought under the unified control of the Akkadian Empire centered on the city of Akkad. At least four generations of kings ruled over the sophisticated empire. And then, quite suddenly, the empire collapsed. One text, written a century after the collapse, noted,

For the first time since the cities were built and founded

The great agricultural tracts produced no grain.

The inundated tracts produced no fish,

The irrigated orchards produced neither syrup nor wine,

The gathered clouds did not rain.

13.1 The Mayan city of Tolum, now in Mexico, was a typical preindustrial city with a prominent central site. As with many early cities around the world, the architecture at the center of the city was monumental and symbolic, connecting the sacred and the profane, the religious and the political. It prospered from the 13th to the 15th century, but the coming of the Spanish brought disease and death.

Archeological research has revealed that the collapse was due to a prolonged drought. The "gathered clouds did not rain" is not a poetical conceit but a record of severe drought.

Around the world, there is evidence of urban collapses due to ecological change. Beginning in the eighth century, many of the great Mayan cities in the Yucatan peninsula were abandoned as wars raged and people fled. A 200-year dry spell, starting around 750, caused a significant decline in regional rainfall. By 930, the Mayan heartland had lost 95 percent of its population. The "Mayan collapse" was caused by widespread drought.

Angkor Thom was the capital of the Khmer Empire, which controlled a large area of what is today Cambodia, Thailand, Laos, and Vietnam from the ninth to the fourteenth century. The city area encompassed more than 385 square miles. At its peak, it housed up to one million people, with more than 1,000 temples. Water collected from the hills was stored and distributed for a wide variety of purposes, including flood control, agriculture, and ritual bathing. A system of overflows and bypasses carried surplus water to the lake to the south. The network of reservoirs was extensive and supplied tremendous amounts of water to the city. The fall of the Khmer Empire in the fourteenth and fifteenth centuries was due to the combination of a dramatic decrease in rainfall in the region and the deleterious impact of the built environments on the surrounding environment. The city's growth led to deforestation, which increased flooding.

The earliest cities, like the cities of today, had an environmental vulnerability. The constant demand for food and water and the risk of climate change and ecological disruption means that most urban empires, sooner or later, collapse (see Figure 13.2).

Urbanization is often described as the geographical redistribution of population from rural areas to urban areas. However, it is not just the spatial reorganization of

13.2 Ruins of Carthage in North Africa. The city was destroyed in the Punic Wars between Rome and Carthage in 146 BCE. It became a Roman city and also a center of early Christianity; it was then destroyed by a Muslim army in 698 CE. The ruins are silent testimony to the rise and fall of cities and urban empires.

13.3 Venice was an important merchant city with trade links throughout Europe and with the Ottoman and Chinese Empires.

society but also the social reorganization of space. Cities incubate social and political change.

The merchant city began to develop in association with the creation of money economy, the extension of trade, and the emergence of a merchant class. In Europe, early merchant cities developed, such as Amsterdam, Bruges, Florence, and Venice (Figure 13.3). The merchant city was a vital cog in the development of international trade and commerce, but also in the creation of a commercial society where private interest was regulated, collective rules were established, and civic communities were forged. The people of the merchant cities created the notion of the public realm and civic society.

A SECOND URBAN REVOLUTION

A second urban revolution began in the late eighteenth century with the creation of the industrial city and unparalleled rates of urban growth. The industrial city was the crucible of early industrial capitalism, giving us factory life and class struggles. Factory production replaced household production, and industry replaced agriculture. The factories of Manchester and other cities in Britain in the early nineteenth century were wonders of the modern world—indeed, it was the world made modern; centuries-old agricultural dominance crumbled in a sudden seismic economic shift. In 1801 almost 70 percent of the British population lived in places smaller than 2,500 population, but by 1851 over 40 percent were living in cities with a population greater than 100,000. New cities were built on greenfield sites, and major cities developed from tiny hamlets.

Although the cities of Britain were at the forefront of the industrial revolution, the rest of Europe and North America were not far behind. Cities like Essen, Cologne, Toronto, and Melbourne began to grow rapidly by the late nineteenth century. Toronto's population increased from 30,000 in 1851 to 181,000 in 1891. Swift economic change and population growth also occurred in cities such as Boston, Pittsburgh, Cleveland, Milwaukee, Cincinnati, and Philadelphia. Industrialization generated unprecedented levels of urbanization. In 1830 Cincinnati's population was 24,800, but by 1850 it had quadrupled to 115,400 and by 1870 it was 216,000. The population of Paterson, New Jersey, increased from 11,334 in 1850 to 125,600 by 1910.

The industrial city created the arena for intense struggle between capital and labor. There were social commentators like Karl Marx who saw the industrial city as the harbinger of social revolution. There were also social reformers who used the appalling conditions of the industrial city to demand more environmental regulations, better public health, and a more livable urban environment. The city, in its various emblematic forms, creates the opportunities, contexts, and laboratories for new social developments, innovative political developments, and far-reaching economic changes. Cities are the accelerants of social, economic, and political change. Modernity emerges in the rise of the city.

THE THIRD URBAN REVOLUTION

Today we are in the midst of the global phenomenon of a third urban revolution. The first was concentrated in the fertile plains of only a few river basins. The second was restricted to cities in countries undergoing rapid industrialization. The third is a truly

Box 13.1 METROPOLITAN UNITED STATES

The US Census Bureau employs the term "metropolitan statistical area" (MSA) to refer to urban areas with a core area of at least 50,000 and economic links to surrounding counties. Using this statistical, rather than political, division of municipal boundaries, it is possible to measure the metropolitanization of the US population. In 1950 the metropolitan population constituted 56.1 percent of the total US population. By 2010, the figure was 83.6 percent. The US population is increasingly and overwhelmingly concentrated in metropolitan areas. More than 90 percent of the country's entire population growth in the last decade occurred within MSAs.

A further 10 percent of the US population lives in micropolitan statistical areas, which contain an urban core of at least 10,000 and, in total, have less than 50,000 population. Only 6.3 percent live outside these two types of urban areas. The United States continues to become a more urban and metropolitan society.

References

Short, J. R. (2012) Metropolitan USA: Evidence from the 2010 Census. *International Journal of Population Research* Article ID 207532, doi:10.1155/2012/207532 http://www.hindawi.com/journals/ijpr/2012/207532/

global phenomenon that picked up pace in the last half of the twentieth century. It is marked by five distinct characteristics.

The first is the sheer scale and pace of change. A majority of the world's population is now urban, and in many countries this new urban majority appeared in less than a generation. In 1900 only 10 percent of the world's population lived in cities. By 2010 it was more than 50 percent, and by 2050 almost 70 percent—more than two out of every three people on the planet will live in cities. Table 13.1 shows the urban percentage in 1950 and 2010 and estimates for 2050. The faster rates of urban growth occur in the developing regions of the world. In 2010 3.5 billion people lived in cities, of whom 2.6 billion lived in the developing world. By 2050 these figures will be respectively 6.2 billion and 5.1 billion. The world's urban population is increasingly living in cities in the developing world.

Table 13.1 ■ PERCENTAGE URBAN, 1950–2050			
	1950	**2010**	**2050**
World	29.4	51.6	67.2
More developed regions	54.5	77.5	85.9
Less developed regions	17.6	46.0	64.1

Source: Population Division of the Department of Economic and Social Affairs of the United Nations Secretariat, *World Population Prospects: The 2010 Revision* and *World Urbanization Prospects: The 2011 Revision* http://esa.un.org/unpd/wup/index.html

The second characteristic is the increasing size of individual cities. Throughout the world, cities have continued to grow larger. In 1800 there were only two cities—London and Beijing—that had more than 1 million inhabitants: by 1900, there were thirteen. Today, there are several hundred cities that exceed one million in population, and there are more than thirty-five that have more than 5 million inhabitants. By 2015, it is estimated that there will be around 400 cities with at least one million inhabitants. The average size of cities has grown dramatically. One of the more visible aspects of contemporary urbanization is the rise of megacities, large urban agglomerations with more than 10 million inhabitants. They are a recent addition to the urban scene. In 1900 no metro region in the world had a population greater than 10 million. In 1950 only New York and Tokyo had populations of more than 10 million. Today, there are twenty-six cities with at least 10 million people. In 1950 the Nigerian city of Lagos had a population of only 320,000. By 1965 it surpassed one million, and in 2002 it became the first sub-Saharan African megacity when it topped 10 million. With an annual population growth rate of 9 percent, it is one of the fastest-growing cities in the world.

Megacities are not just big cities, they are a new distinctive spatial form of social organization that radically transforms the city-nature relationship. Their sheer size exerts a large and heavy environmental footprint. Megacities can impose a heavy environmental toll. Continual city growth generates tremendous rural-to-urban land use changes and associated ecosystem transformations. The increasing population also puts extra pressure on the biophysical systems that provide land, air, and water.

Third, this revolution exhibits a marked metropolitanization. Improvements in transport have allowed dispersal of people and activities away from the tight urban cores of preindustrial and industrial cities. Large metropolitan regions rather than individual cities are the new building blocks of both national and global economies. Three giant urban regions in Asia Pacific, Bangkok (14 million population), Seoul (25 million), and Jakarta (28 million), have between 35 and 75 percent of all foreign direct investment into their respective countries. In China, the three city regions of Beijing, Shanghai, and Hong Kong constitute less than 8 percent of the national population, yet they attract 73 percent of foreign investment and produce 75 percent of all exports. China is less a national economy than the aggregate of three large metropolitan economies. In the United States, ten megapolitan regions, defined as clustered networks of metropolitan regions that have a population of more than 10 million, constitute only 19.8 percent of the nation's land surface yet comprise 67.4 percent of the population.

Population and economic activities have spread beyond the municipal boundaries. In the past fifty years, across the world, small towns have grown into cities and big cities have sprawled into giant metropolitan regions.

Fourth, a distinctive global urban trend is urban sprawl. Big-city regions are now characterized by more dispersed forms of urban development. The steady suburbanization of jobs and residences has extended the urban region further out from central cities. In the United States in 1950, only 23 percent of the US population was living in suburbs. This figure increased to 46.8 percent by 2010. More people live

Box 13.2 MEGALOPOLIS

One of the largest contiguous areas of metropolitan counties is what is sometimes called Megalopolis, a region spanning 600 miles from north of Richmond in Virginia to just north of Portland in Maine and from the shores of the Northern Atlantic to the Appalachians. The region includes the consolidated metropolitan areas of Washington-Baltimore, Philadelphia, New York, and Boston and covers 52,000 square miles, with a 2010 population of 44.6 million. It

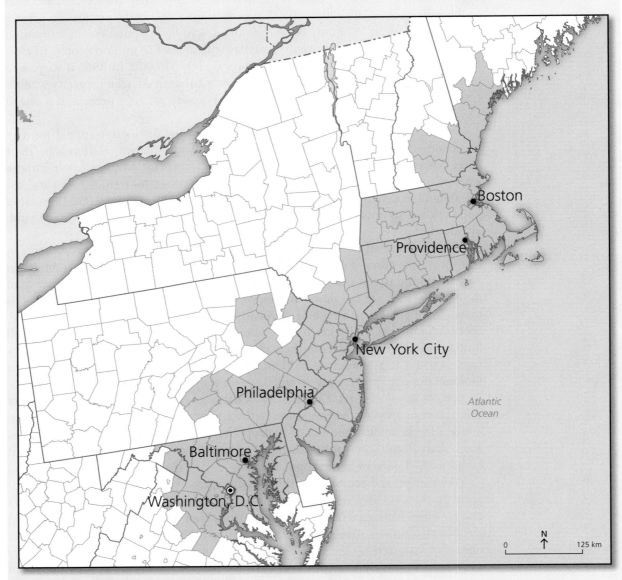

Megalopolis, United States

Box 13.2 CONTINUED

contains just over 14 percent of the entire US population.

In 2000 the combined population of Boston, New York, Philadelphia, and Washington was 10.64 million, and by 2010 this had increased to 10.88 million. Baltimore, with a relatively large manufacturing base, declined from 651,154 in 2000 to 620,961 in 2010.

Megalopolis is overwhelmingly suburban, with three out of every four persons living in the suburbs. Megalopolis, like other large city regions across the country, is a place of increasing racial diversity. In the four combined MSAs that make up this extended region, the percentages of Blacks, Asians, and Hispanics are respectively 20.2, 8.9, and 18.6. The respective figures for the United States are 12.6, 4.8, and 16.3. Megalopolis is one of the most racially diverse regions of the country. In some metro areas, there are more minorities living in the suburbs than in the central city. In the Washington, DC, MSA, for example, there were 857,380 Hispanics living in the suburbs, compared to only 54,749 living in the city. The Hispanic experience in the Washington MSA is predominantly a suburban one. Across the entire region, the suburbs are becoming more racially diverse.

Megalopolis is the destination of significant amounts of immigration from overseas. The foreign-born population increased from 10 percent in 1960 to 23.8 percent in 2010, almost double the national average of 12.4 percent. Migrants are found in both central cities and in suburban areas; particular concentrations can be identified as immigrant gateways. One example is Tyson's Corner, VA, an archetypal edge city located off the Washington Beltway. The population of Tyson's Corner is 19,627, with almost 35 percent foreign-born. Immigrant suburbs are now an important part of the metropolitan United States.

References

Gottmann, J. (1961) *Megalopolis: The Urbanized Northeastern Seaboard of the United States.* New York: Twentieth Century Fund.
Short, J. R. (2011) The Liquid City of Megalopolis. In *The New Blackwell Companion to the City*, ed. G. Bridge and S. Watson, Malden, MA: Blackwell, pp. 26–37.
Short, J. R. (2007) *Liquid City: Megalopolis Revisited.* Washington, DC: Resources for The Future Press/ Johns Hopkins University Press.
Electronic Atlas of Megalopolis http://www.umbc.edu/ges/student_projects/digital_atlas/instructions.htm. Accessed October 19, 2012.

in metropolitan areas, and more of these people are living in extending suburbs. The process, while particularly evident in the developed world, is not limited to it. Consider the case of Shanghai. Since 1991, new residential and industrial complexes have developed along the rural-urban fringe, aided and encouraged by local governments, which are key stakeholders in the land development system. The end result is a more widely dispersed urban system with land development often leapfrogging across the landscape. Shanghai is now a huge polycentric city.

Dispersed urban expansion triggers land cover changes, especially the disappearance or fragmentation of croplands and woodlands, the destruction of both low- and high-quality agricultural lands, and the emergence of a hybrid rural-nonfarm landscape (see Figure 13.4).

13.4 Urban sprawl between Baltimore and Maryland

Sprawl is now associated with a host of negative environmental impacts, including:

- loss of agricultural land in the wake of low-density sprawling development;

- increased impermeable surfaces, which leads to flooding and large discharges of polluted and contaminated water that overwhelm drainage systems and damage ecosystems;

- the heavy use of vehicular traffic, which leads to increased air pollution and global warming.

Sprawl is a form of development that is very often too diffuse to support public transport or easy walking. The heavy, and in some cases total, reliance on private auto transport in the United States, for example, imposes a heavy environmental price in terms of air pollution and the increasing dedication of space for roads and parking. The reliance of a built form precariously balanced on one fossil fuel with large and fluctuating costs raises issues of long-term sustainability. There is also an emerging body of literature that points to the negative public health effects of suburban sprawl, including a link with increased obesity. The promotion of a driving lifestyle leads to less physical activity and an increase in obesity.

There is also the fundamental issue of the long-term sustainability of sprawl. Low-density suburban sprawl is only possible with relatively cheap fuel and lack of accountancy for the environmental impacts. It is unlikely that the cheap gasoline that literally lubricated suburbanization will ever return. Where does that leave low-density suburban sprawl, which is so reliant on large-scale private car usage? The general answer: in a very precarious position. The long-term sustainability of low-density, energy-profligate, heavy-ecological-footprint sprawl is now a matter of serious consideration.

Fifth, there is a distinct feature of urban growth in the rapidly growing cities of the developing world (also referred to as the global South), namely slums. The term "slum" (also called "shantytown," "informal housing," and "squatter housing") refers to unplanned, often illegal, informal housing. Slums arise due to the inability of formal markets and public authorities to provide enough affordable and accessible housing. There are numerous names for these slum settlements. They are called "ranchos" in Venezuela, "pueblos jóvenes" in Peru, "favelas" in Brazil, and "barong-barongs" in the Philippines. A UN survey estimated that around a billion people lived in slums. The figure is estimated to rise to 2 billion by 2030 as people migrate to the cities and urban populations grow.

Box 13.3 SEOUL

The city's population in 1949 was around 2.4 million before it embarked on decades of sustained economic growth fueled by export-led manufacturing and population growth based on rural to urban migration within South Korea. In the 1960s and 1970s, the city population was increasing at the rate of a half million every two years. The enforced industrialization and urbanization led to major environmental damage and social dislocation, but it did lift the majority of South Koreans out of poverty. Authoritarian governments ensured that breakneck economic development was not halted by democratic discussion. Massive urban renewal involved loss of cheap housing, clearance of squatter settlements, the widening of roads, and the channelization of the Han River with high embankments. Seoul was the center of the country's rapid urbanization. The proportion of the nation's population classified as urban increased from 14.5 percent in 1950 to 88.3 percent in 2000.

By 2010, the city population was 10.3 million, while the wider metro area had a population of 25.6 million. Despite the growth of other cities in South Korea, Seoul retains its national prominence, dominating the national economy, politics, art, and culture. The city is moving rapidly towards a postindustrial economy. There was a rapid rise and relative fall in manufacturing employment in the city that peaked at 1.3 million in 1990, 30 percent of the labor force. By 2000, manufacturing constituted only 19 percent of total employment. The city's economy is now dominated by the service sector, which employs 3.6 million people, 80 percent of the city's total workforce. The city has moved from a manufacturing to a service center. It has also spread out as urban growth leapfrogged

Seoul, an older part of the central city that is rapidly transforming

the green belts. A once concentrated city is becoming a polycentric metropolitan region tied together by mass transit and increasing car usage.

Seoul is South Korea's most important global hub. However, the ethnic homogeneity of the city continues to be very obvious. With less than 1 percent foreign-born, the city's ethnic and racial homogeneity is maintained by strong controls on foreign immigration.

References

Kim, K.-J. (ed) (2003) *Seoul: Twentieth Century*. Seoul: Seoul Development Institute.

Some slums go through a development from temporary accommodation built on the most marginal sites to fully formed urban neighborhoods. In the 1950s, some rural migrants moved to Ciudad Nezahualcóyotl, an area on the outskirts of Mexico City, where they built their own homes on appropriated land using whatever materials they could find. Over time, more permanent buildings were constructed. The area was designated a municipality in 1963, allowing the formal provision of public services such as potable water, pavements, sewerage, and electric lighting. By the 1980s, public buildings such as hospitals and schools were being built. In 1995 the area exceeded one million residents. In this process, temporary shelter for recent migrants became a slum and then an integral part of the city. Peter Ward first studied 300 self-builders in neighborhoods in Bogotá and Mexico City in the 1970s. A follow-up study in 2007 allowed him to identify changes. He found that more than four out of every five households stayed in the houses that they built, but densities rose along with the sizes of the extended families, and the values of the properties increased substantially. "Temporary" self-built housing provided stable family accommodation for over forty years as well as an important family asset.

13.5 Informal housing on a steep slope in the Caribbean island of St. Vincent.

There are different types of slums. In Abidjan, in Côte d'Ivoire, where slum dwellers represent one-fifth of the city's population, there are three types of slums. Zoé Bruno, for example, contains buildings of permanent material and basic infrastructure and is only different from the formal areas of the city by the fact of the illegal land occupation. In Blingue, the buildings are made of nonpermanent materials and the area has low levels of infrastructure. In the worst areas, such as Alliodan, makeshift buildings have no infrastructure.

The urban explosion of the past fifty years has forced expansion onto new spaces on more vulnerable sites such as steep hillsides and flood plains or in areas with unstable soil conditions. Many slum structures are erected on such marginal lands because standard, legal housing long ago claimed the best, most secure land in the city (see Figure 13.5). The poor are often forced to settle on land subject to higher risks. Slum homes perched precariously on hillsides are often swept away by heavy rains, which also flood slums located on floodplains. Heavy rain contributes to the landslides and the flooding, but the real causes are the fact that low-income groups could find no land site that was safe and the failure of government to ensure a safer site or to take measures to make existing sites safer. The worst slums often have to occupy the most hazardous sites, on steep slopes and on areas vulnerable to flooding, landslide, and other environmental and social hazards.

The lack of legal ownership makes slum dwellers particularly vulnerable to government clearances. One particularly brutal example of a process repeated throughout the world: on May 19, 2005, the government of Zimbabwe, under the dictatorial control of Robert Mugabe, launched a new urban policy. It was called Operation Murambatsvina, literally "Drive out the rubbish." As part of a nation-wide campaign to beautify the cities, destroy the black market, reduce crime, and undermine the support base of its political opponents, the government authorized the bulldozing of squatter settlements that fringed the city's larger cities. The squatter settlements had long been the main source of opposition to his rule. The campaign destroyed the homes of 700,000 people and wiped out the informal economy that provided a livelihood for 40 percent of the population. Almost 2.4 million poor people were faced with increased economic hardship. Another example: in July 2012 the Lagos state government in Nigeria moved to evict residents of Makoko, a slum neighborhood of around 200,000 people living on dwellings built on stilts in a lagoon. The residents were given seventy-two hours to vacate before men started chopping down the dwellings. City officials argued that the slums were an environmental nuisance, impeded waterfront development, and undermined the megacity status of Lagos. They felt that a 2010 BBC television documentary program, *Welcome to Lagos*, which told the story of Makoko's residents, presented the country and the city in a negative light. In fact, the documentary was a celebration of the ingenuity and vibrancy of slum life in the city. While it noted problems of flooding, irregular power supply, and poor environmental conditions, it was lyrical in its invocation of the resiliency and vitality of marginal groups living in slums on the economic margins. Rather than being a depiction of gloom and darkness, it highlighted the incredible dynamism and energetic entrepreneurship of the slum dwellers.

The process continues: in the build-up to the 2014 World Cup, many of the favelas in Rio de Janeiro are under assault from clearance, forced eviction, and destruction. One plan produced by city authorities envisaged the removal of 13,000 families from 123 different neighborhoods in the city.

Across the urban world, then, we can identify a continuum from slums of hope at one end to slums of despair on the other. Slums of hope provide a platform for rural urban migrants to the city. In slums of despair, residents are imprisoned in webs of multiple deprivation. Both type of slums are vulnerable to assault and destruction from urban development projects.

Box 13.4 SHANGHAI

After the 1842 Treaty of Nanjing, when it was opened up as a port under colonial control, Shanghai became one of the largest shipping ports in the world. It exported food and raw material from the Chinese interior to world markets. Tea, silk, and raw materials were shipped through the city, which became China's major industrial center, with mills, factories, chemical plants, and shipyards. In the 1930s, there were 150,000 workers in textile factories, and the city's population approached 3 million, including 100,000 foreigners. At its pre-Communist peak it was the fifth largest city in the world, a cosmopolitan city with at least sixty different nationalities.

Shanghai became a Communist city on May 25, 1949, when troops of the People's Liberation Army marched in and took it over. The earliest economic plans of the Party aimed to build up heavy industry. The city population quickly grew from 4 million in 1950 to almost 6.5 million in 1960, a staggering 50 percent increase.

During the Cultural Revolution, from 1966 to 1976, more than 30 million urban dwellers were forced to move to and work in the countryside. Shanghai was especially targeted. As a place of foreign influences and conspicuous consumption, it was treated as a dangerous hybrid place—Chinese, yet contaminated with anti-communist tendencies and bourgeois sensibilities. From a peak of 6.4 million in 1961, the city's population declined to 5.4 million in 1978.

In 1984, fourteen coastal "open" cities, including Shanghai, were declared. The reglobalization of Shanghai involved, as with other open cities, the creation of special economic and technological zones to foster concentrations in export-led manufacturing, high-tech industries, and financial services. From 1978 to 2005, the annual growth rate of GDP was close to 10 percent, and average wages grew sixfold. In 1990, a new open economic development zone called Pudong was created. An area

Shanghai. A new skyscraper in the Pudong neighborhood

of former rice paddies is now home to over 3 million people.

There is a frenzy to the remaking of the city. There are the expanding network of inner rings roads and outer motorways, new subway lines, tunnels and bridges, airport upgrades, and new high-speed trains. There are the new spaces of consumption: the malls, shopping centers, and gated communities. At the extremes are exclusive gated communities for the wealthy and enclaves of marginalized migrants. The post-Communist city now exhibits marked social and spatial segregation.

References

Short, J. R. (2012) *Globalization, Modernity and the City*. New York: Routledge.

Cited References

Batuman, E. (2011) The Sanctuary: The World's Oldest Temple and the Dawn of Civilization. *The New Yorker*, December 19 and 26, pp. 72–83.

Sahlins, M. (1972) *Stone Age Economics*. Chicago: Aldine.

Sjoberg, G. (1960) *The Pre-industrial City*. Chicago: Free Press.

Turner. C. and Turner, J. (1999) *Man Corn: Cannibalism and Violence in the Prehistoric Southwest*. Salt Lake City: University of Utah Press.

UN Human Settlements Program (2003) *The Challenge of Slums*. London: Earthscan.

Ward, P. M. (2012) "A Patrimony for the Children": Low-Income Homeownership and Housing (Im)Mobility in Latin American Cities. *Annals of the Association of American Geographers* 102: 1489–1510.

Select Guide to Further Reading

Benton-Short, L. and Short, J. R. (2013) *Cities and Nature*. London: Routledge.

Davis, M. (2006) *Planet of Slums*. London: Verso.

Duncan, J. S. (1990) *The City as Text: The Politics of Landscape Interpretation in the Kandyan Kingdom*. Cambridge: Cambridge University Press.

Gruebner, O., Khan, A., Lautenbach, S., Muller, D., Kramer, A., Lakes, T., and Hostert, P. (2012) Mental Health in the Slums of Dhaka: A Geoepidemiological Study. *BMC Public Health* 12:177 doi:10.1186/1471-2458-12-177

Haug, G., Gunther, D., Peterson, L., Sigman, D., Hughen, K., and Aeschlimann, B. (2003) Climate Change and the Collapse of the Maya Civilization. *Science* 299: 1731–1735.

Kaniewski D., Campo, E. V., and Weiss, H. (2012) Drought is a Recurring Challenge in the Middle East. *Proceedings National Academy of Science* 109: 3862–3867.

Nelson, A. and Lang, R. (2011) *Megapolitan America: A New Vision for Understanding America's Metropolitan Geography*. Chicago: APA Planners.

Schneider, A. and Woodcock, C. E. (2008) Compact, Dispersed, Fragmented, Extensive? A Comparison of Urban Growth in Twenty-five Global Cities Using Remotely Sensed Data, Pattern Metrics and Census Information. *Urban Studies* 45: 659–692.

Short, J. R. (2012) *Globalization, Modernity and the City*. London: Routledge.

Websites

Megacities
http://www.megacitiesproject.org
Urban health
http://www.who.int/topics/urban_health/en
Urban population
http://www.unicef.org/sowc2012/urbanmap/
The United Nations Human Settlements Programme
http://www.unhabitat.org/categories.asp?catid=9,
The urban transformation
http://www.wilsoncenter.org/program/comparative-urban-studies-project
World Bank urban data
http://data.worldbank.org/indicator/SP.URB.TOTL
World urban areas
http://www.demographia.com/db-worldua.pdf

Cities exist not only as singular places but also as nodes in a variety of networks. In this chapter we will explore regional, national, and global networks.

REGIONAL NETWORKS

One of the earliest forms of urban network is the periodic market system. Periodic markets occur in villages and towns when demand density is low and vendors are relatively mobile. At the simplest level they may consist of a seller by the roadside with seasonal wares or produce (see Figure 14.1). There are also the larger weekly, monthly, and annual markets with larger numbers of vendors and customers. There is a geometry to this periodicity, as markets seek to either minimize travel for vendors by bringing them closer together (Figure 14.2A) or maximize demand by spreading markets across space (see Figure 14.2B). A study in northern Nigeria found that markets held on the same day are generally located 10.6 miles apart, whereas markets with meetings two days apart have an average spacing of 3.3 miles.

As demand grows, some traders stay in place, and eventually periodic markets are replaced by fixed markets. Figure 14.3 is a picture of a fixed market in Curaçao that used to be held weekly. However, there are still examples of periodic markets throughout much of the developing world. And even in the rich developed world, farmers' markets continue to attract customers.

With rising demand, fixed markets tend to replace periodic markets. In 1915, C. J. Galpin, who was studying rural communities in Wisconsin, suggested that towns with the same number of services tend to located at regular intervals, and in the surrounding rural areas people tend go to the nearest town to shop for goods and services. The ideal pattern of flat agricultural plain is highlighted in Figure 14.4, where a regular distribution of towns is surrounded by circular complementary regions. There are overlapping complementary regions. If we assume distance minimization by customers, the resultant complementary region of each town takes form of a hexagon, because if we draw a straight line through shared areas the result is a hexagon. Walter Christaller (1893–1969) looked for a similar pattern in southern Germany in the 1930s. He identified what he termed the

14.1 Roadside sale in Jamaica

14.2 Periodic markets

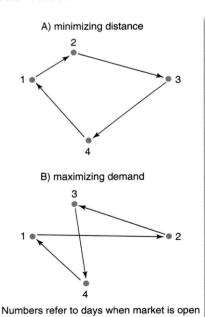

A) minimizing distance

B) maximizing demand

Numbers refer to days when market is open

range and the threshold of a good or service. The range of a good or service is the distance consumers are willing to travel. While a buyer of a car may travel long distances to seek out good bargains, the buyer of a carton of milk will only travel much shorter distances. The threshold of a good is the necessary minimum population to support the continued supply of that good. Car dealers need a larger population to support their business than do milk sellers. People buy cars more infrequently than milk. Higher-order goods and services have larger thresholds and larger ranges than lower-order goods and services. Market towns are distributed in a hierarchy, with higher-order goods and service located in the larger towns. Christaller visualized a range of hexagonal structures depending on whether the system was geared to optimizing markets, minimizing travel, or optimizing administrative boundaries (Figure 14.5).

Christaller's work, first published in 1933 and resuscitated in the 1960s, was seen as a contribution to economic and urban geography. More recently, it has undergone piercing criticism as the context of his work has been uncovered. Christaller joined the German Nazi

14.3 Fixed market in Curaçao

14.4 The Galpin Model

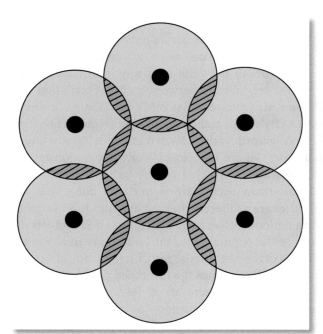

Party in 1940. He joined the Reichskommissariat für die Festigung deutschen Volkstums (Reichskommissariat for the Strengthening of German Nationhood), where he worked on plans to occupy the lands of Czechoslovakia, Poland, and the eastern regions of the USSR. His central place theory was employed to organize and settle the occupied lands. The seemingly innocent geometry of central place theory was devised to organize the Nazi occupation of an Eastern Europe emptied of its original inhabitants. One journalist describes him as "Hitler's geographer." The story of Christaller reminds us of the tangled connections between academics and politics, theory and practice, and the contested politics of space.

Central place theory was extended in a range of case studies. Brian Berry looked at the urban system in rural areas of the US Midwest, while Bromley and Bromley uncovered the hierarchy in a region of Ecuador by looking at bus services. However, it has fallen from favor as a major topic of study. The theory is more suitable for stable agricultural regions of the world. It gives little insight into the massive urbanization or rapid metropolitanization of today.

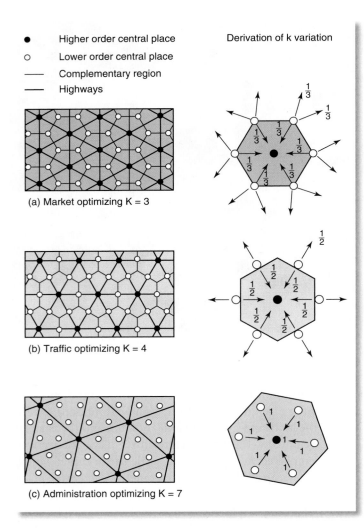

- ● Higher order central place
- ○ Lower order central place
- —— Complementary region
- —— Highways

Derivation of k variation

(a) Market optimizing K = 3

(b) Traffic optimizing K = 4

(c) Administration optimizing K = 7

14.5 Market areas in central place systems

The basics of central place theory, and in particular the notions of complementary region and of the range and threshold of goods and services, are still important tools to uncover some of the socio-spatial relations in urban networks. The measurement and definition of complementary regions allow us identify the effective influence of a city across space. The US Census Bureau, for example, uses commuting patterns to identify city regions.

The changing range and threshold of goods also allow us to understand some of the changes in local urban systems. In many rural areas, small towns are shriveling up and dying. Urban networks are thinning as goods and service provision moves up the urban hierarchy to larger towns and cities. Small towns shrink in economic importance when the range and threshold of goods and services both increase. Urban decline is in part a function of changes in the range and threshold of goods and services.

NATIONAL NETWORKS

Cities are also part of national networks. There are numerous ways to measure a national urban network. One way is to consider the relationship between a city's population and its rank. In a **rank size distribution**, also referred to as Zipf's Law, there is a simple and regular relationship between a city's rank and its population (Figure 14.6). This relationship is found mainly in large countries with a large number of big cities, such as China, India, and the United States. Figure 14.6 plots US city population against expected values according to Zipf's Law.

In contrast, a **primate distribution** occurs when one city dominates the national urban system. Primate cities are a different order of magnitude and significance from all the other cities in a national urban hierarchy. Short and Pinet-Peralta calculate primacy using the ratio of the population of the largest city in a country divided by the combined population of the next two largest cities. A value of 3.0 tells us that the primate city's population is three times the combined population of the next two largest cities. This is a substantial concentration. Table 14.1 notes all the countries with a primacy value above 3.0. Let us consider the most primate urban system to tease out some of the possible causal connections.

14.6 Rank-size in the United States

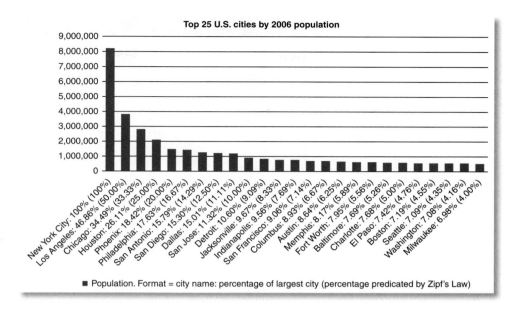

Population. Format = city name: percentage of largest city (percentage predicated by Zipf's Law)

Table 14.1 ■ HIGH URBAN PRIMACY	
Country	**Primacy**
Thailand	9.48
Suriname	8.24
Togo	7.92
Uruguay	7.37
Nigeria	5.94
Uganda	5.94
Ethiopia	5.82
Mongolia	5.67
Peru	5.43
Guinea	5.27
Eritrea	4.98
Namibia	4.80
Argentina	4.76
Mauritania	4.60
UK	4.48
Hungary	4.47

Table 14.1 ■ CONTINUED	
Country	**Primacy**
Armenia	4.33
Côte d'Ivoire	4.24
Madagascar	4.14
Mali	4.04
Nicaragua	3.87
Afghanistan	3.76
Latvia	3.70
Chile	3.69
Georgia	3.49
Iraq	3.34
Myanmar	3.34
Gambia	3.30
Sierra Leone	3.30
Austria	3.27
Haiti	3.26
Greece	3.23
Jamaica	3.22
Tanzania	3.19
Gabon	3.16
Chad	3.14
Central African Republic	3.10
Costa Rica	3.09
Serbia	3.07
Cuba	3.04
Romania	3.02

The population of Thailand exhibits the most pronounced degree of urban primacy. Out of a population of almost 65 million, just over 15 million live in the urban region of Bangkok. Since 1782 the city has been the capital of the country. Bangkok was and remains the center of the country, the unchallenged center of political, intellectual, and religious life. The court was based in the city. There were few other towns

Box 14.1 ESTIMATING CITY POPULATION

An obvious source of urban population data is the United Nations. The UN Department of Economic and Social Affairs: Demographic and Social Statistics available at http://unstats.un.org/unsd/demographic/sconcerns/densurb/urban.aspx lists the populations of the principal cities for most countries in the world. This source has the benefits of ready accessibility, constant updates, and ease of use. The downside is that, as with all international urban data, it is deeply flawed. Different countries take censuses at different times, use different measures (e.g., some use formal urban political boundaries, while others give the data for functional urban agglomerations), and have wildly varying degrees of accuracy. Take the case of Nigeria and its major city of Lagos. At the UN source, accessed in February 2007, the city's population is available only for 1975 and is listed at just over one million. According to the latest official figures in Nigeria, the population of Lagos in 2006 was almost 9 million, but local officials accuse the federal government of deliberately undercounting this southern Nigerian city and its encompassing region to favor the northern part of the country. More neutral observers estimate the current population of Lagos at between 13 million and 15 million.

Henderson has also created a documentation site for world cities data over the period 1960 to 2000, from UN data as well as from world gazetteers and national censuses. This is freely available at http://www.econ.brown.edu/faculty/henderson/worldcities.html. This site has the advantage of providing time series analysis, but, as the website informs readers, the data are based on "incomplete documentation and data only partially cleaned." The data for the United Kingdom include the city data for London but the metropolitan data for Birmingham and Manchester.

A more user-friendly source is available at http://www.citypopulation.de/ which lists the population of all principal cities for most countries. The data are drawn primarily from official censuses and estimates, but even the webmaster reminds the user that the data "are all of varying, and some of suspect accuracy."

Another major problem with urban population data is the distinction between population estimates for the city and for the wider metropolitan region. London's population is calculated with reference to the city boundary. Almost 7.5 million people live within this boundary. Yet its commuting range stretches much wider. The wider city region stretches from the Wash to the Isle of Wight. Within this urban agglomeration live 21 million people, or almost 35 percent of the UK total population.

The "dirty little secret" of global urban research is the poor quality of comparative data, even basic data such as population. Population censuses are of varying degrees of accuracy, are taken at different times, and have differing definitions of city and metropolitan regions. The population figures for most cities around the world are more estimates than precise figures, averages across a wide band of error, and more appropriately used as rough comparisons rather than precise absolute values.

References

Short, J. R., Kim, Y.-H., Kuus, M., and Wells, H. (1996) The Dirty Little Secret of World Cities Research. *International Journal of Urban and Regional Research* 20: 697–717.

of any size. In the past fifty years, this embedded centrality of the city to the wider life of the country has shaped subsequent growth, especially export-led growth. The city became the main transmission hub of economic globalization for the country and the wider region. The centralizing forces of globalization reinforced the national primacy. By 2005, the city was responsible for almost half of all gross domestic product. Thailand is one extended urban region centered in Bangkok. The city is an important global city not only for the country but for the wider region of Southeast Asia.

There is a particular subset of the primate cases in Table 14.1. Ten are from Central or South America—Argentina, Chile, Cuba, Costa Rica, Haiti, Jamaica, Nicaragua, Suriname, Uruguay, and Peru—and nine of the ten are classified as middle-income. These primates all share a colonial history. The centralizing element in the pre-Hispanic imperial and Spanish colonial system (French, English/British, and Dutch in the cases of Haiti, Jamaica, and Suriname respectively) set the conditions for subsequent growth. The largest capital cities were home to the elites, the population center of gravity, and the economic hub of the national space economy. Primacy was reinforced as economies shifted from primary to secondary and then tertiary economic sectors, rural-to-urban migration increased, and foreign investment connected the local to the global. People, jobs, and investment moved to the major city.

Table 14.1 also contains a number of richer countries, including Austria, Hungary, and the United Kingdom. Some of the European primacy pattern reflects the size of imperial cities, including Vienna, Budapest, and London, all centers of far-flung empires rather than just capitals of individual countries. Nineteenth-century Vienna was one of the centers of political power in Europe, the capital of the vast Austro-Hungarian Empire. Vienna flourished as an imperial capital and the most important city in central Europe, but the loss of empire after the First World War (1914–1918) reduced Austria to a small German-speaking state, and Vienna found itself a large city in a small country. Budapest was also the center of a much larger country and empire. After 1920, Hungary forfeited two-thirds of its area. The end result was a large city in a much-reduced country. Nearly one-fifth of Hungary's population lives in Budapest, which is now more than nine times larger than the nation's second-largest city. London was not just the capital of the United Kingdom but the central node in a worldwide formal and informal empire. The retreat from empire and decline of global economic dominance has left a huge city in a relatively small country. The imperial primacy has persisted in a postimperial society. The wealthy, the influential, the movers and shakers live in the city; it is home to royalty, the political elites, those who manufacture the dominant forms of representation, and those who control much of the making and moving of money.

At the other end of the continuum of primacy values are the non-primate distributions. Table 14.2 lists all those countries with a recorded primacy value of less than 0.9. The case of Bolivia disproves the easy assumption of Latin American countries always having primate urban distributions. No simple generalizations can be made, as low primacy is found in the Netherlands as well as India, the United States as well as Venezuela, Canada as well as Benin.

Using aggregate data sets provides only a first glance at urban national networks. If we look at one example in more detail, more complex patterns are revealed. Consider

Table 14.2 ■ LOW URBAN PRIMACY	
Country	**Primacy**
Benin	0.58
South Africa	0.59
Venezuela	0.65
Netherlands	0.70
Egypt	0.72
Australia	0.74
China	0.78
USA	0.84
Bolivia	0.84
India	0.86
Canada	0.89

Australia, which by 2012 had a national population of 22.7 million. At first blush, it appears to have a non-primate distribution, because the largest city, Sydney, has a population of 4.62 million, followed by Melbourne and Brisbane (see Figure 14.7) at 4.13 million and 2.07 million respectively. The primacy value is 0.76. One could deduce that the urban system is evenly distributed. But on closer examination, as shown in Table 14.3, Australia is best depicted as a series of primate states in a federal system.

14.7 Brisbane is one of the large cities in Australia.

Table 14.3 ■ URBAN PRIMACY IN AUSTRALIA	
Country/State	**Primacy**
Australia	0.76
New South Wales	5.44
Queensland	5.32
South Australia	33.48
Tasmania	1.13
Victoria	14.66
Western Australia	11.94

The case of Australia reminds us of the importance of scale, geography, and history. The primacy value for Australia is suggestive of non-primacy, as if activities were evenly distributed throughout the urban system. Yet when we look at the level of individual states, we see there is a marked concentration of activity, enterprise, and population in large cities. The Australian Federation of 1901 brought together a series of hyperprimate economies that the passing of time has done little to change. The major cities continue to dominate their respective states. The geography and (white) history of Australia play an important part. An antipodean gulag for the British soon developed into a colonial enterprise organized and structured through the port cities of the different states. A classic case of colonial spatial organization of a vast country was soon embedded into a series of primate states. The case of Australia shows that reliance solely on national data abstracted from issues of scale, geography, and history has limited explanatory value.

GLOBAL URBAN NETWORKS

Cities are also part of global networks of flows of capital, goods, ideas, and people. Some of the flows have been identified and measured. A substantial body of material has emerged from the work of Peter Taylor and his colleagues at the Globalization and World Cities (GAWC) research network. The website (http://www.lboro.ac.uk/gawc/) lists data sets as well as more than 350 research papers and is an indispensable guide to the metageography of urban networks. In 2000, GAWC collected data on the distribution of 100 global advanced producer service firms, which includes accountancy, advertising, banking/finance, insurance, law, and management consultancy, across 315 cities. They analyzed the resultant data matrix to identify a global urban hierarchy. In 2008, they extended the analysis to 175 firms in 525 cities. The result was a fivefold hierarchy that identified cities as

14.8 The global urban network according to GAWC

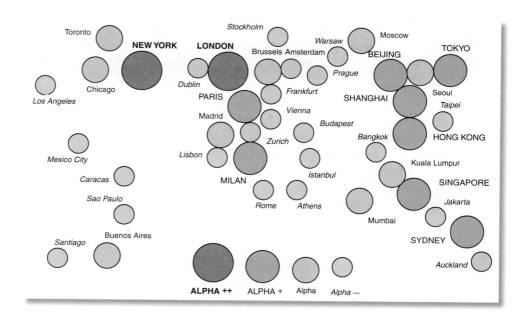

alpha, beta, gamma, high sufficiency, and sufficiency. Figure 14.8 is a cartogram of alpha cities in the network of advanced producer services. Note how New York (NY) and London (LON) dominate. NYLON is an important pivot in the global networks. In 2000, Shanghai was three steps below, in the alpha minus category, while Beijing was only a beta city. In 2008, both Shanghai and Beijing were classified as alpha plus, only one step below NYLON. Both cities are moving into the top tier as China's economic growth, both absolute and relative to the rest of the world, continues apace. The diagram highlights the centers of new metropolitan modernity, the rapidly growing cities of the Far East.

Financial services continue to be concentrated especially in the global cities. At the apex are the supranational centers of London and New York, followed by a second tier of international centers that include Tokyo and Zurich and host centers that attract foreign financial institutions and include such places as Sydney, Toronto, and Vienna.

The globalizing economy creates lots of information, narrative uncertainty, and economic risk that all have to be produced, managed, narrated, explained, and acted upon. Global cities are centers of global epistemic communities of surveillance, knowledge production, and storytelling. Trust, contact networks, and social relations play pivotal roles in the smooth functioning of global business. Spatial propinquity allows these relations to be easily maintained, lubricated, and sustained in an efficient means of communication that helps solve incentive problems, facilitates socialization and learning, and provides psychological motivation. There are positive benefits of face-to-face contact. Global cities are sites of dense networks of interpersonal contact and centers of the important business social capital trust vital to the successful operation of international finance.

Box 14.2 VISUALIZING NATIONAL URBAN NETWORK FLOWS: THE CASE OF THE UNITED STATES

Xingjian Liu and two colleagues estimated the US national urban network from a study of sixty major cities. Using 2010 data, they map four different types of intercity flows, of which two are noted here: internet connectivity and recorded business travel flows.

Note the patterns they reveal.

References

Liu, X., Neal, Z., and Derudder, B. (2012) City Networks in the United States: A Comparison of Four Models. *Environment and Planning A* 44: 255–256. http://www.envplan.com/openaccess/a44496.pdf

Network flows in the United States: internet connectivity

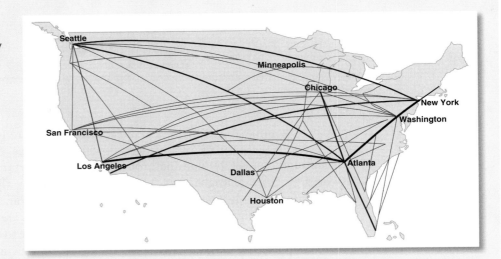

Network flows in the United States: recorded business travel flows

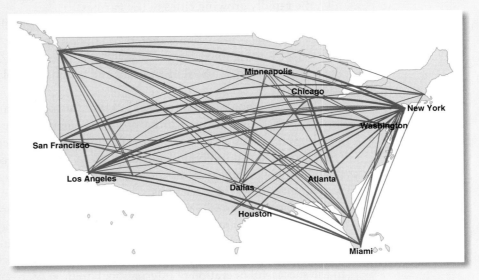

Box 14.3 BLACK HOLES AND LOOSE CONNECTIONS

Networks also have holes. Table 14.4 lists eleven cities which met three criteria: they had a population of over 3 million, were not identified by GAWC as a world city, and did not share their national territory with a world city. They ranged from Tehran, with a population of 10.7 million, to Chittagong, with a population of 3.1 million. There are a number of reasons behind these very large cities' non–world city status. They are the black holes of advanced global capitalism, with many people but not enough affluent consumers or complex industries to support sophisticated producer services. There are also cases of catastrophic decline where there has been an almost complete collapse of civil society. In recent years, Khartoum and Kinshasa, for example, have witnessed the decline of the rule of law and social anarchy. War and social unrest have been the norm rather than the exception. These two cities represent cities that have internally collapsed for all intents and purposes and have been abandoned or bypassed by global capitalism. Sustained social disruption reinforces the global disconnect.

Poverty and social anarchy do not explain all the cases. Tehran and Pyongyang, for example, are cities where national ideologies have not encouraged global economic connections to the advanced capitalist economies.

We can identify three ideal types of large non–world cities: the poor city, the collapsed city, and the excluded city. There are clearly connections between these types, and in

Table 14.4 ■ BLACK HOLES	
City	*Country*
Tehran	Iran
Dhaka	Bangladesh
Khartoum	Sudan
Kinshasa	Congo
Lahore	Pakistan
Baghdad	Iraq
Rangoon	Myanmar
Algiers	Algeria
Abidjan	Ivory Coast
Pyongyang	North Korea
Chittagong	Bangladesh

reality most of the cities listed in the table have elements of all three in differing proportions. It is just as important to identify the black holes and loose connections as to point out the important nodes and connected cities of global urban networks.

References

Short, J. R. (2004) Black Holes and Loose Connections in a Global Urban Network. The *Professional Geographer* 56:295–302.

Vijver, E.V. D., Derudder, B., Bassens, D., and Witlox, F. (2014) Filling Some Black Holes: Modeling the Connection Between Urbanization, Infrastructure, and Global Service Intensity. *The Professional Geographer* 66: 82–90.

Lisa Benton-Short and colleagues also sought to identify a global network, but their work was based on flows of people. They looked at immigration into cities around the world and established an index based on the percentage of foreign-born, the total number of foreign-born, the percentage of foreign-born not from a neighboring country, and the diversity of immigrant home countries. The result was a threefold division into alpha, beta, and gamma cities. There are similarities and differences between the GAWC and the Benton-Short results. Among the similarities: some cities appear in the same category in both analyses. New York and London are alpha cities and sit atop the apex of both hierarchies. Other shared alpha cities include Toronto, Los Angeles, Sydney, and Amsterdam. Differences: while Miami, Melbourne, Vancouver, and Dubai are considered pivotal points of global migration reaching alpha status, in the advanced producer service category they only make it to beta status.

Some of the differences relate to issues of data and data availability. But they also refer to the nature of the global urban network. Networks vary according to the flow. Some flows "pool" in some cities rather than others. Advanced producer services, for example, which can be considered command functions of the globalizing economy, are still concentrated in just a few cities because of the need for social interaction in global financial business deals. The flow of people, while matching the connections in command functions, also has slight differences. National regulations concerning immigration, the demand for labor, and the relative openness of societies to foreign migrants all play a part. The sheer need for labor, whether the global talent pool of specialized knowledge experts or cheap unskilled labor, varies throughout the urban network. The result is a similar but not identical match of command centers with immigration hubs. There is no one fixed global urban hierarchy; it is more a global urban network with different configurations of hierarchy depending on the flows.

Money, people, ideas, goods, and practices do not just flow through the urban network, they are transformed in the process. To be more accurate we should use the term "space of transformative flows." Consider flows of people. The movement through the urban network is not a simple geographical movement; it involves cultural exchanges. These can refer to the new work habits and job practices of the temporary worker as well as the complex cultural transformations of long-term migrants as they adapt to a new milieu and in turn transform their surroundings. Rather than mere transfers, flows along the urban networks are transformative experiences, even in the flows of inanimate things such as of money, goods, and services. A small amount of money in London or New York when remitted back to Ghana or El Salvador can become the source for land and house purchase, enabling a new business or paying for better schooling. Flows through the urban network change the medium and the networks; as people adapt, ideas are tweaked, money is reimagined, and commodities are reappropriated.

Cited References

Benton-Short, L., Price, M., and Friedman S. (2005) Globalization from Below: The Ranking of Global Immigrant Cities. *International Journal of Urban and Regional Research* 29: 945–959.

Berry, B. J. L. (1976) *Geography of Market Centers and Retail Distribution*. Englewood Cliffs: Prentice Hall.

Bromley, R. and Bromley, R. D. F. (1979) Defining Central Place Systems through the Analysis of Bus Services: The Case of Ecuador. *Geographical Journal* 145: 416–436.

Frantzman, S. (2010) Hitler's Geographer: Walter Christaller and Nazi Academics. *The Jerusalem Post,* August 27.
http://www.jpost.com/Magazine/Features/Article.aspx?id=186068

Galpin, C. J. (1915) *The Social Anatomy of an Agricultural Community.* University of Wisconsin Agricultural Experimental Station, Research Bulletin 34.

Hill, P. and Smith, R. H. T. (1972) The Spatial and Temporal Synchronization of Periodic Markets: Evidence from Four Emirates in Northern Nigeria. *Economic Geography* 48: 345–355.

Rössler, M. (1989) Applied Geography and Area Research in Nazi Society: Central Place Theory and Planning, 1933–1945. *Environment and Planning D: Society and Space* 7: 419–431.

Short, J. R. and Pinet-Peralta, L. M. (2010) Urban Primacy: Reopening the Debate. *Geography Compass* 3: 1245–1266.

Select Guide to Further Reading

Alderson, A. S., Beckfield, J., and Sprague-Jones, J. (2010) Intercity Relations and Globalisation: The Evolution of the Global Urban Hierarchy, 1981–2007. *Urban Studies* 47: 1899–1923.

Brenner, N. and Keil, R. (eds.) (2006) *The Global Cities Reader.* New York: Routledge.

Castells, M. (1996) *The Rise of Network Society.* Oxford: Blackwell.

Derudder, B. (2008) Mapping Global Urban Networks: A Decade of Empirical World Cities Research. *Geography Compass* 2: 559–574.

Jefferson, M. (1939) The Law of the Primate City. *Geographical Review* 29: 226–232.

Moomaw, R. and Alwosabi, M. (2004) An Empirical Analysis of Competing Explanations of Urban Primacy Evidence from Asia and the Americas. *Annals of Regional Science* 38: 149–171.

Neal, Z. P. (2010) From Central Places to Network Bases: A Transition in the US Urban Hierarchy, 1900–2000. *City & Community* 10: 49–75.

Taylor, P. J. (2004) *Global City Network.* London: Routledge.

Websites

Comparative urban data is available at
http://www.citypopulation.de/
http://esa.un.org/unpd/wup.html
The Globalization and World Cities (GAWC) website
http://www.lboro.ac.uk/gawc/

15 The Internal Structure of the City

In this chapter, we will focus on the internal structure of the city and, in particular, on four specific themes: the city as investment, as residence, as social context, and as political arena. The chapter ends with a discussion of the major contemporary trends of gentrification, suburban decline, and city marketing.

THE CITY AS INVESTMENT

The city is a site of investment. This investment is cyclical, as capital flows into the building of a city when relative rates of return are high. Building cycles occur on average every eighteen to twenty years. There is distinct periodicity to the building cycle. In the *trough,* there is limited investment and little building. During the *upswing,* the lack of supply just as demand picks up leads to higher levels of construction. At the *peak,* building activity is more feverish, land prices increase, and there is more speculative development (see Figure 15.1). But as the supply expands just as the demand falters, there is a *downswing,* and in more extreme cases a *crash* as prices fall and supply outstrips demand. The cycle then begins again.

Different sectors of the property market may experience slightly differently timed cycles in different places, although what was distinctive about the US housing market crash in 2008 was its national character. Previous housing cycles in the United States had a more regional character. The commercial office property market shows the largest peak and troughs.

Building cycles often align with transport improvements and changes. A building boom in the 1950s was associated with mass car ownership, giving a more dispersed and road-connected character to urban development compared to the higher-density development associated with previous building-boom-associated trams and railways. It is more accurate, then, to speak of a building-transport cycle.

The built form is a visible legacy of the boom of the past. Each major building cycle is also associated with changes in architectural style. Capital is locked into place, with the architecture of the day acting as the equivalent of a date stamp. The very largest and oldest cities have examples of all the major building cycles. A transect through a major city is the equivalent of flipping through the pages of an architectural history text. Some cities, in contrast, experience massive growth only at specific times: the old part of Tallinn in Estonia is a reminder of the city's growth during the Hanseatic League, Venice is filled with buildings built during the Renaissance boom (Figure 15.2),

15.1 Office development in Reading, UK. The project was funded by a pension company eager to place large sums of money in secure, high-return investments.

15.2 Renaissance architecture in Venice, Italy

and the Georgian architecture of Edinburgh is a sign of the city's vitality in the eighteenth century. Housing built in the 1920s boom was influenced by Art Deco and Art Moderne sensibilities, while housing and office buildings constructed in the immediate postwar era were more modernist-inspired. More recent postmodern buildings give an indication of the sites of the latest rounds of investment. Shanghai's postmodern signature buildings indicate its recent rounds of frenzied growth.

THE CITY AS RESIDENCE

We can distinguish between production, supply, and demand for accommodation.

The Production of Housing

15.3 Speculative house-building in Maryland

Housing is produced in a variety of ways. There is the individual contract, whereby a household hires builders to construct a custom-designed dwelling. This is normally very expensive and limited to the very rich. The tiny size of this sector, however, is dwarfed by its architectural importance, as many new residential styles and designs first saw the light of day as individual contracts. Many of the early individual house projects of such famous architects as Frank Gehry, Frank Lloyd Wright, and Le Corbusier influenced changes in overall architectural style. More common is the institutional contract, whereby an institution or a government entity builds dwellings and then rents them out or sells them. Institutional contract production was particularly important during the boom in public housing from the 1950s to the 1970s, when local governments hired builders to construct large projects.

Currently, the two most important forms of production are speculative and self-build. Speculative building involves builders assembling land and constructing dwellings for a general demand rather than for specific customers (Figure 15.3). This form of production is dependent on macroeconomic conditions, especially the interest rate, as builders use borrowed money and sophisticated credit facilities that allow households to purchase homes. Because the system is based on long credit lines, any change in the financial structure reverberates in this sector of the housing market. Wider economic changes, such as major shifts in interest rates, are reflected in the booms and slumps of the speculative housing sector.

In much of the world, incomes are too low, credit facilities for purchasing homes are lacking, and cash-strapped governments are unable and unwilling to provide accommodation. In many cities in the developing world, self-build housing, in which residents simply build their own residences, is an important form of housing production. Areas of self-built housing have a variety of names, including slum, shantytown, informal housing, and squatter housing. Much of this self-build is considered illegal, because the occupiers hold no title to the land, do not pay taxes, and have constructed some form of shelter that does not meet building codes. Because these are illegal structures, they often lack public services such as clean water, sewage, and sanitation infrastructure. Around 1 billion people live in such slums. The figure is estimated to rise to 2 billion by 2030.

The Housing Stock

The rise and fall of the housing stock depends on many factors. There is the natural aging of the housing stock, although the aging process can give older housing the allure of the established, much the same way that antiques have value. Building cycles involve not only the building of the new but often the destruction of the past as old buildings are demolished, or destroyed. The urban renewal projects in the United States from 1949 to 1973 demolished 600,000 units, covering 1,000 densely packed urban square miles and ultimately displaced 2 million people. A program begun with the best of intentions, getting rid of substandard housing, ended up demolishing basically sound housing, destroying functioning neighborhoods, laying the seeds of subsequent inner-city decline, and concentrating poor people—especially poor black people—in increasingly segregated urban neighborhoods. A similar process is occurring in the rapidly growing cities of the Chinese coast. Michael Meyer describes life in the vanishing backstreets of Beijing as they are demolished to make way for malls and new high-rise buildings. From 1990 to 2003, more than half a million residents were evicted from central Beijing, a process that accelerated just before the hosting of the 2008 Summer Olympics.

Around 4 in the afternoon, on January 12, 2010, an earthquake measuring a devastating 7 on the Richter scale occurred in Haiti. Over 300,000 were killed, a similar number were injured, almost a million people were made homeless, and much of the capital city of Port-au-Prince was reduced to rubble. Despite international relief efforts, in 2012 half a million people still lived in temporary shelter, often in appalling conditions. In October and November 2012, Hurricane Sandy etched a destructive path through the Caribbean and along the northeastern Atlantic seaboard. Fifteen thousand homes were destroyed in Cuba, and hundreds of homes were flooded along the New Jersey coast.

The Supply of Housing

Housing supply can be broken down into tenure types. Three main types of tenure can be identified. First is public housing, in which a government agency provides accommodation for citizens. In much of postwar Europe, public housing was an important part of the housing stock. In Scotland, by 1972, for example, more than 80 percent of the housing stock was public housing (Figure 15.4). Public housing

15.4 Public housing in Glasgow, Scotland

was, and in many countries still is, an important part of the social contract between the people and the government. In the United States, by contrast, public housing was always a much smaller percentage of the housing stock and often marginalized to housing the very poorest. Every major US city had "projects," which tended to be large modernist units of public housing providing accommodation for the very poor. Many of them have since been demolished.

One trend is towards a privatization of the public housing stock. In Britain, after 1979 much of the public housing stock was essentially sold off to private residents. A total of 1.6 million units were sold to sitting tenants. The proportion of public housing declined from around 30 percent in 1975, concentrated in the larger urban centers, to around 18 percent by 2011.

Across Western Europe, public housing, sometimes known as social housing, is still an important part of the housing stock, at the highest levels ranging from 40 percent in the Netherlands to 20 percent in Sweden. In Sweden, the 850,000 social housing units are provided by 300 local housing authorities. There are three allocation models: "universal," in which everyone has access to social housing, as in the Netherlands and Sweden, where rents are fixed at market rates with subsidies for the poorest; "restricted," where access is means-tested, as in France and Germany; and "residual," as in the United States, the United Kingdom, and Ireland, where it is reserved for the poorest.

A second form is private renting, whereby landlords rent out property to tenants. Through most of the nineteenth and early twentieth century, this was the dominant tenure form in cities of North America and Europe. Landlords tend to want to raise rents and keep maintenance costs low, while tenants want exactly the opposite. History is studded with landlord-tenant conflicts. Generally, the conflict remains at the level of individual landlord and tenant, but in a few rare cases the

Box 15.1 HOME SWEET HOME

The home is of huge social significance. We spend much of our lives in the home, and our primary emotional and connections are shaped in its domestic arena; where we live and how we live are important determinants of our social position, physical health, and individual well-being. Home is a central element in our socialization into the world. Given its huge significance, there is comparatively little work on the meaning of the home. However, recent work by geographers focuses on the home, where space becomes place and where family relations and gendered and class identities are negotiated, contested, transformed. The home is an active moment in the creation of individual identity, social relations, and collective meaning. The home is a nodal point in a whole series of polarities: journey-arrival, rest-motion, sanctuary-outside, family-community, space-place, inside-outside, private-public, domestic-social, sparetime-worktime, feminine-masculine, heart-mind, Being-Becoming. These are not stable categories; they are both solidified and undermined as they play out their meaning and practice in and through the home. The home is a space riven by ambiguities, a place of paradoxes.

References

Brickell, K. (2012) "Mapping" and "Doing" Critical Geographies of Home. *Progress in Human Geography* 36: 225–244.

Blunt, A. and Dowling, R. (2006) *Home.* New York: Routledge.

Cieraad, I. (ed) (1999) *At Home: An Anthropology of Domestic Space.* Syracuse: Syracuse University Press.

conflict can widen. In Glasgow, Scotland, in 1914–1915, a rent strike broadened into industrial stoppages. Because the country was at war, the government quickly intervened with legislation that limited rent increases and laid the basis for tenant protection and controls on rent that have lasted to the present day. In the United States, rent controls are in operation in around 140 cities. In New York City, rent control has been in operation since 1943 and covers around 185,000 residencies, while rent stabilization, for apartments constructed after 1945, covers around 1 million residences.

Third, and in most affluent countries the largest form of housing supply, is owner occupation, whereby households purchase property. Housing is very expensive in relation to income, so immediate house purchase is beyond the reach of all but the wealthiest. Credit in the form of long-term mortgages is a vital prerequisite for mass homeownership. In the United States, for example, there is a steady encouragement of owner occupation through various encouragements to lenders to provide mortgages. Government-backed agencies such as Fannie Mae and Freddie Mac provide liquidity to the system by purchasing mortgages from banks. Tax policies also encourage homeownership. In the United States, homeowners get exemption from the capital gains tax on house sales and tax relief on mortgage interest payments. These are massive government subsidies that are mostly regressive, in that the richest groups tend to benefit most.

Financial institutions play a key role in owner occupation. Their willingness to lend and the spatial patterns of their lending influence urban housing markets.

In the 1970s, for example, many institutions in the United States restricted their mortgage allocation to lower-income minority neighborhoods. The process was known as redlining, and it meant a lack of housing finance to poorer neighborhoods in the inner city. It became both a cause and effect of inner-city decline, because residential areas denied mortgages tended to deteriorate more rapidly. In 1975 Congress passed the Home Mortgage Disclosure Act in response to evidence that banks were not lending in inner-city minority neighborhoods. Two years later, the 1977 Community Reinvestment Act prodded banks to lend in inner-city communities. Promoting homeownership became a national fixation. From the 1990s onwards, there was a relaxation in lending requirements and banking regulations that led to two developments. The first was a relaxation of strict requirements on borrowers. Previously, most mortgages required a 10 to 20 percent down payment and clear evidence of ability to pay. These were known as prime mortgages. By the mid-2000s, more mortgages were subprime, given to borrowers making no down payment and with fewer verifiable means of income. Inner-city neighborhoods now became a prime site for predatory lending. These subprime mortgages grew in size and importance. By 2006, almost 7 million subprime loans were allocated. The second development was the securitization of mortgages. Previously mortgages had been kept on the books of the lending institutions. With securitization, mortgages were bundled up and sold as a commodity. The emphasis was on generating turnover rather than assessing risk, as the risk was passed onto the next buyer on the chain. It was in the interests of the originating company to allocate as many mortgages as possible and then sell them on. Credit agencies were supposed to assess the risk, but a government inquiry revealed massive abrogation of due diligence by the three main agencies. The result was that toxic mortgages infected the financial system. When the housing bubble burst in 2006–2008, 7 million mortgages went into foreclosure, and banks and other institutions had toxic assets on their books. The net effect was the financial crisis of 2008. The sorry tale reminds us of the importance of the housing finance sector in the overall economy.

The Demand for Housing

Demand for housing varies along a number of dimensions. Perhaps the most important is income and wealth. The private housing market covers a variety of income levels. At the top are the luxurious apartments and palatial houses on sprawling estates. At the bottom are the cheapest apartments and smallest houses. In between are a variety of middle-income areas. The income hierarchy is reflected in the variegated housing market. The more income you have, the more housing you can consume, whether in terms of more space or more prestigious space. Most large cities, for example, have their exclusive neighborhoods where residency is a sign of wealth and achievement. At the other extreme every city has its "bad" neighborhoods with reputations sometimes undeserved but nevertheless an important part of the social geography of the city. The city's housing market can be considered as a space packing problem. The richest get to choose the best housing in the best areas. Groups with successively lower income get less choice, and as income declines, the choices narrow (see Figures 15.5 and 15.6).

15.5 Luxury home in exclusive Palo Alto, California

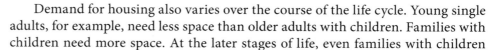

15.6 Modest row houses in inner-city Baltimore

Demand for housing also varies over the course of the life cycle. Young single adults, for example, need less space than older adults with children. Families with children need more space. At the later stages of life, even families with children may shrink in size and hence space requirements as the children mature and leave to start their own lives. This simple stage in the life cycle model of housing demand is undermined by two trends. In the developed world, the average family size is decreasing, so the demand for family style housing is declining while the demand for smaller accommodation for single-person and childless households is increasing. The suburbanization of the US population from 1950 to 1990 was driven in part by the shift of families with children moving to single-family homes in the suburbs, the move in part a decision to get better educational opportunities for their children. Since the 1990s, there has been a move into the city, in part driven by more single-person and childless households for which a house in the suburbs is not as good a choice as a more central location. The second way that the model is undermined is that throughout much of the world the extended family is the norm rather than the nuclear family. Many adults tend to remain with their existing family rather than establishing new independent households. Interestingly, the trend is also reappearing in the richer countries. In the United States, for example, more adult children are remaining longer with their parents than ever before, and sometime returning home after college; the shift is a function of a difficult job market and expensive housing.

It is not only income and stage in the life cycle that affects housing demand; there are also cultural factors. Households vary in their ethnic, racial, and other forms of identity. In some cases, certain ethnic and racial groups are discriminated against. Throughout much of the first two-thirds of the twentieth century, blacks in the United States, to take an obvious example, faced severe discrimination that limited housing choice in the city. Black concentrations in central cities, initially a sign of discrimination, also emerged through time as a platform for political power as the black population found a voice in majority-minority cities such as Baltimore, where blacks made up 63 percent of the population in 2012. In the past fifty years, while formal discrimination has ended there are still marked patterns of segregation. Cities around the world still bear the historical imprint and/or contemporary operation of racial and ethnic segregation. Although apartheid is no longer the formal policy of South African cities, there is still marked residential segregation by race in the social geographies of major South African cities.

Certain groups cluster together in distinct residential areas through choice sometimes as much as constraint. There are many reasons for the clustering, including feelings of security. A neighborhood of similar people can provide a safe platform for entry into a large city.

Part choice, part constraint, racial and ethnic clustering is an important part of the social geography of the city. The geography shifts as new migrant streams enter; old neighborhoods are gentrified or commodified, as in the case of Chinatowns becoming places of Chinese restaurants and festivals rather than places where Chinese people live. Some clusters became centers of entertainment as well as source of identity. There are the well-known Little Italy in New York City and Little Havana in Miami. In Washington, DC, there is Little Ethiopia, home to the largest population of Ethiopians outside Addis Ababa, around 250,000. It is not the formal place of residence of all American Ethiopians but the setting for restaurants and stores that sell Ethiopian food and goods. Little Odessa in Brighton Beach in New York City is home to more than 350,000 people from Russia, Ukraine, and Georgia.

There is also clustering and segregation along religious lines. The geographer Frederick Boal has long studied the segregation between Catholics and Protestants in Belfast. The city was at the frontier zone between an Irish and a British realm. The segregation not only gave a sense of safety during the period of conflict, it was also part of the conflict, as it reinforced group stereotyping and the spatial basis and embodiment of community conflicts.

Severe ethnic national and religious divisions can result in highly segregated cities with borders that scar and divide. In the most severe cases, the lines of segregation are patrolled and policed.

In recent years, sexual identity has also become a basis for residential clustering. In the Paddington district of Sydney, Australia, from the 1970s onwards an inner city neighborhood of small family homes became a favored residence for openly gay households who were discriminated against in much of the city. The neighborhood became a gay-friendly district encouraging an open display of gay identity. As cultural attitudes shifted, the previously transgressive nature of the place was soon commodified and then incorporated the city's economy and national and international image. The annual Mardi Gras festival, initially supported only by the LGBT (lesbian, gay, bisexual, and transgender) community as a celebration of sexual diversity, is now one of the city's biggest cultural events, drawing visitors from around the world. In other cities, such as San Francisco, sexual tolerance is now at the very heart of the city's identity. Elsewhere, in much of the world where LGBT people face open discrimination, there are far fewer opportunities for neighborhoods of sexual diversity and tolerance to flourish. Homosexuality continues to be categorized as a crime in many societies.

Models of the Residential Mosaic

The housing market produces a residential mosaic of different types of neighborhoods. The modeling of the residential mosaic constitutes a consistent theme in urban geography.

Different models focus on different processes. Throughout the twentieth century, a number of different models were proposed. The Burgess model, named after the urban sociologist E. W. Burgess, was based on the experience of Chicago in the first third of the twentieth century, a time of massive immigration from overseas. Burgess saw a process of new migrants moving into the cheaper central city areas and more established residents moving further out (see Figure 15.7). The result was a concentric ring pattern of rising socioeconomic status and increasing family size towards the city's edge. Later, the land economist Homer Hoyt pictured socioeconomic groups arranged in different sectors of the city. Robert Murdie combined

15.7 The process underlying the Burgess model.

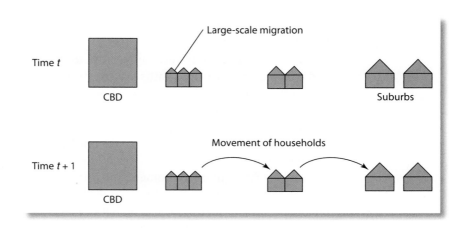

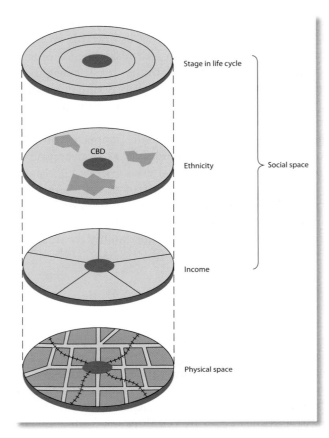

various observations into a layered model of concentric rings of households at different stages in the life cycle, socioeconomic groups in specific sectors, and ethnic, racial, and other minorities in distinct clusters. The composite model is shown in Figure 15.8. These simple patterns have long been overlain by more complex patterns. A more recent composite model, the Hanlon, Short, and Vicino (2010) model is shown in Figure 15.9. Around the central area of this idealized US city, there are pockets of both concentrated poverty and gentrification, and in the inner ring there are suburbs in crisis, with declining prices and aging housing stock. Towards the city's edge there are "boom-burbs" and affluent enclaves. This model reflects the contemporary reality of the heterogeneous US metropolitan areas more accurately than the simplified picture of the traditional models.

THE CITY AS SOCIAL CONTEXT

The human geographer David Seamon argues that we can consider the relationship between people and urban space in terms of three interlinked processes: *movement*, or how people move through space; *rest*, which is the physical attachment to place; and *encounter*, or how we interact in place with other people.

15.8 Murdie's composite model

The Swedish geographer Torsten Hägerstrand realized that we move through both space and time, and he provided a way to map activity in space and time. Figure 15.10 traces the path of two people who leave their homes to go to work, then meet up in a cafe around 4 p.m. Such maps can highlight colocations in time and are enormously useful in tracing the paths we weave through space-time (Figure 15.11).

Much of our activity revolves around fixed pegs in space-time, such as home and work. Our space-time paths are constrained. A prism outlines the space that can be covered in the time available; those with a car will have a much larger prism, as they can cover a larger distance. They can therefore look much further afield for employment. What are the pegs and prisms that constitute your typical day?

We can also think of timed space and spaced times. Certain spaces change through time. Entertainment districts, for example, can remain quiet until the nighttime brings more customers and increased activity. Certain behaviors are more permissible at certain times and places than others. Act rowdily in New Orleans during Mardi Gras, and no big deal. The same activity in Milwaukee on a Sunday afternoon may provoke very different responses.

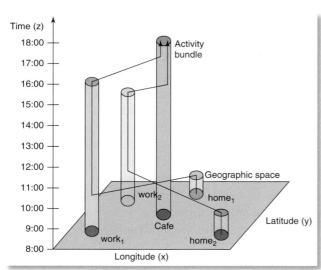

15.9   The Hanlon-Short-Vicino model

15.10   Space-time mappings

How we behave is also influenced by space and place. The sociologist Erving Goffman asks us to think of social activity as a performance and employs spatial metaphors such as "front stage" and "backstage." When we are front stage, in front of strangers, such as a job interview, we are on our best behavior. Backstage, as with friends relaxing, we can let our hair down. The city is a series of stages where different parts of our character are reinforced, highlighted, or suppressed. The city provides opportunities to play a multiplicity of roles, allowing both anonymity and identification, giving us the opportunity to be both performers and audience in a myriad of fleeting and more sustained social interactions. The characterization of the city as stage has unlocked a whole host of useful metaphors, including plot, script, roles, back/front stage, etc., that have been enormously useful to understanding life in the city.

15.11 Space-time traveler. This photograph of a young woman walking through an installation by the artist Jesús Rafael Soto at the Hirshhorn Gallery in Washington, DC, highlights the sense of movement though space.

Other scholars explore the relationships between the official city and the everyday lives we lead. "Strategy" refers to spatial ordering by powerful interests, "tactics" to appropriations and transgressions of ordinary citizens. Through tactics, the strategies of power can be undermined and appropriated. Life in the city is conceptualized as reinforcing both the spatial strategies of the official city and the tactical appropriation and resistance of everyday resistances. To understand the city in all its complexities, we need to connect the official and the everyday, the compliance and resistances embodied in the space-time paths we make across the urban built form and the routes we weave across urban social space.

The third element that David Seamon outlined was encounter, the interaction between people in space. Much of city living is spent with people who are similar to us. Elijah Anderson looks at how people share urban space with people different from themselves. His ethnographic research examines street strategies adopted by different racial-ethnic groups in neighborhoods in Philadelphia. He identifies what he terms "the cosmopolitan canopy," islands of civility in the segregated city. These islands are a space where people of diverse backgrounds come together and interact. In much of the city, people interact with people much like themselves in terms of race and class. The more successful cities have an extensive and variegated cosmopolitan canopy.

Anderson's work is also part of the long tradition of urban ethnography fieldwork that moves through the city with care, recording and noting, making sense of the kaleidoscope of urban experience. This more textured qualitative examination of the city complements the quantitative approach.

BOX 15.2   MEASURING SEGREGATION IN THE CITY

The level of segregation in the city is measured in a variety of ways. The **index of dissimilarity** measures the unevenness in the distribution of two groups across spatial units. The index ranges from 0 to 100, with values closer to 100 indicative of more dissimilarity. Table 15.1 notes the index values for racial groups in counties in the Megalopolis region of the United States from 1960 to 2000.

The dissimilarity in the spatial spread of blacks and whites remains consistently high. In fact, there was an increase in the index for 2000 compared to 1960, which is a staggering finding given the decline of many of the formal and explicit practices of racial discrimination. A striking feature is the persistently high indices for all the groups. For only one pair, Asians and Hispanics, did the index fall below 30, perhaps due to the shared spaces of more recent immigrants. The data reveal persistent segregation between all the groups, increased segregation between blacks and whites from 1960 to 2000, and stable and high levels for whites and Asians, blacks and Asians, and blacks and Hispanics, with a slight decline in segregation levels between whites and Hispanics and Asians and Hispanics.

The **index of segregation** measures the distribution of one group compared to the total population. This index also ranges from 0 to 100, with values closer to 100 indicative of a more segregated distribution.

We can interpret the data in Table 15.2 using the example of the index of 43.3 percent for

Table 15.1 ■ INDEX OF DISSIMILARITY IN MEGALOPOLIS			
	Index of Dissimilarity		
	1960	**1980**	**2000**
Whites/Blacks	43.9	49.9	47.1
Whites/Asians	39.5	38.2	39.2
Whites/Hispanics	na	49.3	42.3
Blacks/Asians	40.2	42.2	41.2
Blacks/Hispanics	na	37.5	36.2
Asians/Hispanics	na	32.9	29.6

Table 15.2 ■ INDEX OF SEGREGATION IN MEGALOPOLIS				
	White	**Black**	**Asian**	**Hispanic**
1960	43.3	43.8	37.8	na
1980	51.2	48.4	35.1	48.4
2000	40.8	42.6	34.2	38.0

Box 15.2 CONTINUED

whites in 1960; this implies that 43.3 percent of whites would have to move to another area to achieve the same distribution as the total population. This is a high value, indicating marked segregation. The high values shown in this table indicate consistently pronounced levels of segregation for all the groups. Whites and blacks were more segregated in 1980 than in 1960,

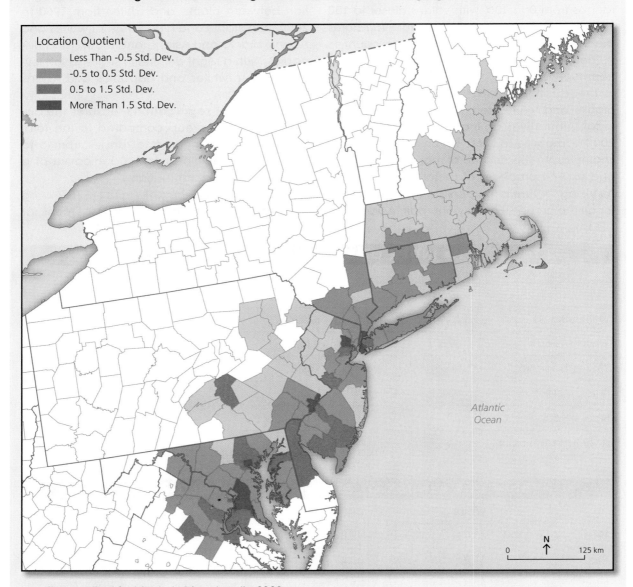

Location quotient for blacks in Megalopolis, 2000

Box 15.2 CONTINUED

then returned to their 1960 pattern in 2000. These data can be interpreted as reflecting the differential nature of suburbanization until 1980: as blacks were moving into the central cities, whites were moving out to the suburbs. The 1980 values indicate the high-water mark of this trend. The 2000 values reflect the greater suburbanization of blacks and consequently slightly less segregation. Asians remained approximately the same, while Hispanics became slightly less segregated in 2000 compared to 1980—in part a function of the wider suburban spread of Hispanics through Megalopolis.

The **location quotient** (LQ) measures the degree of concentration of one group compared to the total population; it is found by dividing the percentage of the subgroup by the total population of each and every spatial unit. Values greater than 1 suggest a higher concentration of the subgroup in that area. Values of less than 1 indicate lower concentrations. LQ values in 1960 were wide, from 0.002 in Perry, PA, to 5.48 in the District of Columbia. By 2000,

the range of values had shrunk somewhat, from 0.028 in Perry to 4.16 in Baltimore City. There was a thin spread of blacks throughout the region and increased concentration in selected cities and suburbs. The map shows the LQ values for blacks in 2000, by standard deviation, and reveals increased concentration in the urban centers and the inner suburban areas around the largest cities.

Each of the different measures provides a different picture of residential segregation and concentration. All of them are very sensitive to the scale of the analysis. Larger observation units, such as the county level, may mask patterns of segregation that are only revealed at the level of census tracts.

References

Johnston, R. J. and Jones, K. (2010) Measuring Segregation: A Cautionary Tale. *Environment and Planning A* 42: 1264–1270.

Short, J. R. (2007) *Liquid City: Megalopolis and the Contemporary Northeast.* Washington, DC: Resources for the Future.

THE CITY AS POLITICAL ARENA

The city is a political arena where different groups and stakeholders compete and cooperate. Let us consider the case of households.

Households have diverse interests. As residents, they want a full range of public goods and services, including clean water, efficient transport systems, and good schools. We can also identify public bads as well as public goods. Public bads are all those unwanted facilities such as trash disposal sites, motorways, and halfway houses for convicted criminals. In many cases, the process is referred to as NIMBY—"not in my backyard." Households individually and collectively seek to attract public goods and deflect or relocate public bads. The process reflects the political power and economic strength of residents' organizations. The rich and powerful live in neighborhoods without toxic waste sites.

It is a consistent finding that toxic facilities are predominately concentrated in lower-income and minority-dominated areas of the city, and major infrastructure projects with negative environmental impacts, such as urban motorways, are more commonly found in poor and minority neighborhoods. Study after study from around the world reveals a correlation between negative environmental impacts and the presence of racial/ethnic minorities. Studies in the United States highlight that race is the most significant variable associated with the location of hazardous waste sites and that the greatest number of commercial hazardous facilities are located in areas with the highest proportion of racial and ethnic minorities. Three out of every five black and Hispanic Americans live in communities with one or more toxic waste sites.

In cities around the world, the poor and the marginal more often than not live in the areas with the worst environmental quality. Social inequalities are expressed and embodied in urban environmental conditions. In Europe, waste facilities are disproportionately located in lower-income areas and in places where ethnic minorities live. Urban environmental inequality is large and pervasive.

Poorer communities have less pleasant urban environments and often bear the brunt of negative externalities. It is through their neighborhoods that motorways are constructed, and it is in their neighborhoods that heavy vehicular traffic can cause elevated lead levels in the local soil and water. There is a direct correlation between socioeconomic status and the quality of the urban environment.

Households are also taxpayers, and as such they want to minimize their taxes while maximizing their benefits. Attitudes to taxation vary, with Scandinavian taxpayers more willing to bear a large load than those in the United States. In all cities in all countries, however, there are limits to the acceptable amount of taxation. Proposition 13, which passed in California in 1978, limited the tax based on property values. Prior to the legislation, increasing property values meant increasing taxes. In a period of rapid house price inflation, taxes skyrocketed. Households organized to place the proposition on the ballot. The effects were felt immediately in reductions in public spending and public services.

Households are also users of services. They want police, fire protection, libraries, and schools. And they want them to be of high quality. So residents have conflicting goals: they want low taxes and quality services. They will fight against increasing taxes but also resist decline in services; they will work with local governments to improve services but fight to resist increasing taxes.

If there is a perception of declining services or increasing taxes, households have a variety of options. The most cited pair of options have been referred to as "exit" and "voice." Choosing the first, households can leave and move to another city or separate municipality. This is more common in the United States, where large metro areas are often balkanized into separate municipalities, often with different tax regimes. People move, if they can, to higher-taxed areas if they believe that the result is better schools and other public services. If households stay, they can choose the second option, to voice their concern, and if they are not heeded they

Box 15.3   POPULATION CHANGE IN US CITIES, 1900–2010

After plotting the individual trajectory of the population size at each successive census of the 100 largest cities in the United States from 1900 to 2010, we identified four model types. The first type of city is *steady decline*. A typical city in this category is Detroit, which experienced a peak of 1.84 million around the mid-twentieth century and then continuous decline; its 2012 population was 701,475 (see figure). The city embodies the rise and rapid fall of the older, under-bounded industrial city. Other cities in this category include Akron, Baltimore, Birmingham, Buffalo, Cincinnati, Cleveland, New Orleans, Rochester, Toledo, and Pittsburgh. These are cities that bear the brunt of an urban

fiscal crisis as the steady loss of population and tax base erodes the revenues of the city. The second model type is *continuous increase*. Here the story is of rising economic and population growth and ease of annexation of surrounding suburban districts. A typical case is San Jose, CA, a Sunbelt city with an expanding economy based largely on information technology. In 1950 the city population was only 95,280, but by 2012 it was 982,765. Decades of spectacular growth, fueled in particular by the Silicon Valley boom in high technology and computer-related industries, have made San Jose one of the most prosperous and economically dynamic cities in the country. The city was

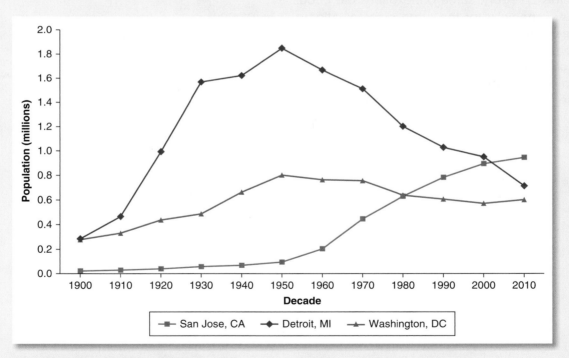

Population change in three US cities

Box 15.3 CONTINUED

also able to annex territory, increasing its area size from 17 square miles in 1950 to 177 in 2010. Other examples of this type include San Diego, Las Vegas, and Orlando. The third model type is what we term *growth interrupted*. Here examples include New York City, Atlanta, San Francisco, and Seattle. These cities' upward population trajectories saw some decline before returning to growth, and eventually surpassed their previous population peak. The figure below plots the trajectory of New York City, where the population was relatively flat from 1950 to 1970 before a twenty-year decline and then resurgence after 1990. The city's areal size remained constant at 303 square miles from 1950 to 2010. In this category, some annexations did occur, but, especially for the large cities of Atlanta, New York, San Francisco, and Seattle, population growth within stable boundaries was the most important process. Finally, there is the *slowly resurgent* city, where previous peaks are not reached but there is a slow and steady

return of population. Examples include Boston, Philadelphia, and Washington, DC. In all three cases, the areal size of the city has remained roughly the same since 1950. Washington, DC's population peaked in 1950, then saw continuous decline until 2000, at which point the city's population began a slow upward resurgence. Cities of this type are big urban areas that did not reach the free fall of continuous decline or the pronounced returned upward trajectory of the growth-interrupted cities. These cities show signs of population recovery—if not quite to past peaks, at least a bending of the curve from decline to upswing.

References

Short, J. R. and Mussman, M. (2014) Population Change in US Cities: Estimating and Explaining the Extent of Decline and Level of Resurgence. *Professional Geographer* 66: 112–123. http://www.tandfonline.com/doi/abs/10.1080/00330124.2013.765297

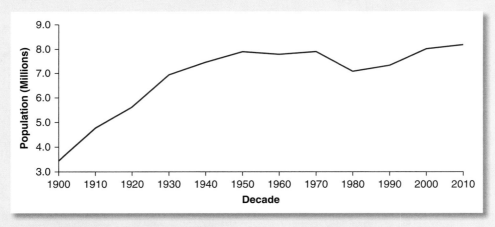

Population change in New York City

15.12 Political protest in Barcelona for Catalan autonomy

can protest. There are three sources of protest: the call for goods and services, the expression of cultural identity (Figure 15.12), and the demand for political power. Collective action can range from the persuasive (petitions) and the collaborative (lobbying elected officials) to the confrontational (including allies, marches, and in extreme cases forms of civil disobedience).

When residents stage a protest, it represents their failure to influence the political process without direct action. The more powerful groups do not need to protest, because their interests are reflected in the political process. That is why we rarely see the very rich and the very powerful taking to the streets; they do not have to. It tends to be the poorer and the more marginalized.

Forms of civil disobedience were evident in the Arab Spring that swept through the cities of the Middle East in 2010–2011 and in the Occupy Wall Street movement that occurred in selected cities in Europe and North America the following year (Figure 15.13).

Protest and uprising are rare. Much of the political life of the city consists of the more banal and everyday operation of political agreements, deal making, and compromise. Clarence Stone identifies what he calls "urban regimes," which he defines as the "informal arrangements that surround and complement the formal workings of governmental authority." Urban regimes consist of informal governing coalitions that make decisions and get things done in a city. Stone developed the notion of urban regime to refer to the informal partnership in Atlanta between city hall and downtown business elites. Political questions of maintaining and extending political support and leadership dominate City Hall, while economic issues of profit and loss concern the business elites. The combination of political and economic logic, with all the ensuing tensions, conflicts, and ambiguities, constitutes the local urban regime. The options and concerns of urban regimes vary over time and space—they may be inclusionary or exclusionary and will vary throughout the metropolitan regions; suburban regimes, for example, are more concerned with preserving property values.

15.13 "Occupy" tents in McPherson Square in Washington, DC. They first went up in October 2011 but were cleared by June 2012.

In the United States, three regime types have been identified: organic, instrumental, and symbolic. *Organic regimes* occur in small towns and suburban districts with a homogeneous population and a strong sense of place; their chief aim is to maintain the status quo. *Instrumental regimes* focus upon specific targets identified in the political partnership between urban governments and business interests. An urban growth machine regime is concerned with securing urban business interests. *Symbolic regimes* occur in cities undergoing rapid changes, including large-scale revitalization, major political change, and image campaigns that try to shift the wider public perception of the city. We should see these three categories as ideal types, with any one city's regime exhibiting characteristics, albeit in different proportions, of each type.

CHANGES IN THE CONTEMPORARY CITY

In the rapidly changing cities of the contemporary world, a number of transnational themes can be noted. Among the many, let us consider three: gentrification, suburban decline, and city branding.

Gentrification

It was the urban scholar Ruth Glass who in 1964 coined the word "gentrification" to refer to a certain form of urban change. A strict definition of the term is the replacement of lower-income households by higher-income households. She employed the term to describe how middle- and upper-class residents moved into working-class areas in London. The term is now used to refer to the movement into city neighborhoods of higher-income households, whether through the replacement of lower-income households in the existing housing stock or in the form of movement into custom-designed buildings. It is now a process found in cities across the world as the more affluent move into central and inner-city neighborhoods previously neglected or inhabited by the poor. It is a process promoted by developers and downtown elites eager to generate business and by city governments eager to lure higher-income households into the city to provide a stronger tax base and a population with higher disposable incomes. Gentrification is often trumpeted as revival, bringing life back into the city. Advocates of the poor and lower-income, in contrast, see gentrification as a form of class warfare over space. Gentrifiers tend to be richer, younger people, while the displaced tend to be older, poorer, and from racial minorities.

In Harlem, home to many poor African Americans in New York City, major construction projects such as Towers on the Park, which opened in 1988, and individual households buying up brownstone dwellings have led to a distinct form of gentrification along the western corridor of central Harlem. Just across the Hudson River from Lower Manhattan sits the small, formerly working-class city of Hoboken, just a quick ferry ride across from New York City's financial district. The process of gentrification began there around 1980. Controls that maintained the presence of lower-income households, such as tenant protection and rent control, became more lax. The housing stock was effectively emptied of lower-income residents in favor of higher-income households, especially those working in the financial services sector in Lower Manhattan, turning what was long a working-class town into a yuppie suburb of Manhattan. The increased employment opportunities in San Francisco from the early 1990s generated an extraordinarily tight housing market. The Mission District, close to the downtown, was particularly vulnerable to gentrification, as it had a relatively cheap housing stock. The area of working-class families and recent Latino immigrants quickly transformed as housing values, rents, and evictions all increased.

The Olde Towne East district, adjacent to downtown Columbus, Ohio, was like many late nineteenth- and early twentieth-century residential areas. Built close to the city, it contained both high-income and middle-income residents in a housing stock that contained some large dwellings. Post–Second World War suburbanization drew off the wealthier residents, and then a mixture of urban renewal and highway construction ripped the heart out of the neighborhood. Originally a stable residential area throughout most of the early twentieth century, by the 1960s the dwelling stock was in decline and most of the residents were low-income African-Americans living in rented accommodation. However, being so close to the downtown and with some substantial housing remaining, the area soon attracted the attention of gay white men seeking to buy and improve housing. In many cities, gentrification has been associated with the coming out of a gay community. In Olde Towne East, the struggle, crystallized between the gay white newcomers and the longer-term residents—mainly low-income African Americans—took

15.14 Gentrification in Paddington: before

a particular form as the new residents sought to have the area designated as historic. For the longer-term low-income residents, this was a financial penalty, as they were often unable to afford the costs of meeting historic preservation codes. The property cost increases forced out many of the older owners and low-income renters. The recent history of this area encapsulates a number of different cleavages, including race, class, income, and sexual orientation, as two marginalized communities fought a turf war over the price and meaning of the residential space.

Gentrification tends to occur when there is recentralization in central city areas. In the case of Sydney, Australia, the immediate post–Second World War years saw a steady suburbanization. The city extended far into distant suburbs, increasing commuting times. Starting in the 1970s, more affluent younger and gay households began buying up the high-density terraced housing in inner-city neighborhoods such as Paddington. The central location reduced commuting times for those working in the city and provided very cheap housing, and the neighborhoods became safe for openly gay people. Paddington is now one of the more fashionable areas of the city (see Figures 15.14 and 15.15).

Gentrification can also be part of a more fundamental rewriting of urban space associated with more aggressive policing, in what is referred to as the punitive turn. This involves, according to proponents, making the streets safe; for critics, it is an aggressive form of policing directed specifically against the poor, minorities, and marginalized people in areas of the city undergoing gentrification. In selected neighborhoods, the gentrified city embodies all these active political moments in a socio-spatial urban transformation that marginalizes the poor and the homeless. Urban policies and market forces combine to promote gentrification, marginalize the poor, and make the homeless disappear from public view.

Suburban Decline

An image persists, especially in the United States, of suburbs as bucolic idylls, different from the grit of the cities. Yet many older postwar suburbs struggle to survive, caught in the stagnant middle between the dynamic processes of urban decentralization, as more distant suburbs are developed, and recentralization, as investment shifts back into the city. The deindustrialization of older suburbs also leaves these places with a smaller economic base for opportunity and mobility. Once prized as the ideal location for families, many older inner suburbs now exhibit symptoms of aging. Those built during the postwar period of mass suburbanization are particularly outdated, as the housing stock now lacks the size and amenities

15.15 Gentrification in Paddington: after

to compete with newer housing on the outer fringe of the metropolitan area or in the redeveloped heart of gentrifying cities. Caught between city gentrification and outer sprawl, many postwar suburbs are currently losing population and the battle for investment resources. Bernadette Hanlon and her colleagues write of the emerging feature of suburban gothic as numerous suburbs in crisis appear on the urban scene.

City Branding

The marketing of cities, also referred to as city branding, has a long history. The frontier town, the resort, the suburb, and the industrial city were all marketed with appropriate images to attract investment and people. In the contemporary world, three new forms can be identified.

The first is the marketing of the postindustrial city. In the wake of the deindustrialization of large swathes of urban North America, Australia, and Europe, formerly industrial cities were placed in the unenviable position of losing investment and jobs. The global shift of manufacturing creates new industrial cities in the developing world but leaves behind industrial cities in the developed world. These industrial cities, or, to be more accurate, these newly postindustrial cities, became associated with the old, the polluted, the past, and the failed. A major theme of marketing these postindustrial cities is to distance them from their recent industrial past. In the case of Syracuse, New York, this involved a new logo for the city that replaced images of smoking factories with a postmodern building skyline and a transformation of a local lake from a dump site to a scene of regeneration. Formerly industrial cities are rebranded in more attractive packages that emphasize the new rather than the old, the fashionably postmodern rather than the merely modern, the postindustrial rather than the industrial, consumption rather than production, spectacle and fun rather than pollution and work. Take the case of Wollongong, an industrial city on the New South Wales coast of Australia. A massive steelworks dominated the urban economy. The steelworks shed 15,000 jobs from the early 1980s to the mid-1990s. The rate of job loss was only one major strand in negative imagery associated with the city in the national imagination and among foreign investors. City leaders decided to rebrand the city in the public imagination. An image campaign was built around the idea of "innovation, creativity and excellence." An important part of the campaign involved the planting half a million trees on the site of the steelworks while the council found funds to clean up the beaches and construct cycle ways. Such "greening" is now an integral part of a city's attempt to shed its hard industrial image for a softer postindustrial imagery.

The second form is the marketing of a city as global. Because of the growing competition, there is constant need to upgrade and improve a city's image. At the top of the global hierarchy, as measured in terms of the concentration of advanced producer services, sit London and New York. Both cities actively position themselves as global cities. In 1965 New York hosted the World's Fair, and after a period of fiscal crisis and economic decline the city was rebranded in 1977 with the successful *I (heart) New York* campaign. In 2012 London hosted the Summer Olympic Games, presenting itself as a multicultural, cosmopolitan, cool city.

The rhetoric of global city branding is often associated with attempts to justify controversial and costly urban redevelopment projects, tax incentives, and business-friendly economic policies.

Darel Paul explores the politics of "global imagineering" in Montreal, Canada, where business interests triumphed, and Minneapolis-St. Paul, Minnesota, where similar interests were trumped by populist politics. In St. Petersburg, Russia, not only was the old Soviet name of Leningrad dropped, the city was actively promoted as an international hub of circulatory capital, host to corporate power, and stage for globalist megaprojects. St. Petersburg was rebranded as an entrepreneurial, economically competitive, globally connected city.

The third form of marketing is presentation as a business-friendly city. As capital becomes ever more mobile and more cities enter the competition, cities need to aggressively promote themselves as good places to do business. Here are some examples from advertisements of US cities in the business press:

Dallas	*The city of choice for business*
Milwaukee	*The city that works for your business*
New York	*The business city that never sleeps*
Phoenix	*Moving business in the right direction*

More specific themes around this general message include emphasizing a pro-business political climate, a skilled labor force, good infrastructure, and accessible location.

The marketing of cities can also involve the construction of buildings by big-name architects, so-called starchitects, and the centrality of "starchitecture" to the symbolic capital of cities. To have a new building by a starchitect denotes cultural heft and global intentionality. Individual buildings and assemblages of certain built forms—museums, art galleries, new airports, and the like—built in the latest style by the hottest architects is an important way for a city to position itself. Perhaps the best-known and most-cited case study is Bilbao in northern Spain. It was a major banking and industrial center that from the 1970s experienced deindustrialization and massive job loss. The old industrial area along the river was a site of abandoned factories. The city authorities began an ambitious urban renewal policy. A centerpiece was the branch of the Guggenheim Museum designed by the famous American architect Frank Gehry. The museum, built along the river, is now an iconic image of the city and a classic case study of using a big-name signature architect designing a major cultural center to successfully rebrand a city (Figure 15.16).

15.16 Guggenheim
Museum in Bilbao

The hosting of events is now a significant part of marketing a city. So-called spotlight events highlight the city for a wider audience: the larger the event, the greater the potential marketing opportunity. World fairs and Olympic Games play an important part in marketing cities. The hosting of events such as films festivals, Expos, and Olympic Games provides opportunities for a city's elites to stage a widely accessible and globally pervasive marketing campaign. In a detailed case study, Claire Colomb explores the marketing of Berlin between 1989 and 2011. She argues that the city was marketed through rebuilding and the staging of a new Berlin. In the inner city, sites were turned into tourist attractions. Place marketing and urban reinvention were intertwined in a symbolic politics of representation.

There is a growing body of critical work that highlights the silences of city marketing. The emphases of most marketing campaigns are on the city as a place of business, less on social inclusivity; more on the profitable city, less on the fair and just city. The dominant themes represent the power of the dominant groups. The more marginal are excluded. In an interesting twist on this finding, however, Jaime Hernandez and Celia Lopez suggest how slums can be used to positively brand a city, in this case Bogotá. They suggest that highlighting rather than ignoring the city's slums can invoke positive responses around ideas of genuine difference, cultural authenticity, and vernacular architecture. The poor and the marginal become less a political threat and more a marketing opportunity. In this case, the ethos of marketing is so pervasive that even the silences are uttered and the problems exposed, not as issues to be solved or addressed but as opportunities to sell and rebrand.

Box 15.4 URBAN SPECTACULARS AND CITY BRANDING

Cities also seek to market themselves through hosting mega-events such as major sporting events, art festivals, and the like. One of the most important mega-events is the Summer Olympic Games.

From humble beginnings in Athens in 1896, when only 200 athletes from fourteen countries competed, with limited press coverage, the modern Olympic Games have now grown to a truly global spectacle involving most countries in the world (Table 15.3).

Hosting the Games involves the provision of venues and the improvement of urban infrastructure. Since Barcelona in 1992 and especially

Table 15.3 ■ THE MODERN SUMMER OLYMPIC GAMES			
Date	Host city	Participants (women)	Countries/National Committees
1896	Athens	200 (0)	14
1900	Paris	1205 (19)	26
1904	St. Louis	687 (6)	13
1908	London	2035 (36)	22
1912	Stockholm	2547 (57)	28
1920	Antwerp	2668 (77)	29
1924	Paris	3092 (136)	44
1928	Amsterdam	3014 (290)	46
1932	Los Angeles	1408 (127)	37
1936	Berlin	4066 (328)	49
1948	London	4099 (385)	59
1952	Helsinki	4925 (518)	69
1956	Melbourne	3184 (371)	67
1960	Rome	5346 (610)	83
1964	Tokyo	5140 (683)	93
1968	Mexico City	5530 (781)	112
1972	Munich	7123 (1058)	121
1976	Montreal	6028 (1247)	92
1980	Moscow	5217 (1124)	80
1984	Los Angeles	5330 (1567)	140

Box 15.4 CONTINUED

Date	Host city	Participants (women)		Countries/National Committees
1988	Seoul	8465	(2186)	159
1992	Barcelona	9634	(2707)	169
1996	Atlanta	10,310	(3513)	197
2000	Sydney	10,651	(4069)	199
2004	Athens	10,625	(4329)	201
2008	Beijing	11,028	(4746)	204
2012	London	10,960	(4676)	204

Table 15.3 ■ CONTINUED

Olympic ring fountain in downtown Atlanta, built for the 2004 Games

since Sydney in 2004, emphasis has also shifted to using the Games as way to undertake urban renewal of industrial and abandoned sites. For the 1992 Games, Barcelona built a new waterfront and upgraded a declining area of the city as well as making numerous improvements throughout the metro area, including new roads, a new sewer system, and the creation or improvement of over 200 parks, plazas, and streets. For the 2000 Games, Sydney built

Box 15.4 CONTINUED

a new road linking the airport to the downtown and constructed the main venue on a previously contaminated inner-city site. Beijing undertook a building frenzy with an estimated $40 billion of Olympic-related buildings and infrastructure, including a new expressway and ring roads, miles of rail and subway tracks, and a $2.2 billion new airport that is the largest in the world. For London 2012, much of the construction of the new sports venues were part of the regeneration of the lower Lea Valley, an area of postindustrial decline.

The Olympics also provide an opportunity to make a modern city. Athens spent close to $16 billion in large-scale public investments in water supply, mass transit, and airport connections to get ready for the 2004 Games. Hosting the Olympics provided the opportunity for citywide, coherent planning to create a modern city. Modernity can come at a cost. The changes often come with increased costs for

city residents unless there is a specific commitment to redistributional outcomes. The Chinese government used the 2008 Games as an opportunity to modernize Beijing. One plan involved the destruction of the old, high-density neighborhoods of small alleyways in the central part of the city, seen by officials as a remnant of a premodern past. Almost 20 square kilometers were destroyed and almost 580,000 people displaced in this one program.

Hosting the Games provides an opportunity for massive urban renewal, major environmental remediation, dramatic infrastructural improvements, and the creation of a positive image across the globe.

References

Gold, J. and Gold, M. (2012) *The Making of Modern Olympic Cities: Critical Concepts in Urban Studies.* New York: Routledge.

Short, J. R. (2008) Globalization, Cities and the Summer Olympics. *City* 12: 321–340.

Cited References

Anderson, E. (1990) *Streetwise: Race, Class, and Change in an Urban Community.* Chicago: University of Chicago Press.

Anderson, E. (2012) *The Cosmopolitan Canopy: Race and Civility in Everyday Life.* New York: W.W. Norton.

Boal, F. (2002) Belfast: Walls Within. *Political Geography* 21: 687–694.

Colomb, C. (2011) *Staging the New Berlin.* London: Routledge.

Goffman, E. (1959) *The Presentation of Self in Everyday Life.* Garden City, NY: Doubleday.

Golubchikov, O. (2010) World-City-Entrepreneurialism: Globalist Imaginaries, Neoliberal Geographies, and the Production of New St. Petersburg. *Environment and Planning A* 42: 626–643.

Hägerstrand, T. (1970) What about People in Regional Science? *Papers of the Regional Science Association* 24: 7–21.

Hanlon, B., Short, J. R., and Vicino, T. J. (2010) *Cities and Suburbs.* New York: Routledge.

Hernandez, J. and Lopez, C. (2011) Is There a Role for Informal Settlements in Branding Cities? *Journal of Place Management and Development* 4: 93–109.

Knox, Paul. (2012) Starchitects, Starchitecture and the Symbolic Capital of World Cities. In *International Handbook of Globalization and World Cities,* Derudder, B., Hoyler, M.,Taylor, P.J., and Witlox, F. (eds.), Northampton, MA: Edward Elgar, pp. 275–283.

Meyer, M. (2008) *The Last Days of Old Beijing.* New York: Walker.

Murdie. R. A. (1969) Factorial Ecology of Metropolitan Toronto. Research Paper 116, Department of Geography, University of Chicago, Chicago.

Paul, D. E. (2004) World Cities as Hegemonic Projects: The Politics of Global Imagineering in Montreal. *Political Geography* 23: 571–596.

Seamon, D. (1979) *A Geography of the Lifeworld.* London: Croom Helm.

Stone, C. N. (1989) *Regime Politics: Governing Atlanta, 1946–1988.* Lawrence: University of Kansas.

Stone, C. N. (2008) Urban Regimes and the Capacity to Govern: A Political Economy Approach. *Journal of Urban Affairs* 15: 1–28.

Select Guide to Further Reading

Barras, R. (2009) *Building Cycles: Growth and Instability.* Oxford: Wiley-Blackwell.

Bieri, D., Knox, P. L., and Wei, F. (2012) Changing Social Ecologies of U.S. Suburban Areas, 1960–2000. http://www-personal.umich.edu/~bieri/docs/SocialEcologies_BKW_Jun12.pdf Accessed Dec. 12, 2012.

Bridge, G. and Watson, S. (eds) (2011) *The New Blackwell Companion to the City.* Chichester: Wiley-Blackwell.

Castells, M. (1989) *The City and Grassroots.* London: Edward Arnold.

Calame, J. and Charlesworth, E. R. (2009) *Divided Cities: Beirut, Belfast, Jerusalem, Mostar, and Nicosia.* Philadelphia: University of Pennsylvania Press.

De Certeau, M. (1984) *The Practice of Everyday Life.* Berkeley and Los Angeles; University of California Press.

Gottlieb, M. (1976) *Long Swings in Urban Development.* New York: National Bureau of Economic Research.

Hall, T. and Barrett, H. (2012) *Urban Geography.* 4th ed. Oxford: Routledge.

Hall, T., Hubbard, P., and Short, J. R. (eds) (2008) *The Sage Companion to the City.* London: Sage.

Harvey, D. (2012) *Rebel Cities: From the Right to the City to the Urban Revolution.* London: Verso.

Immergluck, D. (2011) The Local Wreckage of Global Capital: The Subprime Crisis, Federal Policy and High-Foreclosure Neighborhoods in the US. *International Journal of Urban and Regional Research* 35: 130–146.

Kramer, K. and Short, J. R. (2011) Flânerie and the Globalizing City. *City* 15: 322–342.

Logan, J. and Molotch, H. (2007) *Urban Fortunes: The Political Economy of Place.* Berkeley and Los Angeles: University of California Press. First published 1987.

Martuzzi, M., Mitis, F., and Forastiere, F. (2010) Inequalities, Inequities, Environmental Justice in Waste Management and Health. *European Journal of Public Health* 20: 21–26.

Mikelbank, B. A. (2011) Neighborhood Déjà Vu: Classification in Metropolitan Cleveland, 1970–2000. *Urban Geography* 32: 317–333.

Mohai, P. and Saha, R. (2007) Racial Inequality in the Distribution of Hazardous Waste: A National-Level Reassessment. *Social Problems* 54: 343–370.

Parker, S. (2011) *Cities, Politics and Power.* Oxford: Routledge.

Short, J. R. and Kim, Y.-H. (1998) Urban Crises/Urban Representations: Selling the City in Difficult Times. In Hubbard, P. and Hall, T. (eds) *The Entrepreneurial City*. Chichester: Wiley, pp. 55–75.

United Church of Christ Commission for Racial Justice. (1987) *Toxic Wastes and Race in the United States: A National Report on the Racial and Socio-economic Characteristics of Communities with Hazardous Waste Sites*. New York.

Vicino, T. J., Hanlon, B., and Short, J. J. (2011) A Typology of Urban Immigrant Neighborhoods. *Urban Geography* 32: 383–405.

On gentrification:

Duman, A. (2012) Dispatches from "the Frontline of Gentrification." *City* 16: 672–685.

Lees, L., Slater, T., and Wyly, E. (2010) *The Gentrification Reader*. New York: Routledge.

Short, J. R. (2006) *Alabaster Cities*. Syracuse: Syracuse University Press.

Wyly, E., Newman, K., Schafran, A., and Lee, E. (2010) Displacing New York. *Environment and Planning A* 42: 2602–2623.

On suburban decline:

Hanlon, B. (2009) *Once the American Dream: Inner Ring Suburbs of the Metropolitan United States*. Philadelphia: Temple University Press.

Short, J. R., Hanlon, B. and Vicino, T. (2007) The Decline of Inner Suburbs: The New Suburban Gothic in the United States. *Geography Compass* 1: 641–656.

On city branding:

Dinnie, K. (ed) (2011) *City Branding: Theory and Cases*. New York: Palgrave.

Short, J. R., Benton, L. M., Luce, W. B., and Walton, J. (1993) Reconstructing the Image of an Industrial City. *Annals of Association of American Geographers* 83: 207–224.

Websites

Cities around the world
http://www.fourmilab.ch/earthview/cities.html
Iconic houses
http://www.iconichouses.org/
Resilient cities
http://www.rockefellerfoundation.org/100-resilient-cities

Credits

All photographs © John Rennie Short unless otherwise specified.

Part 1 Opener: NASA Earth Observatory image by Jesse Allen using Landsat data from the U.S. Geological Survey.

1.4: From the Heezen-Tharp Collection, Library of Congress, G9181. C2 1964. H4

2.3: Sheila Terry / Science Source.

2.5: Library of Congress, Moffett.

2.6: Courtesy of the Newberry Library, Chicago, Illinois. Map 6F G4104.C6E2 1895 .G7 sheet 1

Part 2 Opener: © Dinodia/Corbis.

Box 4.1 Figure: After Swartz W, Sala E, Tracey S, Watson R, Pauly D (2010) The Spatial Expansion and Ecological Footprint of Fisheries (1950 to Present). PLoS ONE 5(12): e15143. doi:10.1371/journal.pone.0015143.

4.3: von Grebmer, K., et al. 2012. *2012 Global Hunger Index. Ensuring Sustainable Food Security under Land, Water, and Energy Stresses.* Washington, D.C.: International Food Policy Research Institute. Source: von Grebmer et al. (2012). Reproduced with permission from the International Food Policy Research Institute.

4.4: Source: Food and Agriculture Organization of the United Nations, 2006, Jakob Skoet and Kostas Stamoulis, et al., "The State of Food Insecurity in the World, 2006." [http://www.fao.org/docrep/009/a0750e/a0750e00.htm]. Reproduced with permission.

4.6: Source: Food and Agriculture Organization of the United Nations, 2014. [http://www.fao.org/worldfoodsituation]. Reproduced with permission.

4.7: Adapted by the publisher with permission, from The Global Database on Body Mass Index, [http://apps.who.int/bmi/index.jsp], accessed October 2013.

Box 5.1 Figure: Courtesy of ASPO International.

5.1: US Department of Energy.

5.3: Mauna Loa Observatory, National Oceanic and Atmospheric Administration, Earth System Research Laboratory, Global Monitoring Division.

6.6: Etter, Andres, Clive McAlpine, and Hugh Possingham. "Historical Patterns and Drivers of Landscape Change in Colombia Since 1500: A Regionalized Spatial Approach." *Annals of the Association of American Geographers* 98, 1 (2008): 2–23, Figure 4. DOI: 10.1080/00045600701733911.

6.7: Wilbanks, T. J., & Kates, R. W. (2010). "Beyond adapting to climate change: embedding adaptation in responses to multiple threats and stresses." *Annals of the Association of American Geographers*, 100 (4), 719–728, Figure 1. Ed. Richard Aspinall. DOI: 10.1080/00045608.2010.502408.

Part 3 Opener: Photo by Joergen Geerds.

8.3: Diagram courtesy of Barcelona Field Studies Centre [www.geographyfieldwork.com].

Part 4 Opener: © franckreporter/iStockPhoto

10.10: Jon T. Kilpinen, Valparaiso University.

11.5: Frank Baum, *The Navy Alphabet.*

11.9: From Thomas P.M. Barnett's *The Pentagon's New Map: War and Peace in the Twenty-First Century (2004),* © Barnett Consulting LLC.

Box 12.1 Figure: © Sasi Group (University of Sheffield) and Mark Newman (University of Michigan).

Box 12.2 Figure: Courtesy of The Fund for Peace.

Part 6 Opener: © aleks0649/ iStockPhoto

13.1: Photo by Lisa Benton-Short.

14.8: Courtesy of the GaWC Research Network, Loughborough University.

Box 14.2 Figures: X. Liu *, Z. Neal **, B. Derudder, "City Networks in the United States: A Comparison of Four Models," *Environment and Planning A,* 44 (2), (2012), 255–256, Figures C and D. Pion Ltd, London. [www.pion.co.uk, www.envplan.com]

Index

Page numbers followed by b and *t* indicate information contained in a box or a table on the designated page. Italicized page numbers indicate a figure on the designated page.